Practical Oracle SQL

Mastering the Full Power
of Oracle Database

Kim Berg Hansen

Apress®

Practical Oracle SQL: Mastering the Full Power of Oracle Database

Kim Berg Hansen
Middelfart, Denmark

ISBN-13 (pbk): 978-1-4842-5616-9   ISBN-13 (electronic): 978-1-4842-5617-6
https://doi.org/10.1007/978-1-4842-5617-6

Managing Director, Apress Media LLC: Welmoed Spahr
Acquisitions Editor: Jonathan Gennick
Development Editor: Laura Berendson
Coordinating Editor: Jill Balzano

Cover image designed by Freepik (www.freepik.com)

Distributed to the book trade worldwide by Springer Science+Business Media New York, 233 Spring Street, 6th Floor, New York, NY 10013. Phone 1-800-SPRINGER, fax (201) 348-4505, e-mail orders-ny@springer-sbm.com, or visit www.springeronline.com. Apress Media, LLC is a California LLC and the sole member (owner) is Springer Science + Business Media Finance Inc (SSBM Finance Inc). SSBM Finance Inc is a **Delaware** corporation.

For information on translations, please e-mail rights@apress.com, or visit http://www.apress.com/rights-permissions.

Apress titles may be purchased in bulk for academic, corporate, or promotional use. eBook versions and licenses are also available for most titles. For more information, reference our Print and eBook Bulk Sales web page at http://www.apress.com/bulk-sales.

Any source code or other supplementary material referenced by the author in this book is available to readers on GitHub via the book's product page, located at www.apress.com/9781484256169. For more detailed information, please visit http://www.apress.com/source-code.

Printed on acid-free paper

To
Lis-Karen
for
patience and clearing the dishes

Table of Contents

About the Author xiii

Acknowledgments xv

Introduction xvii

Part I: Core SQL 1

Chapter 1: Correlating Inline Views 3
Brewery products and sales 3
Scalar subqueries and multiple columns 5
Correlating inline view 9
    Outer joining correlated inline view 12
Lessons learned 16

Chapter 2: Pitfalls of Set Operations 17
Sets of beer 18
Set operators 20
    Set concatenation 21
    The three set operators 25
Multiset operators 27
    Multiset union 28
    Multiset intersect 30
    Multiset except 32
Minus vs. multiset except 34
Lessons learned 38

Chapter 3: Divide and Conquer with Subquery Factoring...**39**

Products and sales data...40

Best-selling years of the less strong beers 40

Modularization using the with clause 44

    Multiple uses of the same subquery 47

    Listing column names 51

Lessons learned...55

Chapter 4: Tree Calculations with Recursion...**57**

Bottles in boxes on pallets...57

Multiplying hierarchical quantities...60

    Recursive subquery factoring..61

    Dynamic SQL in PL/SQL function..68

Lessons learned...71

Chapter 5: Functions Defined Within SQL **73**

Table with beer alcohol data...73

Blood alcohol concentration 75

Function with PRAGMA UDF..77

Function in the with clause...80

    Encapsulated in a view...83

Lessons learned...85

Chapter 6: Iterative Calculations with Multidimensional Data **87**

Conway's Game of Life..87

Live neighbor count with the model clause..89

Iterating generations..96

Lessons learned...106

Chapter 7: Unpivoting Columns to Rows **107**

Data received in columns 108

Unpivoting to rows 108

    Do-it-yourself unpivoting..111

    More than one dimension and/or measure 113

Using dimension tables...120

    Dynamic mapping to dimension tables 123

Lessons learned...128

Chapter 8: Pivoting Rows to Columns 131

Tables for pivoting...132

Pivoting single measure and dimension 134

    Do-it-yourself manual pivoting 138

Multiple measures 139

    Multiple dimensions as well 141

Lessons learned...144

Chapter 9: Splitting Delimited Text 145

Customer favorites and reviews 145

Delimited single values..146

    Pipelined table function 147

    Built-in APEX table function...152

    Straight SQL with row generators 153

    Treating the string as a JSON array..155

Delimited multiple values...157

    Custom ODCI table function...157

    Combining apex_string.split and substr...162

    Row generators and regexp_substr 163

    Transformation to JSON...165

Lessons learned...168

Chapter 10: Creating Delimited Text 169

Delimited lists of products 169

String aggregation 171

    Aggregate function listagg 172

    Aggregate function collect 173

    Custom aggregate function stragg...177

    Aggregate function xmlagg 182

When it doesn't fit in a VARCHAR2 184

    Get just the first part of the result 185

    Try to make it fit with reduced data 186

    Use a CLOB instead of a VARCHAR2 187

Lessons learned 190

Part II: Analytic Functions 191

Chapter 11: Analytic Partitions, Ordering, and Windows 193

Sums of quantities 194

Analytic syntax 195

    Partitions 197

    Ordering and windows 199

Flexibility of the window clause 203

Windows on value ranges 206

The danger of the default window 208

Lessons learned 213

Chapter 12: Answering Top-N Questions 215

Top-N of sales data 215

    Which kind of Top-3 do you mean? 217

    The sales data for the beer 218

Traditional rownum method 222

Analytic functions for ranking 222

Fetch only the first rows 225

    Handling of ties 226

    What the row limiting clause cannot do 229

Top-N in multiple partitions 231

    The lateral trick for the row limiting clause 233

Lessons learned 235

Chapter 13: Ordered Subsets with Rolling Sums **237**

Data for goods picking 238

Building the picking SQL 240

    Solving picking an order by FIFO 240

    Easy switch of picking principle 246

    Solving optimal picking route 248

    Solving batch picking 252

    Finalizing the complete picking SQL 262

Lessons learned 264

Chapter 14: Analyzing Activity Logs with Lead **267**

Picking activity log 268

Analyzing departures and arrivals 271

Analyzing picking activity 275

    Complete picking cycle analysis 280

Teaser: row pattern matching 283

Lessons learned 286

Chapter 15: Forecasting with Linear Regression **287**

Sales forecasting 288

    Time series 289

    Calculating the basis for regression 292

    Linear regression 298

    Final forecast 301

Lessons learned 305

Chapter 16: Rolling Sums to Forecast Reaching Minimums **307**

Inventory, budget, and order 307

    The data 310

Accumulating until zero 311

Restocking when minimum reached 315

Lessons learned 322

Part III: Row Pattern Matching 323

Chapter 17: Up-and-Down Patterns 325

The stock ticker example 325

Classifying downs and ups 327

Downs + ups = V shapes 332

    Revisiting if SAME is needed 338

V + V = W shapes 341

    Overlapping W shapes 346

Lessons learned 349

Chapter 18: Grouping Data Through Patterns 351

Two sets of data to group 351

Three grouping conditions 352

    Group consecutive data 353

    Group until gap too large 364

    Group until fixed limit 367

Lessons learned 369

Chapter 19: Merging Date Ranges 371

Job hire periods 371

    Temporal validity 375

Merging overlapping ranges 378

    Attempts comparing to the previous row 379

    Better comparing to the maximum end date 381

    Handling the null dates 386

Lessons learned 388

Chapter 20: Finding Abnormal Peaks 389

Web page counter history 389

The counter data 391

    Patterns in the raw counter data 393

Looking at daily visits 397

    Patterns in daily visits data 399

    More complex patterns... 406

Lessons learned.. 410

Chapter 21: Bin Fitting... **411**

Inventory to be packed in boxes 411

Bin fitting with unlimited number of bins of limited capacity.................................... 413

    Showing where box capacity is too small 422

Bin fitting with limited number of bins of unlimited capacity.................................... 426

Lessons learned.. 433

Chapter 22: Counting Children in Trees **435**

Hierarchical tree of employees 435

Counting subordinates of all levels... 437

    Counting with row pattern matching.. 439

    The details of each match 442

    Fiddling with the output 448

Lessons learned.. 451

Index... **453**

About the Author

Kim Berg Hansen is a database developer from Middelfart in Denmark.

As a youngster originally wanting to work with electronics, he tried computer programming and discovered that the programs he wrote worked well – unlike the electronics projects he soldered that often failed. This led to a VIC-20 with 5 KB RAM and many hours programming in Commodore BASIC.

Having discovered his talent, Kim financed computer science studies at Odense University with a summer job as sheriff of Legoredo while learning methodology and programming in Modula-2 and C. From there he moved into consulting as a developer making customizations to ERP software. That gave him his first introduction to Oracle SQL and PL/SQL, with which he has worked extensively since the year 2000.

His professional passion is to work with data inside the database utilizing the SQL language to the fullest to achieve the best application experience for his application users. With a background fitting programs into 5 KB RAM, Kim hates to waste computing resources unnecessarily.

Kim shares his experience and knowledge by blogging at www.kibeha.dk, presenting at various Oracle User Group conferences, and being the SQL quizmaster at the Oracle Dev Gym. His motivation comes from peers who say "Now I understand" after his explanations and from end users who "can't live without" his application coding. He is an Oracle Certified Expert (OCE) in SQL and an Oracle ACE Director.

Outside the coding world, Kim is married, loves to cook, and is a card-carrying member of the Danish Beer Enthusiasts Association.

Acknowledgments

Uncountable are the number of people inspiring me over the years learning – and eventually teaching – SQL. The space allows me only to acknowledge a few that have been of the greatest importance to me. If you are not mentioned, don't worry; you have still been an invaluable inspiration.

My first and greatest inspiration was – and still is – Tom Kyte. I have learned so much from his books and from AskTom. Without him as my role model, I am not sure I would have gotten involved in the community, sharing knowledge and blogging, and certainly I would not have ended up writing a book.

Second on my list is Steven Feuerstein himself, author of books that many of us consider definitive sources. I thank Steven for giving me the chance to write SQL quizzes for the Oracle Dev Gym (devgym.oracle.com). Teaching is the best way to learn something, and having to come up with new quizzes every week is an opportunity for me to read up on all aspects of SQL.

Everybody involved in sharing knowledge in the community and user groups are also inspirations for me. This is exemplified beautifully by ODTUG and everybody attending the Kscope yearly conferences. I've attended every year since 2010 and I wouldn't have been where I am now without my Kscope network.

Last but definitely not least, I must not forget to acknowledge Stew Ashton. He is the grand master of row pattern matching in SQL, and he has graciously given me permission to take great inspiration for several chapters of Part 3 from his blog (stewashton.wordpress.com).

Introduction

Where do you go to learn SQL?

Well, if I ask myself that same question, of course, the answer is I learn SQL many places: books by Tom Kyte and others, the SQL Reference Manual (that I use daily), conference presentations by experienced developers, blogs, Googling, and much more. But even all of that would not help if I didn't simultaneously simply try writing SQL myself, see where I went wrong, and then try again, and again, and again.

One thing I have noticed in my learning process is that almost all teaching examples are nicely short and sweet in order to facilitate understanding. This is fine as such, but it also sometimes means that it can be harder to relate to daily work.

I had the good fortune of working 16 years at a retail company where the philosophy was never to adapt business practice to whatever the software was capable of, but instead always to customize the software to make the daily business go smarter and smoother. We always went by "of course it is possible to solve, we just need to figure out how." In this atmosphere, I had plenty of practical real tasks to practice on, trying out SQL and changing it piece by piece until I had something that solved the task at hand.

When I have presented about some of these solutions that I developed during those years, I have several times had audience approach me afterward, telling me that suddenly they "saw the light" and understood how analytic functions could help in their work, for example. Until then, they had seen it as some SQL extension that was smart and fancy, but they couldn't relate it to their own tasks they had to solve.

In this book, I will explain a series of tasks, solving them with SQL, explaining in steps how I create that SQL, starting small and building on it until I have a working statement that does not fit on a single PowerPoint slide. The statements I demonstrate here are not trivial examples – but they look more like something you might have to develop yourself in your job.

If you end up with an attitude of "Of course it is possible to solve in SQL," your boss will be happy because he saves a lot on cloud credits with your code using much less CPU. You will be happy because it is much more fun really using your brain to find a good solution.

And I will be happy too and can say: "Mission accomplished!"

What is in this book

This is not a *SQL 101 For Beginners* book. The simplest basics of queries and joins are not covered here – I am assuming that you already have at least some working knowledge of querying a table or two.

It is also not a *Definitive Reference Guide to SQL* book. I am not trying to cover every single piece of syntax in loving detail – not even of those statements and functions that I *do* write about in this book.

Instead *Practical Oracle SQL* is a book with examples of how to solve lots of different tasks using SQL that is a little more complex than what is available in the SQL-92 standard. Each chapter solves a different task, so the chapters do not necessarily need to be read consecutively.

A chapter explains the task; shows the tables, data, and other objects involved; and then walks through developing the solution to the task. Typically this consists of building the SQL step by step from simple to complex. In the course of stepwise walking through the SQL, syntax is explained and examples given of alternatives or caveats where relevant.

All chapters except one (Chapter 6) have as objective a task that is relevant for real application development. The specific examples are shown from the viewpoint of a fictional company that trades beer wholesale, but the techniques can be applied to many other applications. The chapters are divided into three parts based on the SQL technique used to solve the task.

Part 1: Core SQL

The first ten chapters deal with solutions that use a variety of SQL constructs. Everything that does not fit in Part 2 and Part 3 is found in this part.

These chapters cover many techniques: inline view correlation, set operations, with clause and with clause functions, recursive subquery factoring and model clause iteration, pivoting and unpivoting, as well as splitting and creating delimited text.

Part 2: Analytic functions

Analytic functions have been my favorite since I started working with Oracle SQL. I saw a quote (source unknown) from a conference presentation: "If you write on your CV that you know SQL, but you do not use analytic functions, then you are lying." I would hate to solve SQL tasks without having the use of analytic functions, so the six chapters of Part 2 are dedicated to solutions using analytic functions.

Focus is on demonstrating practical tasks that can be solved extremely efficiently, walking through using analytic functions for tasks such as Top-N questions, warehouse picking with rolling sums, analyzing activity logs, and two types of forecasting.

Part 3: Row pattern matching

When in need of SQL that crosses row boundaries, my go-to solution since version 8i has been analytic functions. From version 12.2, `match_recognize` has been added to my toolbox for cases where even an analytic function in SQL would be too convoluted. The six chapters of Part 3 show both using `match_recognize` for the row pattern matching it was designed for and using it for tasks that might not at first glance seem like a case for `match_recognize`.

The tasks covered include finding up-and-down patterns, grouping consecutive data, merging date ranges, finding abnormal peaks, bin fitting, and tree branch calculations.

About the code

The major part of this book is code – SQL, SQL, and more SQL. To really learn from it, you should run the code yourself, play with it, alter it and see what happens, and fool around until you feel confident that you've "got it." Now that wouldn't be fun if you had to type in everything by yourself, so all of the code in the book is available as source files for you.

Source files

You can get the source files for the book from GitHub via the book's page on Apress:

www.apress.com/9781484256169

What you will find is these files:

- `practical_readme.txt`
  A short readme describing the other files.

- `practical_create_schema.sql`

  All the example objects reside in a schema called `practical` (similar to the Oracle-supplied sample schemas `scott` and `hr`). This script creates the `practical` schema with necessary privileges and should be run as a DBA user. If your environment enforces complex passwords, you may need to edit this script to give the `practical` user a more complex password than `practical`.

- `practical_fill_schema.sql`

  Once you have created the `practical` schema, log in as user `practical` – the password is `practical` unless you changed it in the preceding file. Then run this script to create all the example objects – tables, views, types, packages, and so on.

- `practical_clean_schema.sql`

  This script is also to be run as user `practical`. It drops everything that was created with `practical_fill_schema.sql`. You can try things yourself and change the examples and manipulate the data all you want – when you are done, you can return to a fresh example schema by running `practical_clean_schema.sql` followed by `practical_fill_schema.sql`.

- `practical_drop_schema.sql`

  If you want to completely get rid of the example schema `practical`, you can run this script as a DBA user.

- `ch_{chapter_name}.sql`

  Each of the 22 chapters has its own example file with the code from the listings in each chapter. Do note, however, that every listing that is DDL (creation of views, object types, etc.) is not in the chapter SQL file but in `practical_fill_schema.sql` instead. This way every dictionary object is created and dropped together, and the chapter example scripts do not need to worry about cleaning up in the dictionary.

All of the scripts and examples are meant as learning inspiration and should not be installed in productive environments. They are for your use as a learning tool and should be treated as such.

The schema

You should think of the `practical` schema as part of an application used by a fictional company called **Good Beer Trading Co**. Almost all of the examples are based on tasks that such an application could need to do – also in real life. Admitted, a few cases are slightly contrived, but most could have been taken straight from real applications. For example, all techniques shown in Part 2 are directly taken from code I have developed myself during the 16 years I mentioned in the preceding text – I have only adapted them to my `practical` example tables shown in Figure 1.

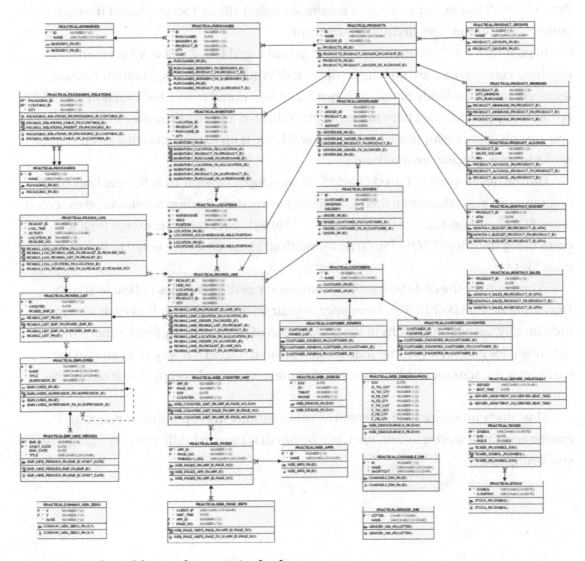

Figure 1. *The tables in the practical schema*

The only table in the schema that has no relation to Good Beer Trading Co is the table `conway_gen_zero` used in Chapter 6. The other tables are all related to the fictional company, each table being used in one or more of the chapters.

Versions and environment

Almost all of the code examples were developed using the Database App Development VM pre-built VirtualBox image that can be downloaded from Oracle, specifically the version that contains Oracle Database 12c Enterprise Edition Release 12.2.0.1.0 – 64bit Production. A few examples require database version 18c or 19c; for those I have used either newer VM images or *livesql.oracle.com*.

In general a lot of the examples shown in Part 1 and Part 2 will work even on database versions that are no longer supported. Where versions higher than 12.2 are required, this is explicitly noted. If relevant, I've also noted from which version specific syntax is supported, but I have not explicitly indicated a from-version for everything. If you are still using unsupported versions, I will leave it up to you to test if a given syntax works in your specific environment.

During development, I used Oracle SQL Developer version 18.2. Screenshots of ER diagrams are also taken from this SQL Developer version. Code examples were executed using SQLcl release 4.2, mostly using `set sqlformat ansiconsole`, except for a few cases using traditional SQL*Plus style formatting. These cases are noted in the source code files.

When you try the code yourself, I recommend opening the files in Oracle SQL Developer or TOAD or PLSQL Developer or your favorite SQL IDE. Run each statement individually, inspecting results in the grid instead of relying on my formatting, which is optimized for getting an output that fits on a printed page. That way you can also very easily alter the statement a bit and try to execute it again and compare changes in the output.

Most diagram figures were created by using various APEX graph and diagram components in a workspace on *apex.oracle.com* that I use to fiddle about working with small APEX pages.

A final word

Maybe you are under the impression that if SQL is slightly more complex than a two-table join, then it is only for geniuses to attempt and you won't even try it. I assure you this is not the case.

Expertise comes from practice. Confidence comes from familiarity. You should just go ahead and write slightly more complex SQL tomorrow, then slightly more the day after, and so on. Over time it will become as familiar to you as whatever other language you've worked in for years, and you will say to yourself: "What was I afraid of?"

I am confident this book will give you a jump start in your journey toward *really* using the power of SQL.

PART I

Core SQL

CHAPTER 1

Correlating Inline Views

Most of the time in SQL, you can simply join tables or views to one another to get the result you want. Often you add inline views and scalar subqueries to the mix, and you can soon create relatively complex solutions to many problems. With analytic functions, you really start to rock 'n' roll and can solve almost anything.

But it can happen from time to time that you have, for instance, a scalar subquery and wish that it could return multiple columns instead of just a single column. You can make workarounds with object types or string concatenation, but it's never really elegant nor efficient.

Also from time to time, you would really like, for example, a predicate inside the inline view to reference a value from a table outside the inline view, which is normally not possible. Often the workaround is to select the column you would like a predicate on in the inline view select list and put the predicate in the join on clause instead. This is often good enough, and the optimizer can often do **predicate pushing** to automatically do what you actually wanted – but it is not always able to do this, in which case you end up with an inefficient query.

For both those problems, it has been possible since version 12.1 to solve them by correlating the inline view with lateral or apply, enabling you in essence to do your own predicate pushing.

Brewery products and sales

In the application schema of the Good Beer Trading Co, I have a couple of views (shown in Figure 1-1) I can use to illustrate inline view correlation.

© Kim Berg Hansen 2020
K. Berg Hansen, *Practical Oracle SQL*, https://doi.org/10.1007/978-1-4842-5617-6_1

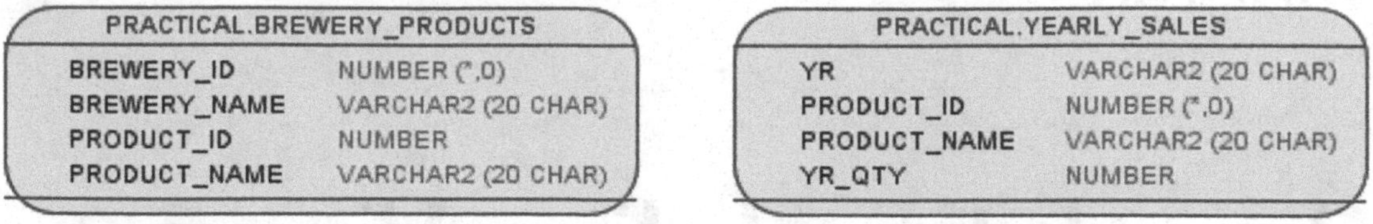

PRACTICAL.BREWERY_PRODUCTS	
BREWERY_ID	NUMBER (*,0)
BREWERY_NAME	VARCHAR2 (20 CHAR)
PRODUCT_ID	NUMBER
PRODUCT_NAME	VARCHAR2 (20 CHAR)

PRACTICAL.YEARLY_SALES	
YR	VARCHAR2 (20 CHAR)
PRODUCT_ID	NUMBER (*,0)
PRODUCT_NAME	VARCHAR2 (20 CHAR)
YR_QTY	NUMBER

Figure 1-1. *Two views used in this chapter to illustrate lateral inline views*

It could just as easily have been tables that I used to demonstrate these techniques, so for this chapter, just think of them as such. The internals of the views will be more relevant in later chapters and shown in those chapters.

View `brewery_products` shows which beers the Good Beer Trading Co buys from which breweries, while view `yearly_sales` shows how many bottles of each beer are sold per year. Joining the two together in Listing 1-1 on `product_id`, I can see the yearly sales of those beers that are bought from Balthazar Brauerei.

Listing 1-1. The yearly sales of the three beers from Balthazar Brauerei

```
SQL> select
  2     bp.brewery_name
  3    , bp.product_id as p_id
  4    , bp.product_name
  5    , ys.yr
  6    , ys.yr_qty
  7  from brewery_products bp
  8  join yearly_sales ys
  9     on ys.product_id = bp.product_id
 10  where bp.brewery_id = 518
 11  order by bp.product_id, ys.yr;
```

This data of 3 years of sales of three beers will be the basis for the examples of this chapter:

BREWERY_NAME	P_ID	PRODUCT_NAME	YR	YR_QTY
Balthazar Brauerei	5310	Monks and Nuns	2016	478
Balthazar Brauerei	5310	Monks and Nuns	2017	582
Balthazar Brauerei	5310	Monks and Nuns	2018	425
Balthazar Brauerei	5430	Hercule Trippel	2016	261
Balthazar Brauerei	5430	Hercule Trippel	2017	344

```
Balthazar Brauerei   5430  Hercule Trippel    2018  451
Balthazar Brauerei   6520  Der Helle Kumpel   2016  415
Balthazar Brauerei   6520  Der Helle Kumpel   2017  458
Balthazar Brauerei   6520  Der Helle Kumpel   2018  357
```

At first I'll use this to show a typical problem.

Scalar subqueries and multiple columns

The task at hand is to show for each of the three beers of Balthazar Brauerei which year
the most bottles of that particular beer are sold and how many bottles that were. I can do
this with two scalar subqueries in Listing 1-2.

Listing 1-2. Retrieving two columns from the best-selling year per beer

```
SQL> select
  2      bp.brewery_name
  3    , bp.product_id as p_id
  4    , bp.product_name
  5    , (
  6        select ys.yr
  7        from yearly_sales ys
  8        where ys.product_id = bp.product_id
  9        order by ys.yr_qty desc
 10        fetch first row only
 11      ) as yr
 12    , (
 13        select ys.yr_qty
 14        from yearly_sales ys
 15        where ys.product_id = bp.product_id
 16        order by ys.yr_qty desc
 17        fetch first row only
 18      ) as yr_qty
 19  from brewery_products bp
 20  where bp.brewery_id = 518
 21  order by bp.product_id;
```

For the data at hand (where there are no ties between years), it works okay and gives me the desired output:

```
BREWERY_NAME         P_ID  PRODUCT_NAME       YR    YR_QTY
Balthazar Brauerei   5310  Monks and Nuns     2017  582
Balthazar Brauerei   5430  Hercule Trippel    2018  451
Balthazar Brauerei   6520  Der Helle Kumpel   2017  458
```

But there are some issues with this strategy:

- The same data in yearly_sales is accessed twice. Had I needed more than two columns, it would have been multiple times.

- Since my order by is not unique, my fetch first row will return a random one (well, probably the first it happens to find using whichever access plan it uses, of which I have no control, so in effect, it could be any one) of those rows that have the highest yr_qty. That means in the multiple subqueries, I have no guarantee that the values come from the same row – if I had had a column showing the profit of the beer in that year and a subquery to retrieve this profit, it might show the profit of a different year than the one shown in the yr column of the output.

A classic workaround is to use just a single scalar subquery like in Listing 1-3.

Listing 1-3. Using just a single scalar subquery and value concatenation

```
SQL> select
  2      brewery_name
  3    , product_id as p_id
  4    , product_name
  5    , to_number(
  6          substr(yr_qty_str, 1, instr(yr_qty_str, ';') - 1)
  7      ) as yr
  8    , to_number(
  9          substr(yr_qty_str, instr(yr_qty_str, ';') + 1)
 10      ) as yr_qty
 11  from (
 12      select
```

```
13          bp.brewery_name
14        , bp.product_id
15        , bp.product_name
16        , (
17              select ys.yr || ';' || ys.yr_qty
18              from yearly_sales ys
19              where ys.product_id = bp.product_id
20              order by ys.yr_qty desc
21              fetch first row only
22          ) as yr_qty_str
23      from brewery_products bp
24      where bp.brewery_id = 518
25  )
26  order by product_id;
```

The scalar subquery is here in lines 16–22, finding the row I want and then selecting in line 17 a concatenation of the values I am interested in. Then I place the entire thing in an inline view (lines 11–25) and split the concatenated string into individual values again in lines 5–10.

The output of this is exactly the same as Listing 1-2, so that is all good, right? Well, as you can see, if I need more than two columns, it can quickly become unwieldy code. If I had been concatenating string values, I would have needed to worry about using a delimiter that didn't exist in the real data. If I had been concatenating dates and timestamps, I'd need to use to_char and to_date/to_timestamp. And what if I had LOB columns or columns of complex types? Then I couldn't do this at all.

So there are many good reasons to try Listing 1-4 as an alternative workaround.

Listing 1-4. Using analytic function to be able to retrieve all columns if desired

```
SQL> select
  2      brewery_name
  3    , product_id as p_id
  4    , product_name
  5    , yr
  6    , yr_qty
  7   from (
  8      select
```

```
 9         bp.brewery_name
10       , bp.product_id
11       , bp.product_name
12       , ys.yr
13       , ys.yr_qty
14       , row_number() over (
15             partition by bp.product_id
16             order by ys.yr_qty desc
17         ) as rn
18     from brewery_products bp
19     join yearly_sales ys
20         on ys.product_id = bp.product_id
21     where bp.brewery_id = 518
22   )
23   where rn = 1
24   order by product_id;
```

This also gives the exact same output as Listing 1-2, just without any scalar subqueries at all.

Here I join the two views in lines 18–20 instead of querying `yearly_sales` in a scalar subquery. But doing that makes it impossible for me to use the `fetch first` syntax, as I need a row per brewery and `fetch first` does not support a partition clause.

Instead I use the `row_number` analytic function in lines 14–17 to assign consecutive numbers 1, 2, 3 … in descending order of `yr_qty`, in effect giving the row with the highest `yr_qty` the value 1 in `rn`. This happens for each beer because of the `partition by` in line 15, so there will be a row with `rn=1` for each beer. These rows I keep with the `where` clause in line 23.

Tip   Much more about analytic functions is shown in Part 2 of the book.

The effect of this is that I can query as many columns from the `yearly_sales` view as I want – here I query two columns in lines 12–13. These can then be used directly in the outer query as well in lines 5–6. No concatenation needed, each column is available directly, no matter the datatype.

This is a much nicer workaround than Listing 1-3, so isn't this good enough? In this case it is fine, but the alternative with correlated inline views can be more flexible for some situations.

Correlating inline view

Listing 1-5 is yet another way to produce the exact same output as Listing 1-2, just this time by correlating an inline view.

Listing 1-5. *Achieving the same with a lateral inline view*

```
SQL> select
  2      bp.brewery_name
  3    , bp.product_id as p_id
  4    , bp.product_name
  5    , top_ys.yr
  6    , top_ys.yr_qty
  7  from brewery_products bp
  8  cross join lateral(
  9      select
 10          ys.yr
 11        , ys.yr_qty
 12      from yearly_sales ys
 13      where ys.product_id = bp.product_id
 14      order by ys.yr_qty desc
 15      fetch first row only
 16  ) top_ys
 17  where bp.brewery_id = 518
 18  order by bp.product_id;
```

The way this works is as follows:

- I do not join brewery_products to yearly_sales directly; instead I join to the inline view top_ys in line 8.

- The inline view in lines 9–15 queries yearly_sales and uses the fetch first row to find the row of the year with the highest sales. But it is *not* executed for *all* beers finding a single row with the

> best-selling year across all beers, for line 13 correlates the yearly_
> sales to the brewery_products on product_id.

- Line 13 would normally raise an error, since it would not make sense in the usual joining to an inline view. But I placed the keyword lateral in front of the inline view in line 8, which tells the database that I want a correlation here, so it should execute the inline view *once for each row* of the correlated outer row source – in this case brewery_products. That means that for each beer, there will be executed an individual fetch first row query, almost as if it were a scalar subquery.

- I then use cross join in line 8 to do the actual joining, which simply is because I need no on clause in this case. I have all the correlation I need in line 13, so I need not use an inner or outer join.

Using this lateral inline view enables me to get it executed for each beer like a scalar subquery, but to have individual columns queried like in Listing 1-4.

You might wonder about the cross join and say, "This isn't a Cartesian product, is it?"

Consider if I had used the traditional join style with a comma-separated list of tables and views and all join predicates in the where clause and no on clauses. In that join style, Cartesian joins happen if you have *no* join predicate at all between two tables/views (sometimes that can happen by accident – a classic error that can be hard to catch).

If I had written Listing 1-5 with traditional style joins, line 8 would have looked like this:

```
...
  7  from brewery_products bp
  8  , lateral(
  9     select
...
```

And with no join predicates in the where clause, it does exactly the same that the cross join does. But because of the lateral clause, it becomes a "Cartesian" join between *each* row of brewery_products and *each* output row set of the correlated inline view as it is executed for each beer. So for each beer, it actually *is* a Cartesian product (think of it as "partitioned Cartesian"), but the net effect is that the total result looks like a correlated join and doesn't appear Cartesian at all. Just don't let the cross join syntax confuse you.

I could have chosen to avoid the confusion of the cross join by using a regular inner join like this:

```
...
 7   from brewery_products bp
 8   join lateral(
 9     select
...
16   ) top_ys
17      on 1=1
18   where bp.brewery_id = 518
...
```

Since the correlation happens inside the lateral inline view, I can simply let the on clause be always true. The effect is exactly the same.

It might be that you feel that both cross join and the on 1=1 methods really do not state clearly what happens – both syntaxes can be considered a bit "cludgy" if you will. Then perhaps you might like the alternative syntax cross apply instead as in Listing 1-6.

Listing 1-6. The alternative syntax cross apply

```
SQL> select
  2      bp.brewery_name
  3    , bp.product_id as p_id
  4    , bp.product_name
  5    , top_ys.yr
  6    , top_ys.yr_qty
  7  from brewery_products bp
  8  cross apply(
  9     select
 10         ys.yr
 11       , ys.yr_qty
 12     from yearly_sales ys
 13     where ys.product_id = bp.product_id
 14     order by ys.yr_qty desc
 15     fetch first row only
```

11

```
16  ) top_ys
17  where bp.brewery_id = 518
18  order by bp.product_id;
```

The output is the same as Listing 1-2 like the previous listings, but this time I am using neither `lateral` nor `join`, but the keywords `cross apply` in line 8. What this means is that for each row in `brewery_products`, the inline view will be *applied*. And when I use `apply`, I am allowed to correlate the inline view with the predicate in line 13, just like using `lateral`. Behind the scenes, the database does exactly the same as a lateral inline view; it is just a case of which syntax you prefer.

The keyword `cross` distinguishes it from the variant `outer apply`, which I'll show in a moment. Here `cross` is to be thought of as "partitioned Cartesian" as I discussed in the preceding text.

Note   You can use the `cross apply` and `outer apply` not only for inline views but also for calling *table functions* (pipelined or not) in a correlated manner. This would require a longer syntax if you use `lateral`. Probably you won't see it used often on table functions, as the table functions in Oracle can be used as a correlated row source in joins anyway, so it is rarely *necessary* to use `apply`, though sometimes it can improve readability.

Outer joining correlated inline view

So far my uses of `lateral` and `apply` have only been of the `cross` variety. That means that in fact I have been cheating a little – it is not *really* the same as using scalar subqueries. It is only because of having sales data for all the beers that Listings 1-2 to 1-6 all had the same output.

If a scalar subquery finds nothing, the value in that output column of the `brewery_products` row will be null – but if a `cross join lateral` or `cross apply` inline view finds no rows, then the `brewery_products` row will not be in the output at all.

What I need to really emulate the output of the scalar subquery method is a functionality like an `outer join`, which I do in Listing 1-7. In this listing, I still find the top year and quantity for each beer, but *only* of those yearly sales that were less than 400.

Listing 1-7. Using outer apply when you need outer join functionality

```
SQL> select
  2      bp.brewery_name
  3    , bp.product_id as p_id
  4    , bp.product_name
  5    , top_ys.yr
  6    , top_ys.yr_qty
  7  from brewery_products bp
  8  outer apply(
  9    select
 10        ys.yr
 11      , ys.yr_qty
 12    from yearly_sales ys
 13    where ys.product_id = bp.product_id
 14    and ys.yr_qty < 400
 15    order by ys.yr_qty desc
 16    fetch first row only
 17  ) top_ys
 18  where bp.brewery_id = 518
 19  order by bp.product_id;
```

In line 14, I make the inline view query only years that had sales of less than 400 bottles. And then in line 8, I changed cross apply to outer apply, giving me this result:

```
BREWERY_NAME          P_ID  PRODUCT_NAME         YR    YR_QTY
Balthazar Brauerei    5310  Monks and Nuns
Balthazar Brauerei    5430  Hercule Trippel      2017  344
Balthazar Brauerei    6520  Der Helle Kumpel     2018  357
```

If I had been using cross apply in line 8, I would only have seen the last two rows in the output.

So outer apply is more correct to use if you want an output that is completely identical to the scalar subquery method. But just like you don't want to use regular outer joins unnecessarily, you should use cross apply if you know for a fact that rows always will be returned.

An outer apply is the same as a left outer join lateral with an on 1=1 join clause, so outer apply cannot support right correlation, only left.

There are cases where an outer join lateral is more flexible than outer apply, since you can actually use the on clause sensibly, like in Listing 1-8.

Listing 1-8. Outer join with the lateral keyword

```
SQL> select
  2      bp.brewery_name
  3    , bp.product_id as p_id
  4    , bp.product_name
  5    , top_ys.yr
  6    , top_ys.yr_qty
  7  from brewery_products bp
  8  left outer join lateral(
  9      select
 10          ys.yr
 11        , ys.yr_qty
 12      from yearly_sales ys
 13      where ys.product_id = bp.product_id
 14      order by ys.yr_qty desc
 15      fetch first row only
 16  ) top_ys
 17      on top_ys.yr_qty < 500
 18  where bp.brewery_id = 518
 19  order by bp.product_id;
```

Since I use lateral in the left outer join in line 8, the inline view is executed once for every beer, finding the best-selling year and quantity, just like most of the examples in the chapter. But in the on clause in line 17, I filter, so I only output a top_ys row if the quantity is less than 500. It gives me this output, which is almost but not quite the same as the output of Listings 1-2 to 1-6:

```
BREWERY_NAME        P_ID  PRODUCT_NAME        YR    YR_QTY
Balthazar Brauerei  5310  Monks and Nuns
Balthazar Brauerei  5430  Hercule Trippel     2018  451
Balthazar Brauerei  6520  Der Helle Kumpel    2017  458
```

Normally the on clause is for the joining of the two tables (or views) and shouldn't really contain a filter predicate. But in this case, it is exactly *because* I do the filtering in the on clause that I get the preceding result. Filtering in different places would solve different problems:

- If the filter predicate is inside the inline view (like Listing 1-7), the problem solved is "For each beer show me the best-selling year and quantity *out of those years that sold less than 400 bottles."*

- If the filter predicate is in the on clause (like Listing 1-8), the problem solved is "For each beer show me the best-selling year and quantity *if that year sold less than 500 bottles."*

- If the filter predicate had been in the where clause right after line 18, the problem solved would have been "For each beer *where the best-selling year sold less than 500 bottles*, show me the best-selling year and quantity." (And then it shouldn't be an outer join, but just an inner or cross join.)

In all, lateral and apply (both in cross and outer versions) have several uses that, though they might be solvable by various other workarounds, can be quite nice and efficient. Typically you don't want to use it if the best access path would be to build the entire results of the inline view first and then hash or merge the join with the outer table (for such a case, Listing 1-4 is often a better solution). But if the best path would be to do the outer table and then nested loop join to the inline view, lateral and apply are very nice methods.

Tip   You will find more examples of doing Top-N queries in Chapter 12, more examples of lateral in Chapters 9 and 12, and examples of using apply on table functions in Chapter 9.

Lessons learned

In this chapter I've shown you some workarounds to some problems and then given you examples of how to solve the same using correlated inline views, so you now know about

- Using keyword `lateral` to enable doing a left correlation inside an inline view

- Distinguishing between `cross` and `outer` versions of joining to the lateral inline view

- Applying the `cross apply` or `outer apply` as alternative syntax to achieve a left correlation

- Deciding whether a correlated inline view or a regular inline view with analytic functions can solve a problem most efficiently

Being able to correlate inline views can be handy for several situations in your application development.

CHAPTER 2

Pitfalls of Set Operations

SQL and set theory are quite related, but in practical daily life, I think many developers (myself included) do not worry too much about theory. Maybe as a consequence thereof, it is typically more seldom that I see the set operators used than joins. Most often you get along with joins fine, but now and again, a well-chosen use of a set operator can be quite nice.

But maybe because we don't use the set operators as much, I see too often code where the developer unwittingly fell into one of the pitfalls that exists, specifically concerning using distinct sets or sets with duplicates.

Most often you see the set operations illustrated with Venn diagrams like Figure 2-1 (normally you'd see them horizontally; I show them vertically as it matches the code and illustrations I use later in the chapter). And it's pretty clear what happens.

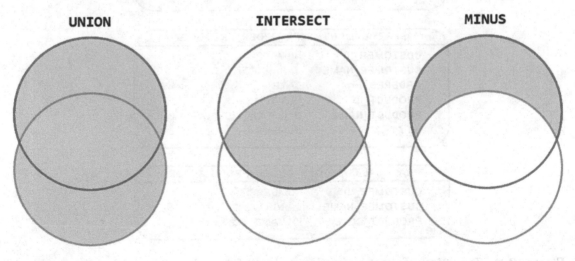

Figure 2-1. *Venn diagrams of the three set operations*

17

© Kim Berg Hansen 2020
K. Berg Hansen, *Practical Oracle SQL*, https://doi.org/10.1007/978-1-4842-5617-6_2

But what often isn't explained as well is that set theory in principle works on *distinct* sets – sets that have no duplicates. In fact the function set in Oracle SQL removes duplicates from a nested table turning it into a proper "set" according to set theory. In the practical life of a developer, it is often that we actually want to work with sets *including* duplicates, but the **set operators** default to working like set theory.

And when you then add that the **multiset operators** default the other way around, confusion can easily abound. This chapter attempts to clear that confusion.

Sets of beer

In the schema for the Good Beer Trading Co, I have some views (shown in Figure 2-2) I can use to demonstrate the set operations. The two views brewery_products and customer_ order_products are both joins of multiple tables, but for the purposes in this chapter, you can think of them as tables, and the internals of the views are irrelevant.

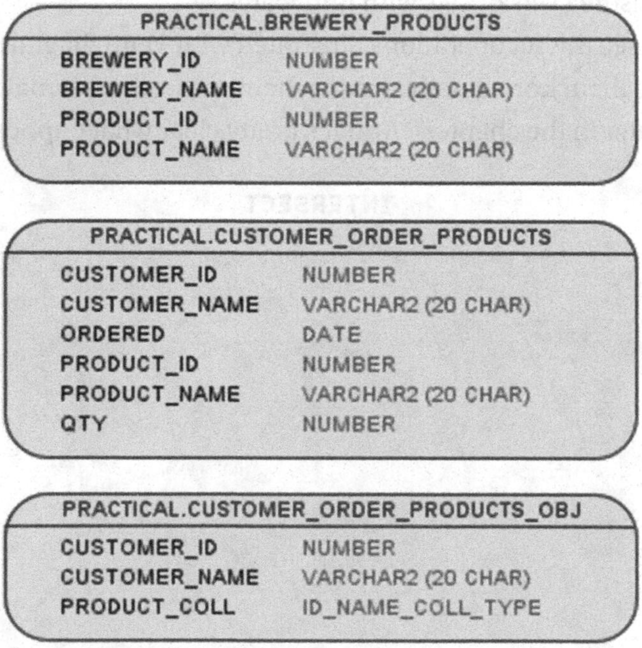

PRACTICAL.BREWERY_PRODUCTS	
BREWERY_ID	NUMBER
BREWERY_NAME	VARCHAR2 (20 CHAR)
PRODUCT_ID	NUMBER
PRODUCT_NAME	VARCHAR2 (20 CHAR)

PRACTICAL.CUSTOMER_ORDER_PRODUCTS	
CUSTOMER_ID	NUMBER
CUSTOMER_NAME	VARCHAR2 (20 CHAR)
ORDERED	DATE
PRODUCT_ID	NUMBER
PRODUCT_NAME	VARCHAR2 (20 CHAR)
QTY	NUMBER

PRACTICAL.CUSTOMER_ORDER_PRODUCTS_OBJ	
CUSTOMER_ID	NUMBER
CUSTOMER_NAME	VARCHAR2 (20 CHAR)
PRODUCT_COLL	ID_NAME_COLL_TYPE

Figure 2-2. *Two views for set examples and one for multiset examples*

View `brewery_products` simply shows which beers are purchased from which breweries. A product will be shown only once per brewery.

View `customer_order_products` shows which beers are sold to which customers, but also includes how much was sold and when, so a product can be shown multiple times per customer.

The last view `customer_order_products_obj` contains the same data as `customer_order_products` but aggregated, so there is only one row per customer containing a nested table column `product_coll` with the product id and name for each time that product has been sold to the customer. The creation of the nested table type and this view is shown in Listing 2-1.

Listing 2-1. Creating the types and view for the multiset examples

```
SQL> create or replace type id_name_type as object (
  2     id      integer
  3   , name    varchar2(20 char)
  4  );
  5  /

Type ID_NAME_TYPE compiled

SQL> create or replace type id_name_coll_type
  2     as table of id_name_type;
  3  /

Type ID_NAME_COLL_TYPE compiled

SQL> create or replace view customer_order_products_obj
  2  as
  3  select
  4     customer_id
  5   , max(customer_name) as customer_name
  6   , cast(
  7        collect(
  8           id_name_type(product_id, product_name)
  9           order by product_id
 10        )
 11        as id_name_coll_type
```

```
12       ) as product_coll
13   from customer_order_products
14   group by customer_id;
```

View CUSTOMER_ORDER_PRODUCTS_OBJ created.

With these views, I can show you the differences between **set** and **multiset** operators.

Set operators

I'm going to use just some of the data, so Listing 2-2 shows you the result of view customer_order_products for two customers.

Listing 2-2. Data for two customers and their orders

```
SQL> select
  2       customer_id as c_id, customer_name, ordered
  3   , product_id  as p_id, product_name , qty
  4   from customer_order_products
  5   where customer_id in (50042, 50741)
  6   order by customer_id, product_id;
```

C_ID	CUSTOMER_NAME	ORDERED	P_ID	PRODUCT_NAME	QTY
50042	The White Hart	2019-01-15	4280	Hoppy Crude Oil	110
50042	The White Hart	2019-03-22	4280	Hoppy Crude Oil	80
50042	The White Hart	2019-03-02	4280	Hoppy Crude Oil	60
50042	The White Hart	2019-03-22	5430	Hercule Trippel	40
50042	The White Hart	2019-01-15	6520	Der Helle Kumpel	140
50741	Hygge og Humle	2019-01-18	4280	Hoppy Crude Oil	60
50741	Hygge og Humle	2019-03-12	4280	Hoppy Crude Oil	90
50741	Hygge og Humle	2019-01-18	6520	Der Helle Kumpel	40
50741	Hygge og Humle	2019-02-26	6520	Der Helle Kumpel	40
50741	Hygge og Humle	2019-02-26	6600	Hazy Pink Cloud	16
50741	Hygge og Humle	2019-03-29	7950	Pale Rider Rides	50
50741	Hygge og Humle	2019-03-12	7950	Pale Rider Rides	100

In the same way, Listing 2-3 shows the output of view `brewery_products` for two breweries.

Listing 2-3. Data for two breweries and the products bought from them

```
SQL> select
  2     brewery_id as b_id, brewery_name
  3   , product_id as p_id, product_name
  4   from brewery_products
  5   where brewery_id in (518, 523)
  6   order by brewery_id, product_id;

B_ID BREWERY_NAME        P_ID PRODUCT_NAME
------ ------------------ ----- ------------------
  518 Balthazar Brauerei  5310 Monks and Nuns
  518 Balthazar Brauerei  5430 Hercule Trippel
  518 Balthazar Brauerei  6520 Der Helle Kumpel
  523 Happy Hoppy Hippo   6600 Hazy Pink Cloud
  523 Happy Hoppy Hippo   7790 Summer in India
  523 Happy Hoppy Hippo   7870 Ghost of Hops
```

In set theory, a set has by definition unique values, a condition that `brewery_products` satisfies.

But in practice in a database, you often don't have unique values. If you look at the data in `customer_order_products`, it is unique when you include the `ordered` date and the `qty` value, but if you only look at product id and name per customer, it is *not* unique.

This difference between real life and set theory is to a certain extent reflected in the set operators.

Set concatenation

In the daily life of a developer, often I am not concerned with set theory, but merely wish to concatenate two sets of rows, in effect just appending one set of rows after the other. This I can do with `union all`, illustrated in Figure 2-3.

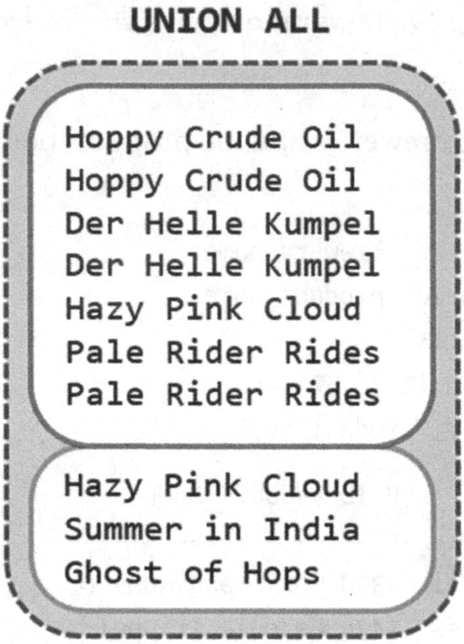

UNION ALL

Figure 2-3. *Union all simply appends one result set after another*

Figure 2-3 shows first seven rows of product names for customer 50741, followed by three rows of product names for brewery 523. Expressed as SQL, this is the code in Listing 2-4.

Listing 2-4. Concatenating the results of two queries

```
SQL> select product_id as p_id, product_name
  2  from customer_order_products
  3  where customer_id = 50741
  4  union all
  5  select product_id as p_id, product_name
  6  from brewery_products
  7  where brewery_id = 523;
```

Simply two select statements are separated with union all, and the output is the two results one after the other:

```
P_ID PRODUCT_NAME
----- -----------------
 4280 Hoppy Crude Oil
 4280 Hoppy Crude Oil
 6520 Der Helle Kumpel
```

```
6520 Der Helle Kumpel
6600 Hazy Pink Cloud
7950 Pale Rider Rides
7950 Pale Rider Rides
6600 Hazy Pink Cloud
7790 Summer in India
7870 Ghost of Hops
```

I selected only the two columns that exist in both views, which makes the output hard to see what rows come from which view. In Listing 2-5 I also select the customer id and name in the first select, but the brewery id and name in the second select.

Listing 2-5. Different columns from the two queries

```
SQL> select
  2     customer_id as c_or_b_id, customer_name as c_or_b_name
  3     , product_id as p_id, product_name
  4  from customer_order_products
  5  where customer_id = 50741
  6  union all
  7  select
  8     brewery_id, brewery_name
  9     , product_id as p_id, product_name
 10  from brewery_products
 11  where brewery_id = 523;
```

Notice that in the first two columns, I give an alias in the first select, but not in the second. That does not matter, since it is the column names or aliases of the first select that are used:

```
C_OR_B_ID C_OR_B_NAME          P_ID PRODUCT_NAME
--------- ------------------- ----- ------------------
    50741 Hygge og Humle       4280 Hoppy Crude Oil
    50741 Hygge og Humle       4280 Hoppy Crude Oil
    50741 Hygge og Humle       6520 Der Helle Kumpel
    50741 Hygge og Humle       6520 Der Helle Kumpel
    50741 Hygge og Humle       6600 Hazy Pink Cloud
    50741 Hygge og Humle       7950 Pale Rider Rides
```

```
50741 Hygge og Humle      7950 Pale Rider Rides
  523 Happy Hoppy Hippo   6600 Hazy Pink Cloud
  523 Happy Hoppy Hippo   7790 Summer in India
  523 Happy Hoppy Hippo   7870 Ghost of Hops
```

A side effect of this is that if I have given a column an alias, then I cannot use the table column name in the order by clause. If I try to append an order by with the table column product_id, I get an error:

```
...
12  order by product_id;

Error starting at line : 1 in command -
...
Error at Command Line : 12 Column : 10
Error report -
SQL Error: ORA-00904: "PRODUCT_ID": invalid identifier
```

Instead I need to use the column alias p_id to get my desired ordering:

```
12  order by p_id;

C_OR_B_ID C_OR_B_NAME          P_ID PRODUCT_NAME
--------- ------------------  ----- ----------------
    50741 Hygge og Humle       4280 Hoppy Crude Oil
    50741 Hygge og Humle       4280 Hoppy Crude Oil
    50741 Hygge og Humle       6520 Der Helle Kumpel
    50741 Hygge og Humle       6520 Der Helle Kumpel
    50741 Hygge og Humle       6600 Hazy Pink Cloud
      523 Happy Hoppy Hippo    6600 Hazy Pink Cloud
      523 Happy Hoppy Hippo    7790 Summer in India
      523 Happy Hoppy Hippo    7870 Ghost of Hops
    50741 Hygge og Humle       7950 Pale Rider Rides
    50741 Hygge og Humle       7950 Pale Rider Rides
```

The union all is a very practical and often used set operator, but there are more.

The three set operators

Using the same data as before, Figure 2-4 illustrates union, intersect, and minus.

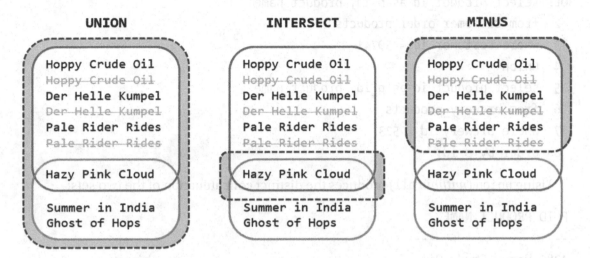

UNION   **INTERSECT**   **MINUS**

Hoppy Crude Oil   Hoppy Crude Oil   Hoppy Crude Oil
~~Hoppy Crude Oil~~   ~~Hoppy Crude Oil~~   ~~Hoppy Crude Oil~~
Der Helle Kumpel   Der Helle Kumpel   Der Helle Kumpel
~~Der Helle Kumpel~~   ~~Der Helle Kumpel~~   ~~Der Helle Kumpel~~
Pale Rider Rides   Pale Rider Rides   Pale Rider Rides
~~Pale Rider Rides~~   ~~Pale Rider Rides~~   ~~Pale Rider Rides~~

Hazy Pink Cloud   Hazy Pink Cloud   Hazy Pink Cloud

Summer in India   Summer in India   Summer in India
Ghost of Hops   Ghost of Hops   Ghost of Hops

Figure 2-4. *Union, intersect, and minus on distinct data*

You may wonder why I show union as a different operator than union all?

In reality it is just the union operator. It is one of the three operators union, intersect, and minus. All three work by design as set theory does: they work on sets with distinct values, so they implicitly remove all duplicates (illustrated by the grayed-out strike-through lines in Figure 2-4). The keyword all tells the union operator *not* to remove duplicates but to keep *all* rows.

What I see a lot in code is unfortunately that union is often used where union all really is wanted. Also in many cases where the values are already distinct, a union unnecessarily performs an implicit distinct where a union all would avoid this overhead.

So my rule of thumb is that it is almost always union all that a SQL developer needs in daily development. Only once in a while is union called for. Therefore, I tend to think of union all and union separately, as it helps me automatically distinguish between when I need one and when I need the other.

Having delivered now my lecture that you most of the time need union all, Listing 2-6 shows you the code for implementing the set operations illustrated in Figure 2-4.

Listing 2-6. Union is a true set operation that implicitly performs a distinct of the query result

```
SQL> select product_id as p_id, product_name
  2  from customer_order_products
  3  where customer_id = 50741
  4  union
  5  select product_id as p_id, product_name
  6  from brewery_products
  7  where brewery_id = 523
  8  order by p_id;
```

Using union (*without* all) produces the distinct concatenation of the two sets:

```
P_ID PRODUCT_NAME
----- ------------------
4280 Hoppy Crude Oil
6520 Der Helle Kumpel
6600 Hazy Pink Cloud
7790 Summer in India
7870 Ghost of Hops
7950 Pale Rider Rides
```

And changing to intersect produces the distinct set of overlapping rows:

```
...
  4  intersect
...
```

```
P_ID PRODUCT_NAME
----- ------------------
6600 Hazy Pink Cloud
```

Finally changing to minus produces the distinct set of the rows of the first select that are *not* in the second select:

```
...
  4  minus
...
```

```
P_ID PRODUCT_NAME
----- --------------------
 4280 Hoppy Crude Oil
 6520 Der Helle Kumpel
 7950 Pale Rider Rides
```

All straightforward, the important thing to remember is that these three operators *always* implicitly remove duplicates. Only by union all can you keep duplicates. (That will change in a future version of the database – see tip at the end of the chapter.)

Multiset operators

Data in a column of a nested table type is known as a collection when used in PL/SQL (that has several types of collections). Within SQL operations, it is known as a **multiset**. Different SQL clients will show these in different formats – Listing 2-7 shows how it looks like in sqlcl and SQL*Plus.

Listing 2-7. The customer product data viewed as a collection type

```
SQL> select
  2     customer_id as c_id, customer_name
  3   , product_coll
  4  from customer_order_products_obj
  5  where customer_id in (50042, 50741)
  6  order by customer_id;
```

I simply query the aggregate view customer_order_products_obj for my two customers and get an output with one row per customer having a column that is a *multiset,* meaning a collection (or array if you will) of product id and names:

```
 C_ID CUSTOMER_NAME   PRODUCT_COLL(ID, NAME)
------ --------------- -----------------------------------------
50042 The White Hart  ID_NAME_COLL_TYPE(ID_NAME_TYPE(4280, 'Ho
                      ppy Crude Oil'), ID_NAME_TYPE(4280, 'Hop
                      py Crude Oil'), ID_NAME_TYPE(4280, 'Hopp
                      y Crude Oil'), ID_NAME_TYPE(5430, 'Hercu
                      le Trippel'), ID_NAME_TYPE(6520, 'Der He
                      lle Kumpel'))
```

27

```
50741 Hygge og Humle   ID_NAME_COLL_TYPE(ID_NAME_TYPE(4280, 'Ho
                       ppy Crude Oil'), ID_NAME_TYPE(4280, 'Hop
                       py Crude Oil'), ID_NAME_TYPE(6520, 'Der
                       Helle Kumpel'), ID_NAME_TYPE(6520, 'Der
                       Helle Kumpel'), ID_NAME_TYPE(6600, 'Hazy
                       Pink Cloud'), ID_NAME_TYPE(7950, 'Pale
                       Rider Rides'), ID_NAME_TYPE(7950, 'Pale
                       Rider Rides'))
```

Note the multiset for each of the customers contains as many rows as there were rows per customer in the output of Listing 2-2, which is by design as this output is simply an aggregation of the Listing 2-2 output. Since I did not include the ordered and qty columns in my multiset, I have duplicates. This enables me to show you how the multiset operators handle this.

Multiset union

The operator multiset union supports the use of either all or distinct keyword, as illustrated in Figure 2-5. With the distinct keyword, it works like the set operator union by removing all duplicates. Using the all keyword has the same effect as in union all of keeping all rows including duplicates.

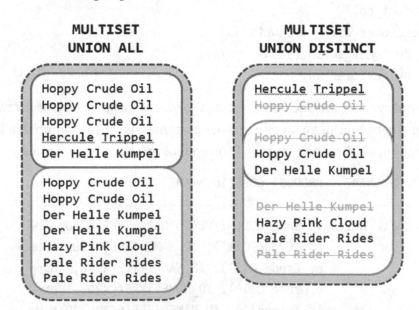

Figure 2-5. *Difference between multiset union all and multiset union distinct*

In Listing 2-8 I do a multiset union between the multisets of customer The White Hart and customer Hygge og Humle.

Listing 2-8. Doing union as a multiset operation on the collections

```
SQL> select
  2      whitehart.product_coll
  3      multiset union
  4      hyggehumle.product_coll
  5        as multiset_coll
  6  from customer_order_products_obj whitehart
  7  cross join customer_order_products_obj hyggehumle
  8  where whitehart.customer_id = 50042
  9  and hyggehumle.customer_id = 50741;
```

Notice I am using neither all nor distinct. But you can see in the output that all rows are there and no duplicates have been removed:

```
MULTISET_COLL(ID, NAME)
----------------------------------------------------------------
ID_NAME_COLL_TYPE(ID_NAME_TYPE(4280, 'Hoppy Crude Oil'), ID_
NAME_TYPE(4280, 'Hoppy Crude Oil'), ID_NAME_TYPE(4280, 'Hopp
y Crude Oil'), ID_NAME_TYPE(5430, 'Hercule Trippel'), ID_NAM
E_TYPE(6520, 'Der Helle Kumpel'), ID_NAME_TYPE(4280, 'Hoppy
Crude Oil'), ID_NAME_TYPE(4280, 'Hoppy Crude Oil'), ID_NAME_
TYPE(6520, 'Der Helle Kumpel'), ID_NAME_TYPE(6520, 'Der Hell
e Kumpel'), ID_NAME_TYPE(6600, 'Hazy Pink Cloud'), ID_NAME_T
YPE(7950, 'Pale Rider Rides'), ID_NAME_TYPE(7950, 'Pale Ride
r Rides'))
```

If I do add the keyword all, I get exactly the same result:

```
...
  3      multiset union all
...
```

Caution   This is the basis of confusion, since the set operator union defaults to distinct behavior, while multiset union defaults to all behavior. To help myself not to make mistakes, I go by the rule of thumb of never relying on the defaults. For multiset, I always include all or distinct. For the set operator union, I have no option of adding a distinct keyword, but I add it in a comment anyway as /*distinct*/ to make it clear to a future me that I didn't accidentally forget an all keyword.

If I change it to distinct, I get an output with all duplicates removed:

```
...
  3      multiset union distinct
...
MULTISET_COLL(ID, NAME)
-------------------------------------------------------------
ID_NAME_COLL_TYPE(ID_NAME_TYPE(4280, 'Hoppy Crude Oil'), ID_
NAME_TYPE(5430, 'Hercule Trippel'), ID_NAME_TYPE(6520, 'Der
Helle Kumpel'), ID_NAME_TYPE(6600, 'Hazy Pink Cloud'), ID_NA
ME_TYPE(7950, 'Pale Rider Rides'))
```

Next up is multiset intersect.

Multiset intersect

Figure 2-6 shows that with multiset intersect, I get the rows that are common to both.

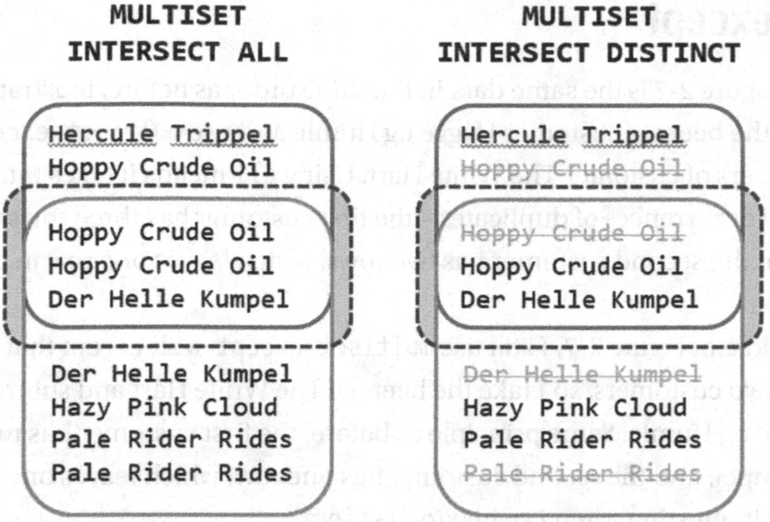

Figure 2-6. *Difference between multiset intersect all and multiset intersect distinct*

And you can see the same in the output if I change the multiset operator of Listing 2-8 to multiset intersect all:

```
...
  3     multiset intersect all
...

MULTISET_COLL(ID, NAME)
-----------------------------------------------------------
ID_NAME_COLL_TYPE(ID_NAME_TYPE(4280, 'Hoppy Crude Oil'),
ID_NAME_TYPE(4280, 'Hoppy Crude Oil'), ID_NAME_TYPE(6520,
'Der Helle Kumpel'))
```

Similarly with the multiset intersect distinct version:

```
...
  3     multiset intersect distinct
...

MULTISET_COLL(ID, NAME)
-----------------------------------------------------------
ID_NAME_COLL_TYPE(ID_NAME_TYPE(4280, 'Hoppy Crude Oil'), ID_
NAME_TYPE(6520, 'Der Helle Kumpel'))
```

Not much surprise here, but it gets more interesting with multiset except.

Multiset except

To the left in Figure 2-7 is the same data in the same order as before, illustrating what is left if I take the beers of customer Hygge og Humle and use `multiset except all` to subtract the beers of customer The White Hart. Using `all` means it takes into account the number of occurrences of duplicates – the first customer has three rows with Hoppy Crude Oil, and the second customer has two rows, which leaves one row in the output of the subtraction.

In the middle of Figure 2-7, I still use `multiset except all`, except that I have swapped the two customers, so I take the beers of The White Hart and subtract the beers of Hygge og Humle. Same principle as before, the first customer has two rows of Der Helle Kumpel, and the second customer has one row, which leaves one row in the output. It gets interesting when I switch to `distinct`.

To the right in Figure 2-7, you can see that when I use `multiset except distinct`, the output no longer contains Der Helle Kumpel. One might think that it should be like removing duplicates from the output of `multiset except all`, but it is not. It is *first* removing duplicates from *both* input sets and *then* doing the subtraction. This means that there can be some values shown using `multiset except all` that *disappear* using `multiset except distinct`.

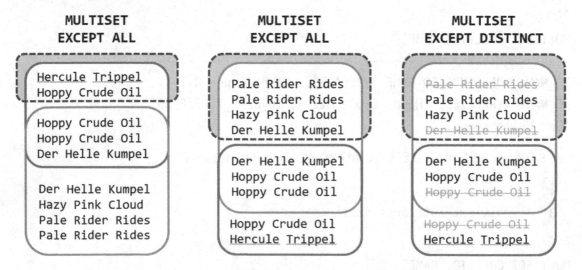

Figure 2-7. *Difference between multiset except all and multiset except distinct*

Showing the same in code, again I simply change the operator of Listing 2-8 to get the left output of Figure 2-7:

```
...
  3     multiset except all
...

MULTISET_COLL(ID, NAME)
-------------------------------------------------------------
ID_NAME_COLL_TYPE(ID_NAME_TYPE(4280, 'Hoppy Crude Oil'), ID_
NAME_TYPE(5430, 'Hercule Trippel'))
```

Swapping the order of the two input nested table columns gives me the middle output of Figure 2-7:

```
SQL> select
  2     hyggehumle.product_coll
  3     multiset except all
  4     whitehart.product_coll
...

MULTISET_COLL(ID, NAME)
-------------------------------------------------------------
ID_NAME_COLL_TYPE(ID_NAME_TYPE(6520, 'Der Helle Kumpel'), ID
_NAME_TYPE(6600, 'Hazy Pink Cloud'), ID_NAME_TYPE(7950, 'Pale
Rider Rides'), ID_NAME_TYPE(7950, 'Pale Rider Rides'))
```

Finally switching to multiset except distinct produces the right output of Figure 2-7, where you notice Der Helle Kumpel is missing:

```
SQL> select
  2     hyggehumle.product_coll
  3     multiset except distinct
  4     whitehart.product_coll
...
```

```
MULTISET_COLL(ID, NAME)
----------------------------------------------------------------
ID_NAME_COLL_TYPE(ID_NAME_TYPE(6600, 'Hazy Pink Cloud'), ID_
NAME_TYPE(7950, 'Pale Rider Rides'))
```

With multiset except, you have the choice between all and distinct as shown here, but that is not the case with the set operator minus.

Minus vs. multiset except

The set operators are typically used more often than the multiset operators, union all probably most of all. But sometimes using minus can be a nice alternative to antijoins (not in and not exists).

I've taken some care to show you the differences between multiset except all and multiset except distinct to lay the ground for Listing 2-9, where I use minus to produce the same output as I did just before with multiset except distinct.

Listing 2-9. Minus is like multiset except distinct

```
SQL> select product_id as p_id, product_name
  2  from customer_order_products
  3  where customer_id = 50741
  4  minus
  5  select product_id as p_id, product_name
  6  from customer_order_products
  7  where customer_id = 50042
  8  order by p_id;
```

Since minus also removes duplicates of the input sets first before doing the subtraction, this output also does not have Der Helle Kumpel in it:

```
 P_ID PRODUCT_NAME
----- ------------------
 6600 Hazy Pink Cloud
 7950 Pale Rider Rides
```

But what if I want an output that takes number of occurrences of duplicates into account? In other words, how can I get a minus all, even if SQL does not support it?

I've shown you that the multiset operators support it, so I can utilize this in Listing 2-10.

Listing 2-10. Emulating minus all using multiset except all

```
SQL> select
  2      minus_all_table.id    as p_id
  3    , minus_all_table.name as product_name
  4    from table(
  5      cast(
  6        multiset(
  7          select product_id, product_name
  8            from customer_order_products
  9           where customer_id = 50741
 10        )
 11        as id_name_coll_type
 12      )
 13      multiset except all
 14      cast(
 15        multiset(
 16          select product_id, product_name
 17            from customer_order_products
 18           where customer_id = 50042
 19        )
 20        as id_name_coll_type
 21      )
 22  ) minus_all_table
 23  order by p_id;
```

Each of the two selects of Listing 2-9 I put inside a multiset function call (lines 6–10 and 15–19), which converts the row set to a multiset (nested table). But I cannot just convert it to a "generic" type; I must use the cast function to specify which nested table type I want to create, in this case id_name_coll_type.

•

That way I now have two multisets, so I can subtract one from the other with multiset except all in line 13. The result of this subtraction I place in the table function in line 4, which turns the multiset (nested table) back into a row set, so the query produces the output that I want:

```
 P_ID PRODUCT_NAME
----- ------------------
 6520 Der Helle Kumpel
 6600 Hazy Pink Cloud
 7950 Pale Rider Rides
 7950 Pale Rider Rides
```

It works nicely, and the techniques shown can be useful from time to time to swap sets and multisets back and forth. But for this specific use case, it is a little bit overkill as I can emulate minus all simpler with the use of an analytic function, as I show in Listing 2-11.

Listing 2-11. Emulating minus all using analytic row_number function

```
SQL> select
  2      product_id as p_id
  3    , product_name
  4    , row_number() over (
  5         partition by product_id, product_name
  6         order by rownum
  7      ) as rn
  8  from customer_order_products
  9  where customer_id = 50741
 10  minus
 11  select
 12      product_id as p_id
 13    , product_name
 14    , row_number() over (
 15         partition by product_id, product_name
 16         order by rownum
```

```
17     ) as rn
18   from customer_order_products
19   where customer_id = 50042
20   order by p_id;
```

What I do here is that I add a column that uses row_number to create a consecutive numbering 1, 2, 3 … for each distinct value combination of product_id and product_name. This way the implicit distinct performed by the minus operator removes *no* rows, since the addition of the consecutive numbers in the rn column makes all rows unique.

That means that the first customer will have two rows with Der Helle Kumpel, one getting rn=1 and the other getting rn=2. While the second customer only has one row, so it gets rn=1. The use of minus then means that the row with rn=1 is subtracted away, but the row with rn=2 stays, as you can see in the output:

```
P_ID PRODUCT_NAME        RN
----- ------------------ --
6520 Der Helle Kumpel     2
6600 Hazy Pink Cloud      1
7950 Pale Rider Rides     1
7950 Pale Rider Rides     2
```

The code in Listing 2-11 might not be much shorter than Listing 2-10, but it is a solution that does not require creating of a nested table type, and the analytic function is less overhead than what is needed for converting collection types back and forth. So until a future SQL release gives us minus all, this is a nice way to emulate it.

Tip   In a future database release (probably 20c), the set operators intersect and except will also support the keyword all, just like union and the multiset operators. Then you won't need a workaround like the ones shown here to emulate minus all, but can do it directly.

Lessons learned

I have explained in detail about the variants of **set** and **multiset** operators with or without `distinct` and `all`, so that hopefully you now will

- Distinguish clearly between union `all` and union, so you won't fall into the mistake of using union when you *don't* want or need duplicates removed.

- Be aware that set operators union, `intersect,` and `minus` default to `distinct` behavior, unlike the multiset operators `multiset union,` `multiset intersect,` and `multiset except` that default to `all` behavior.

- Know how to emulate `minus all` until the day comes where the database version supports it directly.

This knowledge can save you from unwitting mistakes that can be hard to find in development and test environments.

CHAPTER 3

Divide and Conquer with Subquery Factoring

Every programmer has at some point learned about **modularization** – splitting the code into smaller units each solving a distinct part of the whole, typically used in procedural languages as functions and procedures, like in PL/SQL. In SQL there are views to help reduce complexity and provide reusability.

But modularization does not necessarily mean globally accessible and reusable units. For example, in PL/SQL I can create local functions and procedures in the declaration section of another function or procedure. These code units have only local scope and do not exist as objects in the data dictionary – they only serve as local modularization to simplify an otherwise large procedure.

In SQL there is a similar mechanism called **subquery factoring**, also commonly known as **the with clause** or sometimes **common table expressions**, **statement scoped views**, or **named query blocks** (just to mention some of the terms used for this).

The idea is (just like local procedures in a declaration section) to define a "local view" in a kind of "declaration section" of the SQL statement. This "declaration section" itself is **the with clause**, and each "local view" defined in it is called a **named subquery**. It is a very useful technique for local modularization within a single SQL statement.

Tip   The with clause has evolved over versions of the database and can do much more than just what is shown in this chapter. More on that to come in later chapters.

K. Berg Hansen, *Practical Oracle SQL*, https://doi.org/10.1007/978-1-4842-5617-6_3

Products and sales data

To show you an example of modularizing a SQL statement, I will use the tables shown in Figure 3-1.

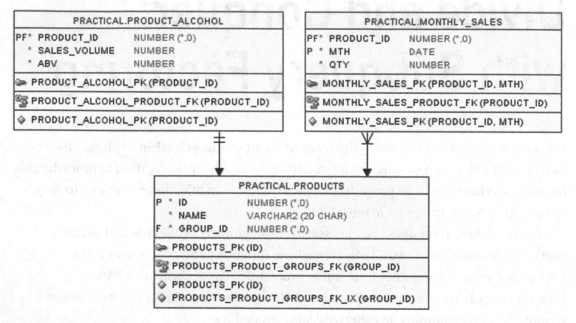

Figure 3-1. *This chapter uses tables product_alcohol and monthly_sales*

In the products table are stored the beers that Good Beer Trading Co are selling. For these, beer information about their alcohol content is in table product_alcohol, and statistics about their monthly sales are in table monthly_sales.

From these data, I will create SQL to find which year sold more than average for the half of the beers that have the lowest alcohol percentage in column abv (alcohol by volume).

Best-selling years of the less strong beers

The Good Beer Trading Co divides their beers into two halves – the half with the lowest alcohol percentage is defined as alcohol class 1, while the stronger half of the beers is alcohol class 2. I find out which are which in Listing 3-1.

Listing 3-1. Dividing the beers into alcohol class 1 and 2

```
SQL> select
  2      pa.product_id as p_id
  3    , p.name         as product_name
  4    , pa.abv
  5    , ntile(2) over (
  6        order by pa.abv, pa.product_id
  7      ) as alc_class
  8  from product_alcohol pa
  9  join products p
 10      on p.id = pa.product_id
 11  order by pa.abv, pa.product_id;
```

The analytic function ntile in lines 5–7 assigns each row into buckets – the number of buckets being the argument. It will be assigned in the order given by the order by clause and such that the rows are distributed as evenly as possible. In this case with ten rows, the first five rows in order by abv will be assigned to bucket 1 and the last five rows to bucket 2:

P_ID	PRODUCT_NAME	ABV	ALC_CLASS
6600	Hazy Pink Cloud	4	1
6520	Der Helle Kumpel	4.5	1
7870	Ghost of Hops	4.5	1
5310	Monks and Nuns	5	1
7950	Pale Rider Rides	5	1
7790	Summer in India	5.5	2
4160	Reindeer Fuel	6	2
5430	Hercule Trippel	6.5	2
4280	Hoppy Crude Oil	7	2
4040	Coalminers Sweat	8.5	2

So now in Listing 3-2, I can take just the beers with the value 1 in alc_class, join them to the monthly_sales table, and aggregate to show me yearly sales.

Listing 3-2. Viewing yearly sales of the beers in alcohol class 1

```
SQL> select
  2      pac.product_id as p_id
  3    , extract(year from ms.mth) as yr
  4    , sum(ms.qty) as yr_qty
  5  from (
  6      select
  7        pa.product_id
  8      , ntile(2) over (
  9          order by pa.abv, pa.product_id
 10        ) as alc_class
 11      from product_alcohol pa
 12  ) pac
 13  join monthly_sales ms
 14      on ms.product_id = pac.product_id
 15  where pac.alc_class = 1
 16  group by
 17      pac.product_id
 18    , extract(year from ms.mth)
 19  order by p_id, yr;
```

As analytic functions cannot be used in a where clause, I need to put the ntile calculation in an inline view in lines 6–11. In line 15, I keep only those with alc_class = 1. The rest is a normal inner join and a group by to give me an output with 3 years of sales for each of the five beers:

P_ID	YR	YR_QTY
5310	2016	478
5310	2017	582
5310	2018	425
6520	2016	415
6520	2017	458
6520	2018	357
6600	2016	121
6600	2017	105
6600	2018	98
7870	2016	552

```
7870   2017   482
7870   2018   451
7950   2016   182
7950   2017   210
7950   2018   491
```

So far so good, now I build further upon that statement, so in Listing 3-3, I can get just those years where a given beer sold more than it sold in an average year for that beer.

Listing 3-3. Viewing just the years that sold more than the average year per beer

```
SQL> select
  2      p_id, yr, yr_qty
  3    , round(avg_yr) as avg_yr
  4  from (
  5      select
  6          pac.product_id as p_id
  7        , extract(year from ms.mth) as yr
  8        , sum(ms.qty) as yr_qty
  9        , avg(sum(ms.qty)) over (
 10              partition by pac.product_id
 11          ) as avg_yr
 12      from (
 13          select
 14              pa.product_id
 15            , ntile(2) over (
 16                  order by pa.abv, pa.product_id
 17              ) as alc_class
 18          from product_alcohol pa
 19      ) pac
 20      join monthly_sales ms
 21          on ms.product_id = pac.product_id
 22      where pac.alc_class = 1
 23      group by
 24          pac.product_id
 25        , extract(year from ms.mth)
 26  )
```

```
27  where yr_qty > avg_yr
28  order by p_id, yr;
```

The code from Listing 3-3 I put inside the inline view in lines 5–25 with the addition of lines 9–11, where I calculate per beer what was sold in an average year using the analytic version of the avg function. This enables me in line 27 to keep only those years where the sales were greater than the average year:

P_ID	YR	YR_QTY	AVG_YR
5310	2017	582	495
6520	2016	415	410
6520	2017	458	410
6600	2016	121	108
7870	2016	552	495
7950	2018	491	294

There is nothing wrong as such with the query in Listing 3-3, but you can see that for each additional inline view I add, the statement becomes more complex and difficult to read. Indentation is absolutely essential to keep track of which select list belongs together with which join and where clause. If the statement grew just a little bigger, you couldn't see the select list and the where clause together without scrolling.

This is where the with clause comes in.

Modularization using the with clause

The with clause allows me to put subqueries at the top of the query, giving them a name, and use them in other places just as if they were views – you can think of it like refactoring in procedural programming, hence the name *subquery factoring*. In Listing 3-4, I refactor Listing 3-3 to use named subqueries in the with clause instead of inline views.

Listing 3-4. Rewriting Listing 3-3 using subquery factoring

```
SQL> with product_alc_class as (
  2      select
  3         pa.product_id
  4      , ntile(2) over (
  5           order by pa.abv, pa.product_id
```

```
 6       ) as alc_class
 7     from product_alcohol pa
 8   ), class_one_yearly_sales as (
 9     select
10         pac.product_id as p_id
11       , extract(year from ms.mth) as yr
12       , sum(ms.qty) as yr_qty
13       , avg(sum(ms.qty)) over (
14           partition by pac.product_id
15       ) as avg_yr
16     from product_alc_class pac
17     join monthly_sales ms
18       on ms.product_id = pac.product_id
19     where pac.alc_class = 1
20     group by
21         pac.product_id
22       , extract(year from ms.mth)
23   )
24   select
25     p_id, yr, yr_qty
26   , round(avg_yr) as avg_yr
27   from class_one_yearly_sales
28   where yr_qty > avg_yr
29   order by p_id, yr;
```

The subquery from the innermost inline view of Listing 3-3 I place in lines 2–7 and give it the name product_alc_class (it is a good idea to use some meaningful names). Then I can refer to product_alc_class in later parts of the query, using it just as if it was a view in the data dictionary. But it is not created in the data dictionary; it is only locally defined within this SQL statement.

The second-level inline view of Listing 3-3 then goes in lines 9–22 and gets the name class_one_yearly_sales in line 8. In line 16, it queries the product_alc_class named subquery in the same place that Listing 3-3 has an inline view.

And the main query in lines 24–29 corresponds to the outer query of Listing 3-3 lines 1–4 and 26–28, just querying the class_one_yearly_sales named subquery instead of an inline view.

The output of Listing 3-4 is identical to Listing 3-3, and the optimizer most likely rewrites the SQL to achieve the same access plan, so what have I gained?

Using the with clause in this simple fashion, I've mostly gained readability – having the select list and where clause close together in lines 24–29, querying a suitably named subquery makes it easier to write, understand, and check the logic of just *this* part of the big query independently. Similarly each of the two named subqueries, they can be looked at individually. It is the same benefits you know from modularizing procedural code locally.

But where Listing 3-4 refactors the *nested* inline views of Listing 3-3 by having the second subquery select from the first and the main query select from the second subquery, I can also rewrite it in an alternative manner in Listing 3-5.

Listing 3-5. Alternative rewrite using independent named subqueries

```
SQL> with product_alc_class as (
  2      select
  3          pa.product_id
  4        , ntile(2) over (
  5              order by pa.abv, pa.product_id
  6          ) as alc_class
  7      from product_alcohol pa
  8  ), yearly_sales as (
  9      select
 10          ms.product_id
 11        , extract(year from ms.mth) as yr
 12        , sum(ms.qty) as yr_qty
 13        , avg(sum(ms.qty)) over (
 14              partition by ms.product_id
 15          ) as avg_yr
 16      from monthly_sales ms
 17      group by
 18          ms.product_id
 19        , extract(year from ms.mth)
 20  )
 21  select
 22      pac.product_id as p_id
```

```
23    , ys.yr
24    , ys.yr_qty
25    , round(ys.avg_yr) as avg_yr
26  from product_alc_class pac
27  join yearly_sales ys
28     on ys.product_id = pac.product_id
29  where pac.alc_class = 1
30  and ys.yr_qty > ys.avg_yr
31  order by p_id, yr;
```

The `product_alc_class` named subquery is unchanged from Listing 3-4. But instead of `class_one_yearly_sales`, I create the simpler `yearly_sales` in lines 8–20, where I calculate the yearly sales of *all* products *without* joining to `product_alc_class`. The two named subqueries in my `with` clause are now not dependent on one another.

In the main query, I simply join the two named subqueries in lines 26–28 and do filtering in the `where` clause in lines 29–30. With this code, I achieve the same output once again as the last two listings.

Listings 3-4 and 3-5 are both examples of using the `with` clause in a manner that could have been solved with inline views. The prime benefit is readability, as the definition of the named subqueries is separated, not inline nested within one another. But there are other benefits to the `with` clause that aren't as easily solvable with inline views.

Multiple uses of the same subquery

One of the issues that potentially can arise from doing something like Listing 3-5 is that I might calculate the yearly sales of all products, even though I only need it done for half of the products. Depending on how the code is written, the optimizer might or might not be smart enough to decide whether or not it is the fastest to just do it for all products, or it might be faster to push the predicates into the subquery to only do it for the desired half.

Sometimes it is not possible to make the query push the predicates. In such cases, I can force it to only calculate yearly sales for the desired products by the method in Listing 3-6.

Listing 3-6. Querying one subquery multiple places

```
SQL> with product_alc_class as (
...
  8  ), yearly_sales as (
...
 16      from monthly_sales ms
 17      where ms.product_id in (
 18          select pac.product_id
 19          from product_alc_class pac
 20          where pac.alc_class = 1
 21      )
...
 25  )
 26  select
...
 31  from product_alc_class pac
 32  join yearly_sales ys
 33      on ys.product_id = pac.product_id
 34  where ys.yr_qty > ys.avg_yr
 35  order by p_id, yr;
```

Listing 3-6 is almost identical to Listing 3-5. But I have added lines 17–21 to make the yearly_sales be calculated only for those products found in the product_alc_class named subquery. Even so I still use product_alc_class in the join in the main query in line 31 – that is okay, as it is allowed to use the named subquery multiple places in the code.

But since the yearly_sales now has been pre-filtered to give me only those for alc_class = 1, I no longer need it in the final where clause in line 34 – I still get the same output as the last three listings.

Note   Strictly speaking, in this particular case, I could avoid joining to product_ alc_class in the main query in Listing 3-6, since I could have queried ys. product_id in the select list instead of pac.product_id. But if there had been more columns in product_alc_class that I needed in the output, then the double usage of the named subquery would be necessary.

A huge benefit of factoring out subqueries in the with clause like this is that the optimizer can decide to treat them in one of two different ways, depending on what it thinks will give the lowest cost:

It can treat them just like views, meaning that the SQL of the named subqueries is basically substituted each place that they are queried.

It can also decide to execute the SQL of a named subquery *only once*, storing the results in a temporary table it creates on the fly and then accessing this temporary table each place that the named subquery is queried.

The with clause allows the optimizer this choice, and (like always when the optimizer is involved) it most often makes a good choice, but sometimes it can make the wrong choice.

To try and see if it is a good idea for the optimizer to do the second method, I can add the *undocumented* hint /*+ materialize */ in line 2 of Listing 3-6 like this:

```
SQL> with product_alc_class as (
  2      select /*+ materialize */
  3          pa.product_id
...
```

With this hint, I force the optimizer to choose the access method of doing a temp table transformation with a load as select as seen in Figure 3-2.

OPERATION	OBJECT_NAME	OPTIONS	CARDINALITY	COST
SELECT STATEMENT			255	31
TEMP TABLE TRANSFORMATION				
LOAD AS SELECT	SYS_TEMP_0FD9D6DFA_611522	(CURSOR DURATION MEMORY)		
WINDOW		SORT	10	4
TABLE ACCESS	PRODUCT_ALCOHOL	FULL	10	3
SORT		ORDER BY	255	27
HASH JOIN			255	26
Access Predicates				
YS.PRODUCT_ID=PAC.PRODUCT_ID				
VIEW			10	2
TABLE ACCESS	SYS.SYS_TEMP_0FD9D6DFA_611522	FULL	10	2
VIEW			255	24
Filter Predicates				
YS.YR_QTY>YS.AVG_YR				
WINDOW		BUFFER	255	24
SORT		GROUP BY	255	24
FILTER				
Filter Predicates				
EXISTS (SELECT 0 FROM (SELECT /*+ CACHE (T1) */ C0 PRODUCT_ID,C1 ALC_CLASS FROM SYS.SYS_TEMP_0FD9D6DFA_611522 T1) PAC W				
TABLE ACCESS	MONTHLY_SALES	FULL	360	3
VIEW			10	2
Filter Predicates				
AND				
PAC.PRODUCT_ID=:B1				
PAC.ALC_CLASS=1				
TABLE ACCESS	SYS.SYS_TEMP_0FD9D6DFA_611522	FULL	10	2

Figure 3-2. *Explain plan showing creation and use of the ad hoc temporary table*

The operations in the explain plan that are nested under the load as select are the execution of the product_alc_class named subquery, whose results then are stored in the on-the-fly created temporary table that is given a sys_temp_* name. This temporary table is then accessed twice in the rest of the explain plan.

The /*+ materialize */ hint is perfect for testing and finding out if you would really like the optimizer to do it this way. If you find this to be the case, but the optimizer prefers (wrongly in *your* opinion) treating your named subquery as a view instead of materializing it, then you might get the idea that you would like to use the hint in your production code as well. An idea I cannot recommend.

It is possible, even likely, that you will be safe using the hint, but it is *always* strongly discouraged to use undocumented hints in production code. You don't have any guarantee from Oracle that it will stay there – it might disappear with no warning at the next upgrade. Then you can use an alternative method to force materialization:

```
SQL> with product_alc_class as (
  2     select
  3        pa.product_id
  4      , ntile(2) over (
  5          order by pa.abv, pa.product_id
```

```
6       ) as alc_class
7       from product_alcohol pa
8       where rownum >= 1
9   ), yearly_sales as (
...
```

In this version of Listing 3-6, I have taken out the /*+ materialize */ hint again, but instead added line 8. A filter clause (that always evaluates as true) on rownum also makes it necessary for the optimizer to materialize the results of the product_alc_class named subquery.

Using where rownum >= 1 or in other ways referencing rownum is a classic trick to prevent view merging. It works because the values assigned to the rownum pseudocolumn could easily be different when view merging is performed compared to when it is not. The optimizer cannot allow itself to perform a query optimization that potentially can change the results, so therefore it cannot allow view merging when using rownum. Hence it must choose to materialize instead. This mechanism works for the with clause as well as for inline or stored views.

Listing column names

So far all my with clauses have contained subqueries that depended on column aliases to specify the column names available when querying the named subqueries.

But I've said that this is a lot like defining a "local view," and you might recall that in the create view statement, you can choose between *explicitly* providing a list of column names and *implicitly* letting the columns get the names of the query column aliases. In the with clause, you can also do both.

Note   In the first database versions that supported the with clause, the implicit column naming was the only way to do it. In version 11.1 the with clause was expanded to allow *recursive* subquery factoring (a topic of a later chapter) in which the explicit column list is mandatory. But the explicit column list can also be used in general; it is not restricted to only recursive subquery factoring.

Listings 3-4, 3-5, and 3-6 all use implicit column naming from column aliases – in Listing 3-7, I show a rewrite of Listing 3-6 that uses explicit lists of column names instead.

Listing 3-7. Specifying column names list instead of column aliases

```
SQL> with product_alc_class (
  2      product_id, alc_class
  3  ) as (
  4    select
  5        pa.product_id
  6      , ntile(2) over (
  7          order by pa.abv, pa.product_id
  8        )
  9    from product_alcohol pa
 10  ), yearly_sales (
 11      product_id, yr, yr_qty, avg_yr
 12  ) as (
 13    select
 14        ms.product_id
 15      , extract(year from ms.mth)
 16      , sum(ms.qty)
 17      , avg(sum(ms.qty)) over (
 18          partition by ms.product_id
 19        )
 20    from monthly_sales ms
 21    where ms.product_id in (
 22        select pac.product_id
 23        from product_alc_class pac
 24        where pac.alc_class = 1
 25    )
 26    group by
 27        ms.product_id
 28      , extract(year from ms.mth)
 29  )
 30  select
```

```
31     pac.product_id as p_id
32   , ys.yr
33   , ys.yr_qty
34   , round(ys.avg_yr) as avg_yr
35  from product_alc_class pac
36  join yearly_sales ys
37     on ys.product_id = pac.product_id
38  where ys.yr_qty > ys.avg_yr
39  order by p_id, yr;
```

For each of my named subqueries in the with clause, I insert between the query name and the as keyword a set of parentheses with a list of column names (lines 1–3 and lines 10–12). This overrules whatever column names and/or aliases returned by the subqueries themselves – I do not even have to provide column aliases, as you can see in line 8 and lines 15–19.

It does not change the output a bit – all listings from Listings 3-3 to 3-7 produce the same output. And in many cases like this, you will not see an explicit column name used, though it can improve productivity a bit – when I do the coding of a subsequent subquery in the statement and need to know which columns of the product_alc_class named subquery are available, it is nice to simply refer to the list in line 2 rather than having to spot what are column names in the code of the select list (that might be long and convoluted).

But there's one common use of the with clause where the explicit column list is extremely handy – that is, for producing test data by selecting from dual like in Listing 3-8.

Listing 3-8. "Overloading" a table with test data in a with clause

```
SQL> with product_alcohol (
 2      product_id, sales_volume, abv
 3  ) as (
 4      /* Simulation of table product_alcohol */
 5    select 4040, 330, 4.5 from dual union all
 6    select 4160, 500, 7.0 from dual union all
 7    select 4280, 330, 8.0 from dual union all
 8    select 5310, 330, 4.0 from dual union all
 9    select 5430, 330, 8.5 from dual union all
10    select 6520, 500, 6.5 from dual union all
```

```
11      select 6600, 500, 5.0 from dual union all
12      select 7790, 500, 4.5 from dual union all
13      select 7870, 330, 6.5 from dual union all
14      select 7950, 330, 6.0 from dual
15  )
16  /* Query to test with simulated data */
17  select
18      pa.product_id as p_id
19    , p.name         as product_name
20    , pa.abv
21    , ntile(2) over (
22          order by pa.abv, pa.product_id
23      ) as alc_class
24  from product_alcohol pa
25  join products p
26      on p.id = pa.product_id
27  order by pa.abv, pa.product_id;
```

Lines 17–27 are the same as Listing 3-1. But I want to test what this query would output *if* the content of the table was something else.

Instead of creating a test table and doing a search-and-replace in my query to make it use the name of the test table, I use the with clause in lines 1–15 to create a named subquery that I give the *same name* as the product_alcohol table. I provide a list of column names in line 2, and then I simply select constant values from dual repeatedly in lines 5–14. It is much more readable *without* having a lot of column aliases cluttering the data list, like the following:

```
...
4       /* Simulation of table product_alcohol */
5       select 4040 as product_id, 330 as sales_volume, 4.5 as abv from
        dual union all
6       select 4160 as product_id, 500 as sales_volume, 7.0 as abv from
        dual union all
...
```

This way I can easily get output from my query using test data, but without changing table names in the query itself:

```
P_ID   PRODUCT_NAME     ABV   ALC_CLASS
5310   Monks and Nuns   4     1
4040   Coalminers Sweat 4.5   1
7790   Summer in India  4.5   1
6600   Hazy Pink Cloud  5     1
7950   Pale Rider Rides 6     1
6520   Der Helle Kumpel 6.5   2
7870   Ghost of Hops    6.5   2
4160   Reindeer Fuel    7     2
4280   Hoppy Crude Oil  8     2
5430   Hercule Trippel  8.5   2
```

This method of including test data in a with clause is also very handy when you ask a question on a forum on the Internet. It makes it a lot easier for people that try to help you, if they can simply execute the query containing data and all, instead of having to create a table, populate it, and *then* try your query. It is not applicable to all situations, of course, but very often it will do nicely.

Lessons learned

The with clause can do many other things too, much of which I'll cover in later chapters. This chapter focused on using it for modularizing a SQL statement so you can

- Divide and conquer by having your SQL split into pieces, each easier to have an overview of.

- View the code of each named subquery as a unit, as opposed to using nested inline views.

- Select from a named subquery more than once in your statement, potentially materializing the result temporarily instead of querying the base tables multiple times.

- Provide column names as a list as alternative to column aliases, particularly to avoid excessive cluttering of the code when using dual for test data.

When learning procedural code, we've all been taught that modularization is key to reduce dangers of complexity – it is no different in SQL. The with clause is a *very* nice tool indeed for local modularization of SQL statements that are just a bit more complex than a simple two-table join.

CHAPTER 4

Tree Calculations with Recursion

Any procedural language I can think of supports some form of recursion. A procedure or function can call itself – if needed repeatedly until some condition has been reached. Typically they'll also support iteration, which is related but not quite the same.

SQL deals with sets of rows, not procedural logic, so how can you do recursion in SQL? It still concerns itself with sets of rows: first find a set of rows; then based on that set of rows, you apply some logic to find a second set of rows; then based on *that* set of rows, you apply the logic *again* (recursively) to find a third set of rows; and so you keep on going until you find no more rows.

The typical use case for such recursion in SQL is hierarchical data. You find the top-level nodes of the tree, then find the child nodes of those, then the grandchild nodes, and so on. Each search for the next level down in the tree is recursively applying a lookup of children based on the rows of the previous level.

In this chapter I primarily focus on SQL recursion in the form of **recursive subquery factoring** that is the most directly applicable method of recursion in SQL. (You can do iterations with the `model` clause – I give examples of this in Chapters 6 and 16. Chapter 16 also gives an example of recursive subquery factoring used in a nonhierarchical manner.)

Here I will show the use of recursion on hierarchical data.

Bottles in boxes on pallets

The Good Beer Trading Co has beers in various sized bottles that are packed in various sized boxes, which might be in larger boxes, which are stacked on pallets. The definitions of those different types of product packaging and relations between them are stored in the tables in Figure 4-1.

K. Berg Hansen, *Practical Oracle SQL*, https://doi.org/10.1007/978-1-4842-5617-6_4

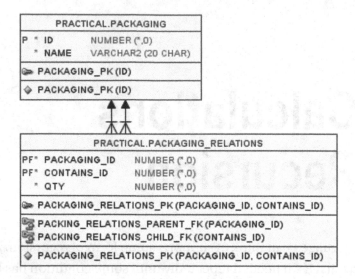

Figure 4-1. *Tables of packaging and how much is in each packaging type*

The packaging table contains the different types and sizes of bottles, boxes, and pallets. These are related to each other in the packaging_relations table, which shows how many of each type of packaging are stored within another type of packaging. Listing 4-1 shows the content of these tables in a hierarchical tree.

Listing 4-1. The hierarchical relations of the different packaging types

```
SQL> select
  2     p.id as p_id
  3   , lpad(' ', 2*(level-1)) || p.name as p_name
  4   , c.id as c_id
  5   , c.name as c_name
  6   , pr.qty
  7  from packaging_relations pr
  8  join packaging p
  9     on p.id = pr.packaging_id
 10  join packaging c
 11     on c.id = pr.contains_id
 12  start with pr.packaging_id not in (
```

```
13     select c.contains_id from packaging_relations c
14  )
15  connect by pr.packaging_id = prior pr.contains_id
16  order siblings by pr.contains_id;
```

In start with in lines 12–14, I start at the top-level pallets, because any packaging that exists as contains_id in packaging_relations is by definition not at the top level. The hierarchy is then traversed by the connect by in line 15.

In the output, you can see that pallet types are defined depending on which box (or mix of boxes) is stacked on the pallets:

P_ID	P_NAME	C_ID	C_NAME	QTY
531	Pallet of L	521	Box Large	12
521	Box Large	502	Bottle 500cl	72
532	Pallet of M	522	Box Medium	20
522	Box Medium	501	Bottle 330cl	36
533	Pallet Mix MS	522	Box Medium	10
522	Box Medium	501	Bottle 330cl	36
533	Pallet Mix MS	523	Box Small	20
523	Box Small	502	Bottle 500cl	30
534	Pallet Mix SG	523	Box Small	20
523	Box Small	502	Bottle 500cl	30
534	Pallet Mix SG	524	Gift Box	16
524	Gift Box	511	Gift Carton	8
511	Gift Carton	501	Bottle 330cl	3
511	Gift Carton	502	Bottle 500cl	2

You can see that a *Pallet of L* contains 12 *Box Large*, which in turn contains 72 *Bottle 500cl* per box.

On the other hand, a *Pallet Mix SG* contains 20 *Box Small*, which in turn contains 30 *Bottle 500cl*, and the pallet also contains 16 *Gift Box*, which contains 8 *Gift Carton* per box, which in turn contains 3 *Bottle 330cl* and 2 *Bottle 500cl* per carton.

From this hierarchy, the goal is for each top-level packaging (the pallets) to find out how many it contains of each lowest-level packaging (the bottles). For *Pallet Mix SG*, I want to know that it contains 20*30+16*8*2 = 856 *Bottle 500cl* plus 16*8*3 = 384 *Bottle 330cl*.

In other words, I need to traverse the branches of the tree and multiply the quantities of each branch.

Multiplying hierarchical quantities

To traverse a hierarchy, the traditional method in Oracle is to use the connect by syntax (as I used in the preceding text in Listing 4-1), so I will try that first in Listing 4-2.

Listing 4-2. First attempt at multiplication of quantities

```
SQL> select
  2      connect_by_root p.id as p_id
  3    , connect_by_root p.name as p_name
  4    , c.id as c_id
  5    , c.name as c_name
  6    , ltrim(sys_connect_by_path(pr.qty, '*'), '*') as qty_expr
  7    , qty * prior qty as qty_mult
  8  from packaging_relations pr
  9  join packaging p
 10      on p.id = pr.packaging_id
 11  join packaging c
 12      on c.id = pr.contains_id
 13  where connect_by_isleaf = 1
 14  start with pr.packaging_id not in (
 15      select c.contains_id from packaging_relations c
 16  )
 17  connect by pr.packaging_id = prior pr.contains_id
 18  order siblings by pr.contains_id;
```

I use the same start with and connect by as Listing 4-1, but the filter on connect_by_isleaf in line 13 makes the output contain *only* the leaves of each branch.

By using connect_by_root in lines 2 and 3, I get the desired effect in this output that p_id is the top-level packaging_id, while c_id is the lowest-level contains_id:

P_ID	P_NAME	C_ID	C_NAME	QTY_EXPR	QTY_MULT
531	Pallet of L	502	Bottle 500cl	12*72	864
532	Pallet of M	501	Bottle 330cl	20*36	720
533	Pallet Mix MS	501	Bottle 330cl	10*36	360
533	Pallet Mix MS	502	Bottle 500cl	20*30	600

534	Pallet Mix SG	502	Bottle 500cl	20*30	600
534	Pallet Mix SG	501	Bottle 330cl	16*8*3	24
534	Pallet Mix SG	502	Bottle 500cl	16*8*2	16

The intermediate rows of the hierarchy (that were visible in the output of Listing 4-1) are omitted from this output, but that does not mean they were skipped. Using `sys_connect_by_path` in line 6, I can see the quantities of all intermediate rows in the `qty_expr` column, which on purpose I delimited with an asterisk so that it visualizes the multiplication that I need to do.

In line 7 of the code, I try to calculate the multiplication in column `qty_mult`, but as you can see, it only works in the first five rows, which are those where I only have two levels to multiply. In the last two rows, I have three levels to multiply, but my output contains just the multiplication of the last two levels.

Probably you spot the error:

```
7    , qty * prior qty as qty_mult
```

I am multiplying `qty` with just the `qty` of the `prior` row. This is patently wrong, and instead I really want to multiply `qty` with the calculated `qty_mult` of the prior row:

```
7    , qty * prior qty_mult as qty_mult
```

But this is unfortunately not supported with the `connect by` syntax, where `prior` only can be used on the table columns and expressions with these, *not* on column aliases of the select list. If I try this modification, I get an error: `ORA-00904: "QTY_MULT": invalid identifier`.

But there is a different way to traverse a tree that is called recursive subquery factoring.

Recursive subquery factoring

Recursive subquery factoring is also sometimes called the recursive `with` clause, as it is a special way of using `with`. Using recursive `with` in Listing 4-3 enables me to do the multiplication I want.

Listing 4-3. Multiplication of quantities with recursive subquery factoring

```sql
SQL> with recursive_pr (
  2      packaging_id, contains_id, qty, lvl
  3  ) as (
  4     select
  5        pr.packaging_id
  6      , pr.contains_id
  7      , pr.qty
  8      , 1 as lvl
  9     from packaging_relations pr
 10     where pr.packaging_id not in (
 11        select c.contains_id from packaging_relations c
 12     )
 13     union all
 14     select
 15        pr.packaging_id
 16      , pr.contains_id
 17      , rpr.qty * pr.qty as qty
 18      , rpr.lvl + 1      as lvl
 19     from recursive_pr rpr
 20     join packaging_relations pr
 21        on pr.packaging_id = rpr.contains_id
 22  )
 23     search depth first by contains_id set rpr_order
 24  select
 25     p.id as p_id
 26   , lpad(' ', 2*(rpr.lvl-1)) || p.name as p_name
 27   , c.id as c_id
 28   , c.name as c_name
 29   , rpr.qty
 30  from recursive_pr rpr
 31  join packaging p
 32     on p.id = rpr.packaging_id
 33  join packaging c
```

```
34     on c.id = rpr.contains_id
35  order by rpr.rpr_order;
```

This is quite a bit longer than using the connect by syntax, but diving into the separate parts should help understanding:

I name my with subquery in line 1 (just as shown in the previous chapter).

When it is a *recursive* with instead of just a normal with, it is mandatory to include the list of column names, as I do in line 2.

Inside the with clause, I need two select statements separated by the union all in line 13.

The first select (lines 4–12) finds the top-level nodes of the hierarchy. This is equivalent to selecting the rows in the start with clause, but can be more complex with, for example, joins.

Recursive subquery factoring does not have a built-in pseudocolumn level, so instead I have my own lvl column, which is initialized to 1 for the top-level nodes in line 8.

The second select (lines 14–21) is the recursive part. It must query itself (line 19) and join to one or more other tables to find child rows.

In the first iteration, the recursive_pr will contain the level 1 nodes found in the preceding text, and the join to packaging_relations in lines 20–21 is equivalent to the connect by and finds the level 2 nodes in the tree. In line 18, I add 1 to the lvl value to indicate this.

In the second iteration, the recursive_pr will give me the level 2 nodes found in the first iteration, and the join finds the level 3 nodes. And so it will be executed repeatedly until no more child rows are found.

This method looks more complex than connect by, but it allows much more flexibility. One of the things it allows is using values calculated on the prior level in the expressions for the next level, as I do in line 17 where I multiply the recursive qty with the qty of the next child row in the tree. This is exactly what I could *not* do in connect by.

Recursive subquery factoring also does not have an order siblings by clause. But line 23 specifies three things: first, how the tree should be searched (depth first is equivalent to how connect by works; breadth first is the other way around and rarely used); second, which column to order siblings by; and, third, the set rpr_order creating a virtual column of that name with an incremental value that can be used in the final order by in line 35 to ensure the entire output is ordered the way I specified.

In the main query beginning line 24, I simply query the recursive subquery and join it to the packaging table to get the packaging names.

In the end I get this output with the qty values that I want:

P_ID	P_NAME	C_ID	C_NAME	QTY
531	Pallet of L	521	Box Large	12
521	Box Large	502	Bottle 500cl	864
532	Pallet of M	522	Box Medium	20
522	Box Medium	501	Bottle 330cl	720
533	Pallet Mix MS	522	Box Medium	10
522	Box Medium	501	Bottle 330cl	360
533	Pallet Mix MS	523	Box Small	20
523	Box Small	502	Bottle 500cl	600
534	Pallet Mix SG	523	Box Small	20
523	Box Small	502	Bottle 500cl	600
534	Pallet Mix SG	524	Gift Box	16
524	Gift Box	511	Gift Carton	128
511	Gift Carton	501	Bottle 330cl	384
511	Gift Carton	502	Bottle 500cl	256

You can see the last two lines have the correct values 384 and 256 instead of the wrong values 24 and 16 that were in the Listing 4-2 output.

But I have another problem with this output – it contains all of the intermediate rows that I do not want to see. Recursive subquery factoring does not have a built-in pseudocolumn connect_by_isleaf and also the operator connect_by_root, so in Listing 4-4, I make a workaround to find leaves using analytic functions.

Listing 4-4. Finding leaves in recursive subquery factoring

```
SQL> with recursive_pr (
  2      root_id, packaging_id, contains_id, qty, lvl
  3  ) as (
  4      select
  5          pr.packaging_id as root_id
  6        , pr.packaging_id
  7        , pr.contains_id
  8        , pr.qty
  9        , 1 as lvl
 10      from packaging_relations pr
 11      where pr.packaging_id not in (
```

```
12          select c.contains_id from packaging_relations c
13      )
14      union all
15      select
16          rpr.root_id
17        , pr.packaging_id
18        , pr.contains_id
19        , rpr.qty * pr.qty as qty
20        , rpr.lvl + 1       as lvl
21      from recursive_pr rpr
22      join packaging_relations pr
23          on pr.packaging_id = rpr.contains_id
24  )
25      search depth first by contains_id set rpr_order
26  select
27      p.id as p_id
28    , p.name as p_name
29    , c.id as c_id
30    , c.name as c_name
31    , leaf.qty
32  from (
33      select
34          rpr.*
35        , case
36              when nvl(
37                      lead(rpr.lvl) over (order by rpr.rpr_order)
38                    , 0
39                  ) > rpr.lvl
40              then 0
41              else 1
42          end as is_leaf
43      from recursive_pr rpr
44  ) leaf
45  join packaging p
46      on p.id = leaf.root_id
```

```
47  join packaging c
48      on c.id = leaf.contains_id
49  where leaf.is_leaf = 1
50  order by leaf.rpr_order;
```

The interesting differences in Listing 4-4 compared to Listing 4-3 are as follows:

I have an extra column root_id in my recursion. In line 5, I initialize this to the packaging_id of the root nodes. And then in line 16, the same value is copied onto all child rows of the same branch. This propagates root_id to all nodes and is the alternative to connect_by_root.

I create an inline view leaf in lines 32–44, in which I create column is_leaf using the calculation in lines 35–42. By using the analytic function lead in line 37, this calculation simply states that if the lvl of the next row in the hierarchical order is greater than the current lvl, then the current row has children and is not a leaf.

I filter on the calculated is_leaf column in line 49 as an alternative to connect_by_isleaf.

And in line 46, I make sure that in the output, I am seeing the root node in the p_id and p_name columns by joining on the root_id instead of packaging_id.

In total this gives me the same seven rows as I got from Listing 4-2, just with correct values of qty:

P_ID	P_NAME	C_ID	C_NAME	QTY
531	Pallet of L	502	Bottle 500cl	864
532	Pallet of M	501	Bottle 330cl	720
533	Pallet Mix MS	501	Bottle 330cl	360
533	Pallet Mix MS	502	Bottle 500cl	600
534	Pallet Mix SG	502	Bottle 500cl	600
534	Pallet Mix SG	501	Bottle 330cl	384
534	Pallet Mix SG	502	Bottle 500cl	256

I'm almost there, but you will notice that lines 5 and 7 in the output both are a quantity of *Bottle 500cl* contained in *Pallet Mix SG* – 600 of them stem from *Box Small*, and 256 stem from *Gift Carton/Gift Box*. I actually want that as a single row, which I take care of in Listing 4-5.

Listing 4-5. Grouping totals for packaging combinations

```
SQL> with recursive_pr (
  2     root_id, packaging_id, contains_id, qty, lvl
  3  ) as (
...
 24  )
 25     search depth first by contains_id set rpr_order
 26  select
 27     p.id as p_id
 28   , p.name as p_name
 29   , c.id as c_id
 30   , c.name as c_name
 31   , leaf.qty
 32  from (
 33     select
 34        root_id, contains_id, sum(qty) as qty
 35     from (
 36        select
 37           rpr.*
 38         , case
 39              when nvl(
 40                   lead(rpr.lvl) over (order by rpr.rpr_order)
 41                 , 0
 42              ) > rpr.lvl
 43              then 0
 44              else 1
 45           end as is_leaf
 46        from recursive_pr rpr
 47     )
 48     where is_leaf = 1
 49     group by root_id, contains_id
 50  ) leaf
 51  join packaging p
 52     on p.id = leaf.root_id
```

```
53   join packaging c
54      on c.id = leaf.contains_id
55   order by p.id, c.id;
```

The recursive subquery is unchanged from Listing 4-4, but the inline view leaf is expanded a bit and is now an inline view inside an inline view, so that I can do a group by in line 49 and sum the quantities in line 34.

The joins to packaging are unchanged; I still find the names of the packaging found from the inline view, but since I have aggregated data, I no longer have the hierarchical order (column rpr_order is gone and wouldn't make sense anyway), so instead I simply order by id columns in line 55. (An alternative could have been to select a min(rpr_order) in the inline view and order by that, but I am content with ordering by id.)

P_ID	P_NAME	C_ID	C_NAME	QTY
531	Pallet of L	502	Bottle 500cl	864
532	Pallet of M	501	Bottle 330cl	720
533	Pallet Mix MS	501	Bottle 330cl	360
533	Pallet Mix MS	502	Bottle 500cl	600
534	Pallet Mix SG	501	Bottle 330cl	384
534	Pallet Mix SG	502	Bottle 500cl	856

This output is what I want – how many of each bottle type is contained within each pallet type.

Using the recursive subquery function is a more flexible way of traversing hierarchies than the connect by syntax, and it will in almost all cases do the job perfectly. But to wrap up the chapter, I'll show you an alternative that in some rare situations might just possibly be preferable.

Dynamic SQL in PL/SQL function

You recall in Listing 4-2 I used sys_connect_by_path to build an expression of the multiplication to take place, like 16*8*3. Wouldn't it be nice simply to evaluate this expression? Well, in Listing 4-6 I do just that.

Listing 4-6. Alternative method using dynamic evaluation function

```
SQL> with
  2      function evaluate_expr(
  3          p_expr varchar2
  4      )
  5          return number
  6      is
  7          l_retval number;
  8      begin
  9          execute immediate
 10              'select ' || p_expr || ' from dual'
 11              into l_retval;
 12          return l_retval;
 13      end;
 14  select
 15      connect_by_root p.id as p_id
 16    , connect_by_root p.name as p_name
 17    , c.id as c_id
 18    , c.name as c_name
 19    , ltrim(sys_connect_by_path(pr.qty, '*'), '*') as qty_expr
 20    , evaluate_expr(
 21          ltrim(sys_connect_by_path(pr.qty, '*'), '*')
 22      ) as qty_mult
 23  from packaging_relations pr
 24  join packaging p
 25    on p.id = pr.packaging_id
 26  join packaging c
 27    on c.id = pr.contains_id
 28  where connect_by_isleaf = 1
 29  start with pr.packaging_id not in (
 30      select c.contains_id from packaging_relations c
 31  )
 32  connect by pr.packaging_id = prior pr.contains_id
 33  order siblings by pr.contains_id;
 34  /
```

The query itself in lines 14–34 is like Listing 4-2, except that in lines 20–22, I call the function `evaluate_expr` using the `sys_connect_by_path` expression as argument.

I could have created a stand-alone or packaged function for this, but I've chosen to put the function in a `with` clause (a feature available from version 12.1) as this ensures the dynamic SQL is *not* called with wrong arguments (think SQL injection). I'll give more examples of this use of PL/SQL in `with` clause in the next chapter.

Inside the `evaluate_expr` function, I simply use the `execute immediate` statement in lines 9–11 to build a dynamic SQL statement that evaluates the multiplication in the parameter string and returns the numeric result. That gives me an output with the correct values in `qty_mult`:

P_ID	P_NAME	C_ID	C_NAME	QTY_EXPR	QTY_MULT
531	Pallet of L	502	Bottle 500cl	12*72	864
532	Pallet of M	501	Bottle 330cl	20*36	720
533	Pallet Mix MS	501	Bottle 330cl	10*36	360
533	Pallet Mix MS	502	Bottle 500cl	20*30	600
534	Pallet Mix SG	502	Bottle 500cl	20*30	600
534	Pallet Mix SG	501	Bottle 330cl	16*8*3	384
534	Pallet Mix SG	502	Bottle 500cl	16*8*2	256

I have not bothered to group this result by `packaging_id` and `contains_id` like in Listing 4-5; I will leave that as an exercise to you.

Note   Listing 4-6 has a slash in line 34, even though line 33 ends with a semicolon. Depending on which client and client version you use, this may be necessary for the client to accept that there was PL/SQL inside a `with` clause. Newest versions should accept the code without a slash, but in the version of `sqlcl` I used, it was needed.

This last SQL statement wasn't really recursion, but you might have situations where even recursion would be hard put to solve your case and a bit of judicious use of PL/SQL makes the solution possible. The thing to remember, however, is that it incurs a punishment whenever runtime context is switched from SQL to PL/SQL and vice versa, though this punishment can in some circumstances be reduced if you put the PL/SQL in a `with` clause as shown here.

This punishment can be irrelevant if the function is called relatively few times compared to the total runtime, but if it is called millions of times, it can be significant. The next chapter dives deeper into this dilemma.

Lessons learned

Hierarchical data is very common, and we all know the classic example of the `scott.emp` table. Oracle has traditionally used the `connect by` syntax, which is not known in other databases, and it is an easy and usually efficient method. But recursive subquery factoring (which is known in other databases as well) can be a lot more flexible and solve things that `connect by` cannot. When you have understood the examples of this chapter, you know how to

- Do SQL recursion by querying initial row set *before* the `union all` (equivalent of `start with`) and joining recursively *after* the `union all` (equivalent of `connect by`).

- Let calculations use calculated values from the previous level of the recursion (rather than only table column values as supported by the `connect by` syntax).

- Emulate `connect_by_root` by propagating the values of the initial row set down through all the levels.

- Emulate `connect_by_isleaf` with analytic `lead` function.

It is still a good idea to know the `connect by` syntax, but knowing recursive subquery factoring allows you to solve problems that `connect by` cannot do.

CHAPTER 5

Functions Defined Within SQL

One of the beauties of the SQL language in Oracle is that it can so easily be extended by writing functions that SQL can call. Typically in PL/SQL, but for special cases, it might also be in C or in Java. With the new multilingual engine, it'll be possible in future versions to write stored procedures and functions in multiple languages.

But the thing to note is that SQL and PL/SQL are executed by two different engines, each with small differences, for example, how variables, datatypes, and memory are handled. Every time SQL calls a PL/SQL function, or vice versa PL/SQL executes static or dynamic SQL, data is passed from one engine to the other with some possible conversion along the way – this is called a context switch.

Context switches are very tiny; normally you wouldn't worry too much about them. But if a function is called a thousand times per second from SQL, it all adds up and can become a noticeable fraction of the time used. In version 12.1, it became possible to minimize this context switch, so it often becomes barely noticeable.

Table with beer alcohol data

To demonstrate this minimal context switch function in SQL, I will use the `product_alcohol` table shown in Figure 5-1.

© Kim Berg Hansen 2020
K. Berg Hansen, *Practical Oracle SQL*, https://doi.org/10.1007/978-1-4842-5617-6_5

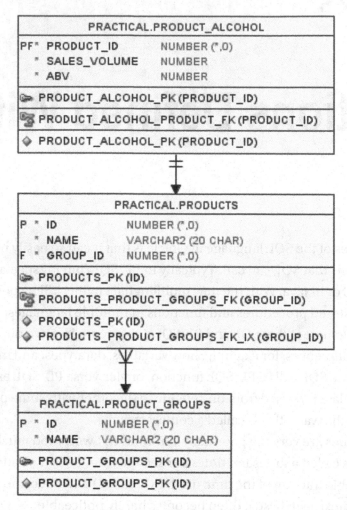

Figure 5-1. *Table product_alcohol contains data for alcohol calculations for the beers*

In this table is stored for each beer the volume (measured in milliliters) in a sales unit (aka a bottle or can) and the ABV (alcohol by volume) percent. In Listing 5-1, I'll show the data for the beers in product group 142, which are the Stouts (relatively strong and very dark beers).

Listing 5-1. The alcohol data for the beers in the Stout product group

```
SQL> select
  2      p.id as p_id
  3    , p.name
  4    , pa.sales_volume as vol
```

```
 5    , pa.abv
 6    from products p
 7    join product_alcohol pa
 8        on pa.product_id = p.id
 9    where p.group_id = 142
10    order by p.id;
```

Reindeer Fuel is in a half-liter bottle (500 milliliter) but only 6% alcohol; the other two are in the standard 0.33-liter bottles but stronger:

P_ID	NAME	VOL	ABV
4040	Coalminers Sweat	330	8.5
4160	Reindeer Fuel	500	6
4280	Hoppy Crude Oil	330	7

This data can be used to find out how much pure alcohol one bottle of beer contains, which is needed to find out how much the blood alcohol concentration (BAC) will be increased by drinking one such bottle.

Blood alcohol concentration

The Good Beer Trading Co must follow a health regulative where each beer must have an indication of how high a concentration of alcohol in your blood that drinking the beer will cause. As this is different for males and females and depends on body weight too, it must be shown both for a male weighing 80 kilograms and a female weighing 60 kilograms.

The BAC (blood alcohol concentration) must be calculated as gram alcohol per milliliter body fluid, measured in percent. Meaning that a BAC of 0.04 shows that 0.04% of the liquid in your body is grams of alcohol. It can be calculated using the Widmark formula.

Widmark formula   Milliliters of drink * ABV/100 = Milliliters alcohol. Milliliters alcohol * 0.789 (specific gravity of alcohol) = Grams alcohol. Body weight * 1000 * Gender liquid ratio = Milliliter fluid in body. (Males are 68% liquids, females 55% liquids.) 100 * Grams alcohol / Milliliter body fluid = BAC.

Putting the Widmark formula into SQL, I can calculate the desired BAC values in Listing 5-2.

Listing 5-2. Calculating blood alcohol concentration for male and female

```
SQL> select
  2      p.id as p_id
  3    , p.name
  4    , pa.sales_volume as vol
  5    , pa.abv
  6    , round(
  7        100 * (pa.sales_volume * pa.abv / 100 * 0.789)
  8          / (80 * 1000 * 0.68)
  9        , 3
 10      ) bac_m
 11    , round(
 12        100 * (pa.sales_volume * pa.abv / 100 * 0.789)
 13          / (60 * 1000 * 0.55)
 14        , 3
 15      ) bac_f
 16   from products p
 17   join product_alcohol pa
 18     on pa.product_id = p.id
 19  where p.group_id = 142
 20  order by p.id;
```

Lines 6–10 calculate the BAC of an 80 kg heavy male, while lines 11–15 do the same for a 60 kg female. The male has more liquid (both because of his gender and his larger weight), so the alcohol is diluted more in his body, and he has a lower BAC.

These two calculations give the columns bac_m and bac_f, which are the two figures Good Beer Trading Co needs to show on the beer labels and packaging:

P_ID	NAME	VOL	ABV	BAC_M	BAC_F
4040	Coalminers Sweat	330	8.5	0.041	0.067
4160	Reindeer Fuel	500	6	0.044	0.072
4280	Hoppy Crude Oil	330	7	0.034	0.055

You can see that if, for example, your country is one of the many that have a legal limit for driving of 0.05% BAC (some countries prefer showing it as per mille instead of percent, so it is 0.5‰ in those countries), all of the beers would cause a 60 kg female to get a ticket for drunk driving if she drove a car after drinking just a single bottle of these strong beers, while an 80 kg male would be below the limit.

Note   This is example data to illustrate a formula encoded in SQL. Actual BAC will vary depending upon more detailed factors in individual bodies and metabolisms, so this should not be used as basis for judging whether you can legally drive a car after drinking a couple beers or not. Use these formulas only as examples for learning SQL – I do not take responsibility for any tickets, and I urge you to drink responsibly.

Anyway, as a developer, you obviously see here that I should take that formula and put it in a function rather than repeat the same code with slightly different numbers twice in this query.

Function with PRAGMA UDF

So at first in Listing 5-3, I'll create a regular (well, almost regular) PL/SQL function for the Widmark formula for BAC calculation. Not that it matters for this demonstration, but I'll follow a best practice of putting the function in a package rather than a stand-alone function, so I've decided to have a package formulas for such functions.

Listing 5-3. Creating a formula package with a bac function

```
SQL> create or replace package formulas
  2  is
  3     function bac (
  4        p_volume in number
  5      , p_abv    in number
  6      , p_weight in number
  7      , p_gender in varchar2
  8     ) return number deterministic;
  9  end formulas;
 10  /
```

Package FORMULAS compiled

```
SQL> create or replace package body formulas
  2  is
  3     function bac (
  4        p_volume in number
  5      , p_abv    in number
  6      , p_weight in number
  7      , p_gender in varchar2
  8      ) return number deterministic
  9      is
 10        PRAGMA UDF;
 11      begin
 12        return round(
 13          100 * (p_volume * p_abv / 100 * 0.789)
 14            / (p_weight * 1000 * case p_gender
 15                                      when 'M' then 0.68
 16                                      when 'F' then 0.55
 17                                  end)
 18          , 3
 19        );
 20    end bac;
 21  end formulas;
 22  /
```

Package Body FORMULAS compiled

All are pretty straightforward, except line 10 in the body. The **UDF pragma** (user-defined function) is available since version 12.1 and tells the compiler that I intend to *primarily* call this function from SQL, rather than call it from PL/SQL.

If I had created the function *without* PRAGMA UDF, it would compile in the normal way, leading to normal context switching when the function is called. When it is compiled *with* PRAGMA UDF, it is compiled in a different manner, which potentially can reduce the overhead of the context switching. How much (if any) overhead reduction there might be is out of my control as a developer. I'll explain more shortly, but first let me show the use of the function.

Using the function is just the same as I would do with a normal function, so in Listing 5-4, I query the BAC using calls to the packaged function.

Listing 5-4. Querying male and female BAC using packaged formula

```
SQL> select
  2      p.id as p_id
  3    , p.name
  4    , pa.sales_volume as vol
  5    , pa.abv
  6    , formulas.bac(pa.sales_volume, pa.abv, 80, 'M') bac_m
  7    , formulas.bac(pa.sales_volume, pa.abv, 60, 'F') bac_f
  8  from products p
  9  join product_alcohol pa
 10     on pa.product_id = p.id
 11  where p.group_id = 142
 12  order by p.id;
```

It gives me the same output as Listing 5-2, no surprises there.

What makes this very easy to use is that I code the function just like I normally would, but as I know the function will be used a lot from SQL and less (or never) from PL/SQL, I simply add the PRAGMA UDF, and the compiler takes care of the rest, potentially saving me from some of the runtime overhead of context switching.

How much benefit the PRAGMA UDF might give is depending on several factors. If the code inside the PL/SQL function only contains something that *could* have been expressed directly in SQL itself (such as the formulas.bac function), the benefit probably is larger, while a more complex function with much PL/SQL functionality or inline SQL might gain less or no benefit. You should test your use cases, but the general rule of thumb is that it won't harm and probably might help a bit if you use the pragma whenever you *know* the function will be almost exclusively used from SQL.

When I compile the function with PRAGMA UDF, I ask the compiler to try and make the function cheaper to call from SQL, if it can. That also means that I do not care if it *might* become slightly more expensive to call from PL/SQL. Again depending on many factors, there might be a slight negative effect here, since a PRAGMA UDF function could expect to receive data in the format the SQL engine delivers it. It might be hardly noticeable, or it might be slightly more – it'll depend on actual circumstances.

But I have another alternative to using a PRAGMA UDF compiled function – I can skip creating a stored function in the database and just specify my function in the query itself.

Function in the with clause

Version 12.1 also allows me to place PL/SQL function (and procedure, but that is rarely useful) code directly inside the with clause of a query, as I do it in Listing 5-5.

Listing 5-5. Querying BAC with a function in the with clause

```
SQL> with
  2     function bac (
  3        p_volume in number
  4      , p_abv    in number
  5      , p_weight in number
  6      , p_gender in varchar2
  7      ) return number deterministic
  8      is
  9      begin
 10         return round(
 11            100 * (p_volume * p_abv / 100 * 0.789)
 12             / (p_weight * 1000 * case p_gender
 13                                  when 'M' then 0.68
 14                                  when 'F' then 0.55
 15                                  end)
 16          , 3
 17          );
 18     end;
 19  select
 20     p.id as p_id
 21   , p.name
 22   , pa.sales_volume as vol
 23   , pa.abv
 24   , bac(pa.sales_volume, pa.abv, 80, 'M') bac_m
 25   , bac(pa.sales_volume, pa.abv, 60, 'F') bac_f
 26  from products p
```

```
27  join product_alcohol pa
28      on pa.product_id = p.id
29  where p.group_id = 142
30  order by p.id
31  /
```

At first is the keyword with, just like in Chapter 3. But then instead of a subquery, lines 2–18 contain the code of the bac function, just as I had it in the package formulas. The defined function can then be called in the SQL as shown in lines 24–25. The output of this query is also the same as Listing 5-2.

A function in the with clause is compiled in the same manner as a PRAGMA UDF function, but it is not stored in the data dictionary as a PL/SQL object; it is only saved along with the query in the shared pool and *cannot* be called from any other SQL or PL/SQL statement.

Note   Line 31 of Listing 5-5 ends the query with slash (/) instead of semicolon (;). Once the parser has detected there is PL/SQL in the with clause, it seems unable (at present) to detect if a semicolon is the end of the statement or part of the PL/SQL code. This might change in future versions, but for now the workaround is to use a slash to make sqlcl or SQL*Plus find the end of the statement.

It's possible to have multiple functions in a single with clause. For example, I might decide to refactor my code and create two helper functions to calculate grams of alcohol and grams of body fluid (same as milliliters) and use those two functions inside my bac function. I can do that in Listing 5-6, which might be longer, but is also a bit more self-documenting.

Listing 5-6. Having multiple functions in one with clause

```
SQL> with
  2      function gram_alcohol (
  3          p_volume in number
  4        , p_abv    in number
  5      ) return number deterministic
  6      is
  7      begin
```

```
 8           return p_volume * p_abv / 100 * 0.789;
 9       end;
10       function gram_body_fluid (
11          p_weight in number
12        , p_gender in varchar2
13        ) return number deterministic
14       is
15       begin
16          return p_weight * 1000 * case p_gender
17                                     when 'M' then 0.68
18                                     when 'F' then 0.55
19                                   end;
20       end;
21       function bac (
22          p_volume in number
23        , p_abv    in number
24        , p_weight in number
25        , p_gender in varchar2
26        ) return number deterministic
27       is
28       begin
29          return round(
30             100 * gram_alcohol(p_volume, p_abv)
31              / gram_body_fluid(p_weight, p_gender)
32          , 3
33          );
34       end;
35   select
...
```

The multiple functions make no difference to the output – it's the same again.

But whether I use a single function or multiple functions, I still have a decision to make. If I want to use a function in multiple SQL statements, I have to create a stored function (with or without PRAGMA UDF), no question about it. But otherwise, why would I ever put it in the with clause instead of using a PRAGMA UDF function?

One reason could be cases where you cannot create stored functions or procedures, for example, either in a read-only database or if you build some tool statements that you wish to run without installing code in databases of your clients.

Another reason could be if the function in some rare cases executes dynamic SQL that for some reason cannot use bind variables, using string concatenated SQL instead. Having the function in the query gives you absolute control of what arguments the function is called with, so you can guard yourself more against SQL injection. The function cannot be called from elsewhere.

A third reason could be functionality that is very specific for a single purpose, where you could choose a different way to encapsulate your code.

Encapsulated in a view

It would be reasonable (in this application) to say that the blood alcohol concentration calculation does not make sense outside the context of a row in the product_alcohol table. If I had been using object-oriented programming, I could say that it would be a *member* method rather than a *static* method.

I can achieve a somewhat similar effect by creating the view in Listing 5-7.

Listing 5-7. Creating a view with the BAC calculations

```
SQL> create view product_alcohol_bac
  2  as
  3  with
  4     function gram_alcohol (
...
 12     function gram_body_fluid (
...
 23     function bac (
...
 37  select
 38     pa.product_id
 39   , pa.sales_volume
 40   , pa.abv
```

```
41   , bac(pa.sales_volume, pa.abv, 80, 'M') bac_m
42   , bac(pa.sales_volume, pa.abv, 60, 'F') bac_f
43  from product_alcohol pa
44  /
```

View PRODUCT_ALCOHOL_BAC created.

In this view, I use the with clause with the three functions from Listing 5-6. The query itself in lines 37–43 only uses the product_alcohol table, selecting all columns of the table plus the two calculated bac_m and bac_f columns.

Now I can make a query joining the products table with the product_alcohol_bac view in Listing 5-8, giving me the desired data directly and simply.

Listing 5-8. Querying BAC data using the view

```
SQL> select
  2       p.id as p_id
  3     , p.name
  4     , pab.sales_volume as vol
  5     , pab.abv
  6     , pab.bac_m
  7     , pab.bac_f
  8  from products p
  9  join product_alcohol_bac pab
 10     on pab.product_id = p.id
 11  where p.group_id = 142
 12  order by p.id;
```

The same output once again:

P_ID	NAME	VOL	ABV	BAC_M	BAC_F
4040	Coalminers Sweat	330	8.5	0.041	0.067
4160	Reindeer Fuel	500	6	0.044	0.072
4280	Hoppy Crude Oil	330	7	0.034	0.055

This method enables me to reuse the logic in other SQL statements by querying the view instead of the table, but still have the logic only in a single place: the view definition.

I could achieve the same by having the view calling the packaged function `formulas.bac` instead of defining the functions in the view, but if it is a functionality that is *so* specific that it is only relevant for this particular query/view definition, then it can be a nice thing to keep everything together and not clutter the data dictionary with stored functions that really never should be called outside this particular SQL.

Lessons learned

Even though the topic of this book is not PL/SQL as such, having the ability to integrate PL/SQL into SQL even tighter than it used to be is a feature you as a SQL developer should be aware of. With this chapter as example, you should now

- Consider if a function is primarily used from SQL and thus could benefit from adding the PRAGMA UDF to the definition.

- Know how to embed "single-use" functions in SQL statements in the with clause.

- Think about if very specific functionality might be better off encapsulated in a view using with clause functions instead of normal stored functions.

For much of your daily development, probably it is the PRAGMA UDF you mostly should think about, but the with clause technique can be very useful if you have situations where you cannot install stored procedures and functions.

CHAPTER 6

Iterative Calculations with Multidimensional Data

You won't find a multitude of real-life examples using the model clause, apart from doing recursion and iteration as I showed in Chapter 4. Recursive subquery factoring came in version 11, but with the model clause, you could do recursion from version 10. However, the real power of the model clause is the way you can address data in multiple dimensions in an array-like fashion, building formulas similar to the way spreadsheets work.

A nested table type in Oracle has a single dimension (index), and the "cell" can be a scalar or a structured type. If you have multiple dimensions, you can nest the nested table types, or you can work with plain SQL – both methods can become hairy for some types of calculations. In the model clause, you work in a sense with arrays that can have multiple dimensions and multiple measures (values) in each cell, and you have a very dense syntax for addressing multiple cells.

The model clause is not the obvious choice for implementation of everything, but I'll show you an example that fits perfectly and uses both multiple dimensions as well as iteration. This example may not be the most useful in itself, but it demonstrates very well the kind of situations where you could consider using the model clause.

Conway's Game of Life

In 1970, British mathematician John Horton Conway devised the Game of Life (also known simply as Life). It is about cells in a two-dimensional grid emulating how cells live and die over generations depending on how crowded things are in the grid. You can see cells populating the grid in Figure 6-1.

© Kim Berg Hansen 2020
K. Berg Hansen, *Practical Oracle SQL*, https://doi.org/10.1007/978-1-4842-5617-6_6

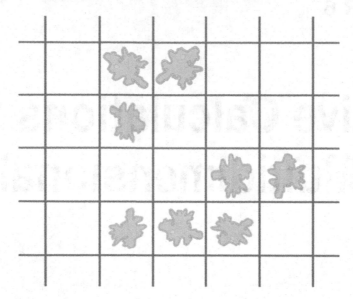

Figure 6-1. *Conway's Game of Life is about life and death of cells in a grid*

The idea is to start with some set of "live" cells (grid cells that are populated by live cellular organisms) and then see how the population evolves over time from generation to generation.

The evolvement is governed by these rules:

- Any live cell with fewer than two live neighbors dies, as if caused by underpopulation.

- Any live cell with two or three live neighbors lives on to the next generation.

- Any live cell with more than three live neighbors dies, as if by overcrowding.

- Any dead cell with exactly three live neighbors becomes a live cell, as if by reproduction.

So in order to find out which cells will be alive in the next generation, you count the number of live neighbors for each cell in this generation and apply the rules. Neighbors are defined as the eight cells that surround a cell (one cell away horizontally, vertically, or diagonally).

Most often you see the Game of Life implemented iteratively in a procedural language – I am going to show you how to do it in a single SQL statement with the model clause.

Note   You can find a fuller explanation of the Game of Life on Wikipedia:
`https://en.wikipedia.org/wiki/Conway%27s_Game_of_Life`.

Live neighbor count with the model clause

I have created a table `conway_gen_zero` for holding all cells in the grid and whether they contain a live cell or not in generation zero. Figure 6-2 shows it has x and y columns for each grid position and column `alive` that contains 1 for a live cell and 0 for a dead (empty) cell.

```
┌─────────────────────────────────────────┐
│ PRACTICAL.CONWAY_GEN_ZERO                │
├─────────────────────────────────────────┤
│ P ⁼ X          NUMBER (*,0)              │
│ P ⁼ Y          NUMBER (*,0)              │
│   ⁼ ALIVE      NUMBER (*,0)              │
├─────────────────────────────────────────┤
│ ⌦ CONWAY_GEN_ZERO_PK (X, Y)             │
├─────────────────────────────────────────┤
│ ◈ CONWAY_GEN_ZERO_PK (X, Y)             │
└─────────────────────────────────────────┘
```

Figure 6-2. *Table for the grid content of generation zero*

To begin with, in Listing 6-1, I populate this table with a 10x10 grid, where the middle of the grid has some live cells in the pattern shown in Figure 6-1.

Listing 6-1. Creating a 10x10 generation zero population

```
SQL> insert into conway_gen_zero (x, y, alive)
  2  select * from (
  3    with numbers as (
  4      select level as n from dual
  5      connect by level <= 10
  6    ), grid as (
  7      select
  8        x.n as x
  9      , y.n as y
 10      from numbers x
 11      cross join numbers y
 12    ), start_cells as (
```

```
13          select  4 x,  4 y from dual union all
14          select  5 x,  4 y from dual union all
15          select  4 x,  5 y from dual union all
16          select  6 x,  6 y from dual union all
17          select  7 x,  6 y from dual union all
18          select  4 x,  7 y from dual union all
19          select  5 x,  7 y from dual union all
20          select  6 x,  7 y from dual
21     )
22     select
23       g.x
24     , g.y
25     , nvl2(sc.x, 1, 0) as alive
26     from grid g
27     left outer join start_cells sc
28        on  sc.x = g.x
29        and sc.y = g.y
30  );
```

100 rows inserted.

I use the techniques of Chapter 3 to make this query in several with clauses:

- numbers in lines 4–5 simply gives me ten rows numbered 1–10.

- grid in lines 7–11 makes a Cartesian join using numbers twice to generate 100 rows with all the (x, y) combinations of a 10x10 grid.

- start_cells in lines 13–20 generates eight rows with the (x, y) coordinates of those cells that are alive in generation zero (the starting population).

- In lines 22–29, the grid is left joined to start_cells, so the result is the 100 rows of the grid with line 25 calculating a 1 (alive) if the cell exists in start_cells and otherwise 0 (dead).

My generation zero population is ready, and in Listing 6-2, I display the population using X for a live cell and space for an empty cell, so you can visually see that this is the cell pattern of Figure 6-1.

Listing 6-2. Vizualizing generation zero

```
SQL> select
  2     listagg(
  3        case alive
  4           when 1 then 'X'
  5           when 0 then ' '
  6        end
  7     ) within group (
  8        order by x
  9     ) as cells
 10  from conway_gen_zero
 11  group by y
 12  order by y;
```

The listagg in lines 2–9 (read more about it in Chapter 10) aggregates a string containing Xs and spaces in order of column x for each column y giving this output:

```
CELLS
----------

  XX
  X
    XX
  XXX
```

Generation zero looks good, so it's time to play around with the model clause in Listing 6-3 to calculate how many live neighbors each cell has.

Listing 6-3. Live neighbor calculation with the model clause

```
SQL> select *
  2  from conway_gen_zero
  3  model
  4  dimension by (
  5     x, y
  6  )
  7  measures (
  8     alive
```

```
 9   , 0 as sum_alive
10   , 0 as nb_alive
11   )
12   ignore nav
13   rules
14   (
15     sum_alive[any, any] =
16        sum(alive)[
17            x between cv() - 1 and cv() + 1
18          , y between cv() - 1 and cv() + 1
19          ]
20     , nb_alive[any, any] =
21        sum_alive[cv(), cv()] - alive[cv(), cv()]
22   )
23   order by x, y;
```

The model clause is built in a set of subclauses:

- dimension by in lines 4–6 states which columns to use as dimensions – or if you wish, indexes in a multidimensional array.

- measures in lines 7–11 are the attributes of each cell in the array. Here I am creating three measures – one is simply the column alive; the two others do not exist in the table but are initialized to zero.

- Then there can be various options of the model clause – in line 12, I'm using ignore nav, which simply states that when a formula tries to use the value of a measure in a cell, any nulls or non-existing values should be treated as a default value that depends on the datatype (in this case, zero for numbers).

- rules beginning in line 13 is a set of formulas that states how I want the values of the measures in each cell to be calculated. I have two formulas here, one for each of the two measures that were not in the table.

- Lines 15–19 calculate sum_alive. Using [any, any] I ask that the measure should be calculated for all cells in the grid. When the formula is calculated for a specific cell, function cv() gives the value of the dimension for that specific cell, and I use this to define a 3x3 grid for which I calculate the sum of measure `alive` in the nine cells in that grid. For example, for the cell in [3, 5], the sum will be calculated over the cells with dimension x between 2 and 4 and dimension y between 4 and 6.

- Lines 20–21 calculate `nb_alive`, which is "neighbors alive." The `sum_alive` calculated in the preceding text is the number of live cells in the nine cells in the 3x3 grid which *includes* the cell itself. So that means I can find the number of *neighbors* alive by subtracting the `alive` value in the cell itself.

The model clause in Listing 6-3 looks very different from normal SQL. It is a quite different way of addressing the data and applying formulas to specified subsets of the data, more similar to arrays in many procedural languages or formulas in spreadsheets, just in the more declarative manner that is the hallmark of SQL.

But I could do the same as Listing 6-3 in normal SQL, if I use a scalar subquery and an inline view. Listing 6-4 provides an example.

Listing 6-4. Live neighbor calculation with the scalar subquery

```
SQL> select
  2      x
  3    , y
  4    , alive
  5    , sum_alive
  6    , sum_alive - alive as nb_alive
  7    from (
  8      select
  9        x
 10      , y
 11      , alive
 12      , (
 13          select sum(gz2.alive)
 14          from conway_gen_zero gz2
 15          where gz2.x between gz.x - 1 and gz.x + 1
 16          and   gz2.y between gz.y - 1 and gz.y + 1
```

```
17           ) as sum_alive
18      from conway_gen_zero gz
19  )
20  order by x, y;
```

Both Listing 6-3 and Listing 6-4 produce the same output – all cells in the grid with the two live counts:

```
 X   Y ALIVE  SUM_ALIVE   NB_ALIVE
--- --- ----- ---------- ----------
 1   1    0       0           0
 1   2    0       0           0
 1   3    0       0           0
...
 5   5    0       4           4
 5   6    0       5           5
 5   7    1       4           3
 5   8    0       3           3
 5   9    0       0           0
 5  10    0       0           0
 6   1    0       0           0
 6   2    0       0           0
 6   3    0       1           1
 6   4    0       1           1
 6   5    0       3           3
...
10   9    0       0           0
10  10    0       0           0
```

`100 rows selected.`

So why do I choose to solve the Game of Life with the model clause instead of plain SQL? For one, it's because the scalar subquery means a lot of repeated reads of the same data over and over. Normally I'd look to analytic functions to avoid such repetitive data access, but the problem here is that I want to sum over a range of *two* dimensions. If, for example, I were to use an analytic sum using the range between 1 preceding and 1 following clause, I could only do that on either x or y dimension, not on both simultaneously.

94

The other reason for solving the Game of Life with the model clause will be clear when I start iterating the calculations over more generations in the game, as doing so is much more complex in plain SQL than in the model clause. Keep reading, and you'll see what I mean.

Before that, however, I'd like to visualize the results of calculations using the listagg technique of Listing 6-2. So in Listing 6-5, I simply take the SQL from either Listing 6-3 or Listing 6-4 and put it in a with clause and then query that instead of the table directly.

Listing 6-5. Displaying the counts grid fashion

```
SQL> with conway as (
...
      /* Content of Listing 6-3 or 6-4 */
...
 24 )
 25 select
 26    listagg(
 27      case alive
 28        when 1 then 'X'
 29        when 0 then ' '
 30      end
 31    ) within group (
 32      order by x
 33    ) cells
 34  , listagg(sum_alive) within group (order by x) sum_alives
 35  , listagg(nb_alive ) within group (order by x) nb_alives
 36  from conway
 37  group by y
 38  order by y;
```

Lines 26–33 are just as they were in Listing 6-2, and then I've added lines 34 and 35 to visualize the content of measures sum_alive and nb_alive, which will work because the values always are single-digit. sum_alive I calculated over a 3x3 grid, so it can be a maximum of 9, and nb_alive can thus be a maximum of 8.

CELLS	SUM_ALIVES	NB_ALIVES
	0000000000	0000000000
	0000000000	0000000000
	0012210000	0012210000
XX	0023310000	0022210000
X	0023432100	0022432100
XX	0023543100	0023532100
XXX	0012443100	0011333100
	0012321000	0012321000
	0000000000	0000000000
	0000000000	0000000000

You can see that in those positions of the grid where there is an X in cells, the digit in nb_alives is one less than sum_alives – just as expected.

So far I've only modeled and calculated neighbor count for generation zero. Now it's time to use that neighbor count to calculate where there will be live cells in the next generation, calculate neighbor count for that generation, and then repeat the process iteratively for generation after generation after ...

Iterating generations

In the beginning of the chapter, I stated the four rules of Conway's Game of Life. They are good for describing Life in terms of simulating a population of cellular organisms. But for implementing the rules in a programming language, it can be helpful to examine the logic of the rules and restate them in the following manner:

- Any cell with exactly two live neighbors keeps the same status (alive or dead) in the next generation.

- Any cell with exactly three live neighbors will be alive in the next generation (no matter if it was alive or dead in this generation).

- Any other cell will be dead in the next generation.

The result of these rules is the same as the original four rules, but there is a great advantage for a programmer: it can easily be stated in an `if` or `case` structure whether a cell is alive or dead in the next generation, based on whether the neighbor count in the current generation is two, three, or anything else. So that I will do in Listing 6-6.

Listing 6-6. Iterating two generations

```
SQL> with conway as (
  2      select *
  3      from conway_gen_zero
  4      model
  5      dimension by (
  6          0 as generation
  7        , x, y
  8      )
  9      measures (
 10          alive
 11        , 0 as sum_alive
 12        , 0 as nb_alive
 13      )
 14      ignore nav
 15      rules upsert all iterate (2)
 16      (
 17          sum_alive[iteration_number, any, any] =
 18              sum(alive)[
 19                  generation = iteration_number
 20                , x between cv() - 1 and cv() + 1
 21                , y between cv() - 1 and cv() + 1
 22              ]
 23        , nb_alive[iteration_number, any, any] =
 24              sum_alive[iteration_number, cv(), cv()]
 25                - alive[iteration_number, cv(), cv()]
 26        , alive[iteration_number + 1, any, any] =
 27              case nb_alive[iteration_number, cv(), cv()]
 28                  when 2 then alive[iteration_number, cv(), cv()]
 29                  when 3 then 1
```

```
30                 else 0
31             end
32     )
33   )
34   select
35     generation
36   , listagg(
37         case alive
38             when 1 then 'X'
39             when 0 then ' '
40         end
41     ) within group (
42         order by x
43     ) cells
44   , listagg(sum_alive) within group (order by x) sum_alives
45   , listagg(nb_alive ) within group (order by x) nb_alives
46   from conway
47   group by generation, y
48   order by generation, y;
```

Compared to Listing 6-3, I have added some things to handle generations of cells:

- In line 6, I have added another dimension generation for a total of three dimensions. This does not exist in the table, so I initialize it with the value zero. That means that the 100 rows in the table will be in the multidimensional array all having zero for generation but x and y values from the table.

- In the rules clause in line 15, I have added upsert all, which states that if I set a value for an existing cell, it will be updated, but if I set a value for a non-existing cell, it will be created. This is needed since I am going to create 100 new cells for every generation I am iterating over.

- In line 15, I have also added iterate (2), which means that the rules will be applied twice.

- As I have added a dimension, I must also expand the indexing used in cell addressing in the formulas for sum_alive and nb_alive in lines 17–25. For the generation dimension, I use the value of iteration_number, which is a number that starts with zero for the first iteration and then increments by one for every iteration. So sum_alive and nb_alive are calculated for the generation that matches the iteration, starting with generation zero.

- In lines 26–31, I apply the three rewritten rules of Conway, where I set the value of alive in the *next* generation using the case structure based on nb_alive in *this* generation. This is where the upsert all is needed, since I am creating new cells with a generation value one higher.

In total, Listing 6-6 produces this output:

GENERATION	CELLS	SUM_ALIVES	NB_ALIVES
0		0000000000	0000000000
0		0000000000	0000000000
0		0012210000	0012210000
0	XX	0023310000	0022210000
0	X	0023432100	0022432100
0	XX	0023543100	0023532100
0	XXX	0012443100	0011333100
0		0012321000	0012321000
0		0000000000	0000000000
0		0000000000	0000000000
1		0000000000	0000000000
1		0000000000	0000000000
1		0012210000	0012210000
1	XX	0023421000	0022321000
1	X X	0034643100	0033633100
1	X XX	0023665200	0022654200
1	XXX	0013564200	0013453200
1	X	0002342100	0002242100
1		0001110000	0001110000

```
1                        0000000000 0000000000
2
2
2
2     XX
2     XX XX
2     X
2     X X
2       X
2
2
```

The content of `cells` (measure `alive`) in generation zero comes directly from the table.

In the first iteration (`iteration_number 0`), the `sum_alive` and `nb_alive` of generation zero are calculated, and the `cells` (`alive`) of generation one are calculated.

In the second iteration (`iteration_number 1`), the `sum_alive` and `nb_alive` of generation one are calculated, and the `cells` (`alive`) of generation two are calculated. Then I do not iterate anymore, so `sum_alive` and `nb_alive` of generation two are not calculated.

Such iteration over multiple generations would have been much more difficult to do with plain SQL. Using a technique like Listing 6-4 combined with recursive subquery factoring (Chapter 4), it would probably be possible, but it would not be very nice and most likely not very performant.

Using the model clause to do this like Listing 6-6 is actually quite declarative, but it is a different way of thinking. Listing 6-6 may look a bit long, but once I have it developed, I can see that I do not actually need to explicitly calculate the intermediate values `sum_alive` and `nb_alive`. I can put those calculations directly into the calculation of `alive`, making a reduced query in Listing 6-7.

Listing 6-7. Reducing the query

```
SQL> with conway as (
  2      select *
  3      from conway_gen_zero
  4      model
  5      dimension by (
```

```
 6        0 as generation
 7      , x, y
 8      )
 9      measures (
10          alive
11      )
12      ignore nav
13      rules upsert all iterate (2)
14      (
15          alive[iteration_number + 1, any, any] =
16              case sum(alive)[
17                      generation = iteration_number,
18                      x between cv() - 1 and cv() + 1,
19                      y between cv() - 1 and cv() + 1
20                  ] - alive[iteration_number, cv(), cv()]
21                  when 2 then alive[iteration_number, cv(), cv()]
22                  when 3 then 1
23                  else 0
24              end
25      )
26 )
27 select
28      generation
29    , listagg(
30          case alive
31              when 1 then 'X'
32              when 0 then ' '
33          end
34      ) within group (
35          order by x
36      ) cells
37 from conway
38 group by generation, y
39 order by generation, y;
```

The reduced query of course does not show the neighbor counts, but I do not need them anymore; they were mostly useful during the development of the code:

```
GENERATION CELLS
---------- ----------
         0
         0
         0
         0     XX
         0     X
         0       XX
         0     XXX
         0
         0
         0
         1
         1
         1
         1     XX
         1     X X
         1     X XX
         1       XXX
         1      X
         1
         1
         2
         2
         2
         2      XX
         2     XX XX
         2     X
         2     X  X
         2       X
         2
         2
```

And now I can play around and try to generate, for example, 25 generations:

```
13     rules upsert all iterate (25)
```

```
GENERATION CELLS
---------- ----------
...
     25    X   X X
     25    XXXX
     25  X  XX  XX
     25 X X   XXX
     25 X X X  XX
     25 X     X X
     25 X XX   X
     25 X    X X
     25          XXX
     25           X
```

260 rows selected.

I can see that the live cells have spread over my entire 10x10 grid, so will it be completely filled if I do 50 generations?

```
13     rules upsert all iterate (50)
```

```
GENERATION CELLS
---------- ----------
...
     50
     50
     50           XX
     50           XX
     50
     50
     50
     50
     50
     50
```

510 rows selected.

Well no, from generation 40 or so, the population starts to decrease, and from generation 46, I have just four cells alive in a stable pattern that will stay like that forever. Partly this is because my grid is much too small and limited – in theory the Game of Life should run on an infinite grid.

Just to round off the playing around with Game of Life, Listing 6-8 puts a different generation zero onto a 6x6 grid. This new starting point gives us an oscillating game, which is interesting to see when you run the iterations.

Listing 6-8. The Toad

```
SQL> truncate table conway_gen_zero;

Table CONWAY_GEN_ZERO truncated.

SQL> insert into conway_gen_zero (x, y, alive)
  2  select * from (
  3    with numbers as (
  4       select level as n from dual
  5       connect by level <= 6
  6    ), grid as (
  7       select
  8          x.n as x
  9        , y.n as y
 10       from numbers x
 11       cross join numbers y
 12    ), start_cells as (
 13       select  4 x,  2 y from dual union all
 14       select  2 x,  3 y from dual union all
 15       select  5 x,  3 y from dual union all
 16       select  2 x,  4 y from dual union all
 17       select  5 x,  4 y from dual union all
 18       select  3 x,  5 y from dual
 19    )
 20    select
 21       g.x
 22     , g.y
 23     , nvl2(sc.x, 1, 0) as alive
```

```
24      from grid g
25      left outer join start_cells sc
26          on  sc.x = g.x
27          and sc.y = g.y
28  );
```

36 rows inserted.

And then I run Listing 6-7 iterating just for two generations:

```
13      rules upsert all iterate (2)
```

In the output, I can see that generation two is identical to generation zero, which means generation three would be identical to generation one, and so on:

```
GENERATION CELLS
---------- ----------
         0
         0    X
         0  X X
         0  X X
         0    X
         0
         1
         1
         1  XXX
         1  XXX
         1
         1
         2
         2    X
         2  X X
         2  X X
         2    X
         2
```

18 rows selected.

This output is an example of what is known as an oscillator with period 2, since it oscillates back and forth between two populations. There are many examples of such oscillators – this one is known as the Toad, visualized in Figure 6-3.

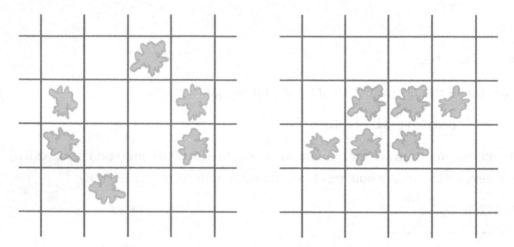

Figure 6-3. *The two states of the Toad oscillator*

Lessons learned

In this chapter I have used an example that is a bit more "for fun" and less practically useful in itself. I have done it, however, as it is a very good showcase of some of the powerful features of the `model` clause, so having read the chapter, you should have an idea about

- Selecting "indexes" for the multidimensional array in `dimension by`

- Defining attributes to carry the values for each cell of the array in `measures`

- Using [] syntax to retrieve data from one or more (with aggregation) cells in `rules`

- Repeating the rules multiple times with `iterate`

- Creating new cells with `upsert all`

With these "building blocks," you can create your own `model` clauses when you have a use case that is suitable for this method of handling data.

CHAPTER 7

Unpivoting Columns to Rows

Ideally, you'd hope always to work with data that's nicely normalized in your relational database, the way they teach in computer science classes. In reality it's quite often not as ideal.

One quite common pattern is to have some data with a bunch of columns, where you'd really like those data as rows with, for example, key-value pairs, where the *key* would be derived from the original column name and the *value* then would be the value from that column.

Personally I like to use the terms **dimension** and **measure** instead of key and value. You might say that's only for data warehousing, but the terms are also used, for example, in the `model` clause in SQL. The advantage, in my opinion, is that it is common to think of multiple dimensions and multiple measures, whereas the key-value terminology most often is used thinking only of a single key and a single value.

The act of turning data in rows into columns is called *pivoting* (which is the topic of the next chapter), so as this is the reverse operation, it is called *unpivoting*. I'll show you unpivoting with examples based on tables that contain data from an external source – that's of course not always the case, but it is not uncommon.

© Kim Berg Hansen 2020
K. Berg Hansen, *Practical Oracle SQL*, https://doi.org/10.1007/978-1-4842-5617-6_7

Data received in columns

To exemplify unpivoting, I am going to use the two tables shown in Figure 7-1.

PRACTICAL.WEB_DEVICES		
P * DAY	DATE	
PC	NUMBER (*,0)	
TABLET	NUMBER (*,0)	
PHONE	NUMBER (*,0)	
⇨ WEB_DEVICES_PK (DAY)		
◇ WEB_DEVICES_PK (DAY)		

PRACTICAL.WEB_DEMOGRAPHICS		
P * DAY	DATE	
M_TW_CNT	NUMBER (*,0)	
M_TW_QTY	NUMBER (*,0)	
M_FB_CNT	NUMBER (*,0)	
M_FB_QTY	NUMBER (*,0)	
F_TW_CNT	NUMBER (*,0)	
F_TW_QTY	NUMBER (*,0)	
F_FB_CNT	NUMBER (*,0)	
F_FB_QTY	NUMBER (*,0)	
⇨ WEB_DEMOGRAPHICS_PK (DAY)		
◇ WEB_DEMOGRAPHICS_PK (DAY)		

***Figure 7-1.** Tables holding incoming data from web provider*

Good Beer Trading Co uses an external service to gather statistics about visitors to the company webshop. This service delivers daily statistical data that are imported into these two tables:

- In table web_devices are saved daily stats about how many visitors to the webshop are from PCs, tablets, and phones, each visitor count stored in a separate column for each device type.

- In table web_demographics are both visitor count as well as the quantity the visitors ended up buying. Both count and quantity are separated into male vs. female visitors, as well as into visitors coming from Twitter campaigns vs. Facebook campaigns. So, for example, column m_tw_cnt is count of male visitors from Twitter, while column f_fb_qty is the quantity bought by female visitors from Facebook.

I'm going to demonstrate various unpivoting methods on these tables.

Unpivoting to rows

First, I take a look at the content of table web_devices in Listing 7-1.

Listing 7-1. Daily web visits per device

```
SQL> select day, pc, tablet, phone
  2  from web_devices
  3  order by day;
```

DAY	PC	TABLET	PHONE
2019-05-01	1042	812	1610
2019-05-02	967	1102	2159

What I want to do now is to *unpivot* these data with a single dimension column containing the device (PC, tablet, or phone) and a single measure column with the visitor count for that device – that is, the value from the corresponding column in the table.

The first method is to use the unpivot clause of the select statement as shown in Listing 7-2.

Listing 7-2. Using unpivot to get dimension and measure

```
SQL> select day, device, cnt
  2  from web_devices
  3  unpivot (
  4     cnt
  5     for device
  6     in (
  7        pc     as 'PC'
  8      , tablet as 'Tablet'
  9      , phone  as 'Phone'
 10     )
 11  )
 12  order by day, device;
```

The unpivot clause consists of three parts:

- First measures must be defined – in this case cnt in line 4. It's a column that does not exist but will be created; I simply define that there should be a single measure, and it is to be called cnt.

- I then define for what dimensions the measures should exist – line 5 with the keyword for followed by dimension name device. Again a non-existing column will be created.

109

- Lastly the in clause in lines 6–10 defines the mapping from the original columns to the new measure and dimension columns. Here I have defined three mappings (lines 7–9) which means there will be generated three output rows for each input row:

  - One row with the value from pc in cnt and the string 'PC' in device

  - One row with the value from tablet in cnt and the string 'Tablet' in device

  - One row with the value from phone in cnt and the string 'Phone' in device

Figure 7-2 shows how the data flows – from the mapping rules in the in clause, the values of the *columns* on the left flow to the measure column and the *literals* on the right flow to the dimension column.

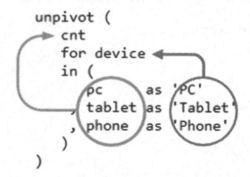

Figure 7-2. *Flow of single dimension and measure values*

Those columns of the original table I specify in the in clause will not be part of the output, as they and their values have been transformed to dimensions and measures. Any *other* column of the table will be output unaltered – in this case that is only the day column, but had there been other columns they would have been there too.

In total Listing 7-2 gives me this output with three rows for each day, one row for each of the three device types, unpivoted just like I wanted it:

DAY	DEVICE	CNT
2019-05-01	PC	1042
2019-05-01	Phone	1610
2019-05-01	Tablet	812

```
2019-05-02   PC       967
2019-05-02   Phone    2159
2019-05-02   Tablet   1102
```

Do-it-yourself unpivoting

But there is another way to unpivot without using the unpivot clause. Before version 10, you had to do it yourself manually, and I'll show you a couple of versions of the manual unpivot. It can be handy to know of it so you can recognize what's happening if you see it in old code. And once in a rare while, there is also the possibility you have something complex that fits less optimally into the unpivot clause and it is easier to implement it this way.

The basic idea in both versions is that I need to generate as many rows as I have values of my dimension. With the unpivot clause, these rows are generated automatically as many as I have expressions in the in list – in Listing 7-3, I generate those three rows manually using select from dual.

Listing 7-3. Manual unpivot using numbered row generator

```
SQL> select
  2      wd.day
  3    , case r.rn
  4        when 1 then 'PC'
  5        when 2 then 'Tablet'
  6        when 3 then 'Phone'
  7      end as device
  8    , case r.rn
  9        when 1 then wd.pc
 10        when 2 then wd.tablet
 11        when 3 then wd.phone
 12      end as cnt
 13  from web_devices wd
 14  cross join (
 15     select level as rn from dual connect by level <= 3
 16  ) r
 17  order by day, device;
```

In the inline view r, I generate three rows in line 15 numbered 1, 2, and 3. With these rows, I do a Cartesian join (line 14) to the web_devices table, so for each and every row in web_devices, I get three rows in the output.

Then I use two case structures for my dimension and measure:

- Lines 3–7 put the literal values for dimension device in the first, second, and third generated row.

- Lines 8–12 put the count values from columns pc, table, and phone in the same rows in measure cnt.

That makes Listing 7-3 produce the exact same output as Listing 7-2, just performed with manual unpivoting.

Listing 7-4 is an alternative manual unpivoting method that also produces the same output.

Listing 7-4. Manual unpivot using dimension style row generator

```
SQL> with devices( device ) as (
  2      select 'PC'     from dual union all
  3      select 'Tablet' from dual union all
  4      select 'Phone'  from dual
  5  )
  6  select
  7      wd.day
  8  , d.device
  9  , case d.device
 10        when 'PC'     then wd.pc
 11        when 'Tablet' then wd.tablet
 12        when 'Phone'  then wd.phone
 13      end as cnt
 14  from web_devices wd
 15  cross join devices d
 16  order by day, device;
```

Where Listing 7-3 generates three numbered rows with case structures defining what data to put in row 1, row 2, and row 3, Listing 7-4 instead generates three rows that already have the values needed for the dimension. Here I chose to put the generator in a with clause in lines 1–5 instead of an inline view, but the effect is the same.

Again I do a Cartesian join with the generated rows in line 15, but now I do not need two `case` structures anymore. As the dimension value, I can directly use the column from the generated rows in line 8, leaving me with a single `case` structure in lines 9–13 for my measure. The difference here is I do not use "row 1, row 2, row 3," but rather the values of the dimension.

Using the with clause also illustrates nicely that `devices` could have been a real table instead of generated rows in a `with` clause – then the query simply would have consisted of lines 6–16. Note, however, that it would not be a *dynamic* unpivoting – even though the dimension values would come from a table, I would still need to hardcode the values into the `case` structure. It *could* be dynamic, but it would require dynamic SQL. I'll show an example of this later in the chapter.

More than one dimension and/or measure

The previous example used table `web_devices` with a single dimension and single measure; now I'll show handling of multiple dimensions and measures. You saw the diagram of table `web_demographics` at the start of the chapter; Listing 7-5 shows you the content.

Listing 7-5. Daily web visits and purchases per gender and channel

```
SQL> select
  2      day
  3    , m_tw_cnt
  4    , m_tw_qty
  5    , m_fb_cnt
  6    , m_fb_qty
  7    , f_tw_cnt
  8    , f_tw_qty
  9    , f_fb_cnt
 10    , f_fb_qty
 11  from web_demographics
 12  order by day;
```

Showing all those columns isn't nicely formatted, but you can see the eight columns that are all combinations of two measures (cnt and qty) for two values of dimension gender (m and f) and two values of dimension channel (tw and fb):

DAY	M_TW_CNT	M_TW_QTY	M_FB_CNT	M_FB_QTY	F_TW_CNT	F_TW_QTY	F_FB_CNT	F_FB_QTY
2019-05-01	1232	86	1017	64	651	76	564	68
2019-05-02	1438	142	1198	70	840	92	752	78

The syntax for using unpivot with multiple dimensions and/or multiple measures is pretty much identical to what I did for single dimension/measure in Listing 7-2 – except that instead of single expressions, I need to use *expression lists*, as I show it in Listing 7-6.

Listing 7-6. Using unpivot with two dimensions and two measures

```
SQL> select day, gender, channel, cnt, qty
  2  from web_demographics
  3  unpivot (
  4    ( cnt, qty )
  5    for ( gender, channel )
  6    in (
  7      (m_tw_cnt, m_tw_qty) as ('Male'  , 'Twitter' )
  8    , (m_fb_cnt, m_fb_qty) as ('Male'  , 'Facebook')
  9    , (f_tw_cnt, f_tw_qty) as ('Female', 'Twitter' )
 10    , (f_fb_cnt, f_fb_qty) as ('Female', 'Facebook')
 11    )
 12  )
 13  order by day, gender, channel;
```

Expression lists are comma-separated lists of expressions inside a set of parentheses – the parentheses are mandatory to identify an expression list, not just a convenience for readability. In the code, I have expression lists in multiple places:

- In line 4, the expression list defines *two* measures, cnt and qty – like before, they are columns that will be created, not columns in the table.

- The expression list in line 5 defines two dimensions in a similar manner.

- Each mapping in lines 7–10 then uses two expression lists each with two columns – first on the left side an expression list with two columns from the table and then on the right an expression list with two literals.

All this leads to an output with four output rows for each input row – since there are four mappings in the in clause:

DAY	GENDER	CHANNEL	CNT	QTY
2019-05-01	Female	Facebook	564	68
2019-05-01	Female	Twitter	651	76
2019-05-01	Male	Facebook	1017	64
2019-05-01	Male	Twitter	1232	86
2019-05-02	Female	Facebook	752	78
2019-05-02	Female	Twitter	840	92
2019-05-02	Male	Facebook	1198	70
2019-05-02	Male	Twitter	1438	142

In Figure 7-3 I show that the flow is still the same – just like in Figure 7-2 – and how the expression lists correspond. Values from the table columns left of the as keyword flow to the measures, literals to the right of the as keyword flow to the dimensions.

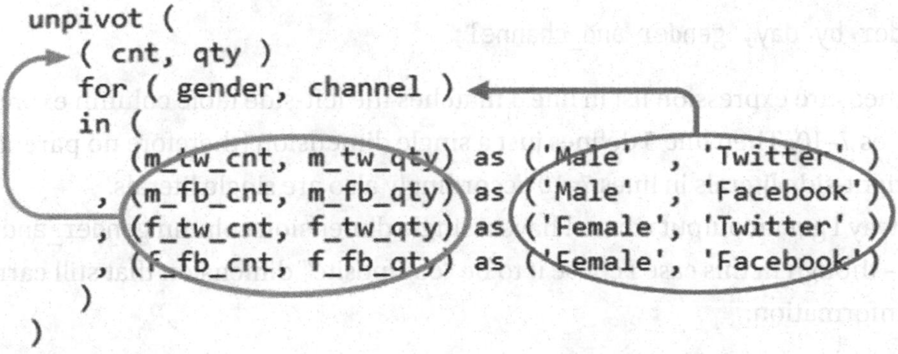

```
unpivot (
   ( cnt, qty )
   for ( gender, channel )
   in (
      (m_tw_cnt, m_tw_qty) as ('Male'  , 'Twitter' )
    , (m_fb_cnt, m_fb_qty) as ('Male'  , 'Facebook')
    , (f_tw_cnt, f_tw_qty) as ('Female', 'Twitter' )
    , (f_fb_cnt, f_fb_qty) as ('Female', 'Facebook')
   )
)
```

Figure 7-3. Flow of multiple dimension and measure values

Looking on the figure also makes it clear that the expression lists with table columns (left) must have the same number of columns as the expression list that defines the measures. Likewise, the expression lists with literals (right) must have the same number of literals as the expression list that defines the dimensions.

But it is not mandatory for the number of dimensions to be equal to the number of measures – you can have many dimensions and few or one measure or vice versa. I'll show you some examples of this.

The first example is Listing 7-7, where I show using a single dimension and two measures.

Listing 7-7. Using unpivot with one composite dimension and two measures

```
SQL> select day, gender_and_channel, cnt, qty
  2  from web_demographics
  3  unpivot (
  4     ( cnt, qty )
  5     for gender_and_channel
  6     in (
  7        (m_tw_cnt, m_tw_qty) as 'Male on Twitter'
  8      , (m_fb_cnt, m_fb_qty) as 'Male on Facebook'
  9      , (f_tw_cnt, f_tw_qty) as 'Female on Twitter'
 10      , (f_fb_cnt, f_fb_qty) as 'Female on Facebook'
 11     )
 12  )
 13  order by day, gender_and_channel;
```

The measure expression list in line 4 matches the left-side table column expression lists in lines 7–10. Then line 5 defines just a single dimension (therefore no parentheses), and the right-side literals in lines 7–10 accordingly also are single literals.

This way I get an output where I have a single dimension column gender_and_channel – though in this case I chose it to be "composite" dimension that still carries two types of information:

DAY	GENDER_AND_CHANNEL	CNT	QTY
2019-05-01	Female on Facebook	564	68
2019-05-01	Female on Twitter	651	76
2019-05-01	Male on Facebook	1017	64

2019-05-01	Male on Twitter	1232	86
2019-05-02	Female on Facebook	752	78
2019-05-02	Female on Twitter	840	92
2019-05-02	Male on Facebook	1198	70
2019-05-02	Male on Twitter	1438	142

Of course I do not necessarily need to do that; I can choose to discard information if I wish and keep just a single "non-composite" dimension keeping only the gender information and discarding the channel, as I show in Listing 7-8.

Listing 7-8. Using unpivot with one single dimension and two measures

```
SQL> select day, gender, cnt, qty
  2  from web_demographics
  3  unpivot (
  4     ( cnt, qty )
  5     for gender
  6     in (
  7        (m_tw_cnt, m_tw_qty) as 'Male'
  8      , (m_fb_cnt, m_fb_qty) as 'Male'
  9      , (f_tw_cnt, f_tw_qty) as 'Female'
 10      , (f_fb_cnt, f_fb_qty) as 'Female'
 11     )
 12  )
 13  order by day, gender;
```

But note that even though I only keep the dimension information on gender with two distinct values, I still get four rows in the output for each input row:

DAY	GENDER	CNT	QTY
2019-05-01	Female	564	68
2019-05-01	Female	651	76
2019-05-01	Male	1017	64
2019-05-01	Male	1232	86
2019-05-02	Female	840	92
2019-05-02	Female	752	78
2019-05-02	Male	1438	142
2019-05-02	Male	1198	70

In other words, repeating the same dimension value literal does *not* automatically aggregate on the dimension. If that is the output I desire, I can use Listing 7-9 to do the aggregation myself.

Listing 7-9. Using unpivot with one aggregated dimension and two measures

```
SQL> select day
  2         , gender
  3         , sum(cnt) as cnt
  4         , sum(qty) as qty
  5  from web_demographics
  6  unpivot (
  7     ( cnt, qty )
  8     for gender
  9     in (
 10        (m_tw_cnt, m_tw_qty) as 'Male'
 11      , (m_fb_cnt, m_fb_qty) as 'Male'
 12      , (f_tw_cnt, f_tw_qty) as 'Female'
 13      , (f_fb_cnt, f_fb_qty) as 'Female'
 14     )
 15  )
 16  group by day, gender
 17  order by day, gender;
```

It is allowed to use `group` by and aggregate functions like `sum` directly in the `unpivot` query – I do not need to wrap it in an inline view. This way I can get just two rows for each original input row – one for each gender:

DAY	GENDER	CNT	QTY
2019-05-01	Female	1215	144
2019-05-01	Male	2249	150
2019-05-02	Female	1592	170
2019-05-02	Male	2636	212

And of course I can also do the other way around – two dimensions with a single measure. In Listing 7-10, for example, I keep just the `cnt` measure and discard the `qty` information.

Listing 7-10. Using unpivot with two dimensions and one measure

```
SQL> select day, gender, channel, cnt
  2  from web_demographics
  3  unpivot (
  4     cnt
  5     for ( gender, channel )
  6     in (
  7        m_tw_cnt as ('Male'  , 'Twitter' )
  8      , m_fb_cnt as ('Male'  , 'Facebook')
  9      , f_tw_cnt as ('Female', 'Twitter' )
 10      , f_fb_cnt as ('Female', 'Facebook')
 11     )
 12  )
 13  order by day, gender, channel;
```

Again you see the match that I use single expression for measure as well as for the left-side table columns and I use expression lists for dimensions and the right-side literals. As you can figure out, I get this output with all eight rows, just no qty column:

DAY	GENDER	CHANNEL	CNT
2019-05-01	Female	Facebook	564
2019-05-01	Female	Twitter	651
2019-05-01	Male	Facebook	1017
2019-05-01	Male	Twitter	1232
2019-05-02	Female	Facebook	752
2019-05-02	Female	Twitter	840
2019-05-02	Male	Facebook	1198
2019-05-02	Male	Twitter	1438

Manual unpivoting can also be done with multiple dimensions and measures, but I will not show you examples of doing this with generated rows using dual like before (that will be left as an exercise for the reader). Instead I will show it using real dimension tables.

Using dimension tables

So I'm going to add two tables to hold the values for my two dimensions: gender_dim and channels_dim defined in Figure 7-4.

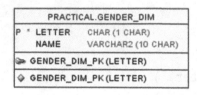

Figure 7-4. Dimension tables

Listing 7-11 shows I've entered the values for male and female in gender_dim:

Listing 7-11. Dimension table for gender

```
SQL> select letter, name
  2  from gender_dim
  3  order by letter;
```

LETTER	NAME
F	Female
M	Male

Likewise, Listing 7-12 shows the values for Twitter and Facebook in table channels_dim.

Listing 7-12. Dimension table for channels

```
SQL> select id, name, shortcut
  2  from channels_dim
  3  order by id;
```

ID	NAME	SHORTCUT
42	Twitter	tw
44	Facebook	fb

Recall that I did manual unpivot before by doing a Cartesian join to some generated rows. When I use my dimension tables in Listing 7-13, I simply do Cartesian joins to both tables, so that for each input row in table web_demographics, I get a row for every combination of rows in gender_dim and channels_dim.

Listing 7-13. Manual unpivot using dimension tables

```
SQL> select
  2       d.day
  3     , g.letter as g_id
  4     , c.id as ch_id
  5     , case g.letter
  6         when 'M' then
  7           case c.shortcut
  8             when 'tw' then d.m_tw_cnt
  9             when 'fb' then d.m_fb_cnt
 10           end
 11         when 'F' then
 12           case c.shortcut
 13             when 'tw' then d.f_tw_cnt
 14             when 'fb' then d.f_fb_cnt
 15           end
 16       end as cnt
 17     , case g.letter
 18         when 'M' then
 19           case c.shortcut
 20             when 'tw' then d.m_tw_qty
 21             when 'fb' then d.m_fb_qty
 22           end
 23         when 'F' then
 24           case c.shortcut
 25             when 'tw' then d.f_tw_qty
 26             when 'fb' then d.f_fb_qty
 27           end
 28       end as qty
 29   from web_demographics d
```

```
30   cross join gender_dim g
31   cross join channels_dim c
32   order by day, g_id, ch_id;
```

Explaining from the bottom up, I do the Cartesian joins with cross join in lines 30 and 31.

Having created four rows for each input row, I use two case constructs for each of my measures – lines 5–16 for cnt and lines 17–28 for qty. Each construct maps values from the dimension tables to specific columns in web_demographics. Should there happen to be more rows in the dimension tables with values that are *not* listed in my case structures, they will generate rows in the output that will have null values in the measures.

And in lines 3 and 4, I get values for my dimensions directly from the dimension tables. Since I have real tables for the dimensions, I choose here to use the primary keys for the dimension tables instead of the textual descriptions – that way this result could, if I wished, be directly inserted into a table having foreign key relationships to the dimension tables:

DAY	G_ID	CH_ID	CNT	QTY
2019-05-01	F	42	651	76
2019-05-01	F	44	564	68
2019-05-01	M	42	1232	86
2019-05-01	M	44	1017	64
2019-05-02	F	42	840	92
2019-05-02	F	44	752	78
2019-05-02	M	42	1438	142
2019-05-02	M	44	1198	70

As a little curiosity, I'd like to mention that I tried doing the case expressions using expression lists like this:

```
5    , case (g.letter, c.shortcut)
6          when ('M', 'tw') then d.m_tw_cnt
7          when ('M', 'fb') then d.m_fb_cnt
8          when ('F', 'tw') then d.f_tw_cnt
9          when ('F', 'fb') then d.f_fb_cnt
10     end as cnt
```

But that gave me an error – this is not supported syntax for the simple case expression. I think it would have been nice, but maybe it will be allowed in a future version, who knows.

As noted earlier, I'm still hard-coding values even when using dimension tables like this – so I'll end the chapter with an example of how it can be made truly dynamic.

Dynamic mapping to dimension tables

To make a truly dynamic unpivoting from values in the dimension tables, I need specifically to generate the mappings to be used in the in clause. To do this, I create the query in Listing 7-14.

Listing 7-14. Preparing column names mapped to dimension values

```sql
SQL> select
  2      s.cnt_col, s.qty_col
  3    , s.g_id, s.gender
  4    , s.ch_id, s.channel
  5    from (
  6      select
  7        lower(
  8          g.letter || '_' || c.shortcut || '_cnt'
  9        ) as cnt_col
 10      , lower(
 11          g.letter || '_' || c.shortcut || '_qty'
 12        )as qty_col
 13      , g.letter as g_id
 14      , g.name as gender
 15      , c.id as ch_id
 16      , c.name as channel
 17      from gender_dim g
 18      cross join channels_dim c
 19    ) s
 20    join user_tab_columns cnt_c
 21      on cnt_c.column_name = upper(s.cnt_col)
 22    join user_tab_columns qty_c
```

```
23     on qty_c.column_name = upper(s.cnt_col)
24  where cnt_c.table_name = 'WEB_DEMOGRAPHICS'
25  and    qty_c.table_name = 'WEB_DEMOGRAPHICS'
26  order by gender, channel;
```

I need each possible combination of values from my two dimension tables, so I use a Cartesian join in lines 17–18. Using the letter and shortcut column values from the two tables, in lines 7–9 and 10–12, I generate the names of the columns in my web_ demographics table. (Strictly speaking I do not really need to use lower function here, I just do it for when I check-read the generated code later.)

Since I could get runtime errors if the values in the dimension tables do not correctly reflect the columns in web_demographics table, I wrap in an inline view and join to user_ tab_columns to make sure I only retrieve columns that exist.

In total the query shows me the data I need for the mappings in the in clause:

CNT_COL	QTY_COL	G_ID	GENDER	CH_ID	CHANNEL
f_fb_cnt	f_fb_qty	F	Female	44	Facebook
f_tw_cnt	f_tw_qty	F	Female	42	Twitter
m_fb_cnt	m_fb_qty	M	Male	44	Facebook
m_tw_cnt	m_tw_qty	M	Male	42	Twitter

Armed with this query, I'm going to use PL/SQL to build dynamic SQL with unpivot. First, I'll turn on serveroutput for debugging purposes:

```
SQL> set serveroutput on
```

And I'll create a sqlcl (or SQL*Plus) bind variable to hold my dynamically generated cursor:

```
SQL> variable unpivoted refcursor
```

Then I'm ready to execute the anonymous PL/SQL block in Listing 7-15 to build dynamic SQL.

Listing 7-15. Dynamically building unpivot query

```
SQL> declare
  2     v_unpivot_sql  varchar2(4000);
  3  begin
  4     for c in (
```

```
 5        select
 6            s.cnt_col, s.qty_col
 7          , s.g_id, s.gender
 8          , s.ch_id, s.channel
 9        from (
10          select
11            lower(
12                g.letter || '_' || c.shortcut || '_cnt'
13              ) as cnt_col
14            , lower(
15                g.letter || '_' || c.shortcut || '_qty'
16              )as qty_col
17            , g.letter as g_id
18            , g.name as gender
19            , c.id as ch_id
20            , c.name as channel
21          from gender_dim g
22          cross join channels_dim c
23        ) s
24        join user_tab_columns cnt_c
25          on cnt_c.column_name = upper(s.cnt_col)
26        join user_tab_columns qty_c
27          on qty_c.column_name = upper(s.cnt_col)
28        where cnt_c.table_name = 'WEB_DEMOGRAPHICS'
29        and   qty_c.table_name = 'WEB_DEMOGRAPHICS'
30        order by gender, channel
31      ) loop
32
33        if v_unpivot_sql is null then
34          v_unpivot_sql := q'[
35            select day, g_id, ch_id, cnt, qty
36            from web_demographics
37            unpivot (
38              ( cnt, qty )
39              for ( g_id, ch_id )
```

```
40                        in (
41                           ]';
42         else
43            v_unpivot_sql := v_unpivot_sql || q'[
44                    , ]';
45         end if;
46
47         v_unpivot_sql := v_unpivot_sql
48                         || '(' || c.cnt_col
49                         || ', ' || c.qty_col
50                         || ') as (''' || c.g_id
51                         || ''', ' || c.ch_id
52                         || ')';
53
54      end loop;
55
56      v_unpivot_sql := v_unpivot_sql || q'[
57                   )
58                   )
59              order by day, g_id, ch_id]';
60
61      dbms_output.put_line(v_unpivot_sql);
62
63      open :unpivoted for v_unpivot_sql;
64  end;
65  /
```

In the query from Listing 7-14, I put in a cursor for loop starting in line 4. In line 33, I check if this is the first row in the loop. If it is, then in lines 34–41, I generate the beginning of the SQL statement I am building. If not, then in lines 43–44, I generate a new line and a comma as separator between the mappings.

Lines 47–52 generate each individual mapping for the in clause, and when the loop is done, lines 56–59 append the final pieces of the SQL to be generated.

Line 61 then sends the generated SQL to the server output for debugging purposes, so I can see here the piece of SQL that was generated in the string variable v_unpivot_sql:

```
select day, g_id, ch_id, cnt, qty
from web_demographics
unpivot (
  ( cnt, qty )
  for ( g_id, ch_id )
  in (
      (f_fb_cnt, f_fb_qty) as ('F', 44)
    , (f_tw_cnt, f_tw_qty) as ('F', 42)
    , (m_fb_cnt, m_fb_qty) as ('M', 44)
    , (m_tw_cnt, m_tw_qty) as ('M', 42)
  )
)
order by day, g_id, ch_id
```

It looks like I want it, with one in clause mapping for each combination of values in my dimension tables. Actually it is just like Listing 7-6, except it uses the primary keys of the two dimension tables instead of descriptive names.

Line 63 of the block opens the bind variable unpivoted (that I created before calling the block) using the dynamically created SQL in the string variable v_unpivot_sql. And then the block is done:

```
PL/SQL procedure successfully completed.
```

And I can see if the cursor retrieves the output I want:

```
SQL> print unpivoted
```

Lo and behold – I get the same output as Listing 7-13 gave me:

DAY	G	CH_ID	CNT	QTY
2019-05-01	F	42	651	76
2019-05-01	F	44	564	68
2019-05-01	M	42	1232	86
2019-05-01	M	44	1017	64
2019-05-02	F	42	840	92
2019-05-02	F	44	752	78
2019-05-02	M	42	1438	142
2019-05-02	M	44	1198	70

The dynamic aspect gets into play, if, for example, the statistics service adds data for Instagram and thus the table web_demographics gets four new columns (counts and quantities for male and female for Instagram).

In such a case, using Listing 7-6 (or Listing 7-13) requires that I add mappings to the code – change the SQL. But if I use the dynamic technique in Listing 7-15, all I need to do is insert data for Instagram in the web_channel dimension table, and the code auto-generates mappings to produce something like

```
in (
    (f_fb_cnt, f_fb_qty) as ('F', 44)
  , (f_in_cnt, f_in_qty) as ('F', 46)
  , (f_tw_cnt, f_tw_qty) as ('F', 42)
  , (m_fb_cnt, m_fb_qty) as ('M', 44)
  , (m_in_cnt, m_in_qty) as ('M', 46)
  , (m_tw_cnt, m_tw_qty) as ('M', 42)
)
```

(Assuming Instagram got id = 46 and shortcut = 'in'.)

This dynamic method opens a cursor using the generated SQL, so it must generate the SQL runtime every single time. Sometimes you may have a requirement for doing this, but in many cases, I would prefer using it as a code generator method.

That way when Instagram columns are added, you first insert Instagram in the dimension table, then you run Listing 7-15 (just with line 63 removed), and finally you take the generated query from the output and copy it to your real code and compile it. You have gained the benefit of dynamically generating code with much less chance of errors, but you do not suffer runtime penalties of building dynamic strings all the time.

If the data change very often, of course, you may need to be completely dynamic. For a case like this, however, it is likely that such changes are rare and only occur along with releasing new application functionality anyway. A generator approach is well suited for such cases.

Lessons learned

Unpivoting is a useful skill, particularly when dealing with data that hasn't been normalized in the usual way of relational databases. In the pages of this chapter, I've shown you different variations on the theme:

- Unpivoting with the three elements of the unpivot clause, measures, dimensions, and mappings

- Using either single expressions or expression lists to unpivot single or multiple measures and/or dimensions

- Manual alternatives to the unpivot clause for use in real old databases or really special circumstances

- Building dynamic unpivot SQL within PL/SQL based on values in dimension tables

If you know the concepts of unpivoting and you can remember (or lookup) the syntax of using for and in in unpivot, you'll find the methods useful for many things.

CHAPTER 8

Pivoting Rows to Columns

The previous chapter was about *unpivoting*, which is the process of turning columns into rows. The opposite operation is called *pivoting*, which – surprise, surprise – is turning rows into columns.

The idea is that you have a resultset with some dimensional values in one or more columns and some facts/measure values in one or more other columns. You'd like the output grouped by some other columns, so you only have one aggregated row for those values, and then the values from your measures should be placed in a set of columns, one for each value of your dimension (or combination of values if you have multiple dimensions).

One thing to remember here is that in SQL, the engine needs at *parse* time to be able to determine names and datatypes of each column. That means that you have to hardcode the dimension values and what column names they should be turned into.

If you wish to have dynamic pivoting, where there automatically will be columns for every dimension value in the data, you need to build it with dynamic SQL similarly to what I showed at the end of the previous chapter. That way there will be a parsing every time you run it, and the column names can then be known at that time. Alternatively the pivot clause supports returning XML instead of columns, which allows you dynamic pivoting without dynamic SQL – which can be an option if an XML output is acceptable. Either way of dynamic pivoting will not be covered in this book.

Tip   In Oracle version 18c or newer, there is a third dynamic pivoting method using polymorphic table functions. I won't be covering PTFs in this book, but Chris Saxon of the Oracle AskTom team has an example of a PTF for dynamic pivoting on Live SQL: `https://livesql.oracle.com/apex/livesql/file/content_HPN95108FSSZD87PXX7MG3LW3.html`.

© Kim Berg Hansen 2020
K. Berg Hansen, *Practical Oracle SQL*, https://doi.org/10.1007/978-1-4842-5617-6_8

Tables for pivoting

The Good Beer Trading Co purchases beer from some breweries, storing the information in the purchases table shown in Figure 8-1, along with dimension lookup tables breweries, products, and product_groups.

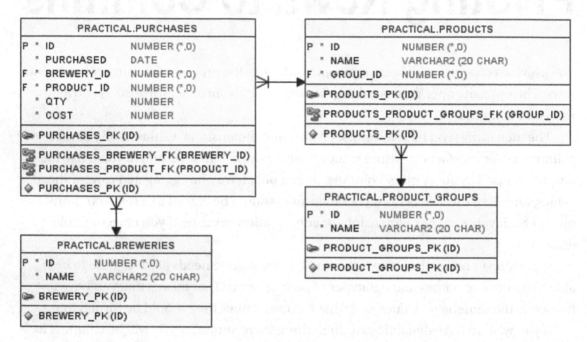

Figure 8-1. Purchases table and associated dimension tables

I'll be demonstrating pivoting data by brewery, product group, and year. To do that, I use the view purchases_with_dims in Listing 8-1, which simply joins the purchases table with the dimension tables.

Listing 8-1. View joining purchases table with the dimensions

```
SQL> create or replace view purchases_with_dims
  2  as
  3  select
  4      pu.id
  5  ,  pu.purchased
  6  ,  pu.brewery_id
  7  ,  b.name as brewery_name
```

```
 8    , pu.product_id
 9    , p.name as product_name
10    , p.group_id
11    , pg.name as group_name
12    , pu.qty
13    , pu.cost
14    from purchases pu
15    join breweries b
16       on b.id = pu.brewery_id
17    join products p
18       on p.id = pu.product_id
19    join product_groups pg
20       on pg.id = p.group_id;
```

View PURCHASES_WITH_DIMS created.

At first I'm going to aggregate the quantity grouped by brewery, product group, and year in Listing 8-2, which is a simple group by without any pivoting at all.

Listing 8-2. Yearly purchased quantities by brewery and product group

```
SQL> select
 2       brewery_name
 3    , group_name
 4    , extract(year from purchased) as yr
 5    , sum(qty) as qty
 6    from purchases_with_dims pwd
 7    group by
 8       brewery_name
 9    , group_name
10    , extract(year from purchased)
11    order by
12       brewery_name
13    , group_name
14    , yr;
```

The output shows me that the company bought from three breweries, two different product groups from each brewery, in three years from 2016 to 2018, resulting in 18 rows for those combinations:

BREWERY_NAME	GROUP_NAME	YR	QTY
Balthazar Brauerei	Belgian	2016	800
Balthazar Brauerei	Belgian	2017	1000
Balthazar Brauerei	Belgian	2018	1000
Balthazar Brauerei	Wheat	2016	500
Balthazar Brauerei	Wheat	2017	500
Balthazar Brauerei	Wheat	2018	400
Brewing Barbarian	IPA	2016	200
Brewing Barbarian	IPA	2017	300
Brewing Barbarian	IPA	2018	500
Brewing Barbarian	Stout	2016	800
Brewing Barbarian	Stout	2017	1000
Brewing Barbarian	Stout	2018	1200
Happy Hoppy Hippo	IPA	2016	1000
Happy Hoppy Hippo	IPA	2017	900
Happy Hoppy Hippo	IPA	2018	800
Happy Hoppy Hippo	Wheat	2016	200
Happy Hoppy Hippo	Wheat	2017	100
Happy Hoppy Hippo	Wheat	2018	100

Now I'd like to have a column for quantity purchased each of the three years instead of a row for each year – this is what pivoting is all about.

Pivoting single measure and dimension

Listing 8-3 shows how I do the pivoting of the years using the pivot clause.

Listing 8-3. Pivoting the year rows into columns

```
SQL> select *
  2  from (
  3     select
  4        brewery_name
```

```
5        , group_name
6        , extract(year from purchased) as yr
7        , sum(qty) as qty
8     from purchases_with_dims pwd
9     group by
10         brewery_name
11        , group_name
12        , extract(year from purchased)
13   ) pivot (
14      sum(qty)
15      for yr
16      in (
17          2016 as y2016
18        , 2017 as y2017
19        , 2018 as y2018
20        )
21   )
22   order by brewery_name, group_name;
```

I built the query of these elements:

- Lines 3–12 simply are the select from Listing 8-2, wrapped in an inline view.

- The pivot keyword in line 13 tells Oracle I want to pivot the data.

- Then I define my measures – in this case only one, the quantity – in line 14. I *must* use an aggregate function here – it can be any aggregate, the one that makes sense in this case is sum.

- After the keyword for in line 15, I define the dimensions I want – here only the year.

- Last, the in clause in lines 16–19 maps in which columns the aggregated measure should be placed for which values of the dimension – columns that do not exist in the table, but will be created in the output.

Shown schematically, you can see in Figure 8-2 that the measure sum(qty) flows to the three column aliases, one for each of the values of the yr dimension.

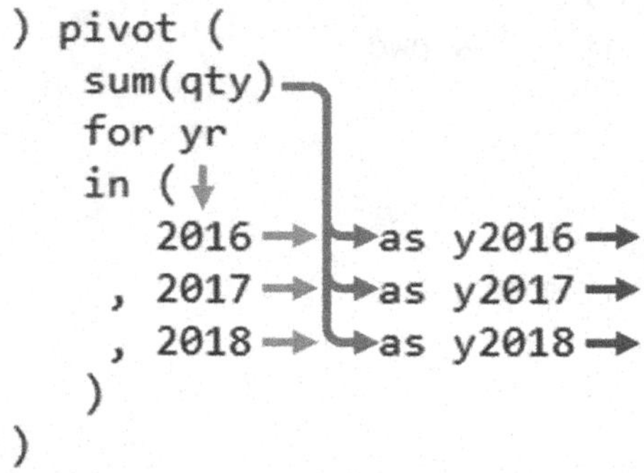

```
) pivot (
    sum(qty)
    for yr
    in (
        2016      as y2016
      , 2017      as y2017
      , 2018      as y2018
    )
)
```

Figure 8-2. *The flows of the pivot clause*

And so I get the output that I desired with 18 aggregated quantities shown in six rows of three quantity columns (one per year) instead of 18 rows:

BREWERY_NAME	GROUP_NAME	Y2016	Y2017	Y2018
Balthazar Brauerei	Belgian	800	1000	1000
Balthazar Brauerei	Wheat	500	500	400
Brewing Barbarian	IPA	200	300	500
Brewing Barbarian	Stout	800	1000	1200
Happy Hoppy Hippo	IPA	1000	900	800
Happy Hoppy Hippo	Wheat	200	100	100

Notice that the yr and qty columns from the inline view are no longer in the output, but brewery_name and group_name are. What happens is that those columns I am referencing in the measures and dimensions in the pivot clause are used for the pivoting. The columns that are left over, they are used for an *implicit* group by.

Since in my inline view I have already grouped the data by brewery, product group, and year, this means that the sum(qty) in line 14 actually always will "aggregate" just a single row of data into each of the year columns, so that aggregation is not really necessary. But I cannot skip it – the pivot clause demands an aggregate function.

What I can do instead is to skip the group by within the inline view and instead let the implicit group by performed by pivot do the aggregation alone, thus avoiding an unnecessary grouping operation. Listing 8-4 simply is the same as Listing 8-3, just with the group by from Listing 8-3 lines 9–12 removed.

Listing 8-4. Utilizing the implicit group by

```
SQL> select *
  2  from (
  3     select
  4        brewery_name
  5      , group_name
  6      , extract(year from purchased) as yr
  7      , qty
  8     from purchases_with_dims pwd
  9  ) pivot (
 10     sum(qty)
 11     for yr
 12     in (
 13        2016 as y2016
 14      , 2017 as y2017
 15      , 2018 as y2018
 16     )
 17  )
 18  order by brewery_name, group_name;
```

Listing 8-4 gives exactly the same output as Listing 8-3; it is just a little bit more efficient from not doing a superfluous grouping operation.

You might think that I could then skip the inline view completely? Well, sometimes it is possible, but not in this case, first because I need to extract the year from the purchased date column and second because the pivot performs an implicit group by on the remaining columns after some of the columns have been used for measures and dimensions.

If I had the yr column in the view and could pivot directly on the purchases_with_ dims view, the grouping would be performed on *all* the columns of the view *except* qty and yr – it would give me the wrong result. The inline view lets me keep *only* the columns I need – those to be used in the pivoting and those to be used for the implicit group by.

To make it a little more clear what's happening behind the scenes with the pivot clause, let me show you pivoting performed manually without pivot.

137

Do-it-yourself manual pivoting

In really old database versions (before version 10), I would have had to do pivoting myself with no help from the pivot clause. Instead I would have had to write a query like Listing 8-5.

Listing 8-5. Manual pivoting without using pivot clause

```
SQL> select
  2      brewery_name
  3    , group_name
  4    , sum(
  5        case extract(year from purchased)
  6          when 2016 then qty
  7        end
  8      ) as y2016
  9    , sum(
 10        case extract(year from purchased)
 11          when 2017 then qty
 12        end
 13      ) as y2017
 14    , sum(
 15        case extract(year from purchased)
 16          when 2018 then qty
 17        end
 18      ) as y2018
 19  from purchases_with_dims pwd
 20  group by
 21      brewery_name
 22    , group_name
 23  order by brewery_name, group_name;
```

I do a group by brewery and product group in lines 20–22. And then I have three case structures for each of the three columns I want, so that all rows in the view from the year 2016 will have the qty value summed in column y2016, all rows from 2017 will be summed in y2017, and 2018 in y2018. The output is exactly the same as Listing 8-4 and Listing 8-3.

This structure is built for me automatically when I use the pivot clause. In Listing 8-4, I defined I wanted to use aggregate function sum on the value from column qty, but such that qty for rows in year 2016 goes to a column I want to be named y2016, and so on. I am *not* defining what to use for the implicit group by – this will be whatever columns are left over, so therefore I am using the inline view to limit the columns that go to the pivot clause rather than use all columns of the view.

Knowing this is the way pivot works will help, when I now show you pivoting with multiple measures by also using the column cost from the table purchases and the view purchases_with_dims, instead of just qty.

Multiple measures

I'm going to extend my query to not only pivot the aggregate quantity but also the aggregate cost. In Listing 8-6, you see I've simply added the cost column in line 8, so I also can add the aggregate measure sum(cost) in line 12.

Listing 8-6. Getting an ORA-00918 error with multiple measures

```
SQL> select *
  2  from (
  3     select
  4         brewery_name
  5       , group_name
  6       , extract(year from purchased) as yr
  7       , qty
  8       , cost
  9     from purchases_with_dims pwd
 10  ) pivot (
 11     sum(qty)
 12   , sum(cost)
 13     for yr
 14     in (
 15         2016 as y2016
 16       , 2017 as y2017
 17       , 2018 as y2018
 18     )
```

```
19  )
20  order by brewery_name, group_name;
```

```
Error at Command Line : 1 Column : 8
Error report -
SQL Error: ORA-00918: column ambiguously defined
```

Why do I get an error saying `column ambiguously defined`? I haven't written the same column alias twice? Well, not directly, but indirectly I have.

What happens is that I have defined two measures with no column aliases. Then I have defined the three year values in the yr dimension and column aliases for them. There will be created a column for every combination, so 2 x 3 = 6 columns. Those six columns will be named *<dimension alias>_<measure alias>*, but if there are no measure aliases, then they will just be named *<dimension alias>*, as you saw in Listings 8-3 and 8-4. There it was okay, but here it means there will be two columns named y2016, two columns y2017, and two columns y2018. Thus the ORA-00918 error.

The solution is to also give the measures column aliases, so, for example, I can do as shown in Figure 8-3, where I alias the measures simply q and c, while the dimension values are aliased with two digits of the year (since those aliases do not start with a letter, they need to be quoted).

This generates therefore the six columns (2 x 3) that are named 16_Q, 16_C, and so on.

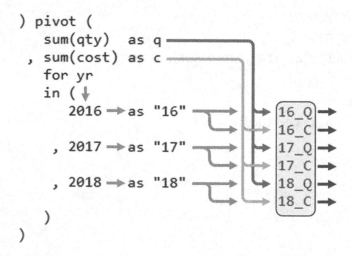

Figure 8-3. *Schematic flow when you have multiple measures*

And to show you it is not just in a schematic diagram it works, I change Listing 8-6 by aliasing the measures and dimension values as shown in Figure 8-3:

```
...
10  ) pivot (
11     sum(qty)  as q
12   , sum(cost) as c
13     for yr
14     in (
15        2016 as "16"
16      , 2017 as "17"
17      , 2018 as "18"
18     )
19  )
...
```

And I get the output I want:

BREWERY_NAME	GROUP_NAME	16_Q	16_C	17_Q	17_C	18_Q	18_C
Balthazar Brauerei	Belgian	800	5840	1000	7360	1000	6960
Balthazar Brauerei	Wheat	500	3280	500	3600	400	2800
Brewing Barbarian	IPA	200	1440	300	1680	500	3920
Brewing Barbarian	Stout	800	5600	1000	6960	1200	8960
Happy Hoppy Hippo	IPA	1000	7360	900	6400	800	5680
Happy Hoppy Hippo	Wheat	200	960	100	800	100	720

(Normally I'd probably pick a little more descriptive column aliases, but using so short aliases makes the lines fit in a book.)

So I've now demonstrated getting pivoted columns as combinations of multiple measures and values of a single dimension. Next up is adding multiple dimensions too.

Multiple dimensions as well

So far I've pivoted only with the year as a dimension, leaving brewery and product group as the columns that are used for implicit group by. Now I'm going to also pivot the product group as a second dimension, leaving only the brewery to be grouped upon.

I have in my data 4 product groups and 3 years, which would mean 12 combinations of dimension values, each showing 2 measures (quantity and cost) for a total of 24 columns. That's a bit large to demo here on a printed page, so in Listing 8-7, I'm reducing the data a bit by selecting only two product groups in line 10 and only two years (2017 and 2018) in lines 11–12.

Listing 8-7. Combining two dimensions and two measures

```
SQL> select *
  2  from (
  3      select
  4          brewery_name
  5        , group_name
  6        , extract(year from purchased) as yr
  7        , qty
  8        , cost
  9      from purchases_with_dims pwd
 10      where group_name in ('IPA', 'Wheat')
 11      and   purchased >= date '2017-01-01'
 12      and   purchased <  date '2019-01-01'
 13  ) pivot (
 14      sum(qty)  as q
 15    , sum(cost) as c
 16      for (group_name, yr)
 17      in (
 18        ('IPA'  , 2017) as i17
 19      , ('IPA'  , 2018) as i18
 20      , ('Wheat', 2017) as w17
 21      , ('Wheat', 2018) as w18
 22      )
 23  )
 24  order by brewery_name;
```

You'll notice that the content of the inline view in lines 3–12 is in principle the same as before; I've simply added a where clause to reduce the dataset I'm pivoting.

The measures q and c in lines 14–15 are also unchanged, just as they were when I only used a single dimension.

Line 16 is different, since here I am no longer just specifying a single column to be my dimension. I am specifying an expression list of two columns instead – group_name and yr.

And since I use an expression list of two columns in my for clause, I also need to use corresponding expression lists of values in the in clause mappings in lines 18–21. Each value expression list (combinations of dimension values) I give a column alias – in this case a very short alias to keep my lines short enough for print; in real life more meaningful aliases should be used.

In total you can see in Figure 8-4 that the combining of the two dimensions I do manually with the expression list and then the combining of the dimension values and the measures automatically creates the columns named with the aliases joined by an underscore.

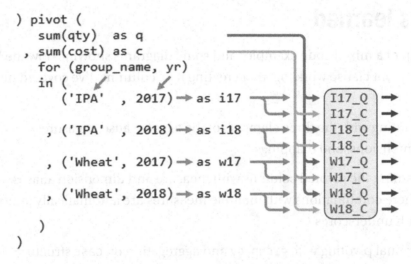

Figure 8-4. *Flows with multiple dimensions just have expression lists instead of single expressions*

And those eight column names you see in the output of Listing 8-7:

BREWERY_NAME	I17_Q	I17_C	I18_Q	I18_C	W17_Q	W17_C	W18_Q	W18_C
Balthazar Brauerei					500	3600	400	2800
Brewing Barbarian	300	1680	500	3920				
Happy Hoppy Hippo	900	6400	800	5680	100	800	100	720

The blanks are because the Good Beer Trading Co does not buy any IPA from Balthazar Brauerei nor any Wheat beers from Brewing Barbarian.

Knowing how the pivoting works as an implicit `group by` as I showed earlier about do-it-yourself manual pivoting, you can also see that in principle, I did not need to reduce the dataset with the `where` clause in lines 10–12. I could simply remove those three lines, and my output would be exactly the same. (Since I do have all three breweries in my output already, if I had had breweries with no purchases at all within the years and product groups I'm after, then there'd be output differences in the form of empty rows.)

However, it would not be a good idea to do so, since the data from the other years and other product groups still would be processed; the implicit case structures would just mean no data from those other years and product groups would be added to the aggregate sums. It would be a waste of CPU cycles and I/O.

Lessons learned

With the help of a mix of code examples and some diagrams showing how the bits and pieces of the pivot clause work together creating new columns, I've covered pivoting topics as

- Pivoting with the three elements of the `pivot` clause, measures, dimensions, and mappings

- Naming the pivoted columns with measure and dimension aliases, where combinations with multiple measures are automatically joined with underscores

- Manual pivoting with `group by` and aggregation on `case` structures to aid understanding of how `pivot` works

- Using expression lists for values from multiple dimensions when pivoting

Pivoting is a very useful tool in your toolbox for a variety of things, quite often simply because users get a much better overview of their data if they do not need to read a lot of rows like the output of Listing 8-2, but can have fewer rows with more columns like the various pivoted outputs in the chapter.

CHAPTER 9

Splitting Delimited Text

Particularly if you get data from somewhere else, it is not uncommon to get it in the form of a string with a list of values separated by some delimiter, typically comma, semicolon, tab, or similar. As you most often don't know the number of elements in the list, you can't just use `substr` to split it into a fixed number of columns. Instead it is normally most useful to be able to turn the list into rows, so you can treat it as a table in your SQL.

Such splitting involves generating rows, which you can do in many ways. I'll show some different methods, ranging from using PL/SQL to loop over the elements of the list and generating a row at a time, over generating all rows at once by selecting from `dual` and retrieving the elements for each row from the list, to pretending the list is JSON and parsing it with native JSON functionality.

Customer favorites and reviews

You would practically never model your tables with a column containing delimited strings (actually I can't think of a use case for it, but it's safer never to say never). You would get such strings from external data sources like files. For demonstration purposes here, the web site of Good Beer Trading Co gives the customers a possibility to choose their favorite beers as well as review beers; the favorites and reviews end up in the `customer_favorites` and `customer_reviews` tables shown in Figure 9-1.

© Kim Berg Hansen 2020
K. Berg Hansen, *Practical Oracle SQL*, https://doi.org/10.1007/978-1-4842-5617-6_9

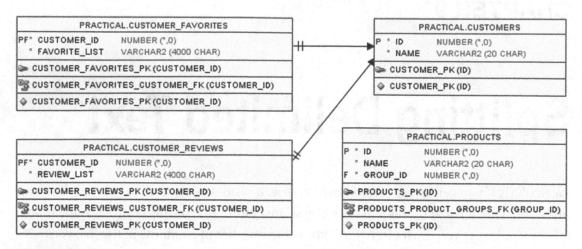

Figure 9-1. *Tables involved in these examples*

Both tables have a proper foreign key to the customers table, but of course cannot have it to the products table, as the product ids are just part of the strings in columns favorite_list and review_list – I show sample data in the upcoming sections. The task at hand is basically to extract out those product ids to be able to join to the products table.

Delimited single values

In Listing 9-1, I examine the data of the customer_favorites table, where column favorite_list contains a comma-separated list of product ids. One customer has saved an empty favorite list.

Listing 9-1. Comma-delimited content of customer_favorites table

```
SQL> select customer_id, favorite_list
  2  from customer_favorites
  3  order by customer_id;

CUSTOMER_ID  FAVORITE_LIST
50042        4040,5310
50741        5430,7790,7870
51007
51069        6520
```

I now need to treat this list as if it was a child table with a row for each of the comma-separated entries. That will enable me to join to the products table (and any other table with a product id column, for that matter). In the rest of this section, I show four different ways to do this.

Pipelined table function

One way that will work also in old database versions (since version 8i) is to extract values from the string in a PL/SQL table function. That requires a collection type (nested table type) and function whose return value is of that type, such as what I create in Listing 9-2.

Listing 9-2. Collection type and pipelined table function

```
SQL> create type favorite_coll_type
  2      as table of integer;
  3  /

Type FAVORITE_COLL_TYPE compiled

SQL> create or replace function favorite_list_to_coll_type (
  2      p_favorite_list   in customer_favorites.favorite_list%type
  3  )
  4      return favorite_coll_type pipelined
  5  is
  6      v_from_pos  pls_integer;
  7      v_to_pos    pls_integer;
  8  begin
  9      if p_favorite_list is not null then
 10          v_from_pos := 1;
 11          loop
 12              v_to_pos := instr(p_favorite_list, ',', v_from_pos);
 13              pipe row (to_number(
 14                  substr(
 15                      p_favorite_list
 16                    , v_from_pos
 17                    , case v_to_pos
 18                          when 0 then length(p_favorite_list) + 1
```

147

```
19                              else v_to_pos
20                  end - v_from_pos
21              )
22          ));
23          exit when v_to_pos = 0;
24          v_from_pos := v_to_pos + 1;
25       end loop;
26    end if;
27  end favorite_list_to_coll_type;
28  /
```

Function FAVORITE_LIST_TO_COLL_TYPE compiled

Collection types can be of object types or scalar types – in this case a scalar type: integer.

I've chosen to make the table function *pipelined* by using the keyword pipelined in line 4.

Inside the function, I create a loop beginning in line 11, where I search for the position of the next comma (the first if it's the first iteration of the loop). Lines 13–22 then pipe a row to the output containing the substr from the previous comma to the found comma (or the end of the string if no comma was found).

If I reach the end of the string (no comma was found), line 23 breaks out of the loop. If there's still something left in the string, line 24 sets the next v_from_pos to be used in the next iteration of the loop.

The loop strategy works if there's at least one element in the comma-separated list. If it's a completely empty list, I make sure in line 9 that I don't start the loop at all – in such a case, no rows will be piped to the output.

Tip   I could have used a regular table function instead of pipelined – then I would have had to build the entire output collection before returning it. But if a table function is meant to be used strictly from SQL and never from PL/SQL, it is almost always a good idea to make it pipelined. This has the advantage of less PGA memory usage as well as the ability to quit processing if the client SQL stops fetching rows from the function. The downside is that you cannot use it in PL/SQL.

Having created my table function, I can use it in Listing 9-3 to split my strings into collections and turn the collections into rows.

Listing 9-3. Using pipelined table function to split string

```
SQL> select
  2     cf.customer_id
  3   , fl.column_value as product_id
  4   from customer_favorites cf
  5     , table(
  6           favorite_list_to_coll_type(cf.favorite_list)
  7         ) fl
  8   order by cf.customer_id, fl.column_value;
```

The table keyword in line 5 takes a collection (nested table) and turns the elements of the collection into rows. If the collection had been of an object type, the columns of the result would have been named like the object attributes, but here the collection is of a scalar type (integer), and then the single column is always called column_value, which in line 3 I give a more meaningful column alias:

CUSTOMER_ID	PRODUCT_ID
50042	4040
50042	5310
50741	5430
50741	7790
50741	7870
51069	6520

But you'll undoubtedly notice that the customer with a blank favorite_list is missing in the output. That's how Listing 9-3 works; I'm joining the customer_favorites table to the row source that is pipelined from my function, and it outputs (correctly) no rows for a blank favorite_list. This is exactly as if I was inner joining to a child table where no rows existed for this customer.

If I want to show the customer with no favorites, I need the equivalent of a left
outer join. But as there are no join predicates, I cannot use the (+) syntax on a
predicate column. Instead Oracle supports putting the (+) syntax directly after the
table(...) call, so I can change line 7 to this:

```
...
 7          )(+) fl
...
```

And that gives me an output that includes the customer with no favorites:

CUSTOMER_ID	PRODUCT_ID
50042	4040
50042	5310
50741	5430
50741	7790
50741	7870
51007	
51069	6520

The row source that's the result of the table function I can of course use for joins
as well, just like if it had been a real child table. I demonstrate this in Listing 9-4, at the
same time showing you how to do ANSI style joins to the table function instead of the
traditional comma used in Listing 9-3.

Listing 9-4. Join the results of the splitting to products

```
SQL> select
  2      cf.customer_id  as c_id
  3    , c.name          as cust_name
  4    , fl.column_value as p_id
  5    , p.name          as prod_name
  6  from customer_favorites cf
  7  cross apply table(
  8      favorite_list_to_coll_type(cf.favorite_list)
  9  ) fl
```

```
10   join customers c
11      on c.id = cf.customer_id
12   join products p
13      on p.id = fl.column_value
14   order by cf.customer_id, fl.column_value;
```

The normal join syntax requires an on clause, which I do not have and do not need. In principle what I need is like a cross join lateral to an inline view, but in ANSI SQL, it has been decided instead to use a special syntax cross apply for this, which I put just before the table keyword in line 7.

The rest is normal SQL with normal joins using the column_value column in the on clause in line 13:

C_ID	CUST_NAME	P_ID	PROD_NAME
50042	The White Hart	4040	Coalminers Sweat
50042	The White Hart	5310	Monks and Nuns
50741	Hygge og Humle	5430	Hercule Trippel
50741	Hygge og Humle	7790	Summer in India
50741	Hygge og Humle	7870	Ghost of Hops
51069	Der Wichtelmann	6520	Der Helle Kumpel

If again I want to include the customer with no favorites, in ANSI SQL I do not use (+), instead I change the cross apply in line 7 to outer apply, which necessitates changing join in line 12 to left outer join:

```
...
 7   outer apply table(
 8      favorite_list_to_coll_type(cf.favorite_list)
 9   ) fl
10   join customers c
11      on c.id = cf.customer_id
12   left outer join products p
13      on p.id = fl.column_value
...
```

151

Customer Boom Beer Bar, who has no favorites, is now included in the output:

```
C_ID   CUST_NAME         P_ID   PROD_NAME
50042  The White Hart    4040   Coalminers Sweat
50042  The White Hart    5310   Monks and Nuns
50741  Hygge og Humle    5430   Hercule Trippel
50741  Hygge og Humle    7790   Summer in India
50741  Hygge og Humle    7870   Ghost of Hops
51007  Boom Beer Bar
51069  Der Wichtelmann   6520   Der Helle Kumpel
```

This first method is a custom built table function for this purpose only. You can also do a generic function, but in fact you don't need to do that. The built-in APEX schema that you probably have in your database has already done this for you, as I'll show next.

Built-in APEX table function

There is APEX API function apex_util.string_to_table(favorite_list, ',') – but it returns a PL/SQL collection type defined in a package, not a nested table type defined in SQL. But it is a deprecated function anyway, so I just mention it so you won't use it, even if you happen to Google it.

Note   As of version 12.2, APEX is not installed in the database by default; rather it is just shipped with the software for easy installation. Even if your company does not use APEX applications as such, I think it is a good idea to install APEX in the database anyway to take advantage of the API packages when you code SQL and PL/SQL. If you wish, you can do it without configuring a web listener (ORDS, embedded PL/SQL gateway, or Oracle HTTP Server).

From APEX version 5.1, the supported function for this is apex_string.split, which returns a SQL nested table type and therefore is good to use in SQL as well. Listing 9-5 is like Listing 9-4, just using the APEX API function instead of the custom function I created before.

Listing 9-5. Splitting with apex_string.split

```
SQL> select
  2      cf.customer_id  as c_id
  3    , c.name              as cust_name
  4    , to_number(fl.column_value) as p_id
  5    , p.name              as prod_name
  6  from customer_favorites cf
  7  cross apply table(
  8      apex_string.split(cf.favorite_list, ',')
  9  ) fl
 10  join customers c
 11      on c.id = cf.customer_id
 12  join products p
 13      on p.id = to_number(fl.column_value)
 14  order by cf.customer_id, p_id;
```

The difference is just the function call in line 8 and then a small detail in line 14, where I utilize the fact that I can use column aliases in the order by clause to order by the more meaningful p_id instead of fl.column_value.

The output of Listing 9-5 is identical to that of Listing 9-4. Both methods call PL/SQL functions to do the actual splitting of the strings, which of course means context switching happening. Next up is a method in straight SQL without the context switching.

Straight SQL with row generators

No matter which method I use, I need to generate rows for each of the elements in the comma-delimited lists. The two previous methods used collections and the table function for this purpose. Another typical method of generating rows is to use a connect by query on dual, and this can be used here as well, as I show in Listing 9-6.

Listing 9-6. Generating as many rows as delimiter count

```
SQL> select
  2      favs.customer_id as c_id
  3    , c.name              as cust_name
  4    , favs.product_id  as p_id
```

```
 5    , p.name                as prod_name
 6  from (
 7    select 8            cf.customer_id
 9      , to_number(
10          regexp_substr(cf.favorite_list, '[^,]+', 1, sub#)
11        ) as product_id
12    from customer_favorites cf
13    cross join lateral(
14       select level sub#
15       from dual
16       connect by level <= regexp_count(cf.favorite_list, ',') + 1
17      ) fl
18  ) favs
19  join customers c
20     on c.id = favs.customer_id
21  join products p
22     on p.id = favs.product_id
23  order by favs.customer_id, favs.product_id;
```

Using cross join lateral in line 13 makes the inline view fl in lines 14–16 be executed for each row in customer_favorites, since I correlate the lateral inline view by using cf.favorite_list in line 16. By counting the number of commas and adding one, the inline view generates exactly the number of rows as there are elements in the comma-separated list.

As I've numbered the fl rows consecutively 1, 2, 3... in column sub#, I can use sub# in regexp_substr in line 10 to extract the first, second, third... occurrence of a "list of at least one character not containing a comma." This is then my product_id which I use to join the products table.

The output of Listing 9-6 is identical to both Listing 9-5 and Listing 9-4.

The preceding simple regular expression works if every element in the list has at least one character (hence the +). If I want it to work also if an element can be blank (meaning two commas in a row in the string), it will not work simply by changing the + to a *, instead I need to switch to slightly more complex regular expression like this:

```
...
10          regexp_substr(
11             cf.favorite_list
12           , '(^|,)([^,]*)'
13           , 1
14           , sub#
15           , null
16           , 2
17          )
...
```

The second group in the expression is like before, just with + changed to *, but I need to state it must follow either the beginning of the string or a comma. As I don't want that preceding comma to be part of the output, I ask for regexp_substr to return to me just the second group (line 16).

Treating the string as a JSON array

A simple comma-separated list of values can become a JSON array as shown in Listing 9-7.

Listing 9-7. Treating the string as a JSON array

```
SQL> select
  2     cf.customer_id  as c_id
  3   , c.name          as cust_name
  4   , fl.product_id   as p_id
  5   , p.name          as prod_name
  6  from customer_favorites cf
  7  outer apply json_table(
  8     '[' || cf.favorite_list || ']'
  9   , '$[*]'
 10     columns (
 11        product_id number path '$'
 12     )
 13  ) fl
 14  join customers c
 15     on c.id = cf.customer_id
```

```
16   left outer join products p
17      on p.id = fl.product_id
18   order by cf.customer_id, fl.product_id;
```

Instead of a PL/SQL table function, I use the SQL function `json_table` in line 7.

The first parameter to `json_table` must be valid JSON, which in this case I can very simply accomplish by surrounding the comma-separated list with square brackets in line 8.

Note   I can keep line 8 very simple only because my values are all numeric. If there had been text values involved, I would have needed to surround the text values with double quotes by replacing commas with quote-comma-quotes and take into consideration escaping any existing quotes. Then I would do as Stew Ashton shows here: `https://stewashton.wordpress.com/2018/06/05/ splitting-strings-a-new-champion/`.

In line 9, I state that there should be one row output from `json_table` for every element in the JSON array. As those elements are simple scalars, the path in line 11 becomes a simple $.

I've shown four methods to split simple delimited strings into rows of scalar values. In most cases, I'd choose between using straight SQL, JSON arrays, and `apex_string. split`. If you have very long strings with many elements, the SQL method of asking for the 1st, 2nd, 3rd...occurrence in `regexp_substr` might become slower for the 50th occurrence – such a case might be better with a function that pipes a row as it traverses the string. On the other hand, if you have many relatively short strings each with few elements, the overhead of occurrence retrieval of elements might be smaller than the comparatively more context switching to PL/SQL.

As always, test your own use case whether SQL or pipelined function is the best. If pipelined function is the answer for you, using built-in `apex_string.split` is often a good choice – creating your own pipelined function would be useful if your database does not have the APEX API packages installed or if you need some special datatype handling.

Now it's time to increase the complexity and look at delimited strings with some more structure in them.

Delimited multiple values

From time to time, I see applications where a string contains data with two delimiters – a row delimiter and a column delimiter. These days that would typically be a JSON string instead, but as data lives on a long time, you might still have to deal with such strings.

As an example here, I've chosen that the customers on the Good Beer Trading Co web site not only can enter their favorite lists, but they can also enter a list of beers that they review, each beer with a score of A, B, or C. This information is stored in column review_list of table customer_reviews, the content of which I show in Listing 9-8.

Listing 9-8. Comma- and colon-delimited content of customer_reviews table

```
SQL> select customer_id, review_list
  2  from customer_reviews
  3  order by customer_id;
```

The row delimiter is a comma, the column delimiter is a colon, so the data is like product:score,product:score,…

```
CUSTOMER_ID  REVIEW_LIST
50042        4040:A,6600:C,7950:B
50741        4160:A
51007
51069        4280:B,7790:B
```

To split up those strings into rows and columns, I'll show you four different methods.

Custom ODCI table function

The first method I'll show involves a pipelined table function again, but not a straightforward one like Listing 9-2.

Instead I am implementing it with the Oracle Data Cartridge Interface (ODCI) that allows me to hook into specific points in the processing of a SQL statement. This means that when the SQL engine hard parses a statement using this function, it will call my code to find out what columns and datatypes will be returned – instead of finding this information from the data dictionary. When a statement is prepared, when a row is fetched, and when the cursor is closed – all these will call my code instead of the standard handling.

Note   This is just one type of ODCI function implementing a custom *pipelined table* function. ODCI can also be used to implement a custom *aggregate* function, which I'll show you in the next chapter.

Here I'll focus on using this ODCI function – all of the details of the PL/SQL is outside the scope of this book. In Listing 9-9, I just show the skeleton of the object type used for implementation of the function.

For the curious reader, the complete code is available in the companion scripts. I describe the internals in detail on my blog: www.kibeha.dk/2015/06/supposing-youve-got-data-as-text-string.html.

Listing 9-9. The skeleton of the object type that implements the ODCI function

```
SQL> create or replace type delimited_col_row as object (
...
14    , static function parser(
15        p_text       in     varchar2
16      , p_cols       in     varchar2
17      , p_col_delim in     varchar2 default '|'
18      , p_row_delim in     varchar2 default ';'
19      ) return anydataset pipelined
20        using delimited_col_row
21
22    , static function odcitabledescribe(
...
28      ) return number
29
30    , static function odcitableprepare(
...
37      ) return number
38
39    , static function odcitablestart(
...
45      ) return number
46
```

```
47    , member function odcitablefetch(
...
51      ) return number
52
53    , member function odcitableclose(
...
55      ) return number
56  )
57  /
```

Type DELIMITED_COL_ROW compiled

```
SQL> create or replace type body delimited_col_row as
...
260  end;
261  /
```

Type Body DELIMITED_COL_ROW compiled

The object type must contain and implement the 5 odci* functions – they will be called by the SQL engine, not by anyone using the type.

The parser function is the one that should be called when you wish to use it. As it references the implementing object type using the syntax using delimited_col_row (line 20), it needs not be inside the object type; if you prefer, it could be implemented as a stand-alone function or in a package.

The object type can be used generically – in Listing 9-10, I use it for this specific case.

Listing 9-10. Using the ODCI table function to parse the delimited data

```
SQL> select cr.customer_id, rl.product_id, rl.score
  2  from customer_reviews cr
  3  outer apply table (
  4      delimited_col_row.parser(
  5        cr.review_list
  6      , 'PRODUCT_ID:NUMBER,SCORE:VARCHAR2(1)'
  7      , ':'
```

```
 8        , ','
 9        )
10  ) rl
11  order by cr.customer_id, rl.product_id;
```

Just like Listing 9-4, I do an apply on my table function – in this case I chose an outer apply instead of a cross apply. The table function delimited_col_row.parser then takes four parameters:

- First, the string that contains my delimited data: cr.review_list

- Then, the specification of the "columns" of each "row" of delimited data, what are their names and datatypes (this should be a literal, not a variable, as this is used at hard parse time, not soft parsing)

- Last, what is the column delimiter and the row delimiter in the data (these same delimiters I use in the column specification in line 6)

When I execute this statement the first time (hard parse), the SQL engine calls my odcitabledescribe function, which parses the second parameter and lets the SQL engine know the table function will return a row set with two columns, product_id and score, of the specified datatypes.

Then the SQL engine runs through odcitableprepare, odcitablestart, odcitablefetch, and odcitableclose. The actual splitting of the string data happens in odcitablefetch, where next row delimiter is found and the data split by the column delimiter, so a "row" is returned. At the end I see this output:

CUSTOMER_ID	PRODUCT_ID	SCORE
50042	4040	A
50042	6600	C
50042	7950	B
50741	4160	A
51007		
51069	4280	B
51069	7790	B

Note that I didn't have to do any column aliasing of a generic column_value – I can use rl.product_id and rl.score directly. I use this in Listing 9-11 for a meaningful join to the products table.

Listing 9-11. Joining with real column names instead of generic column_value

```
SQL> select
  2      cr.customer_id  as c_id
  3    , c.name          as cust_name
  4    , rl.product_id   as p_id
  5    , p.name          as prod_name
  6    , rl.score
  7  from customer_reviews cr
  8  cross apply table (
  9      delimited_col_row.parser(
 10        cr.review_list
 11      , 'PRODUCT_ID:NUMBER,SCORE:VARCHAR2(1)'
 12      , ':'
 13      , ','
 14      )
 15  ) rl
 16  join customers c
 17      on c.id = cr.customer_id
 18  join products p
 19      on p.id = rl.product_id
 20  order by cr.customer_id, rl.product_id;
```

In line 8, I used `cross apply`, so the output doesn't have the customer with no reviews:

C_ID	CUST_NAME	P_ID	PROD_NAME	SCORE
50042	The White Hart	4040	Coalminers Sweat	A
50042	The White Hart	6600	Hazy Pink Cloud	C
50042	The White Hart	7950	Pale Rider Rides	B
50741	Hygge og Humle	4160	Reindeer Fuel	A
51069	Der Wichtelmann	4280	Hoppy Crude Oil	B
51069	Der Wichtelmann	7790	Summer in India	B

Using an ODCI implementation like this allows fine control of all the small details of the implementation. This is well and good, but there are other solutions as well that doesn't need installing a custom ODCI function.

Combining apex_string.split and substr

For the simple delimited list, I showed using `apex_string.split` as an alternative to building your own pipelined table function. There is no such standard alternative for the ODCI function `delimited_col_row.parser` that will handle both rows and columns.

But I can separate handling of columns from handling of rows, as shown in Listing 9-12.

Listing 9-12. Getting rows with apex_string.split and columns with substr

```
SQL> select
  2      cr.customer_id  as c_id
  3    , c.name          as cust_name
  4    , p.id            as p_id
  5    , p.name          as prod_name
  6    , substr(
  7          rl.column_value
  8        , instr(rl.column_value, ':') + 1
  9      ) as score
 10  from customer_reviews cr
 11  cross apply table(
 12      apex_string.split(cr.review_list, ',')
 13  ) rl
 14  join customers c
 15      on c.id = cr.customer_id
 16  join products p
 17      on p.id = to_number(
 18                  substr(
 19                      rl.column_value
 20                    , 1
 21                    , instr(rl.column_value, ':') - 1
 22                  ))
 23  order by cr.customer_id, p_id;
```

I start by splitting the review list into rows in line 12 by using `apex_string.split` with the row delimiter comma. That means that `rl` will have rows with `column_value`, which will contain values with the two columns delimited by a colon – for example, `4040:A`.

Then it is a simple matter of using `substr` to pick out the product id in lines 17–22 and pick out the score in lines 6–9. The output is identical to Listing 9-11.

I've eliminated the custom function, but I'm still incurring a lot of context switches to PL/SQL, so next I'll try to use pure SQL again.

Row generators and regexp_substr

Similar to how I used `apex_string.split` to get the rows and then `substr` to get the columns, I am adapting Listing 9-6 to create Listing 9-13, where I generate rows with dual and use `regexp_substr` to get the columns.

Listing 9-13. Generating as many rows as delimiter count

```
SQL> select
  2      revs.customer_id as c_id
  3    , c.name           as cust_name
  4    , revs.product_id  as p_id
  5    , p.name           as prod_name
  6    , revs.score
  7  from (
  8      select
  9          cr.customer_id
 10        , to_number(
 11            regexp_substr(
 12              cr.review_list
 13            , '(^|,)([^:,]*)'
 14            , 1
 15            , sub#
 16            , null
 17            , 2
 18            )
 19          ) as product_id
 20        , regexp_substr(
 21            cr.review_list
 22          , '([^:,]*)(,|$)'
 23          , 1
```

```
24             , sub#
25             , null
26             , 1
27             ) as score
28       from customer_reviews cr
29       cross join lateral(
30           select level sub#
31           from dual
32           connect by level <= regexp_count(cr.review_list, ',') + 1
33       ) rl
34   ) revs
35   join customers c
36       on c.id = revs.customer_id
37   join products p
38       on p.id = revs.product_id
39   order by revs.customer_id, revs.product_id;
```

The lateral inline view in lines 29–33 is just as I did in Listing 9-6. The trick here is to specify suitable regular expressions in lines 13 and 22 to extract the two columns as what comes *before* and *after* the colon, respectively:

- Line 13 looks for either the beginning of the string or a comma (group 1), followed by zero or more characters that are neither colon nor comma (group 2). Line 17 states the function should return the second group (this needs minimum version 11.2).

- Line 22 looks for zero or more characters that are neither colon nor comma (group 1), followed by either a comma or the end of the string (group 2). Line 26 states the function should return the first group.

Listing 9-13 produces an identical output as Listing 9-11 and Listing 9-12, but does it without PL/SQL calls at all. The cost is more use of regular expression functions, which can be relatively CPU expensive – so to find which performs best, you should test the approaches against your specific use case.

All three solutions so far handle the string as it is, but I also mentioned at the start of the chapter that in many modern applications, such data would be stored as JSON rather than delimited. The database is capable of efficiently handling JSON as well as XML, so here's a fourth method that utilizes this.

Transformation to JSON

The first thing I want to do is to transform the delimited string into some valid JSON. This I do in Listing 9-14, where I transform the delimited pieces into a JSON array of JSON arrays, where each inner array has two elements, the first having the value of the product id and the second having the value of the review score.

Listing 9-14. Turning delimited text into JSON

```
SQL> select
  2      customer_id
  3   , '[["'
  4      || replace(
  5           replace(
  6              review_list
  7            , ','
  8            , '"],["'
  9           )
 10         , ':'
 11         , '","'
 12      )
 13      || '"]]'
 14      as json_list
 15   from customer_reviews
 16   order by customer_id;
```

Let me show you the output before I explain the code:

```
CUSTOMER_ID  JSON_LIST
50042        [["4040","A"],["6600","C"],["7950","B"]]
50741        [["4160","A"]]
51007        [[""]]
51069        [["4280","B"],["7790","B"]]
```

You can see in the output that the code in lines 3–13 transformed the text of `review_list` into *nested* JSON arrays. An *outer* array whose elements correspond to *rows*, where each row itself is an *inner* array whose elements correspond to *columns*.

To do this transformation, the innermost `replace` in lines 5–9 replaces each row delimiter (comma) with the five characters `"],["`, where each character is

- End of inner element

- End of inner array

- Comma as delimiter between elements of the outer array

- Start of new inner array

- Start of new inner element

After that the `replace` in lines 4 and 10–12 replaces each column delimiter (colon) with the three characters `","`, where each character is

- End of inner element

- Comma as delimiter between elements in the inner array

- Start of new inner element

In line 3, the JSON begins with the three characters `[["` for start of outer array, start of inner array, and start of inner element.

Finally in line 13, the JSON ends with the three characters `"]]` for end of inner element, end of inner array, and end of outer array.

Having created the string concatenation expression that transforms the delimited string to JSON, I can now use it in the `json_table` function in Listing 9-15.

Listing 9-15. Parsing JSON with json_table

```
SQL> select
  2      cr.customer_id  as c_id
  3    , c.name          as cust_name
  4    , rl.product_id   as p_id
  5    , p.name          as prod_name
  6    , rl.score
  7  from customer_reviews cr
  8  cross apply json_table (
  9      '[["'
 10      || replace(
 11           replace(
```

```
12              cr.review_list
13              , ','
14              , '"],["'
15           )
16           , ':'
17           , '","'
18           )
19        || '"]]'
20      , '$[*]'
21        columns (
22           product_id  number    path '$[0]'
23         , score       varchar2(1) path '$[1]'
24         )
25     ) rl
26     join customers c
27        on c.id = cr.customer_id
28     join products p
29        on p.id = rl.product_id
30     order by cr.customer_id, rl.product_id;
```

The first parameter to the `json_table` function is the JSON itself, so lines 9–19 are the expression I developed in the previous listing.

The second parameter in line 20 specifies that `json_table` should take as rows all the inner arrays (`*`) in the outer JSON array that is in the root of the JSON string (`$`).

And last in the `column` specification lines 22–23, I state that the first element (`$[0]`) of the inner array is a `number` and should be a column called `product_id`, while the second element (`$[1]`) of the inner array is a `varchar2` and should be a column called `score`.

As you see, this output is identical to the output of the three previous methods:

```
C_ID   CUST_NAME        P_ID   PROD_NAME         SCORE
50042  The White Hart   4040   Coalminers Sweat  A
50042  The White Hart   6600   Hazy Pink Cloud   C
50042  The White Hart   7950   Pale Rider Rides  B
50741  Hygge og Humle   4160   Reindeer Fuel     A
51069  Der Wichtelmann  4280   Hoppy Crude Oil   B
51069  Der Wichtelmann  7790   Summer in India   B
```

As shown before, if I had wanted to show the customer with a blank `review_list`, I change `cross apply` in line 8 to `outer apply`.

Tip   Listing 9-15 can be adapted to use linefeed for row delimiter and comma for column delimiter if you have plain CSV in a CLOB, for example. Alternatively you could look into the `apex_data_parser` package as shown here: `https://blogs.oracle.com/apex/super-easy-csv-xlsx-json-or-xml-parsing-about-the-apex_data_parser-package`.

Using `json_table` requires version 12.1.0.2 or newer. If you have a need for older versions, you'll find in the companion script an example of doing the same thing by transforming to XML and using `xmltable` instead.

Lessons learned

Delimited text is most often a list of values separated by a single delimiter, but it can also be more structured with, for example, both a "row" delimiter and a "column" delimiter. I've shown both types of examples in this chapter along with multiple ways of splitting them, so you can

- Split delimited text with SQL only or built-in PL/SQL functionality.

- Create custom PL/SQL table functions – both regular and the ODCI variant – for special needs.

- Transform the text to JSON and use native JSON parsing.

If you create your own data model, you should use child tables, collections, XML, or JSON rather than relying on storing data as delimited text. But it is common to receive delimited text from places out of your control, in which case any of the shown methods can be useful. Normally using native and built-in functionality is the easiest and the best performant, but for more special use cases, you can test if the other methods are better suited for you.

CHAPTER 10

Creating Delimited Text

You learned in the previous chapter how to take a delimited text and split it to pieces, generating rows with one piece of text per row. Guess what, just like I did a chapter on pivoting after unpivoting, here comes a chapter showing how to take pieces of text in rows and aggregate them into delimited strings.

This is often much liked by users reading reports, where it is easier to get an overview if there is not a lot of repeated data in multiple rows with most columns identical and just a single column with different values. Sometimes you can do pivoting to alleviate that problem, but sometimes you just don't have a fixed number of columns. Outputting a comma-separated string can be the answer for such cases.

Delimited strings can also be useful sometimes for importing elsewhere – for example, a tab- or semicolon-separated string is easy to import in an Excel spreadsheet to produce columns.

There are several ways you can create such delimited text, both using built-in functionality as well as functionality you create yourself. I'll show some of those different ways and their advantages and disadvantages.

Delimited lists of products

As examples, I am going to create text strings with comma-separated lists of product names that the company sells, using the tables shown in Figure 10-1.

© Kim Berg Hansen 2020
K. Berg Hansen, *Practical Oracle SQL*, https://doi.org/10.1007/978-1-4842-5617-6_10

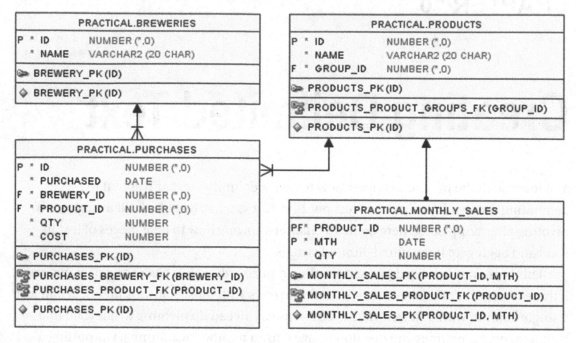

Figure 10-1. *The tables used in this chapter*

For most of the examples in the chapter, I am going to use the tables breweries, products, and purchases joined together in the view brewery_products shown in Listing 10-1. At the end of the chapter, I'll be using monthly_sales and products to create an artificially long string that won't fit in a regular varchar2.

Listing 10-1. View of which products are purchased at which breweries

```
SQL> create or replace view brewery_products
  2  as
  3  select
  4     b.id    as brewery_id
  5   , b.name  as brewery_name
  6   , p.id    as product_id
  7   , p.name  as product_name
  8  from breweries b
  9  cross join products p
 10  where exists (
 11     select null
 12     from purchases pu
```

```
13     where pu.brewery_id = b.id
14     and   pu.product_id = p.id
15  );
```

This view examines all combinations of the breweries and the beers if the beer has been purchased at some time from that brewery. The result – shown in Listing 10-2 – is a list that shows which beer is purchased at which brewery.

Listing 10-2. The breweries and products

```
SQL> select *
  2  from brewery_products
  3  order by brewery_id, product_id;
```

BREWERY_ID	BREWERY_NAME	PRODUCT_ID	PRODUCT_NAME
518	Balthazar Brauerei	5310	Monks and Nuns
518	Balthazar Brauerei	5430	Hercule Trippel
518	Balthazar Brauerei	6520	Der Helle Kumpel
523	Happy Hoppy Hippo	6600	Hazy Pink Cloud
523	Happy Hoppy Hippo	7790	Summer in India
523	Happy Hoppy Hippo	7870	Ghost of Hops
536	Brewing Barbarian	4040	Coalminers Sweat
536	Brewing Barbarian	4160	Reindeer Fuel
536	Brewing Barbarian	4280	Hoppy Crude Oil
536	Brewing Barbarian	7950	Pale Rider Rides

In the next section, I'll show multiple ways to create a variant of this list with just three rows – one for each brewery containing a column with a comma-separated list of all the beer names of that brewery.

String aggregation

You know the function sum is an aggregate function that adds numbers. I'm about to demonstrate various aggregate functions that concatenate strings instead; therefore, this is called *string aggregation*. You can find other methods if you search the Internet or forums – I'll just highlight four methods that each have some pros and cons.

Aggregate function listagg

In version 11.2, a new built-in function appeared called listagg – it is by definition the very function to use for string aggregation (just as sum is the function for additive number aggregation).

It requires a little more syntax than the simple sum function, but it is not hard to use as you can see in Listing 10-3.

Listing 10-3. Using listagg to create product list

```
SQL> select
  2      max(brewery_name) as brewery_name
  3    , listagg(product_name, ',') within group (
  4        order by product_id
  5      ) as product_list
  6  from brewery_products
  7  group by brewery_id
  8  order by brewery_id;
```

In line 3, I use listagg with two parameters: the first is the string column or expression I want to aggregate, and the second (optional) is the delimiter to put between the strings in the aggregated result. If you don't provide a delimiter parameter, the default is null which simply concatenates the strings without any delimiter between them.

After the parameters, the within group is mandatory and requires me to specify an order by (line 4) that tells Oracle in which order the strings should be aggregated.

With those keywords, Listing 10-3 produces this output that has the beers purchased at each brewery in a comma-separated string, where the beers are ordered by product_id:

```
BREWERY_NAME        PRODUCT_LIST
Balthazar Brauerei  Monks and Nuns,Hercule Trippel,Der Helle Kumpel
Happy Hoppy Hippo   Hazy Pink Cloud,Summer in India,Ghost of Hops
Brewing Barbarian   Coalminers Sweat,Reindeer Fuel,Hoppy Crude Oil,Pale
Rider Rides
```

Suppose I want the beers ordered alphabetically in the product list? That's very easy; I just need to change the `order` by clause inside `within group`:

```
...
4          order by product_name
...
```

And now the beers are alphabetically listed:

```
BREWERY_NAME          PRODUCT_LIST
Balthazar Brauerei    Der Helle Kumpel,Hercule Trippel,Monks and Nuns
Happy Hoppy Hippo     Ghost of Hops,Hazy Pink Cloud,Summer in India
Brewing Barbarian     Coalminers Sweat,Hoppy Crude Oil,Pale Rider
Rides,Reindeer Fuel
```

The function `listagg` is easy to use and as a built-in highly performant. There are just a few drawbacks:

- It cannot return a string larger than a `varchar2` – either 4.000 or 32.767 bytes depending on your database setting. (Though there's support for handling such situations – more on that later.)

- Before version 19c, it cannot do a `distinct` aggregation.

- It does not exist in versions before 11.2.

But in all other cases, `listagg` should be your first choice when considering string aggregation. If, however, you *do* find yourself in one of those situations, there are alternatives.

Aggregate function collect

One of the alternatives you can consider if you have one of the special cases is to aggregate into a collection (nested table type) using the `collect` function and then build the string from the collection.

So to make this work, I need to define the two objects shown in Listing 10-4. The first is a nested table type `name_coll_type` of `varchar2` in the size I need – in this case `20 char` – I just need to represent that as `80 bytes`. This is due to a bug – see the note for further explanation.

Listing 10-4. Collection type and function to convert collection to string

```sql
SQL> create or replace type name_coll_type
  2      as table of varchar2(80 byte);
  3  /

SQL> create or replace function name_coll_type_to_varchar2 (
  2      p_name_coll     in name_coll_type
  3    , p_delimiter     in varchar2 default null
  4  )
  5      return varchar2
  6  is
  7      v_name_string  varchar2(4000 char);
  8  begin
  9      for idx in p_name_coll.first..p_name_coll.last
 10      loop
 11        if idx = p_name_coll.first then
 12            v_name_string := p_name_coll(idx);
 13        else
 14            v_name_string := v_name_string
 15                            || p_delimiter
 16                            || p_name_coll(idx);
 17        end if;
 18      end loop;
 19      return v_name_string;
 20  end name_coll_type_to_varchar2;
 21  /
```

The second object I define is the function name_coll_type_to_varchar2 that converts the collection to a delimited string. It simply loops over the elements of the collection and keeps concatenating them unto the string variable to be returned – with a delimiter between each if such parameter has been given.

> **Note**   Type name_coll_type should really be varchar2(20 char), but unfortunately this causes an error due to a bug in Oracle. It is only a problem if you have a database with a multi-byte character set (as I use AL32UTF8) and use char semantics defining your varchar2 columns. This combination confuses collect.
>
> I've seen the bug in versions 12.2 and 18.3, and others have verified it in 11.2. You can see if it has been fixed in future releases on My Oracle Support by searching for bug 29195635. When the bug has been fixed, you can change to the correct datatype – until then the workaround is to use varchar2(80 byte) which is the maximum number of bytes that a varchar2(20 char) can be in AL32UTF8.

So armed with these two objects, I can now use them together with the built-in collect and cast functions as I show in Listing 10-5.

Listing 10-5. Using collect and the created function

```sql
SQL> select
  2      max(brewery_name) as brewery_name
  3    , name_coll_type_to_varchar2(
  4        cast(
  5          collect(
  6              product_name
  7              order by product_id
  8          )
  9          as name_coll_type
 10        )
 11      , ','
 12      ) as product_list
 13   from brewery_products
 14   group by brewery_id
 15   order by brewery_id;
```

How does it work? Well, starting from the inside of the expression, this is what happens:

- The `collect` function in lines 5–8 takes the `product_name` and aggregates it into a collection that'll be ordered by `product_id`. But this is a "generic" collection type used internally by the database; we need to tell which *real* collection type it should be put in.

- So therefore in lines 4 and 9–10, I am using `cast` to specify I want the collection type `name_coll_type`.

- Now I have a collection of the correct type to call function `name_coll_type_to_varchar2` in line 3, and in line 11, I specify that a comma should be used as a delimiter in the resulting string.

The output of Listing 10-5 is identical to that of Listing 10-3 using `listagg`. This method of using `collect` can be a workaround for all three drawbacks of `listagg`:

- It can be used in versions before 11.2.

- It supports distinct in the `collect` function, even you are not yet using version 19c.

- If needed, you can easily make a function `name_coll_type_to_clob` to handle cases where the result won't fit in a `varchar2`.

As I have the APEX packages installed in my database, I can even use this method without having to create my own custom nested table type and function. With the APEX installation comes a type `apex_t_varchar2,` and the package `apex_string` has a function `join` that does the same as my `name_coll_type_to_varchar2` function.

So I can adapt Listing 10-5 to using APEX functionality by just changing lines 3 and 9:

```
...
  3   , apex_string.join(
...
  9           as apex_t_varchar2
...
```

And this will work even if I am not using any APEX applications, just as long as the APEX API packages are installed in my database.

Custom aggregate function stragg

Long before version 11.2 was thought of, a quite common question people would ask of the famous Tom Kyte on *http://asktom.oracle.com* was how to do string aggregation. So Tom developed a custom aggregate function he called `stragg` as an answer to that question, and it has been used by many over the years. Here I'll show a version where I have incorporated a few additions picked up here and there.

Caution   You may possibly find in your database a function called `stragg` in the SYS schema. This is a very little known function based on a C library and installed together with the `dbms_xmlindex` package. It is undocumented and designed specifically for certain tasks in the XML Index implementation. **Do not use it!** There is no guarantee how it works, and it is all too easy to unknowingly call it in an unsupported manner and either get errors or wrong results.

Oracle Data Cartridge Interface (ODCI) is a set of interface functions for doing a rather low-level implementation of functionality that can be used very much like built-ins. Mostly it is used by library authors implementing special functionality in, for example, C, but it can also be used for simpler cases implemented in pure PL/SQL.

As this is a book primarily on SQL, I am not going to waste paper having the entire implementation printed in the book. So I'll show the create statements in the pieces of Listing 10-6, but skip the bulk of the body.

Listing 10-6. Types, type bodies, and function to implement custom aggregate

```
SQL> create or replace type stragg_expr_type as object (
  2     element    varchar2(4000 char)
  3   , delimiter  varchar2(4000 char)
  4   , map member function map_func return varchar2
  5  );
  6  /
```

The original `stragg` by Tom Kyte aggregated simply on a `varchar2` and then hardcoded the delimiter used, since an aggregate function cannot be created with multiple parameters. I am going to aggregate on an object type `stragg_expr_type` instead, allowing me to pass the desired delimiter as a second attribute in the object.

```
SQL> create or replace type body stragg_expr_type
  2  as
  3     map member function map_func return varchar2
  4     is
  5     begin
  6        return element || '|' || delimiter;
  7     end map_func;
  8  end;
  9  /
```

I implement a map member function in my object type, because that allows the database to discover whether two objects are identical or not. And that in turn allows my aggregate function to support the distinct keyword, which is one of the things listagg does not do until version 19c.

```
SQL> create or replace type stragg_type as object
  2  (
  3      aggregated varchar2(4000)
  4  , delimiter  varchar2(4000)
  5
  6  , static function ODCIAggregateInitialize(
  7        new_self    in out stragg_type
  8    ) return number
  9
 10  , member function ODCIAggregateIterate(
 11        self        in out stragg_type
 12      , value       in      stragg_expr_type
 13    ) return number
 14
 15  , member function ODCIAggregateTerminate(
 16        self        in      stragg_type
 17      , returnvalue out     varchar2
 18      , flags       in      number
 19    ) return number
 20
```

```
21   , member function ODCIAggregateMerge(
22       self          in out stragg_type
23       , other_self  in       stragg_type
24       ) return number
25   );
26   /
```

Then I define the type `stragg_type` that is going to implement the actual aggregation. The two attributes I use internally in the implementation. The four functions are determined by the ODCI interface and must be named like shown and with a parameter list exactly as shown (the parameter names may be different, but the order and type of parameters have to match):

- ODCIAggregateInitialize is kind of like a constructor function explicitly called by the database when aggregation is started, so here I create a new instance of the object.

- ODCIAggregateIterate is called by the database with each string that is to be aggregated, so here I add the delimiter and string to the `aggregated` attribute. (In the original `stragg`, the value parameter was simply a `varchar2`; here I am passing a value of type `stragg_expr_type`.)

- ODCIAggregateTerminate is called by the database at the end of the aggregation when it wants the result, and I return the aggregated string here.

- In case the database has decided to split the aggregation job in multiple parts (e.g., in parallel query), each part has called ODCIAggregateInitialize to get an object and then aggregated along with ODCIAggregateIterate. At the end each part will have an object with some strings aggregated in the `aggregated` attribute – the database will then call ODCIAggregateMerge to merge the content, so in this function, I append the `aggregated` of the `other_self` object to the `self` object.

That was the textual description of what I need to implement in the functions, and then I just need to code this in the type body.

```
SQL> create or replace type body stragg_type
  2  is
...
 54  end;
 55  /
```

For the code implementing those four functions in the type body, see the companion script *practical_fill_schema.sql*.

```
SQL> create or replace function stragg(input stragg_expr_type )
  2      return varchar2
  3      parallel_enable aggregate using stragg_type;
  4  /
```

Having create the object type for implementation, the last thing to do is to create the aggregate function stragg itself. The input parameter must be of datatype matching the value parameter of ODCIAggregateIterate function, and the return datatype must match the returnvalue parameter of ODCIAggregateTerminate function.

The aggregate using stragg_type tells the database this is a custom aggregate function that is implemented by the object type stragg_type, so when the database performs aggregation with this function, it will call the ODCI* functions of the type. Keyword parallel_enable specifies the database may use parallelization, because I have implemented ODCIAggregateMerge.

Having created these objects, I am now able to use my custom aggregate function in Listing 10-7.

Listing 10-7. Using stragg custom aggregate function

```
SQL> select
  2      max(brewery_name) as brewery_name
  3    , stragg(
  4          stragg_expr_type(product_name, ',')
  5      ) as product_list
  6  from brewery_products
  7  group by brewery_id
  8  order by brewery_id;
```

Since I declared this function an aggregate function using the ODCI interface, I can use `stragg` in lines 3–5 just like any built-in aggregate function. The input datatype is `stragg_expr_type`, so I use the type constructor with the product name and the comma as delimiter.

Note   The trick of using an object type to pass a delimiter to the aggregate function works nicely, but it does require a bit of self-discipline from me as a developer, since it is up to me to ensure that the delimiter is a constant. In principle I could pass different delimiter values in each row, but that would cause problems in the implementation. I have tried to implement such that the delimiter from the first call to ODCITableIterate is used, but in case of parallelization, there will be multiple calls to ODCITableIterate from different rows. It is therefore important you make sure the delimiter value is constant – the safest is to use a literal.

The output of Listing 10-7 is almost, but not necessarily quite the same as the output I got from `listagg` and `collect`:

```
BREWERY_NAME        PRODUCT_LIST
Balthazar Brauerei  Monks and Nuns,Der Helle Kumpel,Hercule Trippel
Happy Hoppy Hippo   Hazy Pink Cloud,Ghost of Hops,Summer in India
Brewing Barbarian   Coalminers Sweat,Pale Rider Rides,Hoppy Crude
Oil,Reindeer Fuel
```

The product names within the `product_list` column are the same – the result is identical in terms of values. But the order of products within the delimited string is indeterminate with this custom aggregate function – I cannot implement an `order by` clause for `stragg`.

A thing to note here is the behavior if I add the `distinct` clause to the call to `stragg`:

```
...
 4        distinct stragg_expr_type(product_name, ',')
...
```

Suddenly the beers are alphabetically ordered in the product list:

```
BREWERY_NAME          PRODUCT_LIST
Balthazar Brauerei    Der Helle Kumpel,Hercule Trippel,Monks and Nuns
Happy Hoppy Hippo     Ghost of Hops,Hazy Pink Cloud,Summer in India
Brewing Barbarian     Coalminers Sweat,Hoppy Crude Oil,Pale Rider
Rides,Reindeer Fuel
```

This is a side effect of the database having to sort the product names in order to get the distinct values. But it cannot be guaranteed always to be ordered and work like you see here – the database might figure out a way to, for example, use a hash function to do distinct, and then the result will be very unordered.

Aggregate function xmlagg

So you've now seen listagg, collect, and stragg – if that's not enough, Listing 10-8 shows a fourth method of string aggregation using xmlagg.

Listing 10-8. Using xmlagg and extract text from xml

```
SQL> select
  2      max(brewery_name) as brewery_name
  3    , rtrim(
  4        xmlagg(
  5            xmlelement(z, product_name, ',')
  6            order by product_id
  7        ).extract('//text()').getstringval()
  8      , ','
  9      ) as product_list
 10    from brewery_products
 11    group by brewery_id
 12    order by brewery_id;
```

Examining the expression I use here, it works like this:

- In line 5, I create an XML element called z (the name is irrelevant) containing a concatenation of the product name and a comma.

- Using xmlagg in lines 4 and 6, I create an XML snippet that is an aggregation of the z XML elements created in the preceding text – ordered by product id.

- In line 7, I get rid of the XML tags in the snippet, keeping only the text values.

- The aggregated text at this point now has a trailing comma too much, so I get rid of that using rtrim in lines 3 and 8.

All of that together makes Listing 10-8 return the exact same output as listagg and collect in Listings 10-3 and 10-5.

So what's up with this z XML element? What's the purpose of this? Well, if I was to do just the xmlagg(xmlelement(... alone and skip the extract and rtrim, this would be the output for Balthazar Brauerei:

```
<Z>Monks and Nuns,</Z><Z>Hercule Trippel,</Z><Z>Der Helle Kumpel,</Z>
```

You see the XML start and end tags for a series of Z elements, each containing a product name and comma. The actual name I use for the XML tag is irrelevant, so it might as well be as short as possible, because it is stripped away anyway, when I do extract('//text()') on it:

```
Monks and Nuns,Hercule Trippel,Der Helle Kumpel,
```

And now you can see why the rtrim is necessary to remove the comma at the end.

Creating the z XML element is the nice way to behave when using xmlagg. But there is actually an alternative that can save you from needing to do the extract to strip away XML tags.

The function xmlparse takes xml as text and transforms it to XMLType datatype. Normally it will check if it is good XML, but it also supports the keyword wellformed, by which you tell the database "trust me, this is good XML, you do not need to check it." So I can replace the use of `xmlelement` with `xmlparse` and thereby skip having to use extract:

```
...
4       xmlagg(
5           xmlparse(content product_name || ',' wellformed)
6           order by product_id
7       ).getstringval()
...
```

This will directly give me the output with no XML tags, ready to use the `rtrim` function to get rid of the last comma:

```
Monks and Nuns,Hercule Trippel,Der Helle Kumpel,
```

Why would you consider using `xmlagg` when you have the other alternatives I've shown? Partly it is nice in older databases that string aggregation is possible with `xmlagg` without having to install your own datatypes; partly it is one of the ways to handle very long aggregations, as I'll show you now.

When it doesn't fit in a VARCHAR2

The string aggregations I've shown so far will all fail, if the aggregated output is longer than the maximum length of a `varchar2` – normally 4000 bytes, but could be 32.767 bytes if your database `max_string_size` is set to extended.

What to do then if you need larger output? To show you that, I'm going to use the table `monthly_sales` and join it to the `products` table.

I have monthly sales data for 3 years for each of my 10 products, so 360 rows in this table. Imagine I need to output the product name for each of those rows in a fixed length format – that is, each product name padded with spaces so it fills exactly 20 characters without using any delimiters. The result is a single string 7200 characters.

In Listing 10-9, I attempt to generate this string using `listagg` – as I use no `group by,` I should get a single row with a single column in the output having this 7.200-character fixed length list of 360 product names.

Listing 10-9. Getting ORA-01489 with listagg

```
SQL> select
  2     listagg(rpad(p.name, 20)) within group (
  3        order by p.id
  4     ) as product_list
  5  from products p
  6  join monthly_sales ms
  7     on ms.product_id = p.id;

Error starting at line : 1 in command -
Error report -
ORA-01489: result of string concatenation is too long
```

But it fails in my database where a varchar2 can be at most 4.000 bytes long. To work around this, I have different options.

Get just the first part of the result

Sometimes I do not actually need to get the entire result; it is sufficient to get what *can* fit in a varchar2 and an indication that there is more than could be shown. In version 12.2, the listagg function was enhanced to provide just this functionality, as I show in Listing 10-10.

Listing 10-10. Suppressing error in listagg

```
SQL> select
  2     listagg(
  3        rpad(p.name, 20)
  4        on overflow truncate '{more}' with count
  5     ) within group (
  6        order by p.id
  7     ) as product_list
  8  from products p
  9  join monthly_sales ms
 10     on ms.product_id = p.id;
```

Compared to Listing 10-9, I have simply added line 4:

- Keywords on `overflow` is used to specify what the database should do if the result of the aggregation becomes too long to fit a `varchar2`. The default is `on overflow error`, which gives the error in Listing 10-9.

- `truncate` specifies that instead of raising an error, it should return only what will fit in a `varchar2` and truncate the rest. Note it never truncates in the middle of a string in the list – the string that causes the overflow so the output won't fit, that string will be truncated in its entirety.

- The literal `'{more}'` will be appended to the result if it was truncated. If I do not specify a literal, the default is an ellipsis (three dots) `'...'`.

- `with count` causes a count of how many elements (not characters) were truncated to be appended. The default is `without count`.

This addition of line 4 causes Listing 10-10 to run without error and give me this output instead with a single string almost 4000 characters long (most of them omitted here to save paper):

```
PRODUCT_LIST
Coalminers Sweat    Coalminers Sweat    ...[[3880 characters removed]]...
Der Helle Kumpel    Der Helle Kumpel    {more}(162)
```

So for cases where it is enough to know there is more than could fit, this is a nice enhancement to `listagg`. But what if that is not the case? Then I have other possibilities.

Try to make it fit with reduced data

There can be cases where the reason it won't fit with `listagg` is that the data is not unique, and you do not actually need to see each individual occurrence of the duplicated data – once is enough. When your database is version 19c or later, you can do `distinct` string aggregation, making the fewer occurrences possibly fit inside a `varchar2`.

Listing 10-11 is like Listing 10-9; I just added the keyword `distinct` in the `listagg` function call, which is a new feature in version 19c.

Listing 10-11. Reducing data with distinct

```
SQL> select
  2      listagg(distinct rpad(p.name, 20)) within group (
  3        order by p.id
  4      ) as product_list
  5    from products p
  6    join monthly_sales ms
  7      on ms.product_id = p.id;
```

Since the 7200 character string in this case contains a whole lot of repetitions, doing `distinct` gives me a string with just 200 characters:

```
PRODUCT_LIST
Coalminers Sweat     Der Helle Kumpel    Ghost of Hops       Hazy Pink Cloud
Hercule Trippel      Hoppy Crude Oil     Monks and Nuns      Pale Rider
Rides    Reindeer Fuel      Summer in India
```

If I had not had a 19c database, I could have used an inline view with a `select distinct` and then performed my `listagg` aggregation on the result of the inline view.

For cases where a `distinct` set of data makes the aggregated result small enough, `listagg` supports it in version 19c or later. But there can also be cases where you really *do* need the aggregated result to be larger than a `varchar2` – then you need a `clob`.

Use a CLOB instead of a VARCHAR2

One way to use a clob is to use the collect function shown earlier and then create a function `name_coll_type_to_clob` instead of the `name_coll_type_to_varchar2` I have shown. I'll leave that as an exercise to you, as it is not much that need to be changed, if you want to try it.

But in Listing 10-12, I'll instead show you how to aggregate to a `clob` using the built-in function `xmlagg` – then you do not need to create any function of your own.

Listing 10-12. Using xmlagg to aggregate to a clob

```
SQL> select
  2      xmlagg(
  3        xmlparse(
```

```
 4              content rpad(p.name, 20) wellformed
 5           )
 6        order by product_id
 7      ).getclobval() as product_list
 8  from products p
 9  join monthly_sales ms
10     on ms.product_id = p.id;
```

This is very like what I did in Listing 10-8, just using getclobval() in line 7 instead of getstringval(). That is really all that is necessary to get a clob instead of varchar2 from an xmltype, and the result is the 7200 character string I want (shown here with most of it cut away):

PRODUCT_LIST

```
Coalminers Sweat    Coalminers Sweat    ...[[7120 characters removed]]...
Pale Rider Rides    Pale Rider Rides
```

If my database is version 18c or later, I can get the same output as Listing 10-12 by using json_arrayagg as alternative to xmlagg. I show an example in Listing 10-13.

Listing 10-13. Using json_arrayagg to aggregate to a clob

```
SQL> select
  2      json_value(
  3        replace(
  4          json_arrayagg(
  5            rpad(p.name, 20)
  6            order by product_id
  7            returning clob
  8          )
  9        , '","'
 10        , ''
 11        )
 12      , '$[0]' returning clob
 13    ) as product_list
 14  from products p
 15  join monthly_sales ms
 16     on ms.product_id = p.id;
```

If you didn't create your own name_coll_type_to_clob and you have APEX installed in the database, you also have an APEX function that can be used, as I show in Listing 10-14.

Listing 10-14. Using apex_string.join_clob to aggregate to a clob

```
SQL> select
  2      apex_string.join_clob(
  3        cast(
  4          collect(
  5            rpad(p.name, 20)
  6            order by p.id
  7          )
  8          as apex_t_varchar2
  9        )
 10      , ''
 11      , 12 /* dbms_lob.call */
 12      ) as product_list
 13  from products p
 14  join monthly_sales ms
 15    on ms.product_id = p.id;
```

This is a function that can be used just like apex_string.join that I showed you earlier in the chapter. Since apex_string.join_clob returns a temporary clob, it has an extra parameter compared to apex_string.join to indicate the life span of the temporary clob, accepting the same values as dbms_lob.createtemporary. In line 11, I state that the clob just lives for the duration of the call.

Until perhaps a future listagg implementation might possibly implement clob support, xmlagg, json_arrayagg, and apex_string.join_clob are all valid methods to use. The JSON functionality in the database has generally been tuned from version to version, so in the most recent database versions, the JSON functions are typically the fastest solution.

Lessons learned

I've shown both built-in and custom-made methods of string aggregation enabling you to

- Use built-in `listagg` function as the preferred method, except for the special cases where it will not work.

- Create a nested table type and a function (or use APEX built-ins) to use the `collect` aggregate function as an alternative.

- Use a custom created aggregate function `stragg`.

- Do string aggregation both in `varchar2` and `clob` with various built-in functions.

All of the methods can be good to know for special circumstances, but my recommendation is in general to stick to `listagg` if you can. The built-in functionality normally outperforms anything you can build yourself – unless the circumstances are very special.

PART II

Analytic Functions

CHAPTER 11

Analytic Partitions, Ordering, and Windows

A wise man once said in a conference presentation that if you put SQL on your resume and do not know analytic functions, you are lying. I can only agree. It would be similar to stating you know Windows and have never worked with a newer windows version than Windows 95.

I use analytic functions almost daily when developing. There are so many cases where they either are necessary to create a SQL solution at all (the alternative being a slow procedural solution instead) or at the very least make the SQL much more performant than not using analytic functions (often cases of many self-joins leading to multiple lookups of the same data).

The fantastic bit about analytic functions is that you can retrieve or reference values across rows – you are not restricted to values in the row itself when doing calculations. You can use different subclauses of analytic functions in different combinations to achieve this.

The basics of these subclauses, and how they work together, are shown in this chapter. The rest of Part 2 contains different use cases of analytic functions solving tasks that often would be hard without.

© Kim Berg Hansen 2020
K. Berg Hansen, *Practical Oracle SQL*, https://doi.org/10.1007/978-1-4842-5617-6_11

Sums of quantities

To showcase the different subclauses of an analytic function call, I'll be using the orderlines table shown in Figure 11-1.

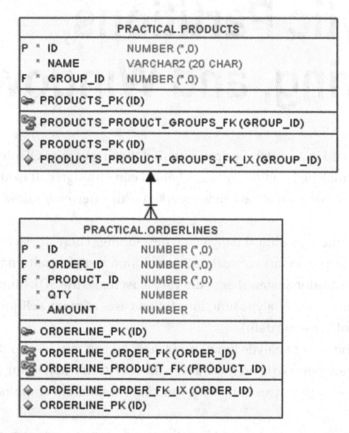

Figure 11-1. *Orderlines table of how much of each product is ordered by customers*

The orderlines table contains how much is in order from customers for each of the beers in the products table. In the example queries of this chapter, I'll join the two tables just to make it easier to spot the two different beers whose data I show in Listing 11-1.

Listing 11-1. Content of orderlines table for two beers

```
SQL> select
  2     ol.product_id as p_id
  3   , p.name        as product_name
  4   , ol.order_id   as o_id
```

```
 5    , ol.qty
 6  from orderlines ol
 7  join products p
 8     on p.id = ol.product_id
 9  where ol.product_id in (4280, 6600)
10  order by ol.product_id, ol.qty;
```

P_ID	PRODUCT_NAME	O_ID	QTY
4280	Hoppy Crude Oil	423	60
4280	Hoppy Crude Oil	427	60
4280	Hoppy Crude Oil	422	80
4280	Hoppy Crude Oil	429	80
4280	Hoppy Crude Oil	428	90
4280	Hoppy Crude Oil	421	110
6600	Hazy Pink Cloud	424	16
6600	Hazy Pink Cloud	426	16
6600	Hazy Pink Cloud	425	24

I'll make a lot of different sums of the qty column. With the basic ideas you can apply to most of the analytic functions, sum is just a handy example.

Analytic syntax

I'm sure you have seen Figure 11-2 in the SQL Reference Manual, showing that all analytic functions use the keyword over followed by parentheses surrounding an analytic clause.

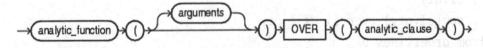

Figure 11-2. *Basic analytic function syntax diagram*

Many functions are aggregate functions when used without over and become analytic when you add over. The interesting bits happen within the analytic clause shown in Figure 11-3.

Figure 11-3. *The three parts that make up the analytic clause*

The analytic clause has three parts:

- **query_partition_clause** to split the data into partitions and apply the function separately to each partition

- **order_by_clause** to apply the function in a specific order and/or provide the ordering that the *windowing_clause* depends upon

- **windowing_clause** to specify a certain window (fixed or moving) of the ordered data in the partition

But you'll notice that the three parts are all optional in the syntax diagram, so the analytic clause itself is allowed to be empty. Listing 11-2 shows what happens then.

Listing 11-2. The simplest analytic function call is a grand total

```
SQL> select
  2      ol.product_id as p_id
  3    , p.name        as product_name
  4    , ol.order_id   as o_id
  5    , ol.qty
  6    , sum(ol.qty) over () as t_qty
  7  from orderlines ol
  8  join products p
  9      on p.id = ol.product_id
 10  where ol.product_id in (4280, 6600)
 11  order by ol.product_id, ol.qty;
```

I've just taken Listing 11-1 and added line 6: a sum of the qty column as analytic function (recognizable by the over keyword) with an empty analytic clause. The output becomes:

P_ID	PRODUCT_NAME	O_ID	QTY	T_QTY
4280	Hoppy Crude Oil	423	60	536
4280	Hoppy Crude Oil	427	60	536
4280	Hoppy Crude Oil	422	80	536
4280	Hoppy Crude Oil	429	80	536
4280	Hoppy Crude Oil	428	90	536
4280	Hoppy Crude Oil	421	110	536
6600	Hazy Pink Cloud	424	16	536
6600	Hazy Pink Cloud	426	16	536
6600	Hazy Pink Cloud	425	24	536

The t_qty column simply contains the sum of all the qty values – not of the entire table, but of those rows that satisfy the where clause.

When executing a SQL statement, evaluation of analytic functions happens *after* the rows have been found (where clause evaluation) and also *after* any group by aggregation that may be in the statement. Therefore, analytic functions cannot be used in the where, group by, and having clauses. But they can be used in the order by clause, if you need to.

The empty analytic clause means that no partitioning has been defined, so there is just a single partition containing all the rows. Also no ordering and windowing have been defined, so the entire partition is the window on which the sum function is applied. Therefore it becomes the grand total.

Often, though, I'd like to apply the analytic function on smaller subsets, which I'll show next.

Partitions

There are two ways to split the rows into smaller subsets for analytic functions, each serving different purposes. The first is partitioning with the *query_partition_clause* shown in Figure 11-4.

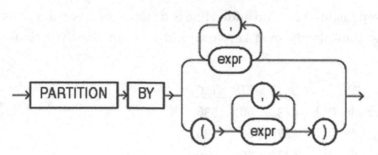

Figure 11-4. *Syntax diagram for the query_partition_clause*

You can use one or more expressions to do the partitioning, where there will be created a partition for each distinct value in the expression(s). Each partition is completely separated, and the analytic function evaluated in one partition cannot see data in any other partition.

Note   You'll see that Listing 11-3 is the same as Listing 11-2, only changed in the analytic function call. This goes for most of the examples in the chapter – if nothing else is indicated, they are copies of Listing 11-2 with just the changed function call shown.

I show a simple example of using partition by in Listing 11-3.

Listing 11-3. Creating subtotals by product with partitioning

```
...
 6   , sum(ol.qty) over (
 7        partition by ol.product_id
 8   ) as p_qty
...
```

The analytic clause is no longer empty; I have added line 7 to create a partition for each beer, and the grand totals now apply within each partition only. This way p_qty is a grand total per product:

P_ID	PRODUCT_NAME	O_ID	QTY	P_QTY
4280	Hoppy Crude Oil	423	60	480
4280	Hoppy Crude Oil	427	60	480
4280	Hoppy Crude Oil	422	80	480

4280	Hoppy Crude Oil	429	80	480
4280	Hoppy Crude Oil	428	90	480
4280	Hoppy Crude Oil	421	110	480
6600	Hazy Pink Cloud	424	16	56
6600	Hazy Pink Cloud	426	16	56
6600	Hazy Pink Cloud	425	24	56

That's nice, but I can be much more creative with the second form of splitting the data into subsets – windowing with the *order_by_clause* and *windowing_clause*.

Ordering and windows

For the *order_by_clause* syntax shown in Figure 11-5, the authors of the SQL Reference Manual have copied the syntax for the regular order by in a query.

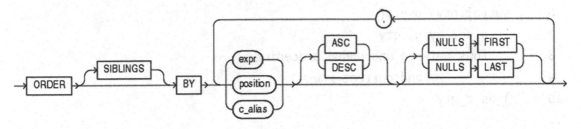

Figure 11-5. *Syntax diagram for the order_by_clause*

But it isn't quite the truth. When you read the following description in the manual, it is explained that keyword siblings cannot be used, and you also cannot use *position* and *c_alias* for an analytic order by.

For some analytic functions, *query_partition_clause* and *order_by_clause* are all there are – the third subclause is unavailable. But for many, you also have the *windowing_clause* (Figure 11-6) available. To use windowing, you must have filled the *order_by_clause*.

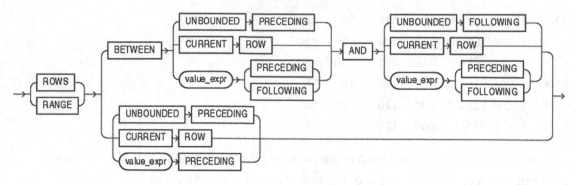

Figure 11-6. *Syntax diagram for the windowing_clause*

I'll do a running total in Listing 11-4 by using both ordering and windowing.

Listing 11-4. Creating a running sum with ordering and windowing

```
...
 6    , sum(ol.qty) over (
 7         order by ol.qty
 8         rows between unbounded preceding
 9                  and current row
10      ) as r_qty
...
15  order by ol.qty;
```

Line 7 contains my order by and lines 8–9 my window specification. I specify that when the analytic sum is to be evaluated on a given row, the sum should be applied to a rolling window of all the preceding rows up to and including the current row. To see easily what happens, I change the order by in line 15 to match the order by in line 7, giving me an output with r_qty being a running sum of qty:

P_ID	PRODUCT_NAME	O_ID	QTY	R_QTY
6600	Hazy Pink Cloud	426	16	16
6600	Hazy Pink Cloud	424	16	32
6600	Hazy Pink Cloud	425	24	56
4280	Hoppy Crude Oil	427	60	116
4280	Hoppy Crude Oil	423	60	176
4280	Hoppy Crude Oil	422	80	256
4280	Hoppy Crude Oil	429	80	336

```
4280  Hoppy Crude Oil   428   90  426
4280  Hoppy Crude Oil   421   110  536
```

The qty of each row is added as the rows are processed in order, resulting in the running sum. When the ordering is not unique, whichever row the database happens to access first will be added first. The first two lines of the output might have shown o_id 424 before 426 instead, if the access plan had been such that 424 was accessed first.

I can change the order by in line 15 back to the same ordering as Listing 11-2 (and most other examples), ordering by product_id first, then qty:

...

```
15  order by ol.product_id, ol.qty;
```

Now my output is ordered differently, but the running sum is *still* calculated with the order by in the analytic sum, namely, qty alone. You'll see, for example, that the two first lines of the previous output are now near the end, but o_id 426 still has a value of 16 in r_qty and o_id 424 a value of 32 and so on:

P_ID	PRODUCT_NAME	O_ID	QTY	R_QTY
4280	Hoppy Crude Oil	423	60	176
4280	Hoppy Crude Oil	427	60	116
4280	Hoppy Crude Oil	422	80	256
4280	Hoppy Crude Oil	429	80	336
4280	Hoppy Crude Oil	428	90	426
4280	Hoppy Crude Oil	421	110	536
6600	Hazy Pink Cloud	424	16	32
6600	Hazy Pink Cloud	426	16	16
6600	Hazy Pink Cloud	425	24	56

Having analytics applied in a different order than the output itself is a useful technique in a quite a few situations.

Tip   The lower half of Figure 11-6 shows the shortcut syntax. When you have a window that is rows between *something* and current row, you can simply use rows *something*, and it will default to using *something* as start row and current row as end row of the window. In Listing 11-4, I could have replaced lines 8–9 with a single line containing rows unbounded preceding. Personally I like to always use the between syntax, but you can use the shortcut if you like. It is only syntactical difference, and the result is identical.

Of course I can combine all three clauses in a single call, as I do it in Listing 11-5.

Listing 11-5. Combining partitioning, ordering, and windowing

```
...
 6   , sum(ol.qty) over (
 7        partition by ol.product_id
 8        order by ol.qty
 9        rows between unbounded preceding
10                 and current row
11      ) as p_qty
...
```

I partition in line 7 by product_id and order in line 8 by qty, so the window in lines 8–9 gives me a running sum for each beer, which the output shows nicely since I kept the usual query ordering of product_id, qty:

P_ID	PRODUCT_NAME	O_ID	QTY	P_QTY
4280	Hoppy Crude Oil	423	60	60
4280	Hoppy Crude Oil	427	60	120
4280	Hoppy Crude Oil	422	80	200
4280	Hoppy Crude Oil	429	80	280
4280	Hoppy Crude Oil	428	90	370
4280	Hoppy Crude Oil	421	110	480
6600	Hazy Pink Cloud	424	16	16
6600	Hazy Pink Cloud	426	16	32
6600	Hazy Pink Cloud	425	24	56

Windowing is very handy and often used for running totals, but the window can be much more flexible than that.

Flexibility of the window clause

The running totals in the previous two listings was *up to and including current row*, which is quite normal. But the window does not need to include the current row, as I show in Listing 11-6 that calculates running total of all previous rows.

Listing 11-6. Window with all previous rows

```
...
 6   , sum(ol.qty) over (
 7         partition by ol.product_id
 8         order by ol.qty
 9         rows between unbounded preceding
10                  and 1 preceding
11     ) as p_qty
...
```

In line 10, I replaced the current row with 1 preceding, meaning the window is all rows *up to and including the row just before the current row*:

P_ID	PRODUCT_NAME	O_ID	QTY	P_QTY
4280	Hoppy Crude Oil	423	60	
4280	Hoppy Crude Oil	427	60	60
4280	Hoppy Crude Oil	422	80	120
4280	Hoppy Crude Oil	429	80	200
4280	Hoppy Crude Oil	428	90	280
4280	Hoppy Crude Oil	421	110	370
6600	Hazy Pink Cloud	424	16	
6600	Hazy Pink Cloud	426	16	16
6600	Hazy Pink Cloud	425	24	32

You'll notice that means that p_qty is null on the first row of each partition, since there are no preceding rows at that point.

Windows can also look *ahead* in the data rather than just look at the preceding rows.
I can change the window specification of Listing 11-6 to a window starting at the current
row and including all the following rows in the partition:

```
...
 9          rows between current row
10                          and unbounded following
...
```

That gives me a reversed running total:

```
P_ID  PRODUCT_NAME     O_ID  QTY  P_QTY
4280  Hoppy Crude Oil  423   60   480
4280  Hoppy Crude Oil  427   60   420
4280  Hoppy Crude Oil  422   80   360
4280  Hoppy Crude Oil  429   80   280
4280  Hoppy Crude Oil  428   90   200
4280  Hoppy Crude Oil  421   110  110
6600  Hazy Pink Cloud  424   16   56
6600  Hazy Pink Cloud  426   16   40
6600  Hazy Pink Cloud  425   24   24
```

Again I do not only need to include the current row; I can also do a window of all
rows *yet to come*:

```
...
 9          rows between 1 following
10                          and unbounded following
...
```

The null value at the end of each partition indicates there are no rows following:

```
P_ID  PRODUCT_NAME     O_ID  QTY  P_QTY
4280  Hoppy Crude Oil  423   60   420
4280  Hoppy Crude Oil  427   60   360
4280  Hoppy Crude Oil  422   80   280
4280  Hoppy Crude Oil  429   80   200
4280  Hoppy Crude Oil  428   90   110
4280  Hoppy Crude Oil  421   110
```

```
6600   Hazy Pink Cloud   424   16   40
6600   Hazy Pink Cloud   426   16   24
6600   Hazy Pink Cloud   425   24
```

I can give the window bounds in both ends to sum, for example, the values from the previous row, the current row, and the following row:

```
...
 9          rows between 1 preceding
10                    and 1 following
...
```

P_ID	PRODUCT_NAME	O_ID	QTY	P_QTY
4280	Hoppy Crude Oil	423	60	120
4280	Hoppy Crude Oil	427	60	200
4280	Hoppy Crude Oil	422	80	220
4280	Hoppy Crude Oil	429	80	250
4280	Hoppy Crude Oil	428	90	280
4280	Hoppy Crude Oil	421	110	200
6600	Hazy Pink Cloud	424	16	32
6600	Hazy Pink Cloud	426	16	56
6600	Hazy Pink Cloud	425	24	40

Or I can make a window that is unbounded in both ends:

```
...
 9          rows between unbounded preceding
10                        and unbounded following
...
```

But this makes little sense, as the totally unbounded window is the entire partition, which means that the order by clause actually does not make a difference to the output, which is the same as I got from Listing 11-3 that had no order by and no windowing clause:

P_ID	PRODUCT_NAME	O_ID	QTY	P_QTY
4280	Hoppy Crude Oil	423	60	480
4280	Hoppy Crude Oil	427	60	480
4280	Hoppy Crude Oil	422	80	480

```
4280   Hoppy Crude Oil   429    80    480
4280   Hoppy Crude Oil   428    90    480
4280   Hoppy Crude Oil   421   110    480
6600   Hazy Pink Cloud   424    16     56
6600   Hazy Pink Cloud   426    16     56
6600   Hazy Pink Cloud   425    24     56
```

So for the completely unbounded window, I recommend just skipping order by and windowing clause.

In the syntax diagram, you saw that a window could be specified using either rows between or range between. As I gave several examples of, a rows between window is determined by a number of rows before or after the current row. It is different with range between.

Windows on value ranges

If I want, I can specify a window not as "two rows before to two rows after the current row" but instead as "those rows where the *value* is from 20 less to 20 more than the value in the current row." This I can do with range between like Listing 11-7.

Listing 11-7. Range window based on qty value

```
...
 6    , sum(ol.qty) over (
 7         partition by ol.product_id
 8         order by ol.qty
 9         range between 20 preceding
10                   and 20 following
11      ) as p_qty
...
```

When I specify between 20 preceding and 20 following in lines 9–10, I ask that the window will contain those rows where the value is the same as the value in the current row plus/minus 20. But the value of what?

The value that range will use is the value of the column used in the order by in the analytic function. Therefore, in order to use range windows, the order by column must be a number or a date/timestamp.

The column I calculate the total of in the sum function does not have to be the same as the one I use for ordering and range, but in practice, it often is, giving me an output where you can see both third and fourth rows get a sum of 370, as it is the sum of all the rows in the partition with values between 80-20=60 and 80+20=100:

P_ID	PRODUCT_NAME	O_ID	QTY	P_QTY
4280	Hoppy Crude Oil	423	60	280
4280	Hoppy Crude Oil	427	60	280
4280	Hoppy Crude Oil	422	80	370
4280	Hoppy Crude Oil	429	80	370
4280	Hoppy Crude Oil	428	90	360
4280	Hoppy Crude Oil	421	110	200
6600	Hazy Pink Cloud	424	16	56
6600	Hazy Pink Cloud	426	16	56
6600	Hazy Pink Cloud	425	24	56

Even range windows do not have to include the current row value; I can also specify I want the window to contain those rows with a qty value between the current qty + 5 and the current qty + 25:

```
...
 9           range between  5 following
10                      and 25 following
...
```

P_ID	PRODUCT_NAME	O_ID	QTY	P_QTY
4280	Hoppy Crude Oil	423	60	160
4280	Hoppy Crude Oil	427	60	160
4280	Hoppy Crude Oil	422	80	90
4280	Hoppy Crude Oil	429	80	90
4280	Hoppy Crude Oil	428	90	110
4280	Hoppy Crude Oil	421	110	
6600	Hazy Pink Cloud	424	16	24
6600	Hazy Pink Cloud	426	16	24
6600	Hazy Pink Cloud	425	24	

Running totals can be performed with `range` windows as well:

```
...
 9          range between unbounded preceding
10                         and current row
...
```

But notice how the running totals are identical for the rows that have same qty value:

P_ID	PRODUCT_NAME	O_ID	QTY	P_QTY
4280	Hoppy Crude Oil	423	60	120
4280	Hoppy Crude Oil	427	60	120
4280	Hoppy Crude Oil	422	80	280
4280	Hoppy Crude Oil	429	80	280
4280	Hoppy Crude Oil	428	90	370
4280	Hoppy Crude Oil	421	110	480
6600	Hazy Pink Cloud	424	16	32
6600	Hazy Pink Cloud	426	16	32
6600	Hazy Pink Cloud	425	24	56

Compare this output to the output of Listing 11-5, where the first two rows have values in p_qty of 60 and 120, respectively. Here they both have 120.

That is because of the nature of the `range` window, which gives a different meaning to the term `current row`. It no longer specifically means *the* current row, but rather the *value of* the current row. (In my opinion it would have been nice to use wording like `current value` for `range` windows, but that is unfortunately not supported syntax.)

So you see `range` windows using the `current row` can actually *include following rows* in case of value ties. This leads me to showing you a pitfall that is all too easy to fall into.

The danger of the default window

In Figure 11-3, you can see that it is possible to use `order by` *without* specifying a windowing clause. That leads to a default windowing clause, which might surprise you. In Listing 11-8, I show you the difference between the default, `range between,` and `rows between.`

Listing 11-8. Comparing running sum with default, range, and rows window

```
SQL> select
  2      ol.product_id as p_id
  3    , p.name            as product_name
  4    , ol.order_id   as o_id
  5    , ol.qty
  6    , sum(ol.qty) over (
  7         partition by ol.product_id
  8         order by ol.qty
  9         /* no window - rely on default */
 10      ) as def_q
 11    , sum(ol.qty) over (
 12         partition by ol.product_id
 13         order by ol.qty
 14         range between unbounded preceding
 15                   and current row
 16      ) as range_q
 17    , sum(ol.qty) over (
 18         partition by ol.product_id
 19         order by ol.qty
 20         rows between unbounded preceding
 21                   and current row
 22      ) as rows_q
 23  from orderlines ol
 24  join products p
 25     on p.id = ol.product_id
 26  where ol.product_id in (4280, 6600)
 27  order by ol.product_id, ol.qty;
```

I have three analytic function calls here:

- Column def_q in lines 6–10 uses order by but leaves the windowing clause empty.

- Column range_q in lines 11–16 uses the range between window for a running total.

- Column rows_q in lines 17–22 uses the rows between window for a running total.

You see in the output that def_q and range_q are identical:

P_ID	PRODUCT_NAME	O_ID	QTY	DEF_Q	RANGE_Q	ROWS_Q
4280	Hoppy Crude Oil	423	60	120	120	60
4280	Hoppy Crude Oil	427	60	120	120	120
4280	Hoppy Crude Oil	422	80	280	280	200
4280	Hoppy Crude Oil	429	80	280	280	280
4280	Hoppy Crude Oil	428	90	370	370	370
4280	Hoppy Crude Oil	421	110	480	480	480
6600	Hazy Pink Cloud	424	16	32	32	16
6600	Hazy Pink Cloud	426	16	32	32	32
6600	Hazy Pink Cloud	425	24	56	56	56

Yes, if you have an *order_by_clause*, the default for the *windowing_clause* is range between unbounded preceding and current row.

I have seen many blog and forum posts showing a running total as something like sum(col1) over (order by col2) and leaving it at that. And when you test your code with this default window, often you get the result you expect, as the difference in output only occurs when there are duplicates in the values. So you might not spot the error until the code has gone into production.

Note   It is not just a problem when there are duplicate values. Even if your order by is unique, using default range between windows for running totals can potentially incur some overhead by evaluation of the analytic function, impacting performance. This is because rows between can be executed more optimally by the SQL engine, while range between requires the SQL engine to "look ahead" in the rows and see if possibly any following rows have the same value. For more detailed explanation of this, see a blog post I did a while back: `www.kibeha.dk/2013/02/rows-versus-default-range-in-analytic.html`.

In my opinion, the default ought to have been `rows between`, as in my experience, this is by far the most used window specification. It is *very* often I use `rows between` and only once in a rare while `range between`.

So my best practice rule of thumb is that whenever I have an `order by` clause, I always *explicitly* write the windowing clause, *never* relying on the default. Even for those rare cases where my window actually happens to be `range between unbounded preceding and current row`, I still write it explicitly. This tells the future me, or any developers maintaining my code in the future, that the `range between` is desired. If I see code where the windowing clause is absent, I always wonder if it is really meant to be `range between` or if it is simply a misunderstood copy-paste from a forum post.

This applies only to analytic functions that support the windowing clause, of course. And I also do not use it if my window is the entire partition, then I simply omit `order by` and windowing clause rather than write `rows between unbounded preceding and unbounded following`.

But even though Listing 11-5 adheres to this rule of thumb, there is another issue with it: the fact that it is possibly to get a different output from the same data in different executions of the code, because the rows with duplicate values might be in different order in the output depending on the access plan used by the optimizer.

This issue does not strictly influence the correctness of the solution, but users are liable to question the correctness when they observe different outputs (even if both outputs are correct). So I make it my best practice to make the combination of the columns used in `partition by` and `order by` unique in the analytic function (when using `rows between`, not applicable to `range between`). This makes the output *deterministic*, so the user can verify he gets the same result in each run.

Listing 11-9 represents both these best practices for doing running totals.

Listing 11-9. A best practice for a running sum

```
SQL> select
  2      ol.product_id as p_id
  3    , p.name        as product_name
  4    , ol.order_id   as o_id
```

```
 5    , ol.qty
 6    , sum(ol.qty) over (
 7          partition by ol.product_id
 8          order by ol.qty, ol.order_id
 9          rows between unbounded preceding
10                      and current row
11      ) as p_qty
12   from orderlines ol
13   join products p
14      on p.id = ol.product_id
15   where ol.product_id in (4280, 6600)
16   order by ol.product_id, ol.qty, ol.order_id;
```

In reality I am only interested in the qty ordering within each product_id partition (as in Listing 11-5), but the combination of those two columns is not unique, making the output nondeterministic. Therefore, I add order_id to both order by clauses (lines 8 and 16):

P_ID	PRODUCT_NAME	O_ID	QTY	P_QTY
4280	Hoppy Crude Oil	423	60	60
4280	Hoppy Crude Oil	427	60	120
4280	Hoppy Crude Oil	422	80	200
4280	Hoppy Crude Oil	429	80	280
4280	Hoppy Crude Oil	428	90	370
4280	Hoppy Crude Oil	421	110	480
6600	Hazy Pink Cloud	424	16	16
6600	Hazy Pink Cloud	426	16	32
6600	Hazy Pink Cloud	425	24	56

This ensures a deterministic output.

And in this case the statement can even execute using only a single sorting operation, since the columns in the analytic partition by followed by the columns in the analytic order by match the columns in the final order by in line 16. This enables the optimizer to skip the final ordering, as the analytic function evaluation has already ordered the data correctly.

Lessons learned

This chapter introduced the basic elements of the three subclauses of analytic functions. Although I've shown it specifically using the sum function, you can generalize to other analytic functions and use what you've learned about

- Using partition by to split rows into parts where the analytic function is applied within each part separately.

- Using the windowing clause in conjunction with order by to create moving windows of rows to calculate, for example, running totals.

- Understanding that the *default* windowing clause is rarely a good match for your use case, so always using an *explicit* windowing clause is a good idea.

With a good understanding of these subclauses, you can make analytic functions solve many otherwise difficult tasks for you. The following chapters in this part of the book are dedicated to several such solutions.

CHAPTER 12

Answering Top-N Questions

I think it is extremely few developers that haven't been asked to create a Top-N report. The questions by the business that can be classified as a Top-N question are legion such as the following:

- Which of our products sell the most?

- Which user profiles create the most tweets?

- Which sales employees generate most leads?

- Which hotels in the chain have the least complaints?

The last one could strictly speaking be called a Bottom-N question, but that is in principle exactly the same. For a Top-N report, you order the data by a specific *descending* order and pick the Top-N rows of data. If you want a Bottom-N report, you simply order the data by a specific *ascending* order and still pick the Top-N rows of data. In SQL terms, it simply is a matter of doing `order by col_name desc` vs. `order by col_name asc`. So I'm just going to show Top-N examples – Bottom-N you can get by replacing `desc` with `asc`.

To demonstrate the Top-N SQL, I'm using the first question from the preceding list: Which of our products sell the most?

Top-N of sales data

As my Good Beer Trading company sells beer, the marketing department has asked me to find out the Top-3 best-selling beers the company sells, so they can do a campaign with a pedestal like Figure 12-1.

© Kim Berg Hansen 2020
K. Berg Hansen, *Practical Oracle SQL*, https://doi.org/10.1007/978-1-4842-5617-6_12

Figure 12-1. *Top-3 beers by total sales*

Now that's a quite naïve question they gave me here, so I need to get back to them and ask them to specify what they mean. Do I determine the ordering in terms of quantity or amount sold? Is it all-time best sellers they want or from a specific year? What should I do if there are ties where two or more beers have sold the same?

Often the easiest way for me as a developer to get the detailed specification I need is to give them examples, since they sometimes won't understand why "Top-3 best-selling beers" is an ambiguous question.

Which kind of Top-3 do you mean?

Particularly there's ambiguity concerning what to do in case of ties. Generally there are three cases:

- Top-rows rule: "*I want exactly 3 rows.*"

  In such a case, I need to explain to the business that this means they will not see, for example, a fourth row that has exactly the same value as the third row. For such a tie, the output will not show both rows, but only one of them. In this case, either it will be a random one or the business needs to decide a tiebreaker rule to determine which one to output.

- Olympic rule: "*I want gold, silver, and bronze the Olympic way.*"

  By the rules often used in sports competitions, if, for example, there's a tie for first place, two gold medals are given, then the silver medal is skipped, and the third guy gets a bronze medal. Using this rule can lead to more than three rows in the output, for example, when there is a tie for bronze, in which case there will be one first place, one second place, and two third places for a total of four rows in the output.

- Top-values rule: "*I want all that have the Top-3 values.*"

  With the previous rule, if there's a tie for second place, there'll be a gold medal and two silver medals, but no bronze medal. This rule states that no matter how many ties there are for first value, ties for second value, and ties for third value, the output should contain all the rows that have the Top-3 values.

All of these Top-3 rules can be handled in SQL – I'll demonstrate how.

The sales data for the beer

Figure 12-2 shows the tables with the beer sales data per month and the beer product names.

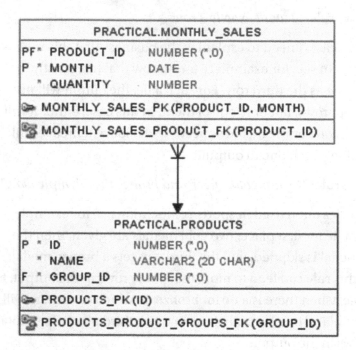

Figure 12-2. *Tables holding monthly sales for products*

I'll be doing Top-N queries both on the total sales of the products and the sales for each year (there's sales data for 2016, 2017, and 2018), and in Listing 12-1, I have a couple of views that aggregate the monthly sales.

Listing 12-1. Views for aggregating sales on total and year level

```
SQL> create or replace view total_sales
  2  as
  3  select
  4     ms.product_id
  5   , max(p.name) as product_name
  6   , sum(ms.qty) as total_qty
  7  from products p
  8  join monthly_sales ms
```

```
 9       on ms.product_id = p.id
10   group by
11       ms.product_id;
```

View TOTAL_SALES created.

```
SQL> create or replace view yearly_sales
  2  as
  3  select
  4      extract(year from ms.mth) as yr
  5    , ms.product_id
  6    , max(p.name) as product_name
  7    , sum(ms.qty) as yr_qty
  8  from products p
  9  join monthly_sales ms
 10      on ms.product_id = p.id
 11  group by
 12      extract(year from ms.mth), ms.product_id;
```

View YEARLY_SALES created.

Querying the total_sales view, I can order it by total_qty desc in Listing 12-2.

Listing 12-2. A view of the total sales data

```
SQL> select product_name, total_qty
  2  from total_sales
  3  order by total_qty desc;
```

That shows me the ten beers from the products table, and I can visually see here which beers are the Top-3 best-selling beers. Since we have a tie for second place, then by the top-rows and the Olympic rules, it's the first three rows, and by the top-values rule, it's the first four rows:

PRODUCT_NAME	TOTAL_QTY
Reindeer Fuel	1604
Ghost of Hops	1485
Monks and Nuns	1485
Der Helle Kumpel	1230

```
Hercule Trippel    1056
Summer in India    961
Pale Rider Rides   883
Coalminers Sweat   813
Hazy Pink Cloud    324
Hoppy Crude Oil    303
```

I could query the yearly_sales view the same way:

```
SQL> select yr, product_name, yr_qty
  2  from yearly_sales
  3  order by yr, yr_qty desc;
```

But in Listing 12-3, I'm going to use the pivoting technique from Chapter 8 to show the ranking of the beers in columns for each year. Not that it is necessary for doing Top-N queries, but it visualizes the difference in the data over the three years.

Listing 12-3. A view of the yearly sales data (manually formatted, not ansiconsole)

```
SQL> select *
  2  from (
  3     select
  4        yr, product_name, yr_qty
  5      , row_number() over (
  6         partition by yr
  7         order by yr_qty desc
  8        ) as rn
  9     from yearly_sales
 10  )
 11  pivot (
 12     max(product_name) as prod
 13   , max(yr_qty)
 14     for yr in (
 15        2016, 2017, 2018
 16     )
 17  )
 18  order by rn;
```

I'm getting a little ahead of myself with the use of analytic function row_number in lines 5–8. I'll explain more in a little while, but what it does here is assigning the numbers 1–10 to each beer *within each year* in order of quantity sold. This number (rn) is then used for the implicit group by in the pivot, so I get an output with ten rows numbered 1–10 having two columns for each year – the name of the beer and the quantity sold:

RN	2016_PROD	2016	2017_PROD	2017	2018_PROD	2018
1	Ghost of Hops	552	Monks and Nuns	582	Reindeer Fuel	691
2	Monks and Nuns	478	Reindeer Fuel	582	Pale Ride r Rides	491
3	Der Helle Kumpel	415	Ghost of Hops	482	Hercule T rippel	451
4	Summer in India	377	Der Helle Kumpel	458	Ghost of Hops	451
5	Reindeer Fuel	331	Hercule T rippel	344	Monks and Nuns	425
6	Coalminer s Sweat	286	Summer in India	321	Der Helle Kumpel	357
7	Hercule T rippel	261	Coalminer s Sweat	227	Coalminer s Sweat	300
8	Pale Ride r Rides	182	Pale Ride r Rides	210	Summer in India	263
9	Hazy Pink Cloud	121	Hazy Pink Cloud	105	Hoppy Cru de Oil	132
10	Hoppy Cru de Oil	99	Hoppy Cru de Oil	72	Hazy Pink Cloud	98

I've made the beer name columns narrow with sqlcl column formatting to get line breaks in the names instead of line breaks that put 2018 data below 2016 and 2017. This way doesn't break names as nice, but the quantities are aligned to make it easy to observe the ordering in each year and where the ties are. Notice there's a tie for first place in 2017 and a tie for third place in 2018.

Traditional rownum method

Before analytic functions, a traditional method for a Top-N query was to do an inline view with the desired order by clause and then filter on rownum <= in the outer query, as I show in Listing 12-4.

Listing 12-4. Top-3 using inline view and filter on rownum

```
SQL> select *
  2  from (
  3     select product_name, total_qty
  4     from total_sales
  5     order by total_qty desc
  6  )
  7  where rownum <= 3;
```

This method gives me the Top-3 beers according to the top-rows rule:

PRODUCT_NAME	TOTAL_QTY
Reindeer Fuel	1604
Monks and Nuns	1485
Ghost of Hops	1485

It works fine and is performant – the optimizer recognizes the construct and will do as little work as possible to get only the desired three rows.

However, this method cannot as easily help us with the Olympic rule and the top-values rule. For those it is much easier to use analytic functions.

Analytic functions for ranking

In Listing 12-5, I am rewriting Listing 12-4, just using the analytic function row_number in line 5 instead of the construct with rownum. As an analytic function cannot be used inside the where clause, I still need to use an inline view.

Listing 12-5. Top-3 using inline view and filter on row_number()

```
SQL> select *
  2  from (
  3     select
  4        product_name, total_qty
  5        , row_number() over (order by total_qty desc) as ranking
  6     from total_sales
  7  )
  8  where ranking <= 3
  9  order by ranking;
```

The output is the same as I got from Listing 12-4 – it is still the top-rows rule I am applying for my Top-3 output:

PRODUCT_NAME	TOTAL_QTY	RANKING
Reindeer Fuel	1604	1
Monks and Nuns	1485	2
Ghost of Hops	1485	3

But row_number is not the only analytic function I can use for ranking my data; I have two other analytic functions at my disposal too. Listing 12-6 compares the three functions.

Listing 12-6. Comparison of the three analytic ranking functions

```
SQL> select
  2     product_name, total_qty
  3  , row_number() over (order by total_qty desc) as rn
  4  , rank() over (order by total_qty desc) as rnk
  5  , dense_rank() over (order by total_qty desc) as dr
  6  from total_sales
  7  order by total_qty desc;
```

The three functions correspond directly to the three ranking rules I've mentioned:

- row_number - Implements the top-rows rule

- rank   - Implements the Olympic rule

- dense_rank - Implements the top-values rule

Which I can see in the output:

PRODUCT_NAME	TOTAL_QTY	RN	RNK	DR
Reindeer Fuel	1604	1	1	1
Ghost of Hops	1485	2	2	2
Monks and Nuns	1485	3	2	2
Der Helle Kumpel	1230	4	4	3
Hercule Trippel	1056	5	5	4
Summer in India	961	6	6	5
Pale Rider Rides	883	7	7	6
Coalminers Sweat	813	8	8	7
Hazy Pink Cloud	324	9	9	8
Hoppy Crude Oil	303	10	10	9

I simply get consecutive numbers when I use row_number.

When I use rank, a row can follow one of two rules: if it is a tie with the previous row, it gets the *same ranking* as the previous row; if it is not a tie, it gets the same ranking *as if it had been* using row_number. This makes it "skip" rankings in the Olympic fashion, like here where we have two beers ranked second place and then the next one is ranked fourth place.

Lastly with dense_rank, a row can also follow one of two rules: again if it is a tie with the previous row, it gets the *same ranking* as the previous row; but if it is not a tie, the row here gets the ranking of the previous row *plus one*. Therefore, rankings are not skipped, but a consecutive ranking is assigned to each unique value, thus implementing the top-values rule.

Armed with these different analytic functions, it is easy for me to switch between the different ranking rules. Listing 12-5 gave me the top-rows rule – I can simply change line 5 to rank to use the Olympic rule:

```
5       , rank() over (order by total_qty desc) as ranking
```

In this case, the output is the same three beers; the only difference is that the second and third rows both are ranked as second place:

PRODUCT_NAME	TOTAL_QTY	RANKING
Reindeer Fuel	1604	1
Ghost of Hops	1485	2
Monks and Nuns	1485	2

Or alternatively I can change line 5 to dense_rank to use the top-values rule:

```
5        , dense_rank() over (order by total_qty desc) as ranking
```

This gives me a Top-3 report with an output of four rows, since there are two rows both having the second place ranked value:

```
PRODUCT_NAME        TOTAL_QTY   RANKING
Reindeer Fuel       1604        1
Monks and Nuns      1485        2
Ghost of Hops       1485        2
Der Helle Kumpel    1230        3
```

With these three analytic functions, I can answer Top-N questions with all three rules, so I'm happy. The only slight hitch is that I still need to write inline views and filter rows in the outer query. Could I write less? The answer is yes.

Fetch only the first rows

In version 12 came along a new syntax to the select statement – the *row limiting clause*. It's also known as fetch first, since that's the syntax used as you can see in Listing 12-7.

Listing 12-7. Fetching only the first three rows

```
SQL> select product_name, total_qty
  2  from total_sales
  3  order by total_qty desc
  4  fetch first 3 rows only;
```

With this syntax, I skip the inline view; I just write my query with a suitable order by clause and append the fetch first clause to state I only want the first three rows, which is then what I get in the output:

```
PRODUCT_NAME        TOTAL_QTY
Reindeer Fuel       1604
Ghost of Hops       1485
Monks and Nuns      1485
```

Doing `rows only` gave me a result according to the first-rows rule. In effect this is simply "syntactic sugar" that makes it easier and simpler to write such a Top-N query, but underneath the database is automagically rewriting Listing 12-7 to perform the same operation as an inline view with a `row_number` function like Listing 12-5. The two listings work and perform identically; the difference is only that Listing 12-7 is shorter and easier to write and read.

The row limiting clause has another option instead of `rows only` – I can choose to do `rows with ties`:

```
4  fetch first 3 rows with ties;
```

The definition is that when the three rows have been fetched, it checks if there are further rows with the same value (ties) – if yes, then these are also output. For the data here, this is not the case, so I get the same output:

```
PRODUCT_NAME      TOTAL_QTY
Reindeer Fuel     1604
Ghost of Hops     1485
Monks and Nuns    1485
```

The rule from the rows with ties definition is implemented underneath as an inline view with a `rank` function call, as that rule matches the Olympic rule I've shown – it is just stated differently.

But how does that compare to the tie handling of the analytic functions according to the three ranking rules I showed before? I'll dive a little deeper into the handling of ties with some examples from the yearly sales data.

Handling of ties

In Listing 12-8, I am comparing the three analytic ranking functions for the sales of year 2018 (similar to how I compared them for total sales in Listing 12-6). As I can show my point just with the first five rows instead of showing all ten beers, I use `fetch first` in line 9 just because it's so easy that way to save paper in the book.

Listing 12-8. Comparison of analytic functions for 2018 sales

```
SQL> select
  2      product_name, yr_qty
  3    , row_number() over (order by yr_qty desc) as rn
  4    , rank() over (order by yr_qty desc) as rnk
  5    , dense_rank() over (order by yr_qty desc) as dr
  6  from yearly_sales
  7  where yr = 2018
  8  order by yr_qty desc
  9  fetch first 5 rows only;
```

In 2018 I have a tie for third place, as I can see here in the output:

PRODUCT_NAME	YR_QTY	RN	RNK	DR
Reindeer Fuel	691	1	1	1
Pale Rider Rides	491	2	2	2
Hercule Trippel	451	3	3	3
Ghost of Hops	451	4	3	3
Monks and Nuns	425	5	5	4

So in Listing 12-9, I can use line 5 to apply the top-rows rule and get the first three rows as they are ranked by the row_number function (the rn column in the preceding output).

Listing 12-9. Fetching first three rows for 2018

```
SQL> select product_name, yr_qty
  2  from yearly_sales
  3  where yr = 2018
  4  order by yr_qty desc
  5  fetch first 3 rows only;
```

And yes, I get the desired three rows in the output:

PRODUCT_NAME	YR_QTY
Reindeer Fuel	691
Pale Rider Rides	491
Hercule Trippel	451

But hang on – I could also get this output instead, since Ghost of Hops and Hercule Trippel both sold 451 in 2018:

```
PRODUCT_NAME        YR_QTY
Reindeer Fuel        691
Pale Rider Rides     491
Ghost of Hops        451
```

The query in Listing 12-9 has an *indeterminate* output – which of these two outputs I get will in principle be random; in practice whether I get Hercule Trippel or Ghost of Hops in the third line depends on which of the two beers the database happens to find first in the order that it happens to access the data. That will be highly dependent on which access plan the optimizer chooses.

The problem is not only when using fetch first with rows only, it applies equally when I myself use the row_number function. In the output from Listing 12-8, Hercule Trippel and Ghost of Hops might have swapped places – I cannot know.

Typically business users dislike a report whose output "changes overnight" when supposed be identical, which might happen if, for example, statistics gathering made the optimizer choose a different access path the next day. In other words, users don't like indeterminate output. A best practice when using row_number or fetch first with rows only can be to always make the order by deterministic by adding some tiebreaker rule, for example, stating that in case of ties always display the one with the first product id:

```
order by yr_qty desc, product_id
```

But I prefer instead to convince the business user that he really doesn't want to use the first-rows rule; instead he most likely would like, for example, to use the Olympic rule, which I then can implement easily by using with ties instead of rows only:

```
4   order by yr_qty desc
5   fetch first 3 rows with ties;
```

And then I get an output of four rows showing *both* Hercule Trippel and Ghost of Hops:

```
PRODUCT_NAME        YR_QTY
Reindeer Fuel        691
Pale Rider Rides     491
Hercule Trippel      451
Ghost of Hops        451
```

Now in that output, it is actually *indeterminate* in which *order* Hercule Trippel and Ghost of Hops are displayed. As I remarked before, users dislike that, so it can be tempting to "fix" this by making sure the order by is deterministic:

```
4  order by yr_qty desc, product_id
5  fetch first 3 rows with ties;
```

But that would be a *wrong* approach, since when the order by is deterministic, there *are no ties* by definition, so the output then is *not* what I want:

```
PRODUCT_NAME        YR_QTY
Reindeer Fuel       691
Pale Rider Rides    491
Hercule Trippel     451
```

When I want ties to be displayed in my output, I'll have to live with a nondeterministic output when I use fetch first. If I cannot live with that, I'll have to code the inline view with the rank function manually, since that gives me higher control and enables me to use the *nondeterministic* order by in the analytic function call and a *deterministic* order by in the outer query.

What the row limiting clause cannot do

So with ties in the fetch first row limiting clause handles ties like if I use analytic function rank. But let me change Listing 12-8 to show the year 2017 instead of 2018:

```
7  where yr = 2017
```

This time I have a tie for first place:

```
PRODUCT_NAME        YR_QTY  RN  RNK  DR
Monks and Nuns      582     1   1    1
Reindeer Fuel       582     2   1    1
Ghost of Hops       482     3   3    2
Der Helle Kumpel    458     4   4    3
Hercule Trippel     344     5   5    4
```

Let me try to use fetch first with ties for 2017 in Listing 12-10.

Listing 12-10. Fetching with ties for 2017

```
SQL> select product_name, yr_qty
  2  from yearly_sales
  3  where yr = 2017
  4  order by yr_qty desc
  5  fetch first 3 rows with ties;
```

I get those rows where column RNK is <= 3:

PRODUCT_NAME	YR_QTY
Monks and Nuns	582
Reindeer Fuel	582
Ghost of Hops	482

In other words this is like the Olympic rule for handling ties. If I want to use the first-values rule to get all rows that have the Top-3 values, I can*not* do it with the row limiting clause. There simply does not exist syntax like:

```
fetch first 3 values with ties;  /* <-- Invalid syntax */
```

Instead I need to manually create my inline view and use dense_rank as shown in Listing 12-11.

Listing 12-11. Using dense_rank for what fetch first cannot do

```
SQL> select *
  2  from (
  3     select
  4        product_name, yr_qty
  5      , dense_rank() over (order by yr_qty desc) as ranking
  6     from yearly_sales
  7     where yr = 2017
  8  )
  9  where ranking <= 3
 10  order by ranking;
```

Now I'm getting the four rows from 2017 that have the Top-3 values:

```
PRODUCT_NAME        YR_QTY  RANKING
Monks and Nuns      582       1
Reindeer Fuel       582       1
Ghost of Hops       482       2
Der Helle Kumpel    458       3
```

The row limiting clause is a very handy shortcut for Top-N queries, but it can only do the top-rows or Olympic rule, internally implementing it like an inline view with row_number or rank analytic functions. If you want top-values rule, you do it yourself with dense_rank.

Top-N in multiple partitions

So far I've executed a Top-N query either for the total sales or for a specific year in the yearly sales. In either case, I ended up with just the "top" rows of the entire row set.

But suppose I'd like to see the Top-3 best-selling beers for each of the years. Of course I could write a query for each year, perhaps putting them together with union all to get it all in one output.

But Listing 12-12 shows a much easier way using the partition by clause in line 6.

Listing 12-12. Ranking with row_number within each year

```
SQL> select *
  2  from (
  3    select
  4      yr, product_name, yr_qty
  5    , row_number() over (
  6        partition by yr
  7        order by yr_qty desc
  8      ) as ranking
  9    from yearly_sales
 10  )
 11  where ranking <= 3
 12  order by yr, ranking;
```

With the `partition by`, assignment of `row_number` values happens *within* each partition:

- The data is split into partitions – one for each distinct value of `yr`.

- In each partition, the data is ordered by `yr_qty desc` and consecutive numbers 1, 2, 3, … assigned.

This is what I utilize in Listing 12-3 some pages back in the chapter to get numbers 1-10 assigned to beers within each year, so I could `pivot` and list the beers in order per year in columns side by side.

But here in Listing 12-12, I am not pivoting; instead I filter on the result of the inline view, so I only keep those rows that have got `row_number` 1, 2, and 3 within each year:

YR	PRODUCT_NAME	YR_QTY	RANKING
2016	Ghost of Hops	552	1
2016	Monks and Nuns	478	2
2016	Der Helle Kumpel	415	3
2017	Monks and Nuns	582	1
2017	Reindeer Fuel	582	2
2017	Ghost of Hops	482	3
2018	Reindeer Fuel	691	1
2018	Pale Rider Rides	491	2
2018	Hercule Trippel	451	3

That gave me nine rows (three beers per each of three years) that are a Top-3 report per year by the first-rows rule.

I can easily change line 5 to use the `rank` function and get me a Top-3 report per year by the Olympic rule:

```
5       , rank() over (
```

That gives me ten rows, since in 2018 there are four beers with ranking <= 3:

YR	PRODUCT_NAME	YR_QTY	RANKING
2016	Ghost of Hops	552	1
2016	Monks and Nuns	478	2
2016	Der Helle Kumpel	415	3
2017	Monks and Nuns	582	1
2017	Reindeer Fuel	582	1

```
2017   Ghost of Hops      482      3
2018   Reindeer Fuel      691      1
2018   Pale Rider Rides   491      2
2018   Hercule Trippel    451      3
2018   Ghost of Hops      451      3
```

And the first-values rule I implement with a dense_rank in line 5:

```
5         , dense_rank() over (
```

This produces 11 rows, since with this rule I have four beers with ranking <= 3 both in 2017 and 2018:

```
YR     PRODUCT_NAME       YR_QTY  RANKING
2016   Ghost of Hops      552      1
2016   Monks and Nuns     478      2
2016   Der Helle Kumpel   415      3
2017   Monks and Nuns     582      1
2017   Reindeer Fuel      582      1
2017   Ghost of Hops      482      2
2017   Der Helle Kumpel   458      3
2018   Reindeer Fuel      691      1
2018   Pale Rider Rides   491      2
2018   Hercule Trippel    451      3
2018   Ghost of Hops      451      3
```

All in all, using analytic functions in inline views makes it very easy to either choose a total Top-N report or put in partition by and get a Top-N per year (or whatever you use for partition key or keys).

Using the row limiting clause, this is not quite so easy.

The lateral trick for the row limiting clause

fetch first does not support partition by, so basically you cannot do it but have to write it with analytic functions as shown in Listing 12-12.

But there is a trick that can allow you to emulate the behavior by using a lateral join to correlate an inline view, if you have some row source that defines your "manual partitions."

In Listing 12-13 lines 3–5, I create an inline view years that hardcodes three "partitions" – the three years 2016, 2017, and 2018. Then I have another inline view top_sales that is a Top-3 query using fetch first, and in this inline view, I filter on the year in line 10. I can do this correlation in line 10 because of the cross join lateral in line 7, which means that inline view top_sales is executed once *for each* of the rows from inline view years.

Listing 12-13. Using fetch first in a laterally joined inline view

```
SQL> select top_sales.*
  2  from (
  3     select 2016 as yr from dual union all
  4     select 2017 as yr from dual union all
  5     select 2018 as yr from dual
  6  ) years
  7  cross join lateral (
  8     select yr, product_name, yr_qty
  9     from yearly_sales
 10     where yearly_sales.yr = years.yr
 11     order by yr_qty desc
 12     fetch first 3 rows with ties
 13  ) top_sales;
```

Using this lateral trick and with ties, Listing 12-13 produces the same ten rows as Listing 12-12 did when I used rank:

YR	PRODUCT_NAME	YR_QTY
2016	Ghost of Hops	552
2016	Monks and Nuns	478
2016	Der Helle Kumpel	415
2017	Monks and Nuns	582
2017	Reindeer Fuel	582
2017	Ghost of Hops	482
2018	Reindeer Fuel	691
2018	Pale Rider Rides	491
2018	Hercule Trippel	451
2018	Ghost of Hops	451

Depending on the data and indexes and such, this could easily perform worse than the analytic method in Listing 12-12. If everything is right, it can perform just as well, but not faster. So is there really any use for this?

Well, the main difference is that the analytic function method of Listing 12-12 requires you to be able to specify an expression resulting in a set of unique values to `partition by` – while Listing 12-13 can correlate with an arbitrarily complex `where` clause in line 10.

I admit that using, for example, `case` structure, you can make very complex expressions for partitioning, so it will be a very rare case where the complexity is such that Listing 12-13 is needed – but it's nice to know the option is there, just in case.

Lessons learned

In this chapter I've used sales data to exemplify Top-N queries, along the way providing you insight in

- The three different Top-N query types: top-rows, Olympic, and top-values

- Implementing these with analytic functions `row_number`, `rank,` and `dense_rank`

- Using the shortcut `fetch first` row limiting clause for the first two types

- Doing Top-N per subsets of data with `partition by` in analytic functions

These methods will help you in many use cases, not just sales data.

CHAPTER 13

Ordered Subsets with Rolling Sums

One of the most useful features of analytic functions is the flexibility of the window clause, enabling aggregation of particular subsets of the data within a specific order. A classic subset that can be used for many purposes is the set of data from the beginning until the current row – if, for example, the sum aggregate function is used on that subset, you get an accumulated sum or rolling sum or running total (many names for the same thing).

The use cases are plenty; many financial reports need running totals. But a different practical use case that has been extremely helpful in my work involves a slight variation of the running total, where I use the sum of all the *previous* rows to keep selecting rows until I have selected *just* sufficiently large subset to cover the sum I need – in this case until I have picked enough goods in the warehouse to cover the order by a customer.

The complete case in this chapter will demonstrate the use of analytic functions to solve three problems simultaneously:

- Picking goods from the inventory in a certain order – most notably in first-in, first-out (FIFO) order

- Ordering the picking list to make the operator drive optimally through the warehouse

- Batch picking multiple orders

It can all be done in a single SQL statement, and I'll show the gradual building of the statement by solving the first problem and then expanding the statement adding the solutions to the second and third problems.

© Kim Berg Hansen 2020
K. Berg Hansen, *Practical Oracle SQL*, https://doi.org/10.1007/978-1-4842-5617-6_13

Data for goods picking

When you look at Figure 13-1, there are a lot of tables, mostly to show you a fairly realistic data model. For demonstration purposes, I could have simplified this a lot, but I will do that with a view, as you'll see shortly.

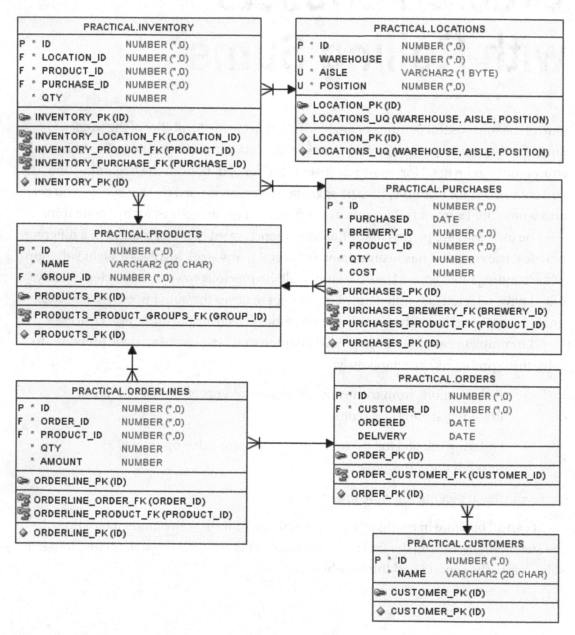

Figure 13-1. *The tables used in this chapter*

In the inventory table is stored how many of a given product are currently stored in a given location and from which purchase did that quantity originate (thereby giving us the age of quantity in that location). Basically that's just foreign keys to locations, products, and purchases tables and then a qty column.

Then there are customers who have given orders that have orderlines specifying which products they are buying, how many, and for how much.

To simplify working with these tables, I create the view inventory_with_dims shown in Listing 13-1. This simply joins the inventory table with the three referenced tables, so that I have all relevant information (product name, purchase date, warehouse, aisle, position) for each inventory row.

Listing 13-1. View joining inventory with other relevant tables

```
create or replace view inventory_with_dims
as
select
    i.id
  , i.product_id
  , p.name as product_name
  , i.purchase_id
  , pu.purchased
  , i.location_id
  , l.warehouse
  , l.aisle
  , l.position
  , i.qty
from inventory i
join purchases pu
    on pu.id = i.purchase_id
join products p
    on p.id = i.product_id
join locations l
    on l.id = i.location_id;
```

When I build my picking SQL statement, I'll be using this view together with the orderlines table.

Building the picking SQL

For the first two parts of the problem, I will just pick a single order, the order with id = 421. In Listing 13-2, I'll just show you the data of that order.

Listing 13-2. Data for the order I am going to pick

```
SQL> select
  2     c.id           as c_id
  3   , c.name         as c_name
  4   , o.id           as o_id
  5   , ol.product_id  as p_id
  6   , p.name         as p_name
  7   , ol.qty
  8  from orders o
  9  join orderlines ol
 10     on ol.order_id = o.id
 11  join products p
 12     on p.id = ol.product_id
 13  join customers c
 14     on c.id = o.customer_id
 15  where o.id = 421
 16  order by o.id, ol.product_id;
```

As you see here in the output, the White Hart pub has ordered 110 of Hoppy Crude Oil and 140 of Der Helle Kumpel:

```
C_ID    C_NAME             O_ID  P_ID  P_NAME             QTY
50042   The White Hart     421   4280  Hoppy Crude Oil    110
50042   The White Hart     421   6520  Der Helle Kumpel   140
```

Then it's time to start building an analytic SQL statement.

Solving picking an order by FIFO

The first thing I do is I join the orderlines of order 421 with the inventory_with_dims view in Listing 13-3.

(Bear with me that I'm using very short column aliases, but it's an easy way to get a *sqlcl* output with very narrow columns that fits nicely on print.)

Listing 13-3. Possible inventory to pick – in order of purchase date

```
SQL> select
  2      i.product_id as p_id
  3    , ol.qty        as ord_q
  4    , i.qty         as loc_q
  5    , sum(i.qty) over (
  6          partition by i.product_id
  7          order by i.purchased, i.qty
  8          rows between unbounded preceding and current row
  9      )              as acc_q
 10    , i.purchased
 11    , i.warehouse   as wh
 12    , i.aisle       as ai
 13    , i.position    as pos
 14   from orderlines ol
 15   join inventory_with_dims i
 16      on i.product_id = ol.product_id
 17   where ol.order_id = 421
 18   order by i.product_id, i.purchased, i.qty;
```

In lines 5–9 I am doing a rolling sum of the inventory quantity, partitioned by product and ordered by purchase date. And for those cases with multiple rows having the same purchase date, I add the quantity to the ordering, so I get to clean out smaller quantities in the warehouse first.

In this query, the final order by in line 18 matches the columns of the partition by followed by order by in the analytic function. This is not necessary (later I will change this on purpose), but when they match like here, then the optimizer can do both with a single sorting operation.

The output shows me for each of the two ordered products all of the inventory in purchase order, and in column acc_q (accumulated quantity), I can see the rolling sum:

P_ID	ORD_Q	LOC_Q	ACC_Q	PURCHASED	WH	AI	POS
4280	110	36	36	2018-02-23	1	C	1
4280	110	39	75	2018-04-23	1	D	18
4280	110	35	110	2018-06-23	2	B	3
4280	110	34	144	2018-08-23	2	C	20
4280	110	37	181	2018-10-23	1	A	4
4280	110	19	200	2018-12-23	2	C	7
6520	140	14	14	2018-02-26	2	B	5
6520	140	14	28	2018-02-26	1	A	29
6520	140	20	48	2018-02-26	1	C	13
6520	140	24	72	2018-02-26	2	B	26
6520	140	26	98	2018-04-26	2	D	9
6520	140	48	146	2018-04-26	1	A	16
6520	140	70	216	2018-06-26	1	C	5
6520	140	21	237	2018-08-26	2	C	31
6520	140	48	285	2018-08-26	1	D	19
6520	140	72	357	2018-10-26	2	A	1
6520	140	43	400	2018-12-26	1	B	32

So this looks just like what I need, right? When the rolling sum is larger than the ordered quantity, I've got enough, right? I'm going to try that in Listing 13-4 by wrapping Listing 13-3 in an inline view and filtering in the where clause.

Listing 13-4. Filtering on the accumulated sum

```
SQL> select *
  2  from (
...
 20  )
 21  where acc_q <= ord_q
 22  order by p_id, purchased, loc_q;
```

Did I get the right result? No, not quite:

P_ID	ORD_Q	LOC_Q	ACC_Q	PURCHASED	WH	AI	POS
4280	110	36	36	2018-02-23	1	C	1
4280	110	39	75	2018-04-23	1	D	18
4280	110	35	110	2018-06-23	2	B	3
6520	140	14	14	2018-02-26	2	B	5
6520	140	14	28	2018-02-26	1	A	29
6520	140	20	48	2018-02-26	1	C	13
6520	140	24	72	2018-02-26	2	B	26
6520	140	26	98	2018-04-26	2	D	9

Product 4280 is OK; it just happens that the rolling sum exactly matches the ordered quantity of 110 after picking at three locations. But product 6520 only gets to pick 98, where it should get 140? If you look back at the previous output, you'll see that by the next location (1 A 16), the rolling sum becomes 146, which is greater than 140 so that row is not included in the output, even though I need to pick most of the quantity of that location.

The problem is that I cannot in the where clause create a filter that will include the *first* row where the rolling sum is greater than the ordered quantity, but not any *more* rows than that.

But what I can do is to create a rolling sum that accumulates the *previous* rows only, rather than including the current row. This is simply done in Listing 13-5 by simply changing the window end point of Listing 13-3 from current row to 1 preceding in line 8.

Listing 13-5. Accumulated sum of only the previous rows

```
...
5    , sum(i.qty) over (
6        partition by i.product_id
7        order by i.purchased, i.qty
8        rows between unbounded preceding and 1 preceding
9    )              as acc_prv_q
...
```

The rolling sums in this output is pushed one row down when compared to the output of Listing 13-3:

P_ID	ORD_Q	LOC_Q	ACC_PRV_Q	PURCHASED	WH	AI	POS
4280	110	36		2018-02-23	1	C	1
4280	110	39	36	2018-04-23	1	D	18
4280	110	35	75	2018-06-23	2	B	3
4280	110	34	110	2018-08-23	2	C	20
4280	110	37	144	2018-10-23	1	A	4
4280	110	19	181	2018-12-23	2	C	7
6520	140	14		2018-02-26	2	B	5
6520	140	14	14	2018-02-26	1	A	29
6520	140	20	28	2018-02-26	1	C	13
6520	140	24	48	2018-02-26	2	B	26
6520	140	26	72	2018-04-26	2	D	9
6520	140	48	98	2018-04-26	1	A	16
6520	140	70	146	2018-06-26	1	C	5
6520	140	21	216	2018-08-26	2	C	31
6520	140	48	237	2018-08-26	1	D	19
6520	140	72	285	2018-10-26	2	A	1
6520	140	43	357	2018-12-26	1	B	32

This means that the row of product 6520 in location 1 A 16 that was missing in the output of Listing 13-4 is now within the window of rows where acc_prv_q is less than ord_q, so I can create Listing 13-6 that correctly filters what I need. It is the solution to the first problem of the three described at the beginning of the chapter.

Listing 13-6. Filtering on the accumulation of previous rows

```
SQL> select
  2      wh, ai, pos, p_id
  3    , least(loc_q, ord_q - acc_prv_q) as pick_q
  4    from (
  5      select
  6          i.product_id as p_id
  7        , ol.qty        as ord_q
  8        , i.qty         as loc_q
```

```
 9        , nvl(sum(i.qty) over (
10            partition by i.product_id
11            order by i.purchased, i.qty
12            rows between unbounded preceding and 1 preceding
13          ), 0)          as acc_prv_q
14        , i.purchased
15        , i.warehouse  as wh
16        , i.aisle      as ai
17        , i.position   as pos
18      from orderlines ol
19      join inventory_with_dims i
20        on i.product_id = ol.product_id
21      where ol.order_id = 421
22  )
23  where acc_prv_q < ord_q
24  order by wh, ai, pos;
```

In lines 9–13, I do the rolling sum of previous rows, but note that I need to use nvl to turn the null of the first row into a zero – otherwise, the where clause in line 23 will fail.

That where clause you can read as "As long as the previous row(s) have *not yet* picked enough to fulfill the order, I need to include this row in the output."

In line 3, I calculate how much needs to be picked at the location of each row. I know how much still needs to be picked; it's the ordered quantity (ord_q) minus what has already been picked in the previous rows (acc_prv_q). If this is smaller than what is on the location (loc_q), that is what I need to pick. But if it is greater, then of course I can only pick as much as is on the location. In other words, I need to pick the smaller of the two numbers, which I can do with the least function.

Finally I've cleaned up the select list only saving what's necessary to put on the picking list, and in line 23, I'm ordering the rows in location order:

WH	AI	POS	P_ID	PICK_Q
1	A	16	6520	42
1	A	29	6520	14
1	C	1	4280	36
1	C	13	6520	20
1	D	18	4280	39

2	B	3	4280	35
2	B	5	6520	14
2	B	26	6520	24
2	D	9	6520	26

The picking operator can now take this list and drive around the warehouse picking the goods as specified. He'll follow the route shown in Figure 13-2.

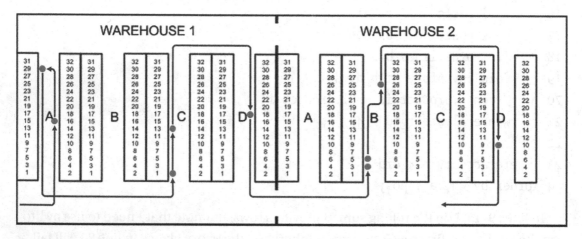

Figure 13-2. *The result of the first version of the FIFO picking query*

This route has the problem that after having picked the first two locations in aisle A, he needs to start "from the bottom" in aisle C. That means he either has to turn around (as shown in the figure) or he could take an unnecessary drive "down" aisle B. Neither is really satisfactory, and I'll come back to the solution of this in a little while.

Easy switch of picking principle

But first I'd like to stress the point that the order by of the query itself and the order by within the analytic function do not have to be identical, as they were in Listing 13-3; they can be different like in the picking list query of Listing 13-6, where I use this fact to select the inventory in FIFO order with the analytic order by, but give the output of the selected rows in location order.

This separation means that I can easily switch picking principle simply by changing my analytic order by, but still get an output in location order.

So for these examples, imagine that beers can keep indefinitely, so it does not matter if I use the first-in, first-out principle or not.

I could then use a picking principle saying that I want to prioritize locations close to the starting point of the driver to give him a short picking route. I just need to change line 11 in Listing 13-6:

```
...
 11            order by i.warehouse, i.aisle, i.position
...
```

Selecting inventory to pick in location order gives a short route; he does not have to enter warehouse 2 at all:

WH	AI	POS	P_ID	PICK_Q
1	A	4	4280	37
1	A	16	6520	48
1	A	29	6520	14
1	B	32	6520	43
1	C	1	4280	36
1	C	5	6520	35
1	D	18	4280	37

Or I could use as picking principle that I want the smallest number of picks:

```
...
 11            order by i.qty desc
...
```

This will pick from inventories with large quantities first, making it possible to fulfill the order with just five picks:

WH	AI	POS	P_ID	PICK_Q
1	A	4	4280	37
1	C	1	4280	34
1	C	5	6520	68
1	D	18	4280	39
2	A	1	6520	72

But if I pick from large quantities first, then over time the warehouse will be full of locations that have just a small quantity that was "left over" from previous picks. I could choose a picking principle that will clean up such small quantities, freeing the locations for new inventory:

```
...
11              order by i.qty
...
```

Ordering by quantity ascending instead of descending helps cleaning out locations in the warehouse, but of course then the operator has to pick in more places:

WH	AI	POS	P_ID	PICK_Q
1	A	29	6520	14
1	B	32	6520	21
1	C	1	4280	22
1	C	13	6520	20
2	B	3	4280	35
2	B	5	6520	14
2	B	26	6520	24
2	C	7	4280	19
2	C	20	4280	34
2	C	31	6520	21
2	D	9	6520	26

As you can see, having separated the order by that selects the inventory from the order by that controls the picking order, it is easy to switch picking strategies.

With that point made, back to solving the routing problem of Figure 13-2.

Solving optimal picking route

Simply ordering the output in location order means the picking operator needs to drive in the same direction ("upward") in every aisle – this is not optimal. I'd like him to switch directions so that every other aisle he drives "down."

But it is not so simple that I can just say up in aisle A and C, down in aisle B and D. Instead I need it to be up in the first, third, fifth...aisle he visits and then down in the second, fourth, sixth...aisle he visits.

To do that, I start by expanding Listing 13-6 with an extra column giving each visited aisle a consecutive number (Listing 13-7).

Listing 13-7. Consecutively numbering visited warehouse aisles

```
SQL> select
  2     wh, ai
  3   , dense_rank() over (
  4         order by wh, ai
  5     ) as ai#
  6   , pos, p_id
  7   , least(loc_q, ord_q - acc_prv_q) as pick_q
  8   from (
...
 26   )
 27   where acc_prv_q < ord_q
 28   order by wh, ai, pos;
```

The analytic function dense_rank in lines 3–5 gives the same rank to rows that have the same value in the columns used in the order by. And unlike rank, dense_rank does not skip any numbers (as I showed in Chapter 12); it assigns the ranks consecutively.

So using warehouse and aisle in the order by in dense_rank, the ai# column contains the "visited aisle number" I want:

WH	AI	AI#	POS	P_ID	PICK_Q
1	A	1	16	6520	42
1	A	1	29	6520	14
1	C	2	1	4280	36
1	C	2	13	6520	20
1	D	3	18	4280	39
2	B	4	3	4280	35
2	B	4	5	6520	14
2	B	4	26	6520	24
2	D	5	9	6520	26

That enables me to wrap Listing 13-7 in an inline view to create Listing 13-8 with an odd-even ordering logic.

Listing 13-8. Ordering ascending and descending alternately

```
SQL> select *
  2  from (
...
 30  )
 31  order by
 32     wh, ai#
 33   , case
 34        when mod(ai#, 2) = 1 then +pos
 35                              else -pos
 36     end;
```

First, I order by warehouse and visited aisle, but then within each aisle, I use the case
structure in lines 33–36 to order the positions *ascending* in odd numbered aisles and
descending in even numbered aisles:

WH	AI	AI#	POS	P_ID	PICK_Q
1	A	1	16	6520	42
1	A	1	29	6520	14
1	C	2	13	6520	20
1	C	2	1	4280	36
1	D	3	18	4280	39
2	B	4	26	6520	24
2	B	4	5	6520	14
2	B	4	3	4280	35
2	D	5	9	6520	26

That gives the operator a better picking route as you can see in Figure 13-3,
so Listing 13-8 is the solution to the second of my three problems.

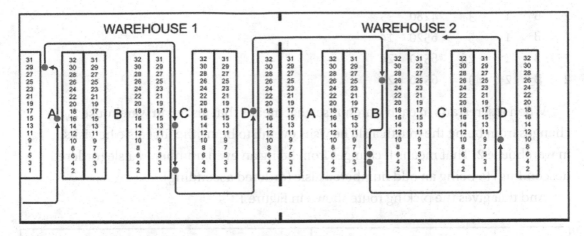

Figure 13-3. *Alternating position order of odd/even visited aisles*

Again I can show a variation where I can adapt the query very easily to match changing conditions. In Figure 13-3, you see a door between warehouses 1 and 2 both at the bottom and at the top, but what happens if there's only a door at the bottom and it's closed at the top?

A small change to the dense_rank call of Listing 13-8 produces Listing 13-9.

Listing 13-9. Restarting aisle numbering within each warehouse

```
...
5        , dense_rank() over (
6              partition by wh
7              order by ai
8          ) as ai#
...
```

All I've done is to change an order by warehouse and aisle into a partition by warehouse and order by aisle. The result is that the ranks assigned in column ai# restart from 1 in each warehouse:

WH	AI	AI#	POS	P_ID	PICK_Q
1	A	1	16	6520	42
1	A	1	29	6520	14
1	C	2	13	6520	20
1	C	2	1	4280	36
1	D	3	18	4280	39

2	B	1	3	4280	35
2	B	1	5	6520	14
2	B	1	26	6520	24
2	D	2	9	6520	26

When `ai#` restarts in each warehouse, that means that aisle B in warehouse 2 changes from being the fourth aisle he visits overall to being the first aisle he visits in warehouse 2. That means it changes from being an even numbered aisle (ordered descending) to being an odd numbered aisle (ordered ascending).

And that gives the picking route shown in Figure 13-4.

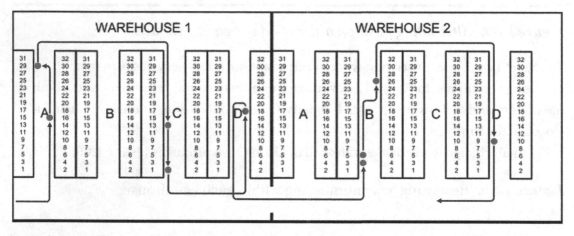

Figure 13-4. *What happens when there is just one door between warehouses*

The first two problems are now solved, so I'll now move on to the third and last problem.

Solving batch picking

It's all well and good that I now can pick a single order by FIFO with a good picking route, but to work efficiently, I need the picking operator to be able to pick multiple orders simultaneously in a single drive through the warehouses.

So I'm going to use Listing 13-2 again to show order data, just this time for two other orders. In real life, I'd probably model a "picking batch" table to use for specifying which orders are to be included in a batch, but here I'm just coding the two order ids using `in`:

```
...
15  where o.id in (422, 423)
...
```

And it shows me two pubs that each have ordered a quantity of both Hoppy Crude Oil and Der Helle Kumpel:

C_ID	C_NAME	O_ID	P_ID	P_NAME	QTY
51069	Der Wichtelmann	422	4280	Hoppy Crude Oil	80
51069	Der Wichtelmann	422	6520	Der Helle Kumpel	80
50741	Hygge og Humle	423	4280	Hoppy Crude Oil	60
50741	Hygge og Humle	423	6520	Der Helle Kumpel	40

I can start simple in Listing 13-10 by just finding the total quantities ordered for each product and then applying the FIFO picking method of Listing 13-6 to those totals.

Listing 13-10. FIFO picking of the total quantities

```
SQL> with orderbatch as (
  2     select
  3        ol.product_id
  4      , sum(ol.qty) as qty
  5     from orderlines ol
  6     where ol.order_id in (422, 423)
  7     group by ol.product_id
  8  )
  9  select
 10     wh, ai, pos, p_id
 11   , least(loc_q, ord_q - acc_prv_q) as pick_q
 12  from (
 13     select
 14        i.product_id as p_id
 15      , ob.qty       as ord_q
 16      , i.qty        as loc_q
 17      , nvl(sum(i.qty) over (
 18           partition by i.product_id
 19           order by i.purchased, i.qty
 20           rows between unbounded preceding and 1 preceding
 21        ), 0)        as acc_prv_q
 22      , i.purchased
 23      , i.warehouse  as wh
```

```
24        , i.aisle       as ai
25        , i.position    as pos
26      from orderbatch ob
27      join inventory_with_dims i
28          on i.product_id = ob.product_id
29  )
30  where acc_prv_q < ord_q
31  order by wh, ai, pos;
```

Using the with clause, I create the orderbatch subquery in lines 1–8 that simply is an aggregation of the ordered quantities per product. The rest of the query is identical to Listing 13-6, except that it uses orderbatch in line 26 instead of table orderlines.

The output is a picking list showing what needs to be picked to fulfill the two orders:

WH	AI	POS	P_ID	PICK_Q
1	A	16	6520	22
1	A	29	6520	14
1	C	1	4280	36
1	C	13	6520	20
1	D	18	4280	39
2	B	3	4280	35
2	B	5	6520	14
2	B	26	6520	24
2	C	20	4280	30
2	D	9	6520	26

But there's a slight problem for the picking operator – he can see how much to pick, but not how much of that he needs to pack in each order.

To figure that out, I need to calculate some quantity intervals in Listing 13-11.

Listing 13-11. Quantity intervals for each pick out of total per product

```
SQL> with orderbatch as (
...
  8  )
  9  select
 10      wh, ai, pos, p_id
 11    , least(loc_q, ord_q - acc_prv_q) as pick_q
```

```
12    , acc_prv_q + 1          as from_q
13    , least(acc_q, ord_q) as to_q
14    from (
15      select
16          i.product_id as p_id
17        , ob.qty        as ord_q
18        , i.qty         as loc_q
19        , nvl(sum(i.qty) over (
20              partition by i.product_id
21              order by i.purchased, i.qty
22              rows between unbounded preceding and 1 preceding
23          ), 0)          as acc_prv_q
24        , nvl(sum(i.qty) over (
25              partition by i.product_id
26              order by i.purchased, i.qty
27              rows between unbounded preceding and current row
28          ), 0)          as acc_q
29        , i.purchased
30        , i.warehouse  as wh
31        , i.aisle      as ai
32        , i.position   as pos
33      from orderbatch ob
34      join inventory_with_dims i
35          on i.product_id = ob.product_id
36    )
37    where acc_prv_q < ord_q
38    order by p_id, purchased, loc_q, wh, ai, pos;
```

The inline view in lines 14–36 is almost the same as before, but I have added
an extra rolling sum in lines 24–28, so I now have both a rolling sum of the previous rows
in acc_prv_q and a rolling sum that includes the current row in acc_q.

With those I can in lines 12–13 calculate the from and to quantity intervals for the row, showing you this output that I've ordered in line 38 so that you easily can see what happens with the intervals:

WH	AI	POS	P_ID	PICK_Q	FROM_Q	TO_Q
1	C	1	4280	36	1	36
1	D	18	4280	39	37	75
2	B	3	4280	35	76	110
2	C	20	4280	30	111	140
1	A	29	6520	14	1	14
2	B	5	6520	14	15	28
1	C	13	6520	20	29	48
2	B	26	6520	24	49	72
2	D	9	6520	26	73	98
1	A	16	6520	22	99	120

With these quantity intervals, you can read that the 36 to be picked in the first row are numbers 1-36 out of the total 140 to be picked of product 4280, the 39 in the next row are then numbers 37-75 out of the 140, and so on.

If you've a keen eye, you may have spotted that in Listing 13-11, I am actually doing a superfluous analytic function call, since I am using a call both to calculate rolling sum of previous rows and to calculate rolling sum including the current row. But the latter could also be calculated as the rolling sum of previous rows + the quantity in the current row.

So in Listing 13-12, I've changed slightly to only do the rolling sum of previous rows in order to save an analytic function call.

Listing 13-12. Quantity intervals with a single analytic sum

```
SQL> with orderbatch as (
...
  8  )
  9  select
 10     wh, ai, pos, p_id
 11   , least(loc_q, ord_q - acc_prv_q) as pick_q
 12   , acc_prv_q + 1                   as from_q
 13   , least(acc_prv_q + loc_q, ord_q) as to_q
 14  from (
```

```
15    select
16       i.product_id as p_id
17     , ob.qty        as ord_q
18     , i.qty         as loc_q
19     , nvl(sum(i.qty) over (
20          partition by i.product_id
21          order by i.purchased, i.qty
22          rows between unbounded preceding and 1 preceding
23       ), 0)          as acc_prv_q
24     , i.purchased
25     , i.warehouse   as wh
26     , i.aisle       as ai
27     , i.position    as pos
28    from orderbatch ob
29    join inventory_with_dims i
30       on i.product_id = ob.product_id
31  )
32  where acc_prv_q < ord_q
33  order by p_id, purchased, loc_q, wh, ai, pos;
```

The inline view again only contains the acc_prv_q (as it used to), and then in line 13, I am using acc_prv_q + loc_q instead of the acc_q I no longer have. The result of Listing 13-12 is identical to that of Listing 13-11.

Having quantity intervals for the picks is not enough; I also need similar quantity intervals for the orders, as I show in Listing 13-13.

Listing 13-13. Quantity intervals for each order out of total per product

```
SQL> select
  2     ol.order_id    as o_id
  3   , ol.product_id  as p_id
  4   , ol.qty
  5   , nvl(sum(ol.qty) over (
  6        partition by ol.product_id
  7        order by ol.order_id
  8        rows between unbounded preceding and 1 preceding
  9     ), 0) + 1       as from_q
```

```
10    , nvl(sum(ol.qty) over (
11         partition by ol.product_id
12         order by ol.order_id
13         rows between unbounded preceding and 1 preceding
14      ), 0) + ol.qty as to_q
15   from orderlines ol
16   where ol.order_id in (422, 423)
17   order by ol.product_id, ol.order_id;
```

I'm skipping the inline view here and instead calculate from_q directly in lines 5–9 and to_q in lines 10–14. In both calculations, I'm doing a rolling sum of all previous rows, so that when I'm using the exact same analytic function expression twice, the SQL engine will recognize this and only perform the analytic call once.

The output shows me then that the 80 of product 4280 that is ordered in order 422 are numbers 1-80 out of the 140, just like the picking quantity intervals before.

O_ID	P_ID	QTY	FROM_Q	TO_Q
422	4280	80	1	80
423	4280	60	81	140
422	6520	80	1	80
423	6520	40	81	120

With the two sets of quantity intervals, I can join them where they overlap and that way see how many of each pick go to what order. Listing 13-14 brings the code together.

Listing 13-14. Join overlapping pick and order quantity intervals

```
SQL> with olines as (
  2     select
  3        ol.order_id    as o_id
  4      , ol.product_id  as p_id
  5      , ol.qty
  6      , nvl(sum(ol.qty) over (
  7           partition by ol.product_id
  8           order by ol.order_id
  9           rows between unbounded preceding and 1 preceding
 10        ), 0) + 1        as from_q
 11      , nvl(sum(ol.qty) over (
```

```
12          partition by ol.product_id
13          order by ol.order_id
14          rows between unbounded preceding and 1 preceding
15       ), 0) + ol.qty as to_q
16    from orderlines ol
17    where ol.order_id in (422, 423)
18 ), orderbatch as (
19    select
20       ol.p_id
21     , sum(ol.qty) as qty
22    from olines ol
23    group by ol.p_id
24 ), fifo as (
25    select
26       wh, ai, pos, p_id, loc_q
27     , least(loc_q, ord_q - acc_prv_q) as pick_q
28     , acc_prv_q + 1                   as from_q
29     , least(acc_prv_q + loc_q, ord_q) as to_q
30    from (
31      select
32         i.product_id as p_id
33       , ob.qty       as ord_q
34       , i.qty        as loc_q
35       , nvl(sum(i.qty) over (
36           partition by i.product_id
37           order by i.purchased, i.qty
38           rows between unbounded preceding and 1 preceding
39         ), 0)        as acc_prv_q
40       , i.purchased
41       , i.warehouse  as wh
42       , i.aisle      as ai
43       , i.position   as pos
44      from orderbatch ob
45      join inventory_with_dims i
46        on i.product_id = ob.p_id
47      )
```

```
48      where acc_prv_q < ord_q
49 )
50 select
51      f.wh, f.ai, f.pos, f.p_id
52    , f.pick_q, f.from_q as p_f_q, f.to_q as p_t_q
53    , o.o_id  , o.from_q as o_f_q, o.to_q as o_t_q
54 from fifo f
55 join olines o
56      on o.p_id = f.p_id
57      and o.to_q >= f.from_q
58      and o.from_q <= f.to_q
59 order by f.p_id, f.from_q, o.from_q;
```

I build the query using three with clause subqueries:

- First I create olines, which is Listing 13-13 calculating the quantity intervals for the orderlines.

- Then orderbatch, similar to how I did it in Listing 13-12, except that I do the aggregation using olines in line 22 instead of the orderlines table, since olines already has the desired orderlines.

- The third subquery is fifo, which also comes from Listing 13-12 and takes care of building the FIFO picks including quantity intervals.

The main query then is a join of fifo and olines on the product id and on overlapping quantity intervals. In the resulting output, you see the from/to intervals for the picks as p_f_q/p_t_q and for the orderlines as o_f_q/o_t_q (short column names are good for print):

WH	AI	POS	P_ID	PICK_Q	P_F_Q	P_T_Q	O_ID	O_F_Q	O_T_Q
1	C	1	4280	36	1	36	422	1	80
1	D	18	4280	39	37	75	422	1	80
2	B	3	4280	35	76	110	422	1	80
2	B	3	4280	35	76	110	423	81	140
2	C	20	4280	30	111	140	423	81	140
1	A	29	6520	14	1	14	422	1	80
2	B	5	6520	14	15	28	422	1	80
1	C	13	6520	20	29	48	422	1	80

2	B	26	6520	24		49	72	422	1	80
2	D	9	6520	26		73	98	422	1	80
2	D	9	6520	26		73	98	423	81	120
1	A	16	6520	22		99	120	423	81	120

In the first row, all 36 go to order 422. Likewise in the second row, all 39 go to order 422.

But the next 35 picked are numbers 76-110 (out of 140), which overlaps both with order 422 (numbers 1-80) and order 423 (numbers 81-140). You can see from those overlaps that 5 of the 35 (numbers 76-80) should go to order 422 and the 30 of the 35 (numbers 81-110) should go to order 423.

In Listing 13-15, I calculate this as well as clean up the query a bit to not show the intermediate calculation columns.

Listing 13-15. How much quantity from each pick goes to which order

```
SQL> with olines as (
...
 18  ), orderbatch as (
...
 24  ), fifo as (
...
 49  )
 50  select
 51      f.wh, f.ai, f.pos, f.p_id
 52    , f.pick_q, o.o_id
 53    , least(
 54        f.loc_q
 55      , least(o.to_q, f.to_q) - greatest(o.from_q, f.from_q) + 1
 56      ) as q_f_o
 57  from fifo f
 58  join olines o
 59      on o.p_id = f.p_id
 60      and o.to_q >= f.from_q
 61      and o.from_q <= f.to_q
 62  order by f.p_id, f.from_q, o.from_q;
```

Lines 53–56 calculate the "quantity for order" (q_f_o) by taking either the quantity that is on the location or the "size of the interval overlap," whichever is the smaller of the two. The result is this output with all the necessary information for the picking operator:

WH	AI	POS	P_ID	PICK_Q	O_ID	Q_F_O
1	C	1	4280	36	422	36
1	D	18	4280	39	422	39
2	B	3	4280	35	422	5
2	B	3	4280	35	423	30
2	C	20	4280	30	423	30
1	A	29	6520	14	422	14
2	B	5	6520	14	422	14
1	C	13	6520	20	422	20
2	B	26	6520	24	422	24
2	D	9	6520	26	422	8
2	D	9	6520	26	423	18
1	A	16	6520	22	423	22

That solved the third problem; now all that is needed to complete the solution is to combine the solutions of problems 2 and 3, so the picking operator also can do the batch picking in an efficient picking route.

Finalizing the complete picking SQL

I have Listing 13-15 for batch picking and Listing 13-8 for a good picking route. Combining the two in Listing 13-16 gives me the complete solution.

Listing 13-16. The ultimate FIFO batch picking SQL statement

```
SQL> with olines as (
...
 18 ), orderbatch as (
...
 24 ), fifo as (
...
 49 ), pick as (
 50    select
```

```
51        f.wh, f.ai
52      , dense_rank() over (
53          order by wh, ai
54      ) as ai#
55      , f.pos, f.p_id
56      , f.pick_q, o.o_id
57      , least(
58          f.loc_q
59        , least(o.to_q, f.to_q) - greatest(o.from_q, f.from_q) + 1
60      ) as q_f_o
61    from fifo f
62    join olines o
63      on o.p_id = f.p_id
64      and o.to_q >= f.from_q
65      and o.from_q <= f.to_q
66  )
67  select
68      p.wh, p.ai, p.pos
69    , p.p_id, p.pick_q
70    , p.o_id, p.q_f_o
71  from pick p
72  order by p.wh
73         , p.ai#
74         , case
75             when mod(p.ai#, 2) = 1 then +p.pos
76                                    else -p.pos
77         end;
```

The with clause subqueries olines, orderbatch, and fifo are the same as
Listing 13-15. Then the main query from Listing 13-15 I have put into subquery pick in
lines 49–66.

I've added the calculation of the "visited aisle number" ai# (from Listing 13-8) in
lines 52–54.

Then the main query is simply selecting the necessary information from the `pick` subquery and using the `order` by from Listing 13-8 to give an optimal picking route:

WH	AI	POS	P_ID	PICK_Q	O_ID	Q_F_O
1	A	16	6520	22	423	22
1	A	29	6520	14	422	14
1	C	13	6520	20	422	20
1	C	1	4280	36	422	36
1	D	18	4280	39	422	39
2	B	26	6520	24	422	24
2	B	5	6520	14	422	14
2	B	3	4280	35	422	5
2	B	3	4280	35	423	30
2	C	20	4280	30	423	30
2	D	9	6520	26	422	8
2	D	9	6520	26	423	18

Where a location is repeated on the list, like 2 B 3, you can see that it shows 35 should be picked, 5 of which are to be placed in the package for order 422 and 30 are for the package for order 423.

With this list, the picking operator will be led in a good route through the warehouses, picking products for a batch of multiple orders, where the products have been selected by the first-in, first-out principle.

In total this is practically a complete warehouse goods picking app in a single SQL statement.

Lessons learned

This chapter has shown you the building of a single SQL app with multiple uses of analytic functions that have given you knowledge on

- Using the window clause to apply analytic `sum` to a subset of the rows to find the subset that gives a sufficiently large result

- Calculating intervals with analytic rolling sums to find overlapping intervals

- Assigning `dense_rank` to results for alternating ascending and descending ordering

When you understand how to build a statement like this piece by piece with analytic functions, you can create many similar statements that contain a lot of business logic, thereby achieving an app with a lot better performance than extracting the data and doing the same logic procedurally.

CHAPTER 14

Analyzing Activity Logs with Lead

Logs can be many things, and sometimes you are lucky that each line of the log is self-contained and has all the data you need to analyze the log. But most often a row in a log table pinpoints that at *this* exact moment in time, *this* specific activity occurred – and the interesting fact you need to analyze is how long time there was *between* rows in the log.

This is where analytic functions lag and lead come in very handy, as they can be used on a given row to retrieve information from previous rows (lag) or next rows (lead) in a given order. You can often choose to use either lag or lead depending on how you build your logic, but most often the deciding factor will be *when* the row is inserted in the activity log. If the row is inserted at the start of the activity, the time of the activity is the time between this row and the *next* row, so lead is the sensible choice. Contrariwise, if the row is inserted when the activity is finished, the time of the activity is the time between the *previous* row and this row, and then the use of lag makes sense.

Where I worked when I created this type of code first, there was an automatic warehouse with robot picking, so the operator stood in a fixed position, boxes came on a conveyor belt to him, he picked products, the box moved away, and a new one came. Departures and arrivals of the boxes were logged, which meant that the time from a box arrived until it departed was the time used for picking, while the time from the box departed until the next box arrived was waiting time. With the use of lead SQL similar to what I show here, we could analyze when there was too much waiting time and use that information to tune the robot warehouse.

The Good Beer Trading Co in this book does not have a robot warehouse, but I showed picking optimization in the previous chapter. Now I can follow up in this chapter with analyzing how much time was used picking vs. driving around in the warehouse.

267

© Kim Berg Hansen 2020
K. Berg Hansen, *Practical Oracle SQL*, https://doi.org/10.1007/978-1-4842-5617-6_14

Picking activity log

In Chapter 13 I showed how Good Beer Trading Co can calculate efficient picking lists for picking beers in the warehouse for multiple orders. When the warehouse operators start picking some orders, they do not just print the output from the queries in Chapter 13; instead a picking list is created in table `picking_list`, and the query output is stored in table `picking_line`, these two tables shown in Figure 14-1.

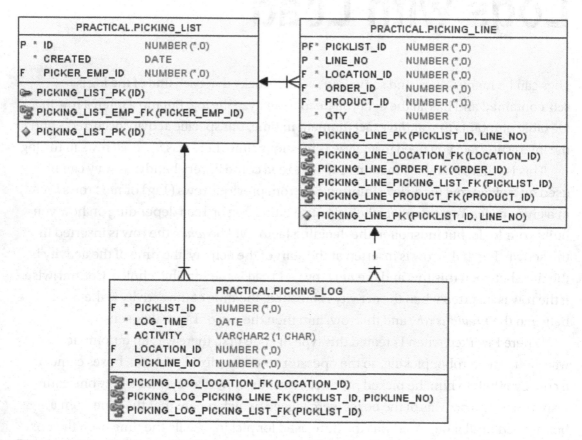

Figure 14-1. *Tables to hold picking lists and logs for doing the picking*

Then after the picking list with corresponding picking lines has been created and printed, the picking operator drives off on his electric picking cart. As he drives along and picks the beers in the warehouse, he scans barcodes on the location shelves and the beers to register his activity – this activity is stored in table `picking_log`, the contents of which you can see in Listing 14-1.

Listing 14-1. Content of the activity log for picking lists

```
SQL> select
  2      list.picker_emp_id as emp
  3    , list.id            as list
  4    , log.log_time
  5    , log.activity       as act
  6    , log.location_id    as loc
  7    , log.pickline_no    as line
  8  from picking_list list
  9  join picking_log log
 10    on log.picklist_id = list.id
 11  order by list.id, log.log_time;
```

I join with the `picking_list` table in order to retrieve the employee id, so that in my statistical reports, I can compare and see which operator works the fastest, so (s)he can teach the others:

EMP	LIST	LOG_TIME	ACT	LOC	LINE
149	841	2019-01-16 14:05:11	D		
149	841	2019-01-16 14:05:44	A	16	
149	841	2019-01-16 14:05:52	P	16	1
149	841	2019-01-16 14:06:01	D	16	
149	841	2019-01-16 14:06:20	A	29	
149	841	2019-01-16 14:06:27	P	29	2
...					
149	841	2019-01-16 14:13:00	D	233	
149	841	2019-01-16 14:14:41	A		
152	842	2019-01-19 16:01:12	D		
152	842	2019-01-19 16:01:48	A	16	
152	842	2019-01-19 16:01:53	P	16	1
...					
152	842	2019-01-19 16:08:58	D	212	
152	842	2019-01-19 16:09:23	A	233	
152	842	2019-01-19 16:09:34	P	233	11
152	842	2019-01-19 16:09:42	P	233	12

```
152    842    2019-01-19 16:09:53   D      233
152    842    2019-01-19 16:11:42   A
```

63 rows selected.

In the `activity` column of the table (`act` in the output) can be stored either D for departure, A for arrival, or P for pick. When he drives off from a location, he scans the location barcode, and a row with D is inserted in the table. Upon arrival at the next location, again he scans the location barcode, and a row with A is created. Then he picks one or more picking lines at that location, each time scanning the beer which creates a P row.

There's a little variation at each end. When he sets off on his picking tour, a D row is inserted with a `null` location. When he's done and returns to his origin, an A row is similarly inserted with a `null` location.

Apart from that variation, the work follows a repetitive cycle as shown in Figure 14-2.

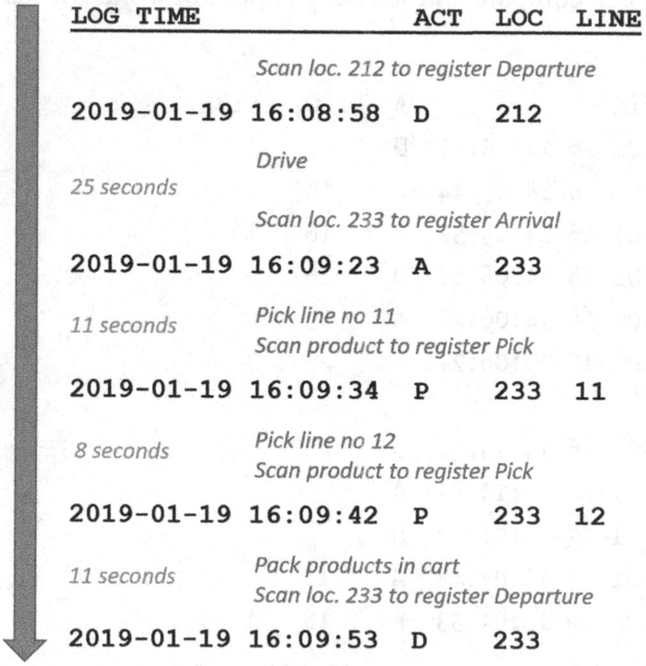

LOG TIME		ACT	LOC	LINE
	Scan loc. 212 to register Departure			
2019-01-19 16:08:58		D	212	
25 seconds	*Drive*			
	Scan loc. 233 to register Arrival			
2019-01-19 16:09:23		A	233	
11 seconds	*Pick line no 11* *Scan product to register Pick*			
2019-01-19 16:09:34		P	233	11
8 seconds	*Pick line no 12* *Scan product to register Pick*			
2019-01-19 16:09:42		P	233	12
11 seconds	*Pack products in cart* *Scan loc. 233 to register Departure*			
2019-01-19 16:09:53		D	233	

Figure 14-2. *Timeline of part of the picking log*

You can see how he works, scanning locations and beers as he goes along, and this cycle repeats. It will always be D->A->P->D, with the possibility of there being more than one P in a cycle.

But the interesting thing to analyze is the number of seconds *between* rows and also figuring out that the 25 seconds is driving, the 11+8 seconds is picking, and the last 11 seconds is packing. I'll show you all of that, but I start simply by figuring out driving and working (lumping picking and packing together).

Analyzing departures and arrivals

First, I will simply analyze departures and arrivals, where the time between a departure and an arrival is *driving* time and the time between an arrival and a departure is *work* time (later I'll look at the picking and packing part of the work time). In Listing 14-2, I look at just the D and A activities.

Listing 14-2. Departures and arrivals with lead function calls

```
SQL> select
  2      list.picker_emp_id as emp
  3    , list.id           as list
  4    , log.log_time
  5    , log.activity      as act
  6    , log.location_id   as loc
  7    , to_char(
  8        lead(log_time) over (
  9          partition by list.id
 10          order by log.log_time
 11        )
 12      , 'HH24:MI:SS'
 13      ) as next_time
 14    , to_char(
 15        lead(log_time, 2) over (
 16          partition by list.id
 17          order by log.log_time
 18        )
 19      , 'HH24:MI:SS'
 20      ) as next2_time
 21  from picking_list list
 22  join picking_log log
```

```
23      on log.picklist_id = list.id
24  where log.activity in ('D', 'A')
25  order by list.id, log.log_time;
```

I restrict the data to D and A activities in line 24.

Using lead in lines 8–11 gives me what is the log_time of the next row, and adding the parameter 2 to the lead call in line 15 gives me the log_time of the next row after that:

EMP	LIST	LOG_TIME	ACT	LOC	NEXT_TIME	NEXT2_TIME
149	841	2019-01-16 14:05:11	D		14:05:44	14:06:01
149	841	2019-01-16 14:05:44	A	16	14:06:01	14:06:20
149	841	2019-01-16 14:06:01	D	16	14:06:20	14:06:35
149	841	2019-01-16 14:06:20	A	29	14:06:35	14:07:16
...						
149	841	2019-01-16 14:11:26	D	163	14:12:42	14:13:00
149	841	2019-01-16 14:12:42	A	233	14:13:00	14:14:41
149	841	2019-01-16 14:13:00	D	233	14:14:41	
149	841	2019-01-16 14:14:41	A			
152	842	2019-01-19 16:01:12	D		16:01:48	16:02:04
152	842	2019-01-19 16:01:48	A	16	16:02:04	16:02:19
...						
152	842	2019-01-19 16:09:53	D	233	16:11:42	
152	842	2019-01-19 16:11:42	A			

```
42 rows selected.
```

You notice that the last row of each partition (picking list) has null in next_time, and the two last rows have null in next2_time. That makes sense and is OK for my purpose.

Using lead twice in this manner gives me that each D row has the time of a complete Depart – Arrive – Depart picking cycle. Likewise each A row has the time of a complete Arrive – Depart – Arrive cycle. I only need one of the two, so I choose to work with Depart–Arrive–Depart cycles in Listing 14-3.

Listing 14-3. Depart–Arrive–Depart cycles

```
SQL> select
  2     emp, list
  3   , log_time as depart
  4   , to_char(next_time , 'HH24:MI:SS') as arrive
  5   , to_char(next2_time, 'HH24:MI:SS') as next_depart
  6   , round((next_time  - log_time )*(24*60*60)) as drive
  7   , round((next2_time - next_time)*(24*60*60)) as work
  8  from (
  9     select
 10       list.picker_emp_id as emp
 11     , list.id                 as list
 12     , log.log_time
 13     , log.activity        as act
 14     , lead(log_time) over (
 15           partition by list.id
 16           order by log.log_time
 17       ) as next_time
 18     , lead(log_time, 2) over (
 19           partition by list.id
 20           order by log.log_time
 21       ) as next2_time
 22     from picking_list list
 23     join picking_log log
 24       on log.picklist_id = list.id
 25     where log.activity in ('D', 'A')
 26  )
 27  where act = 'D'
 28  order by list, log_time;
```

Listing 14-2 I use in the inline view and simply keep only the D rows in line 27 – I have all the data I need in those rows and can skip the A rows.

Then I can give my time columns meaningful names in lines 3–5 (had I chosen A-D-A cycles instead of D-A-D cycles, the names would have been different). And that makes it easy to calculate the number of seconds used for drive and for work in lines 6–7 (the rounding is just because the calculations otherwise would have shown a small inevitable rounding error in the 20th decimal or so):

EMP	LIST	DEPART	ARRIVE	NEXT_DEPART	DRIVE	WORK
149	841	2019-01-16 14:05:11	14:05:44	14:06:01	33	17
149	841	2019-01-16 14:06:01	14:06:20	14:06:35	19	15
...						
149	841	2019-01-16 14:11:26	14:12:42	14:13:00	76	18
149	841	2019-01-16 14:13:00	14:14:41		101	
152	842	2019-01-19 16:01:12	16:01:48	16:02:04	36	16
152	842	2019-01-19 16:02:04	16:02:19	16:02:37	15	18
...						
152	842	2019-01-19 16:08:58	16:09:23	16:09:53	25	30
152	842	2019-01-19 16:09:53	16:11:42		109	

```
21 rows selected.
```

The *last* row of each picking list (partition) has a null value in next_depart, which makes the work calculation become null too. As shown before, the picker starts at the null location and ends at the null location, so after having picked the *last* product on the picking list, he registers a departure from that location and an arrival at the null location, indicating he is done and there is no next_depart. So the last D-A-D picking cycle is incomplete; it is only D-A. (If I had chosen to use A-D-A cycles, it would have been the *first* row that would be incomplete, having only D-A.)

Listing 14-3 gives me the details for each picking cycle. I can then simply aggregate these data in Listing 14-4 to give me some statistics on how efficient the employee has worked on each picking list.

Listing 14-4. Statistics per picking list

```
SQL> select
  2     max(emp) as emp
  3   , list
  4   , min(log_time) as begin
  5   , to_char(max(next_time), 'HH24:MI:SS') as end
  6   , count(*) as drives
  7   , round(
  8         avg((next_time - log_time )*(24*60*60))
```

```
 9        , 1
10        ) as avg_d
11      , count(next2_time) as stops
12      , round(
13            avg((next2_time  - next_time)*(24*60*60))
14          , 1
15          ) as avg_w
16      from (
...
34      )
35      where act = 'D'
36      group by list
37      order by list;
```

I take the query from Listing 14-3 and tack on a group by in line 36 and then simply choose which aggregates I am interested in in the select list:

```
EMP   LIST  BEGIN                END       DRIVES  AVG_D  STOPS  AVG_W
149   841   2019-01-16 14:05:11  14:14:41  10      42.9   9      15.7
152   842   2019-01-19 16:01:12  16:11:42  11      41.5   10     17.4
```

Here I chose to show the average number of seconds used to drive between picking locations and the average number of seconds used working (picking and packing) at each stop. I could just as easily have used min, max, median, sum, and so on, but I leave that as an exercise for the reader. It is more interesting to move on to analyzing the data when I also want to include the picking activity.

Analyzing picking activity

It is possible for me to use a similar technique with lead to include the picking activity, as I show in Listing 14-5.

Listing 14-5. Including picking activity

```
SQL> select
  2      emp, list
  3    , to_char(depart, 'HH24:MI:SS') as depart
  4    , to_char(arrive, 'HH24:MI:SS') as arrive
```

```
 5    , to_char(pick1 , 'HH24:MI:SS') as pick1
 6    , to_char(
 7        case when pick2 < next_depart then pick2 end
 8      , 'HH24:MI:SS'
 9      ) as pick2
10    , to_char(next_depart, 'HH24:MI:SS') as next_dep
11    , round((arrive      - depart)*(24*60*60)) as drv
12    , round((next_depart - arrive)*(24*60*60)) as wrk
13    from (
14      select
15        list.picker_emp_id as emp
16      , list.id            as list
17      , log.activity       as act
18      , log.log_time       as depart
19      , lead(log_time) over (
20            partition by list.id
21            order by log.log_time
22        ) as arrive
23      , lead(
24            case log.activity when 'P' then log_time end
25        ) ignore nulls over (
26            partition by list.id
27            order by log.log_time
28        ) as pick1
29      , lead(
30            case log.activity when 'P' then log_time end, 2
31        ) ignore nulls over (
32            partition by list.id
33            order by log.log_time
34        ) as pick2
35      , lead(
36            case log.activity when 'D' then log_time end
37        ) ignore nulls over (
38            partition by list.id
39            order by log.log_time
```

```
40          ) as next_depart
41      from picking_list list
42      join picking_log log
43          on log.picklist_id = list.id
44  )
45  where act = 'D'
46  order by list, depart;
```

I have here four calls to lead, which for any D row will give me the following:

- Lines 19–22 give me the next row after the D row, which always will be an A row.

- Lines 23–28 give me the next P row after the D row by using a case expression to return null for all rows that are *not* P rows, enabling me to skip those rows using ignore nulls.

- Lines 29–34 are almost identical, just adding parameter 2 in line 30 to get the *second* P row after the D row.

- Lines 35–40 finally use the case and ignore nulls technique to get me the next D row after the current D row.

All that gives me an output very similar to that of Listing 14-3, just adding columns for the time of the first and second (if any) picks:

EMP	LIST	DEPART	ARRIVE	PICK1	PICK2	NEXT_DEP	DRV	WRK
149	841	14:05:11	14:05:44	14:05:52		14:06:01	33	17
149	841	14:06:01	14:06:20	14:06:27		14:06:35	19	15
...								
149	841	14:11:26	14:12:42	14:12:53		14:13:00	76	18
149	841	14:13:00	14:14:41				101	
152	842	16:01:12	16:01:48	16:01:53		16:02:04	36	16
...								
152	842	16:07:03	16:07:12	16:07:16	16:07:22	16:07:34	9	22
152	842	16:07:34	16:08:44	16:08:49		16:08:58	70	14
152	842	16:08:58	16:09:23	16:09:34	16:09:42	16:09:53	25	30
152	842	16:09:53	16:11:42				109	

21 rows selected.

I *could* then start calculating how many seconds were spent picking and packing out of the `wrk` seconds, but it is not really a good way to continue, as this code only works if the worker picks *at most* two picking lines at each stop on the route. And it's a bad idea to try to keep adding multiple `lead` calls to try and create columns `pick1` to `pick<n>`. I want to try something else instead.

When I don't know how many picks there might be for each stop, it is better to work with rows instead of columns. But then I somehow need to know which rows belong together in a picking cycle. I can do that with `last_value` in Listing 14-6.

Listing 14-6. Identifying cycles

```
SQL> select
  2      list.picker_emp_id as emp
  3    , list.id              as list
  4    , last_value(
  5        case log.activity when 'D' then log_time end
  6      ) ignore nulls over (
  7        partition by list.id
  8        order by log.log_time
  9        rows between unbounded preceding and current row
 10      ) as begin_cycle
 11    , to_char(log_time, 'HH24:MI:SS') as act_time
 12    , log.activity as act
 13    , lead(activity) over (
 14        partition by list.id
 15        order by log.log_time
 16      ) as next_act
 17    , round((
 18        lead(log_time) over (
 19          partition by list.id
 20          order by log.log_time
 21        ) - log_time
 22      )*(24*60*60)) as secs
 23  from picking_list list
```

```
24  join picking_log log
25     on log.picklist_id = list.id
26  order by list.id, log.log_time;
```

The case expression in line 5 that I use as parameter for last_value will only have the log_time value for D rows, otherwise null. So on a D row, the output of the last_value call will be the log_time of the row. On the next row, the ignore nulls clause in line 6 makes last_value go back and find the last non-null value, which was the log_time of the D row. This repeats on each subsequent row until a new D row is reached, making all rows belonging together in the same picking cycle have the same value in column begin_cycle.

With lead calls in lines 13–22, I calculate on each row what is the activity of the *next* row and how many seconds did *this* activity last. In total I get an output with all the details for every row, but ready to be grouped by each cycle:

```
EMP  LIST  BEGIN_CYCLE          ACT_TIME  ACT  NEXT_ACT  SECS
149  841   2019-01-16 14:05:11  14:05:11  D    A         33
149  841   2019-01-16 14:05:11  14:05:44  A    P         8
149  841   2019-01-16 14:05:11  14:05:52  P    D         9
149  841   2019-01-16 14:06:01  14:06:01  D    A         19
149  841   2019-01-16 14:06:01  14:06:20  A    P         7
149  841   2019-01-16 14:06:01  14:06:27  P    D         8
...
149  841   2019-01-16 14:13:00  14:13:00  D    A         101
149  841   2019-01-16 14:13:00  14:14:41  A
152  842   2019-01-19 16:01:12  16:01:12  D    A         36
152  842   2019-01-19 16:01:12  16:01:48  A    P         5
152  842   2019-01-19 16:01:12  16:01:53  P    D         11
...
152  842   2019-01-19 16:08:58  16:08:58  D    A         25
152  842   2019-01-19 16:08:58  16:09:23  A    P         11
152  842   2019-01-19 16:08:58  16:09:34  P    P         8
152  842   2019-01-19 16:08:58  16:09:42  P    D         11
152  842   2019-01-19 16:09:53  16:09:53  D    A         109
152  842   2019-01-19 16:09:53  16:11:42  A

63 rows selected.
```

   Now I have what I need to do some analysis that includes picking and packing activities, no matter how many picks there are at each stop.

Complete picking cycle analysis

I could use a group by on the emp, list, and begin_cycle to get data for each picking cycle, but in this case, it can be a little easier in Listing 14-7 to use the *implicit* grouping that is performed by pivot.

Listing 14-7. Grouping cycles by pivoting

```
SQL> select *
  2    from (
  3      select
  4        list.picker_emp_id as emp
  5      , list.id              as list
  6      , last_value(
  7          case log.activity when 'D' then log_time end
  8        ) ignore nulls over (
  9          partition by list.id
 10          order by log.log_time
 11          rows between unbounded preceding and current row
 12        ) as begin_cycle
 13      , lead(activity) over (
 14          partition by list.id
 15          order by log.log_time
 16        ) as next_act
 17      , round((
 18          lead(log_time) over (
 19            partition by list.id
 20            order by log.log_time
 21          ) - log_time
 22        )*(24*60*60)) as secs
 23      from picking_list list
 24      join picking_log log
 25        on log.picklist_id = list.id
 26    ) pivot (
```

```
27   sum(secs)
28   for (next_act) in (
29       'A' as drive    -- D->A
30     , 'P' as pick     -- A->P or P->P
31     , 'D' as pack     -- P->D
32     )
33   )
34   order by list, begin_cycle;
```

I wrap Listing 14-6 in an inline view and use the pivot operator on the result. But since pivot makes implicit group by on all columns not used in the pivot clause itself, I do need to leave out columns act_time and act from Listing 14-6, as they would have ruined the implicit grouping.

If you look again at Figure 14-2, you see there are four possible combinations of the activity on one row and the activity on the next row. The seconds going from a D row to an A row are spent driving, seconds going from an A row to a P row are picking, seconds going from a P row to a P row are *also* picking, and finally the seconds going from a P row to a D row are spent packing.

This means that I can pivot on the next_act column in line 28 with the three different values creating virtual columns drive, pick, and pack. Line 30 represents both picking cases: A->P and P->P.

So with the sum in place in line 27, I get an output with each picking cycle just like the output of Listing 14-3, except I now have the working time split up into pick and pack, where the pick column may contain time from one or more rows of the picking log:

EMP	LIST	BEGIN_CYCLE	DRIVE	PICK	PACK
149	841	2019-01-16 14:05:11	33	8	9
149	841	2019-01-16 14:06:01	19	7	8
...					
149	841	2019-01-16 14:11:26	76	11	7
149	841	2019-01-16 14:13:00	101		
152	842	2019-01-19 16:01:12	36	5	11
...					
152	842	2019-01-19 16:08:58	25	19	11
152	842	2019-01-19 16:09:53	109		

21 rows selected.

I could have included a count(*) measure in the pivot clause if I wanted to show also how many picks at each stop rather than just the total seconds used for picking at the stop.

And just as Listing 14-4 aggregated data from Listing 14-3, I use Listing 14-8 to aggregate the data of Listing 14-7.

Listing 14-8. Statistics per picking list on the pivoted cycles

```
SQL> select
  2      max(emp) as emp
  3    , list
  4    , min(begin_cycle) as begin
  5    , count(*) as drvs
  6    , round(avg(drive), 1) as avg_d
  7    , count(pick) as stops
  8    , round(avg(pick), 1) as avg_pick
  9    , round(avg(pack), 1) as avg_pack
 10  from (
...
 34  ) pivot (
 35      sum(secs)
 36      for (next_act) in (
 37          'A' as drive   -- D->A
 38        , 'P' as pick    -- A->P or P->P
 39        , 'D' as pack    -- P->D
 40      )
 41  )
 42  group by list
 43  order by list;
```

A nice little thing to note here is that I do *not* need to wrap Listing 14-7 in another inline view; I can add the group by directly after the pivot. Actually that means that *two* grouping operations will be performed, first the implicit one in the pivot and then the explicit one in line 42 where I group by each picking list:

EMP	LIST	BEGIN	DRVS	AVG_D	STOPS	AVG_PICK	AVG_PACK
149	841	2019-01-16 14:05:11	10	42.9	9	7.1	8.6
152	842	2019-01-19 16:01:12	11	41.5	10	7.8	9.6

As before, you can play around yourself doing other aggregates than simply count and avg; you know the technique now.

I could end the chapter here, but I just want to give you a little teaser on what you'll see when you get to Part 3 of this book.

Teaser: row pattern matching

The match_recognize clause (formally known as **row pattern matching**) is a very powerful tool in the SQL developer's toolbox. The entire Part 3 is dedicated to various ways to use this clause.

But what I have been showing in this chapter *is* actually detecting and grouping on a *pattern* in the data – a cyclic pattern of activities going from D to A to one or more P and back to D. I have used some useful tricks in the analytic function toolbox by deliberately making null values for the ignore nulls clause to create groups of cycles, but it is actually relatively obscure what the code in Listing 14-7 and 14-8 does.

With row pattern matching, I can make a SQL statement in Listing 14-9 that at first glance might seem even more obscure, but once you know match_recognize, this is actually (trust me on this) more readable.

Listing 14-9. Identifying picking cycles with row pattern matching

```
SQL> select
  2     *
  3  from (
  4     select
  5        list.picker_emp_id as emp
  6      , list.id            as list
  7      , log.log_time
```

```
 8        , log.activity        as act
 9      from picking_list list
10      join picking_log log
11         on log.picklist_id = list.id
12   )
13   match_recognize (
14      partition by list
15      order by log_time
16      measures
17         max(emp) as emp
18       , first(log_time) as begin_cycle
19       , round(
20            (arrive.log_time - first(depart.log_time))
21          * (24*60*60)
22         ) as drive
23       , round(
24            (last(pick.log_time) - arrive.log_time)
25          * (24*60*60)
26         ) as pick
27       , round(
28            (next(last(pick.log_time)) - last(pick.log_time))
29          * (24*60*60)
30         ) as pack
31      one row per match
32      after match skip to last arrive
33      pattern (depart arrive pick* depart{0,1})
34      define
35         depart as act = 'D'
36       , arrive as act = 'A'
37       , pick   as act = 'P'
38   )
39   order by list;
```

I will not dive deep into the syntax at this point, but I invite you to come back here after you have read Part 3 and read this listing again and see if you do not agree that (with suitable knowledge of the syntax) it is more clear what the code does.

But the important thing you can note here is that in lines 34–37, I make some *definitions* that a row with `act = 'D'` is called `depart` and similar for `arrive` and `pick`, and then in line 33, I can easily state that one picking cycle contains a `depart`, followed by an `arrive`, followed by zero or more `pick`, and followed by zero or one `depart`. You'll notice the similarity to regular expression syntax. (The *zero or more* and *zero or one* parts are to handle the incomplete picking cycle that ends each picking tour.)

And just as Listing 14-9 produces the same output as Listing 14-7, I can get the same statistical output from Listing 14-10 that I got in Listing 14-8.

Listing 14-10. Statistics per picking list with row pattern matching

```
SQL> select
  2      max(emp) as emp
  3    , list
  4    , min(begin_cycle) as begin
  5    , count(*) as drvs
  6    , round(avg(drive), 1) as avg_d
  7    , count(pick) as stops
  8    , round(avg(pick), 1) as avg_pick
  9    , round(avg(pack), 1) as avg_pack
 10    from (
...
 19    )
 20    match_recognize (
...
 45    )
 46    group by list
 47    order by list;
```

I hope I have wetted your appetite for Part 3 of the book. Come back to this and play with this code when you are done with Part 3.

Lessons learned

The techniques of this chapter are classic examples of how analytic functions enable you to use data from across rows for inter-row calculations. In particular you have seen

- The use of lead to fetch data from the next row or lead with an optional parameter to fetch from the nth next row

- The use of the ignore nulls clause of lead to fetch data from the next row with a non-null value, where you can customize the value to be non-null only on those rows you want lead to fetch data from

- The use of last_value with the ignore nulls clause to set up a common value on a group of rows that belong together and grouping or pivoting on that common value

These are all techniques useful in many situations, and if it becomes too complex to use these techniques, I recommend looking into using match_recognize (the topic of Part 3) as an alternative that often fits these situations very nicely.

CHAPTER 15

Forecasting with Linear Regression

Some years ago at the retail company I worked at then, our data analyst came up to me. She was working on forecasting how much each of our products would sell in the next 12 months and wanted to know if I could help develop a piece of SQL to do this.

Such forecasting can be done with a multitude of different models, each suitable to different types of data and circumstances. She had experimented with tools and researched and ran tests of the models on selected products and done whatever magic analysts do to make discoveries in our data. In the course of this, she found that a very suitable model for such sales forecasting in our case was a time series model with seasonal adjustment and exponential smoothing.

To help me understand this model and implement it, she brought me an Excel spreadsheet in which she had 3 years of monthly sales data for one of our products and then a series of columns that successively calculated the intermediate steps in the model, ending with the forecast for the next year.

The problem for her was that this spreadsheet was nice but could only operate on a single product. We had 100.000 products we needed to forecast. Therefore she really wished the forecast could be performed right inside the database with SQL.

With the help of analytic functions for averaging and linear regression, I could implement the same forecasting model in SQL, doing a series of calculations that emulated the calculations of each separate column of the spreadsheet. In this chapter I will show you this step by step.

© Kim Berg Hansen 2020
K. Berg Hansen, *Practical Oracle SQL*, https://doi.org/10.1007/978-1-4842-5617-6_15

Note   The spreadsheet made by our analyst that I used as basis for developing this SQL was based on the work by Robert Nau, Fuqua School of Business, Duke University, who has written about it here, where you can download a similar spreadsheet: *http://people.duke.edu/~rnau/411outbd.htm.*

Sales forecasting

To demonstrate this time series forecasting model, I am going to use monthly sales data for the beers that my fictional Good Beer Trading Co sells. I have those data in the tables of Figure 15-1.

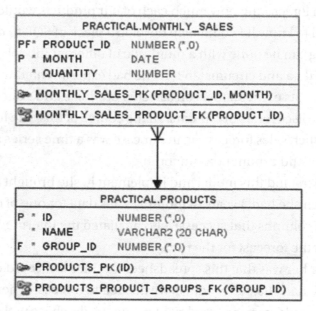

Figure 15-1. *Table with monthly sales for products*

There are more beers in the products table, but I am going to concentrate on two that have a nice seasonal variation in their sales – one sold primarily wintertime and one sold primarily summertime. Listing 15-1 shows the two beers queried by primary key id values.

Listing 15-1. The two products for showing forecasting

```
SQL> select id, name
  2  from products
  3  where id in (4160, 7790);
```

So you can see that if I query sales data for product ids 4160 and 7790, I will get data for Reindeer Fuel and Summer in India:

```
ID NAME
---------- --------------------
   4160 Reindeer Fuel
   7790 Summer in India
```

I have the sales data for 2016, 2017, and 2018, and besides having nice seasonal variations, Reindeer Fuel is selling a bit more each year, while Summer in India is selling a bit less. Now it's time to try and apply this time series forecasting model to the data and forecast the sales of 2019.

Time series

The first thing to do in time series forecasting is to build the time series, which is a set of consecutive data each being exactly one time unit apart. In this case I am using months for time unit. I have 3 years = 36 months of actual data, and I want to forecast 1 year = 12 months, so I need to create a time series of 48 rows for each beer in Listing 15-2.

Listing 15-2. Building time series 2016–2019 for the two beers

```
SQL> select
  2      ms.product_id
  3    , mths.mth
  4    , mths.ts
  5    , extract(year from mths.mth) as yr
  6    , extract(month from mths.mth) as mthno
  7    , ms.qty
  8  from (
  9      select
 10        add_months(date '2016-01-01', level - 1) as mth
 11      , level as ts --time series
 12      from dual
 13      connect by level <= 48
 14  ) mths
```

```
15  left outer join (
16      select product_id, mth, qty
17      from monthly_sales
18      where product_id in (4160, 7790)
19  ) ms
20      partition by (ms.product_id)
21      on  ms.mth = mths.mth
22  order by ms.product_id, mths.mth;
```

The inline view mths in lines 9–13 creates 48 rows, one for each month in 2016–2019. The column mth contains the month as a date datatype, which I need to join with the sales data. Column ts contains consecutive numbers 1–48, which I can think of as number of "time unit," in this case number of months.

Inline view ms in lines 16–18 simply queries the monthly_sales table for the two products I'm after – when I'm happy with my model, I can simply remove line 18 and run for all products instead of only two.

The left outer join between the two inline views is *partitioned* in line 20 on the product id, which means that the 48 rows of mths will be outer joined individually to each product – first outer joined to the 36 rows of product 4160 and then outer joined to the 36 rows of product 7790.

In total I get 96 rows in the output, partially shown here:

```
PROD MTH        TS    YR MTHNO  QTY
---- -------   ---  ----- ------ ----
4160 2016-01    1   2016      1   79
4160 2016-02    2   2016      2  133
...
4160 2018-11   35   2018     11   73
4160 2018-12   36   2018     12  160
4160 2019-01   37   2019      1
4160 2019-02   38   2019      2
...
4160 2019-11   47   2019     11
4160 2019-12   48   2019     12
7790 2016-01    1   2016      1    4
7790 2016-02    2   2016      2    6
...
```

7790	2018-11	35	2018	11	3
7790	2018-12	36	2018	12	5
7790	2019-01	37	2019	1	
7790	2019-02	38	2019	2	
...					
7790	2019-11	47	2019	11	
7790	2019-12	48	2019	12	

96 rows selected.

For each product, the first 36 rows contain actual sales data in column qty and then 12 rows (ts = 37–48) with null in qty – these 12 rows are to be filled with the forecast sales as I continue developing the query.

In the preceding output, I only showed parts of the rows; since it is easier for us humans to grasp such data if presented visually, the complete result set I show in Figure 15-2.

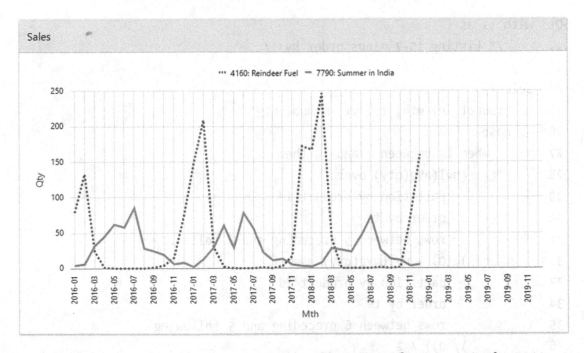

Figure 15-2. *The monthly sales 2016–2018 plus rows in the time series for 2019 forecast*

The two lines are the sales for the two beers, and then at the end, there is the 12 months I'm going to forecast. So let me start by generating the values I need for the linear regression.

Calculating the basis for regression

In principle I could just do a linear regression on the sales data just as they are, but that would just give me a straight line in 2019, not a forecast that takes into account that the beers sell well in specific seasons of the year. With the forecasting model I've chosen, I will get a forecast that takes into account the seasons and the trend over the years and smooths out irregular outliers.

The first value I need to calculate is the *centered moving average*, so I take my time series code from Listing 15-2 and place it in a with clause named s1. That enables me to select from s1 in Listing 15-3.

Listing 15-3. Calculating centered moving average

```
SQL> with s1 as (
...       /* Listing 15-2 minus order by */
 23  )
 24  select
 25     product_id, mth, ts, yr, mthno, qty
 26   , case
 27        when ts between 7 and 30 then
 28           (nvl(avg(qty) over (
 29              partition by product_id
 30              order by ts
 31              rows between 5 preceding and 6 following
 32           ), 0) + nvl(avg(qty) over (
 33              partition by product_id
 34              order by ts
 35              rows between 6 preceding and 5 following
 36           ), 0)) / 2
 37        else
 38           null
```

```
39     end as cma -- centered moving average
40   from s1
41   order by product_id, mth;
```

What happens here is the following:

- In lines 28–31, I calculate the average quantity sold in a moving window of 12 months `between 5 preceding and 6 following`. That's the monthly average sales measured over a year, but slightly "off center," since I have 5 months before, then the current month, and then 6 months after.

- So in lines 32–26, I calculate another monthly average sales measured over a year, but this time `between 6 preceding and 5 following`, so I'm slightly off center in the other direction.

- Adding these two together and dividing by two (lines 28, 32, and 36) gives me the average of these two "off center" averages, and that is what is called *centered moving average*.

- If I calculated this for all 36 months of my sales data, I would get wrong values at both ends, because they would not be calculated for the entire 12-month periods. Therefore, I use a case structure in lines 26–27 and 37–38 to skip the first 6 months and the last 6 months of the 36 and only calculate `cma` for month numbers 7–30 (that's the `ts`-time series–column).

So when I plot in `cma` on the graph in Figure 15-3, you can see it's a slowly rising line covering the "middle" two years of the sales period. (To keep the graphs clearly separable, from now I'm only showing one of the beers – Reindeer Fuel. At the end of the chapter, I'll show the final graphs for both beers.)

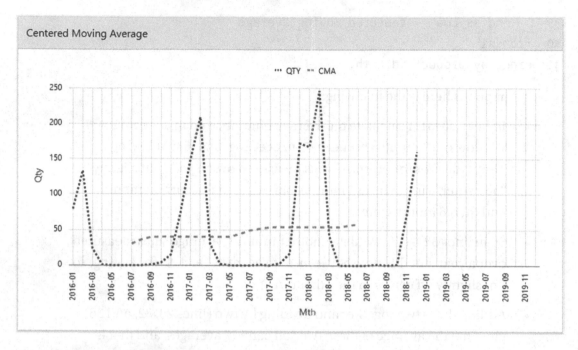

Figure 15-3. *Centered moving average for Reindeer Fuel*

Having calculated cma, I put that calculation into a new with clause named s2 and proceed to calculate *seasonality factor* in Listing 15-4.

Listing 15-4. Calculating seasonality factor

```
SQL> with s1 as (
...      /* Listing 15-2 minus order by */
 23  ), s2 as (
...      /* Listing 15-3 final query minus order by */
 41  )
 42  select
 43     product_id, mth, ts, yr, mthno, qty, cma
 44   , nvl(avg(
 45        case qty
 46           when 0 then 0.0001
 47           else qty
 48        end / nullif(cma, 0)
```

```
49      ) over (
50          partition by product_id, mthno
51      ),0) as s -- seasonality
52  from s2
53  order by product_id, mth;
```

Basically the seasonality factor is how much the monthly sales is higher or lower than the average month. But there's a little more to it than just taking `qty/cma`:

- The model does not like months with zero sales – they will skew the data in later steps and make the forecast wrong, so my little workaround for this in lines 45–48 is to make any zeroes become a very small value instead. In my final result, I'll be rounding to integers anyway, so I will end up forecasting zeroes; I just need to use small values instead of zeroes in the intermediate calculations.

- To avoid potential division by zero errors, in line 48, I use `nullif` to turn any zeroes into `null`. There will also be rows where `cma` itself is `null`, so with this I make sure that the result of the division becomes `null` both where `cma` is `null` and where `cma` is zero.

- The seasonal variations might vary a bit from year to year (different weather, which month contains Easter, and so on), so I want a seasonality factor that is an average over the years, but *by month*. In other words, for January, I want the average seasonality of January 2016, January 2017, and January 2018; for February, the average of all Februaries; and so on. This is accomplished in lines 44 and 49–51 with an analytic `avg` call that partitions by product and `mthno` – which was calculated as `extract(month from mths.mth)`, so it contains 1, 2,...12.

That calculation produces this output (partially reproduced), where you can see that the values of column s (seasonality factor) repeat, so all Januaries have the same value and so on. Note in particular that due to the `avg` being partitioned on `mthno`, s has values also in those months where `cma` is `null` (or zero). This is crucial both for the next step (deseasonalizing) and the final step (reseasonalizing):

PROD	MTH	TS	YR	MTHNO	QTY	CMA	S
4160	2016-01	1	2016	1	79		3.3824
4160	2016-02	2	2016	2	133		4.8771
...							
4160	2017-01	13	2017	1	148	40.3	3.3824
4160	2017-02	14	2017	2	209	40.3	4.8771
...							
4160	2018-01	25	2018	1	167	54.1	3.3824
4160	2018-02	26	2018	2	247	54.1	4.8771
...							
4160	2019-01	37	2019	1			3.3824
4160	2019-02	38	2019	2			4.8771
...							

Armed with a seasonality factor in every month of the time series, once again I put the code in with clause s3 and calculate deseasonalizing in Listing 15-5.

Listing 15-5. Deseasonalizing sales data

```
SQL> with s1 as (
...       /* Listing 15-2 minus order by */
 23 ), s2 as (
...       /* Listing 15-3 final query minus order by */
 41 ), s3 as (
...       /* Listing 15-4 final query minus order by */
 53 )
 54 select
 55     product_id, mth, ts, yr, mthno, qty, cma, s
 56   , case when ts <= 36 then
 57       nvl(
 58         case qty
 59           when 0 then 0.0001
 60           else qty
 61         end / nullif(s, 0)
 62       , 0)
```

```
63     end as des -- deseasonalized
64  from s3
65  order by product_id, mth;
```

Deseasonalizing ("taking the season out of the data") basically just is dividing the quantity with the seasonality factor. Once again I avoid problems with zeroes by turning them into a small value (lines 58–61) and avoid potential division by zero errors with a nullif call in line 61.

In Figure 15-4 you can see that I have values in column des for all 36 months and the line follows more or less the cma line (centered moving average). The more identical the seasonal variations was in each year, the closer the des line will match the cma line.

Mostly the variations here are due to the zero sales that were turned into small values, where you'll see a sharp spike followed by a sharp dip (or vice versa). But since the average of the spike and the dip hits the cma fairly well, it will even out in the next step (as I'll show you). If I had left the zeroes (perhaps turning into null to avoid division by zero), I would have skewed the data and messed up the model.

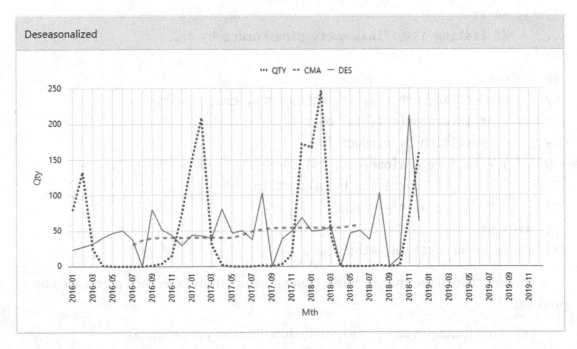

Figure 15-4. *Deseasonalized sales for Reindeer Fuel*

This deseasonalized line on the graph is now representing a somewhat smoothed out version of monthly average sales over a year taking into account seasonal variations averaged over the years. Next step is creating a straight line as closely as possible matching the des line.

Linear regression

As you may have guessed by now, in Listing 15-6, I put the previous calculations into with clause s4 and proceed to perform linear regression.

Listing 15-6. Calculating trend line

```
SQL> with s1 as (
...      /* Listing 15-2 minus order by */
 23  ), s2 as (
...      /* Listing 15-3 final query minus order by */
 41  ), s3 as (
...      /* Listing 15-4 final query minus order by */
 53  ), s4 as (
...      /* Listing 15-5 final query minus order by */
 65  )
 66  select
 67     product_id, mth, ts, yr, mthno, qty, cma, s, des
 68   , regr_intercept(des, ts) over (
 69        partition by product_id
 70     ) + ts * regr_slope(des, ts) over (
 71                 partition by product_id
 72              ) as t -- trend
 73  from s4
 74  order by product_id, mth;
```

I am using two of the analytic linear regression functions here, each partitioned by product:

- Both functions accept two parameters, first the **y** coordinate of the graph and second the **x** coordinate. In my case the des (deseasonalized) value is the y coordinate, while ts (time series) is the x coordinate. I cannot use month directly; it must be a numeric datatype, so ts with a unit of 1 month is perfect.

- Lines 68–70 use `regr_intercept`, which gives me the *interception point* between the y axis and the interpolated straight line. In other words, the y value where x = 0.

- Lines 70–72 use `regr_slope`, which gives me the *slope* of the interpolated straight line. The slope is how much the y value increases (or decreases if negative) when the x value increases by 1. Since my x axis has a unit of 1 month, the slope therefore is how much the graph goes up (or down) per month.

- So in total lines 68–72 calculate the y value where x = 0 (`regr_intercept`) and for each month add the number of months (`ts`) times how much it goes up (or down) per month (`regr_slope`).

Plotted on the graph in Figure 15-5, I have now a straight trend line t that has a value in all 48 months.

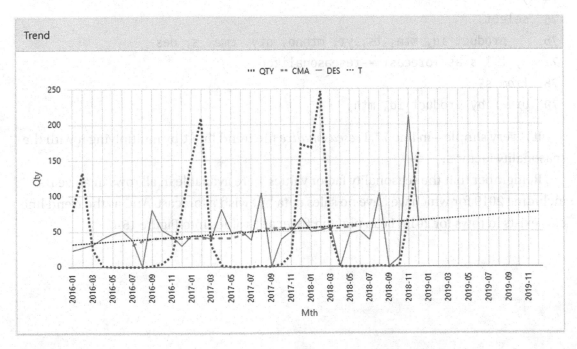

Figure 15-5. *Trend line for Reindeer Fuel by linear regression*

I shove the calculation so far into with clause s5 in Listing 15-7, and I can now do the final step in the forecast.

Listing 15-7. Reseasonalizing trend ➤ forecast

```
SQL> with s1 as (
...      /* Listing 15-2 minus order by */
 23  ), s2 as (
...      /* Listing 15-3 final query minus order by */
 41  ), s3 as (
...      /* Listing 15-4 final query minus order by */
 53  ), s4 as (
...      /* Listing 15-5 final query minus order by */
 65  ), s5 as (
...      /* Listing 15-6 final query minus order by */
 74  )
 75  select
 76     product_id, mth, ts, yr, mthno, qty, cma, s, des
 77   , t * s as forecast --reseasonalized
 78  from s5
 79  order by product_id, mth;
```

It is very simple – in line 77, I *reseasonalize* the trend line t by multiplying it with the seasonality factor s.

Remember that the seasonality factor values were available in all rows in all years, including 2019 for which we have no sales data but wish a forecast. And as the trend line also exists in rows for 2019, I can plot the forecast values into Figure 15-6.

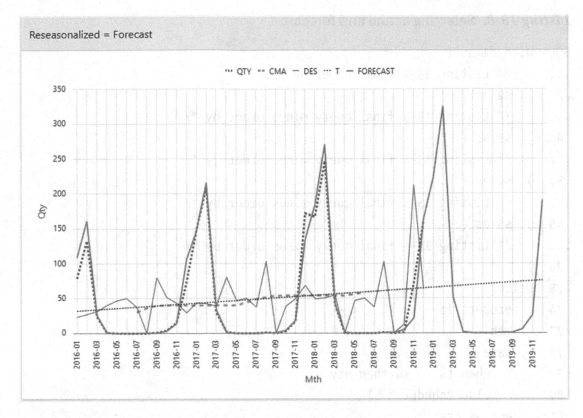

Figure 15-6. *Reseasonalized forecast for Reindeer Fuel*

Having both qty and forecast values plotted in the same graph enables me visually to check if the model fits my data reasonably well. The closer the two lines match in 2016–2018, the more I can trust the forecast in 2019. In this case, it looks like it fits fairly well.

Final forecast

Having satisfied myself that the model looks like it fits my data, I'm going to clean up a little and not retrieve the columns with all the intermediate calculations, but instead in Listing 15-8, I just get the relevant information for showing my users the actual and forecast sales quantity.

Listing 15-8. Selecting actual and forecast

```
SQL> with s1 as (
...       /* Listing 15-2 minus order by */
 23 ), s2 as (
...       /* Listing 15-3 final query minus order by */
 41 ), s3 as (
...       /* Listing 15-4 final query minus order by */
 53 ), s4 as (
...       /* Listing 15-5 final query minus order by */
 65 ), s5 as (
...       /* Listing 15-6 final query minus order by */
 74 )
 75 select
 76     product_id
 77   , mth
 78   , case
 79       when ts <= 36 then qty
 80       else round(t * s)
 81     end as qty
 82   , case
 83       when ts <= 36 then 'Actual'
 84       else 'Forecast'
 85     end as type
 86 from s5
 87 order by product_id, mth;
```

I simply select the product and month, and then I use a case structure twice to give me a qty column and a type column:

- Lines 78–81 give me actual sold quantity for the first 36 months and the forecast (reseasonalized trend) for the last 12 months. As I cannot sell fractional beers, I'm rounding the forecast to integers.

- Lines 82–85 populate the type column with **Actual** for the first 36 months and **Forecast** for the last 12 months to allow me to distinguish what the contents of qty represent.

That way I produce a simpler output:

```
PROD MTH       QTY TYPE
---- -------   ---- --------
4160 2016-01    79 Actual
4160 2016-02   133 Actual
...
4160 2018-11    73 Actual
4160 2018-12   160 Actual
4160 2019-01   222 Forecast
4160 2019-02   325 Forecast
...
4160 2019-11    26 Forecast
4160 2019-12   191 Forecast
7790 2016-01     4 Actual
7790 2016-02     6 Actual
...
7790 2018-11     3 Actual
7790 2018-12     5 Actual
7790 2019-01     1 Forecast
7790 2019-02     7 Forecast
...
7790 2019-11     3 Forecast
7790 2019-12     3 Forecast

96 rows selected.
```

In Figure 15-7 I plot these into a graph, where I show the results for both beers (same as I showed in Figure 15-2, just now with the forecast added in).

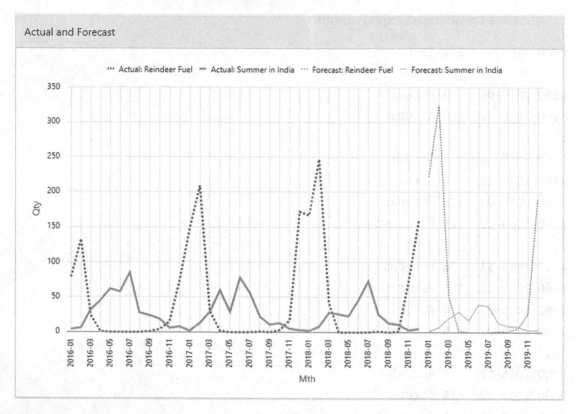

Figure 15-7. *The monthly sales 2016–2018 plus the forecasts for 2019*

For Reindeer Fuel I've shown all the details in the previous pages, and here I only show the actual sales and the 2019 forecast. But even without the details in this graph, you can still visually see that it is a beer selling well in the winter time, it sells a little more each year, and the 2019 forecast graph matches the shape of the other years, just a little higher.

The other beer, Summer in India, sells well in the summertime and sells a little less each year, and the 2019 forecast is shaped like the other years, just a little lower.

All in all, for these two beers, this forecasting model looks quite good; and being entirely developed in SQL with analytic functions, it performs quite well indeed. At the job I mentioned at the start of the chapter, I forecasted 100,000 products by inserting 1.2 million rows to a forecast table using `insert into…select…`in 1½ minute.

Other products with a less nice seasonal variation profile might not fit as well into this forecasting model. This is where you probably need statistical tools instead of plain SQL in order to discover which forecasting models fit best to which products (or whatever you are forecasting).

However, it can still be a nice option to use the tools in a discovery phase, and once you have categorized your products into a handful of different models, maybe it can still make sense then to implement this handful of models using the power of SQL to be able to efficiently process lots of data without needing to pull them out of the database.

Lessons learned

Forecasting is a science, and one small chapter in a book on SQL will not make you a forecasting expert, but even with such a small appetizer on the forecasting topic, I've shown you some things about

- Chaining calculations in multiple `with` clauses as an alternative to nested inline views

- Building time series data with consecutive rows one time unit apart

- Averaging with moving windows and averaging the same period across different years

- Calculating linear regression with `regr_intercept` and `regr_slope`

- Combining these techniques to implement a forecasting model in SQL

Though this chapter has shown just a single forecasting model, this should help you implement other similar time series–based regressions in SQL, if you have the formulas and you have the need for speed and efficiency higher than many external forecasting tools can offer.

CHAPTER 16

Rolling Sums to Forecast Reaching Minimums

If you have a steady consumption rate, it is easy to forecast how far you can go with that rate – for example, if you know your car on average drives 20 kilometers per liter fuel and it has 30 liters left in the tank, you can simply multiply to know that you can drive 600 kilometers before you run out of fuel.

But if the consumption is not steady, you need something else. If the Good Beer Trading Co sells a particular seasonal Christmas beer, it is not simply a steady 100 beers sold per month – June will sell very few of those beers, while December sells hundreds. For such a case, you estimate (perhaps using the techniques of the previous chapter) what you think you are going to sell and store it as a *forecast* or sales budget.

Once you have forecast you are going to sell 150 in January, 100 in February, 250 in March, and so on, you need to figure out that the 400 you have in stock in your inventory will dwindle to 250 by the end of January and to 150 by the end of February and be sold out a little later than the middle of March. Figuring this out is the topic of this chapter.

Inventory, budget, and order

In the Good Beer Trading Co example, I'm going to demonstrate the case of forecasting when the inventory reaches zero (or a minimum) given that I know how many beers are in order (waiting to be picked from the inventory) and how many beers are budgeted to be sold (assumed to be picked at some point).

I'll use month as the time granularity, budgeting sales quantities per month. For this demonstration purpose, I don't need to go to weekly or daily data, but you can easily adapt the methods to finer time granularity if you need it. I will use the data in the tables shown in Figure 16-1.

© Kim Berg Hansen 2020
K. Berg Hansen, *Practical Oracle SQL*, https://doi.org/10.1007/978-1-4842-5617-6_16

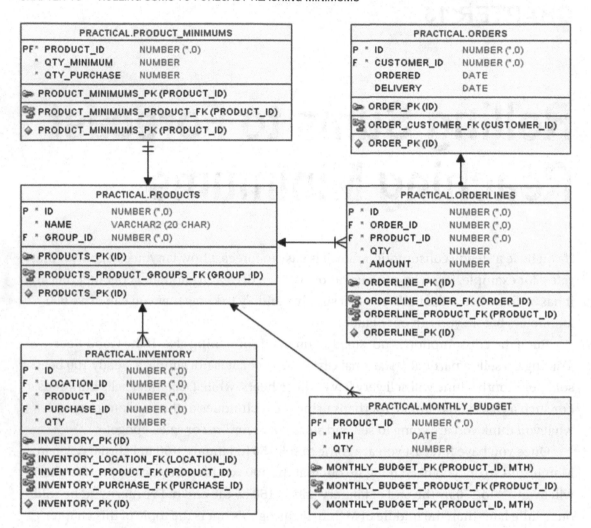

Figure 16-1. *The tables used in the examples of this chapter*

From table `inventory`, I know what quantity of each beer is in stock, table `monthly_budget` shows me the quantity each beer is expected to sell per month, and how much has been ordered (but *not yet* picked and therefore not yet taken from the stock) is in table `orderlines`. Table `product_minimums` I'll get back to later in the chapter.

You'll notice the `inventory` table contains quantities per location (I used the table in the FIFO picking in Chapter 13), but for this purpose, I just need the total quantity in stock per beer. To make that easier, I create the view `inventory_totals` in Listing 16-1 aggregating the inventory per beer.

Listing 16-1. View of total inventory per product

```sql
SQL> create or replace view inventory_totals
  2  as
  3  select
  4      i.product_id
  5  , sum(i.qty) as qty
  6  from inventory i
  7  group by i.product_id;

View INVENTORY_TOTALS created.
```

Similarly for the quantities in order, I do not need specific orderlines. I just need how many of each beer each month, so I aggregate those figures in view monthly_orders in Listing 16-2.

Listing 16-2. View of monthly order totals per product

```sql
SQL> create or replace view monthly_orders
  2  as
  3  select
  4      ol.product_id
  5  , trunc(o.ordered, 'MM') as mth
  6  , sum(ol.qty) as qty
  7  from orders o
  8  join orderlines ol
  9     on ol.order_id = o.id
 10  group by ol.product_id, trunc(o.ordered, 'MM');

View MONTHLY_ORDERS created.
```

Those are the tables and views I'm going to be using; now I'll show the data in them.

The data

I'll use two beers for the examples of this chapter: Der Helle Kumpel and Hazy Pink Cloud. They have the total inventory shown in Listing 16-3.

Listing 16-3. The inventory totals for two products

```
SQL> select it.product_id, p.name, it.qty
  2  from inventory_totals it
  3  join products p
  4      on p.id = it.product_id
  5  where product_id in (6520, 6600)
  6  order by product_id;

PRODUCT_ID  NAME            QTY
6520        Der Helle Kumpel  400
6600        Hazy Pink Cloud   100
```

This is totals in stock as of January 1, 2019. Then I have a monthly sales budget for the year 2019 (Listing 16-4).

Listing 16-4. The 2019 monthly budget for the two beers

```
SQL> select mb.product_id, mb.mth, mb.qty
  2  from monthly_budget mb
  3  where mb.product_id in (6520, 6600)
  4  and mb.mth >= date '2019-01-01'
  5  order by mb.product_id, mb.mth;

PRODUCT_ID  MTH          QTY
6520        2019-01-01   45
6520        2019-02-01   45
6520        2019-03-01   50
...
6520        2019-10-01   50
6520        2019-11-01   40
6520        2019-12-01   40
6600        2019-01-01   20
```

```
6600          2019-02-01   20
6600          2019-03-01   20
...
6600          2019-10-01   20
6600          2019-11-01   20
6600          2019-12-01   20

24 rows selected.
```

Product 6520 is expected to sell a bit more in the summer months, while product 6600 is expected to sell a steady 20 per month.

But I don't just have the expected quantities; I also have in Listing 16-5 the quantities that have already been ordered in the first months of 2019.

Listing 16-5. The current monthly order quantities

```
SQL> select mo.product_id, mo.mth, mo.qty
  2  from monthly_orders mo
  3  where mo.product_id in (6520, 6600)
  4  order by mo.product_id, mo.mth;

PRODUCT_ID   MTH          QTY
6520         2019-01-01   260
6520         2019-02-01   40
6600         2019-01-01   16
6600         2019-02-01   40
```

The thing to note here is that in January, product 6520 has been ordered much more than what was expected.

Given these data, I'll now make some SQL to find out when we run out of beers for those two products.

Accumulating until zero

One of the really useful things you can do with analytic functions is the rolling (accumulated) sum that I've shown before. In Listing 16-6, I use it again.

Listing 16-6. Accumulating quantities

```
SQL> select
  2     mb.product_id as p_id, mb.mth
  3   , mb.qty b_qty, mo.qty o_qty
  4   , greatest(mb.qty, nvl(mo.qty, 0)) as qty
  5   , sum(greatest(mb.qty, nvl(mo.qty, 0))) over (
  6         partition by mb.product_id
  7         order by mb.mth
  8         rows between unbounded preceding and current row
  9     ) as acc_qty
 10  from monthly_budget mb
 11  left outer join monthly_orders mo
 12     on mo.product_id = mb.product_id
 13     and mo.mth = mb.mth
 14  where mb.product_id in (6520, 6600)
 15  and mb.mth >= date '2019-01-01'
 16  order by mb.product_id, mb.mth;
```

In line 4, I calculate the monthly quantity as whichever is the greatest of *either* the budgeted quantity *or* the ordered quantity. In the following output, you see January for product 6520 has o_qty as the greatest (making qty = 260), while January for product 6600 has b_qty as the greatest (making qty = 20.)

The idea is that if the ordered quantity is the smallest, there hasn't yet been orders to match the budget, but it's still expected to rise until budget is reached. But when the ordered quantity is the greatest, I know the budget has been surpassed, so I don't expect it to become greater yet.

So this quantity is then what I accumulate with the analytic sum in lines 5–9, so I end up with column acc_qty that shows me accumulated how much I expect to pick from the inventory:

P_ID	MTH	B_QTY	O_QTY	QTY	ACC_QTY
6520	2019-01-01	45	260	260	260
6520	2019-02-01	45	40	45	305
6520	2019-03-01	50		50	355
...					

6520	2019-11-01	40		40	775
6520	2019-12-01	40		40	815
6600	2019-01-01	20	16	20	20
6600	2019-02-01	20	40	40	60
6600	2019-03-01	20		20	80
...					
6600	2019-11-01	20		20	240
6600	2019-12-01	20		20	260

In Listing 16-7, I use this accumulated quantity to calculate what's the expected inventory for each month (if I don't restock along the way).

Listing 16-7. Dwindling inventory

```
SQL> select
  2     mb.product_id as p_id, mb.mth
  3   , greatest(mb.qty, nvl(mo.qty, 0)) as qty
  4   , greatest(
  5       it.qty - nvl(sum(
  6         greatest(mb.qty, nvl(mo.qty, 0))
  7       ) over (
  8         partition by mb.product_id
  9         order by mb.mth
 10         rows between unbounded preceding and 1 preceding
 11       ), 0)
 12   , 0
 13   ) as inv_begin
 14   , greatest(
 15       it.qty - sum(
 16         greatest(mb.qty, nvl(mo.qty, 0))
 17       ) over (
 18         partition by mb.product_id
 19         order by mb.mth
 20         rows between unbounded preceding and current row
 21       )
 22   , 0
 23   ) as inv_end
```

```
24   from monthly_budget mb
25   left outer join monthly_orders mo
26      on mo.product_id = mb.product_id
27      and mo.mth = mb.mth
28   join inventory_totals it
29      on it.product_id = mb.product_id
30   where mb.product_id in (6520, 6600)
31   and mb.mth >= date '2019-01-01'
32   order by mb.product_id, mb.mth;
```

Lines 4–13 calculate how much quantity was in stock at the beginning of the month, while lines 14–23 calculate how much at the end of the month:

P_ID	MTH	QTY	INV_BEGIN	INV_END
6520	2019-01-01	260	400	140
6520	2019-02-01	45	140	95
6520	2019-03-01	50	95	45
6520	2019-04-01	50	45	0
6520	2019-05-01	55	0	0
...				
6600	2019-01-01	20	100	80
6600	2019-02-01	40	80	40
6600	2019-03-01	20	40	20
6600	2019-04-01	20	20	0
6600	2019-05-01	20	0	0
...				

You see how the inventory dwindles until it reaches zero. As I use month for time granularity, in principle I can only state that the inventory will reach zero at some point during that month. But if I assume that the budgeted sales will be evenly distributed throughout the month, I can also in Listing 16-8 make a *guesstimation* of which day that zero will be reached.

Listing 16-8. Estimating when zero is reached

```
SQL> select
  2      product_id as p_id, mth, inv_begin, inv_end
  3    , trunc(
```

```
 4        mth + numtodsinterval(
 5                   (add_months(mth, 1) - 1 - mth) * inv_begin / qty
 6                 , 'day'
 7                 )
 8      ) as zero_day
 9   from (
...
41   )
42   where inv_begin > 0 and inv_end = 0
43   order by product_id;
```

I wrap Listing 16-7 in an inline view and use `inv_begin` / `qty` in line 5 to figure out how large a fraction of the estimated monthly sales can be fulfilled by the inventory at hand at the beginning of the month. When I assume evenly distributed sales, this is then the fraction of the number of days in the month that I have sufficient stock for.

Filtering in line 42 gives me as output just the rows where the inventory becomes zero:

P_ID	MTH	INV_BEGIN	INV_END	ZERO_DAY
6520	2019-04-01	45	0	2019-04-27
6600	2019-04-01	20	0	2019-04-30

In reality, however, I wouldn't let the inventory reach zero. I'd set up a minimum quantity that I mustn't get below of (as a buffer in case I underestimated sales), and every time I get to the minimum quantity, I must buy more beer and restock the inventory.

Restocking when minimum reached

In table `product_minimums`, I have parameters for the inventory handling of each product. Listing 16-9 shows the table content for the two beers I use for demonstration.

Listing 16-9. Product minimum restocking parameters

```
SQL> select product_id, qty_minimum, qty_purchase
  2    from product_minimums pm
  3   where pm.product_id in (6520, 6600)
  4   order by pm.product_id;
```

Column qty_minimum is my inventory buffer – I plan that the inventory should never get below this. Column qty_purchase is the number of beers I buy every time I restock the inventory:

PRODUCT_ID	QTY_MINIMUM	QTY_PURCHASE
6520	100	400
6600	30	100

With this I am ready to write SQL that can show me when I need to purchase more beer and restock throughout 2019.

This is not simply done with analytic functions, since I cannot use the result of an analytic function inside the analytic function itself to add more quantity. This would mean an unsupported type of recursive function call; it cannot be done. But I can do it with **recursive subquery factoring** instead of analytic functions as shown in Listing 16-10.

Listing 16-10. Restocking when a minimum is reached

```
SQL> with mb_recur(
  2      product_id, mth, qty, inv_begin, date_purch
  3    , p_qty, inv_end, qty_minimum, qty_purchase
  4  ) as (
  5      select
  6        it.product_id
  7      , date '2018-12-01' as mth
  8      , 0 as qty
  9      , 0 as inv_begin
 10      , cast(null as date) as date_purch
 11      , 0 as p_qty
 12      , it.qty as inv_end
 13      , pm.qty_minimum
 14      , pm.qty_purchase
 15      from inventory_totals it
 16      join product_minimums pm
 17        on pm.product_id = it.product_id
 18      where it.product_id in (6520, 6600)
 19  union all
 20      select
```

```
21        mb.product_id
22      , mb.mth
23      , greatest(mb.qty, nvl(mo.qty, 0)) as qty
24      , mbr.inv_end as inv_begin
25      , case
26          when mbr.inv_end - greatest(mb.qty, nvl(mo.qty, 0))
27                  < mbr.qty_minimum
28          then
29              trunc(
30                mb.mth
31              + numtodsinterval(
32                  (add_months(mb.mth, 1) - 1 - mb.mth)
33                    * (mbr.inv_end - mbr.qty_minimum)
34                    / mb.qty
35                  , 'day'
36                )
37            )
38        end as date_purch
39      , case
40          when mbr.inv_end - greatest(mb.qty, nvl(mo.qty, 0))
41                  < mbr.qty_minimum
42          then mbr.qty_purchase
43        end as p_qty
44      , mbr.inv_end - greatest(mb.qty, nvl(mo.qty, 0))
45        + case
46            when mbr.inv_end - greatest(mb.qty, nvl(mo.qty, 0))
47                    < mbr.qty_minimum
48            then mbr.qty_purchase
49            else 0
50          end as inv_end
51      , mbr.qty_minimum
52      , mbr.qty_purchase
53    from mb_recur mbr
54    join monthly_budget mb
55      on mb.product_id = mbr.product_id
56      and mb.mth = add_months(mbr.mth, 1)
```

```
57    left outer join monthly_orders mo
58        on mo.product_id = mb.product_id
59        and mo.mth = mb.mth
60 )
61 select
62    product_id as p_id, mth, qty, inv_begin
63  , date_purch, p_qty, inv_end
64 from mb_recur
65 where mth >= date '2019-01-01'
66 and p_qty is not null
67 order by product_id, mth;
```

I start in lines 5–18 by setting up one row per product containing what is the inventory when I start, along with the parameters for minimum quantity and how much to purchase. I set this row as being in December 2018 with the inventory in the inv_end column – that way it will function as a "primer" row for the recursive part of the query in lines 20–59.

In the recursive part I do:

- Join to the monthly budget for the *next* month in line 56. The first iteration here will find January 2019 (since my "primer" row was December 2018), and then each iteration will find the next month until there are no more budget rows.

- The inv_begin of this next month in the iteration is then equal to the inv_end of the previous month, so that's a simple assignment in line 24.

- Lines 44–50 calculate the inv_end, which is the beginning inventory (previous inv_end) *minus* the quantity picked that month *plus* a possible restocking. If the beginning inventory minus the quantity would become less than the minimum, I add the quantity I will be purchasing for restocking.

- To show on the output how much I need to purchase for restocking, I separate this case structure out in lines 39–43.

- And in lines 25–28, I use the same case condition to calculate an estimated date of the month where the restocking by purchasing more beer should take place.

Line 65 removes the "primer" rows from the output (they are not interesting), and line 66 gives me just those months where I need to restock:

P_ID	MTH	QTY	INV_BEGIN	DATE_PURCH	P_QTY	INV_END
6520	2019-02-01	45	140	2019-02-25	400	495
6520	2019-10-01	50	115	2019-10-10	400	465
6600	2019-03-01	20	40	2019-03-16	100	120
6600	2019-08-01	20	40	2019-08-16	100	120

I am now able to plan when I need to purchase more beers to restock the inventory.

In Listing 16-10, I used recursive subquery factoring. The way I did it means that for the budget and orders, there will be a series of repeated small lookups to the tables for each month. Depending on circumstances, this might be perfectly fine, but in other cases, it could be bad for performance.

Listing 16-11 shows an alternative method of recursion (or rather, *iteration*) with the model clause instead, where a different access plan can be used by the optimizer.

Listing 16-11. Restocking with model clause

```
SQL> select
  2      product_id as p_id, mth, qty, inv_begin
  3    , date_purch, p_qty, inv_end
  4    from (
  5      select *
  6      from monthly_budget mb
  7      left outer join monthly_orders mo
  8        on mo.product_id = mb.product_id
  9        and mo.mth = mb.mth
 10      join inventory_totals it
 11        on it.product_id = mb.product_id
 12      join product_minimums pm
 13        on pm.product_id = mb.product_id
 14      where mb.product_id in (6520, 6600)
 15      and mb.mth >= date '2019-01-01'
 16      model
 17      partition by (mb.product_id)
```

```
18      dimension by (
19          row_number() over (
20              partition by mb.product_id order by mb.mth
21          ) - 1 as rn
22      )
23      measures (
24          mb.mth
25        , greatest(mb.qty, nvl(mo.qty, 0)) as qty
26        , 0 as inv_begin
27        , cast(null as date) as date_purch
28        , 0 as p_qty
29        , 0 as inv_end
30        , it.qty as inv_orig
31        , pm.qty_minimum
32        , pm.qty_purchase
33      )
34      rules sequential order iterate (12) (
35          inv_begin[iteration_number]
36            = nvl(inv_end[iteration_number-1], inv_orig[cv()])
37        , p_qty[iteration_number]
38            = case
39                  when inv_begin[cv()] - qty[cv()]
40                      < qty_minimum[cv()]
41                  then qty_purchase[cv()]
42              end
43        , date_purch[iteration_number]
44            = case
45                  when p_qty[cv()] is not null
46                  then
47                      trunc(
48                          mth[cv()]
49                        + numtodsinterval(
50                              (add_months(mth[cv()], 1) - 1 - mth[cv()])
51                              * (inv_begin[cv()] - qty_minimum[cv()])
52                              / qty[cv()]
```

```
53                        , 'day'
54                    )
55                )
56            end
57        , inv_end[iteration_number]
58            = inv_begin[cv()] + nvl(p_qty[cv()], 0) - qty[cv()]
59        )
60    )
61    where p_qty is not null
62    order by product_id, mth;
```

With this method I do not need "primer" rows and repeated monthly lookups. Instead I grab all the data I need in one go in lines 5–15, rather like if I was using analytic functions. And then I can use model:

- Lines 19–21 create a consecutive numbering that I can use as dimension ("index") in my measures. I deliberately make it have the values 0–11 instead of 1–12, because that fits how iteration_number is filled when using iteration.

- In the measures in lines 24–32, I set up the "variables" I need to work with.

- In the rules clause, I can then perform all my calculations. In line 34, I specify that I want my calculations to be performed in the order I have typed them, and they should be performed 12 times. That means that within each of the 12 iterations, I can use the pseudocolumn iteration_number, and it will increase from 0 to 11.

- The first rule to be executed is lines 35–36, where I set inv_begin to the inv_end of the previous month (in the first iteration, this will be null, so with nvl I set it to the original inventory in the first month).

- If the inventory minus the quantity is less than the minimum, then in lines 37–42, I set p_qty to the quantity I need to purchase.

- If I *did* find a p_qty (line 45), the rule in lines 43–56 calculates the day I need to purchase and restock.

- And lines 57–68 calculate the inv_end by using the other measures.

The 12 iterations and calculations are quite similar to what I did in the recursive subquery factoring, except that I use measures indexed by a dimension where the data in those measures have all been filled initially before I start iterating and calculating.

This method will for some cases enable more efficient access of the tables – but at the cost of using more memory to keep all the data and work with them in the `model` clause (potentially needing to spill some to disk if you have huge amounts of data here.) Whether Listing 16-10 or 16-11 is the best will depend on the case – you'll need to test the methods yourself.

Lessons learned

Analytic functions are extremely useful and can solve a lot of things, including rolling sums to find when you reach some minimum. But it cannot do all, so in this chapter, I showed you a mix of

- Subtracting a rolling sum from a starting figure to discover when a minimum (or zero) has been reached

- Using recursive subquery to repeatedly replenish the dwindling figure whenever minimum has been reached

- Using the model clause to accomplish the same with an alternative data access plan

Though it's a mix of techniques, all in all they should help you solve similar cases in the future.

PART III

Row Pattern Matching

CHAPTER 17

Up-and-Down Patterns

Using `match_recognize` is also known as *row pattern matching* for a reason – it is very applicable for situations where you have data nicely ordered in, for example, a time series that can be depicted with a value on the y axis and the time on the x axis of a graph. Visually on a graph is an easy way for us humans to look for patterns – `match_recognize` can do the same with SQL.

It doesn't necessarily have to be time on the x axis, and there could be multiple values on the y axis – the thing to remember is that if you as human would visualize something on line graphs and look for patterns on the graphs, you can code SQL to go through the data a lot faster than your eyes can spot patterns visually.

This chapter exemplifies this approach step by step, so that at the end you can apply the technique for similar pattern searching on other types of data.

The stock ticker example

In the Oracle Data Warehousing Guide, pattern matching examples are given using stock ticker data, because they are a nice example of data with a value that changes over time, where analysts look for specific patterns like V and W shapes that can indicate if it's time to buy or sell shares. I'll do the same.

In the `practical` schema, I have created the tables shown in Figure 17-1 for storing information on stock and their prices. The examples in the chapter only concern themselves with the `ticker` table, but for completeness, the `stock` table is created too.

K. Berg Hansen, *Practical Oracle SQL*, https://doi.org/10.1007/978-1-4842-5617-6_17

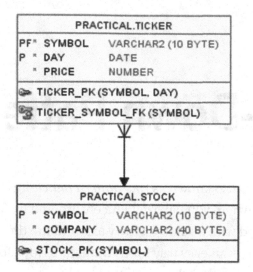

Figure 17-1.   *The ticker table used in this chapter*

I have created a fictional stock symbol BEER for my Good Beer Trading Co. In the ticker table, I've inserted the end-of-day stock prices for three weeks of stock trading in April 2019, depicted on the graph in Figure 17-2.

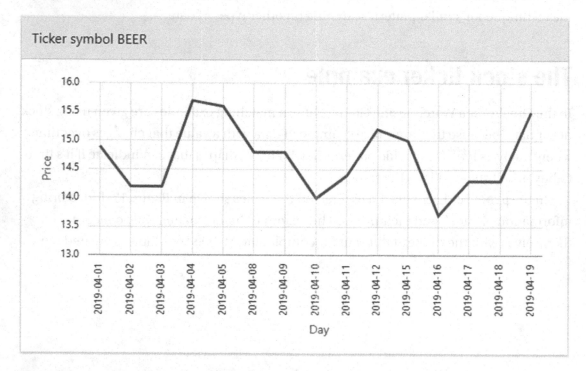

Figure 17-2.   *Graphical depiction of the data in the TICKER table*

Those 15 days of stock prices will be the basis for my walk-through of pattern matching for up-and-down patterns.

Classifying downs and ups

When developing a pattern matching query, I typically start simple.

Almost always I'll know beforehand what I want to partition by, as well as the ordering the data needs to be in for the pattern matching to make sense. For example, for the stock ticker data, I want to look for patterns within each symbol value separately, so I will use partition by for that purpose (this data only contains a single symbol, but there might have been more). And the patterns I'm looking for deal with how the data changes over time, so I do order by the day column (within each symbol).

Then I build my first skeleton query (shown in Listing 17-1), where I define how I want my rows to be classified and have the simplest possible pattern enabling me to test if my definitions are as I want them.

Listing 17-1. Classifying the rows

```
SQL> select *
  2   from ticker
  3   match_recognize (
  4     partition by symbol
  5     order by day
  6     measures
  7       match_number() as match
  8     , classifier()   as class
  9     , prev(price)    as prev
 10     all rows per match
 11     pattern (
 12       down | up
 13     )
 14     define
 15       down as price < prev(price)
 16     , up   as price > prev(price)
 17   )
 18   order by symbol, day;
```

Apart from the `partition` by and `order` by, I like to go over the clauses from the bottom going up – that makes more sense to me.

So in lines 15 and 16, I am defining that if the price in a row is less than the price in the previous row, the row is to be classified as a `down` row, but if the price is greater than the previous, the row is to be classified as an `up` row.

The pattern in row 12 is as simple as possible – a match consists of a single row that is either a `down` row or an `up` row (the | sign is used for logical *or* in the `pattern`.) This is of course not the pattern I will end up with; it is merely a convenient pattern to test if my classification definitions give me what I want.

Since my pattern in this case only gives a single row for each match, I'd get the same number of rows in my output if I chose one `row` `per` `match` in line 10 instead of the `all` `rows` `per` `match` I use here. But a difference is that one `row` would only output the columns used in `partition` and `order` by as well as the measures, while `all` `rows` output all columns of the table. That helps for debugging while developing, even if I know that my final desired result will use one `row` `per` `match`.

Lines 7–9 define what measures I want in the output (besides the table columns). Function `match_number()` shows me which rows belong together in a match (in this case always single rows in a match, but later that will change). Function `classifier()` shows me which classification definition the row got, which is what I want to see if I got right. And lastly in line 9, I output the previous price, so I can double-check that the correlation between price and previous price matches the classification.

Running the query in Listing 17-1 gives this output:

SYMBOL	DAY	MATCH	CLASS	PREV	PRICE
BEER	2019-04-02	1	DOWN	14.9	14.2
BEER	2019-04-04	2	UP	14.2	15.7
BEER	2019-04-05	3	DOWN	15.7	15.6
BEER	2019-04-08	4	DOWN	15.6	14.8
BEER	2019-04-10	5	DOWN	14.8	14
BEER	2019-04-11	6	UP	14	14.4
BEER	2019-04-12	7	UP	14.4	15.2
BEER	2019-04-15	8	DOWN	15.2	15
BEER	2019-04-16	9	DOWN	15	13.7
BEER	2019-04-17	10	UP	13.7	14.3
BEER	2019-04-19	11	UP	14.3	15.5

I can see that my rows are classified correctly according to the definition I made. But I notice I'm not really matching all rows here, only 11 out of 15. For one thing I am not finding the rows where the price is *equal* to the previous price. So I try changing my definitions in lines 15 and 16 to use less-than-or-equal and greater-than-or-equal:

```
...
15        down as price <= prev(price)
16      , up   as price >= prev(price)
...
```

SYMBOL	DAY	MATCH	CLASS	PREV	PRICE
BEER	2019-04-02	1	DOWN	14.9	14.2
BEER	2019-04-03	2	DOWN	14.2	14.2
BEER	2019-04-04	3	UP	14.2	15.7
BEER	2019-04-05	4	DOWN	15.7	15.6
BEER	2019-04-08	5	DOWN	15.6	14.8
BEER	2019-04-09	6	DOWN	14.8	14.8
BEER	2019-04-10	7	DOWN	14.8	14
BEER	2019-04-11	8	UP	14	14.4
BEER	2019-04-12	9	UP	14.4	15.2
BEER	2019-04-15	10	DOWN	15.2	15
BEER	2019-04-16	11	DOWN	15	13.7
BEER	2019-04-17	12	UP	13.7	14.3
BEER	2019-04-18	13	DOWN	14.3	14.3
BEER	2019-04-19	14	UP	14.3	15.5

I got more rows in my output now; those rows with a price equal to the previous price are included. But it is maybe not the best idea, since looking at match numbers 12, 13, and 14, that is definitely an *upward*-going trend on the graph, but my definition has classified the row in match 13 as DOWN.

My problem is that rows with an unchanged price potentially match *both* of my definitions, so with the simple *or* pattern I have used, such rows will be classified as the first classifier in the pattern that evaluates to true. This may not always be a problem as I'll show later, but for now I will try changing my definitions to be mutually exclusive by adding a same classification (remembering to add it to the *or* pattern):

```
...
11    pattern (
12       down | up | same
13    )
14    define
15       down as price < prev(price)
16     , up   as price > prev(price)
17     , same as price = prev(price)
...
```

And I get the same rows as the last output, just this time classified three ways: DOWN, UP, and SAME:

SYMBOL	DAY	MATCH	CLASS	PREV	PRICE
BEER	2019-04-02	1	DOWN	14.9	14.2
BEER	2019-04-03	2	SAME	14.2	14.2
BEER	2019-04-04	3	UP	14.2	15.7
BEER	2019-04-05	4	DOWN	15.7	15.6
BEER	2019-04-08	5	DOWN	15.6	14.8
BEER	2019-04-09	6	SAME	14.8	14.8
BEER	2019-04-10	7	DOWN	14.8	14
BEER	2019-04-11	8	UP	14	14.4
BEER	2019-04-12	9	UP	14.4	15.2
BEER	2019-04-15	10	DOWN	15.2	15
BEER	2019-04-16	11	DOWN	15	13.7
BEER	2019-04-17	12	UP	13.7	14.3
BEER	2019-04-18	13	SAME	14.3	14.3
BEER	2019-04-19	14	UP	14.3	15.5

I'm still not entirely happy, as I'm not seeing the very first row in the output. Since it has no previous row, it can never satisfy any of the three definitions, so how to handle that? It is fairly easy by adding a fourth classification to the pattern in line 12:

```
...
12       down | up | same | strt
...
```

Now you'll be expecting me to add `strt` to the definitions in the `define` clause, but that is not needed here. If the pattern matching hits a definition in the pattern that is not defined, it is simply assumed always to be true. So the first row cannot match any of the three defined classifications, and the matching then attempts to see if it matches `strt`, and it does, since any row can do that.

Therefore I see classifier `strt` for the first row in the output, which now contains all 15 rows:

SYMBOL	DAY	MATCH	CLASS	PREV	PRICE
BEER	2019-04-01	1	STRT		14.9
BEER	2019-04-02	2	DOWN	14.9	14.2
BEER	2019-04-03	3	SAME	14.2	14.2
BEER	2019-04-04	4	UP	14.2	15.7
BEER	2019-04-05	5	DOWN	15.7	15.6
BEER	2019-04-08	6	DOWN	15.6	14.8
BEER	2019-04-09	7	SAME	14.8	14.8
BEER	2019-04-10	8	DOWN	14.8	14
BEER	2019-04-11	9	UP	14	14.4
BEER	2019-04-12	10	UP	14.4	15.2
BEER	2019-04-15	11	DOWN	15.2	15
BEER	2019-04-16	12	DOWN	15	13.7
BEER	2019-04-17	13	UP	13.7	14.3
BEER	2019-04-18	14	SAME	14.3	14.3
BEER	2019-04-19	15	UP	14.3	15.5

A thing to note is that it *does* matter where in the `pattern` I place such an undefined classification. For example, I could have placed it at the beginning of my *or* list of classifications:

```
...
12          strt | down | up | same
...
```

As the matching is lazy and short circuit evaluates the pattern, it'll begin by seeing if the row matches the definition of `strt`, which is undefined, and therefore any row matches it, so I'm getting an immediate match, and `down`, `up,` and `same` are never evaluated. I get an output that isn't very helpful:

SYMBOL	DAY	MATCH	CLASS	PREV	PRICE
BEER	2019-04-01	1	STRT		14.9
BEER	2019-04-02	2	STRT	14.9	14.2
BEER	2019-04-03	3	STRT	14.2	14.2
BEER	2019-04-04	4	STRT	14.2	15.7
BEER	2019-04-05	5	STRT	15.7	15.6
BEER	2019-04-08	6	STRT	15.6	14.8
BEER	2019-04-09	7	STRT	14.8	14.8
BEER	2019-04-10	8	STRT	14.8	14
BEER	2019-04-11	9	STRT	14	14.4
BEER	2019-04-12	10	STRT	14.4	15.2
BEER	2019-04-15	11	STRT	15.2	15
BEER	2019-04-16	12	STRT	15	13.7
BEER	2019-04-17	13	STRT	13.7	14.3
BEER	2019-04-18	14	STRT	14.3	14.3
BEER	2019-04-19	15	STRT	14.3	15.5

But I'm reasonably happy with the query so far, classifying my rows into down, up, same, and strt – it's now time to start using these classifications for some pattern matching.

Downs + ups = V shapes

By now I've made the definitions down, up, and same – it's time to put those together in a pattern to look for specific patterns of rows. I'd like to find where the price is going down (or staying the same within a downward slope) for a period, followed by going up (or staying the same within an upward slope) for a period – in other words a V shape in the graph.

As discussed in the previous chapter, syntax for the pattern clause is very similar to regular expressions, so a period of at least one down-or-same price can be defined as (down | same)+ and then followed by (up | same)+ for a period of at least one up-or-same price, leading to the pattern shown in line 12 of Listing 17-2.

Listing 17-2. Searching for V shapes

```
SQL> select *
  2  from ticker
  3  match_recognize (
  4    partition by symbol
  5    order by day
  6    measures
  7      match_number() as match
  8    , classifier()   as class
  9    , prev(price)     as prev
 10    all rows per match
 11    pattern (
 12      (down | same)+ (up | same)+
 13    )
 14    define
 15      down as price < prev(price)
 16    , up   as price > prev(price)
 17    , same as price = prev(price)
 18  )
 19  order by symbol, day;
```

The output no longer has a unique match_number() for each row as in all the previous queries; this time I get three distinct matches, one for each of the three V shapes in the graph:

SYMBOL	DAY	MATCH	CLASS	PREV	PRICE
BEER	2019-04-02	1	DOWN	14.9	14.2
BEER	2019-04-03	1	SAME	14.2	14.2
BEER	2019-04-04	1	UP	14.2	15.7
BEER	2019-04-05	2	DOWN	15.7	15.6
BEER	2019-04-08	2	DOWN	15.6	14.8
BEER	2019-04-09	2	SAME	14.8	14.8
BEER	2019-04-10	2	DOWN	14.8	14
BEER	2019-04-11	2	UP	14	14.4
BEER	2019-04-12	2	UP	14.4	15.2
BEER	2019-04-15	3	DOWN	15.2	15

BEER	2019-04-16	3	DOWN	15	13.7
BEER	2019-04-17	3	UP	13.7	14.3
BEER	2019-04-18	3	SAME	14.3	14.3
BEER	2019-04-19	3	UP	14.3	15.5

Having a pattern now that matches multiple rows, it makes sense to condense the output to show me one row per match, like in Listing 17-3 in line 11. But then I need some other changes as well.

In the measures, I now use navigational functions first and last in lines 8–9 to get the first and last day of each match, and I use aggregate count in line 10 to find how many days each match covers.

Using one row per match, I also no longer get all columns in the output; here I only get what I use in partition by as well as all the measures, which means that in the order by in line 20, I cannot use column day, but need to use measure first_day.

Listing 17-3. Output a single row for each match

```
SQL> select *
  2  from ticker
  3  match_recognize (
  4     partition by symbol
  5     order by day
  6     measures
  7       match_number() as match
  8     , first(day)     as first_day
  9     , last(day)      as last_day
 10     , count(*)       as days
 11     one row per match
 12     pattern (
 13        (down | same)+ (up | same)+
 14     )
 15     define
 16        down as price < prev(price)
 17      , up   as price > prev(price)
 18      , same as price = prev(price)
 19  )
 20  order by symbol, first_day;
```

My output is now condensed to a single row with data for each of the three V shapes in the graph:

SYMBOL	MATCH	FIRST_DAY	LAST_DAY	DAYS
BEER	1	2019-04-02	2019-04-04	3
BEER	2	2019-04-05	2019-04-12	6
BEER	3	2019-04-15	2019-04-19	5

But hang on; I'm not quite happy with this – each matched V shape seems to start a day too late? When I mark out the three matches on the graph in Figure 17-3, it is quite clear I'm not getting the entire V shape.

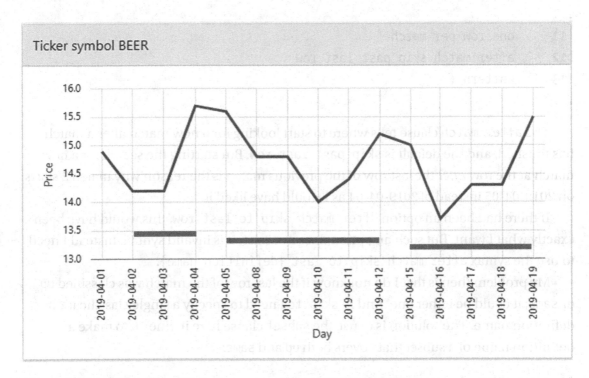

Figure 17-3. *The three V shapes not quite entirely matched*

OK, I can try adding a STRT to my pattern to match any row as the beginning of the V shape. I simply add that to my `pattern` in line 13:

```
...
13        strt (down | same)+ (up | same)+
...
```

And it helps for the first match, but not the second and third:

SYMBOL	MATCH	FIRST_DAY	LAST_DAY	DAYS
BEER	1	2019-04-01	2019-04-04	4
BEER	2	2019-04-05	2019-04-12	6
BEER	3	2019-04-15	2019-04-19	5

The reason is that I have not defined what `match_recognize` should do after it has found a match – where should it start looking for the next match. When I do not specify anything, it defaults to jumping to the row *right after* the match and starts looking there. It behaves just as if I had specified this line 12 in the query:

```
...
11      one row per match
12      after match skip past last row
13      pattern (
...
```

The `after match` clause tells where to start looking for a new match after a match has finished, and the default is `skip past last row`. But starting the search for a new match at the row *after* the last row of the previous match is the reason why match 2 starts on 2019-04-05 instead of 2019-04-04 as I would have liked it.

If there had been an option `after match skip to last row`, this would have been exactly what I want. But such an option does not exist; it is invalid syntax. Instead I need to use the syntax `after match skip to last {definition name}`.

My problem then is that I do not know if the last row of the match was classified `up` or `same`; it could be either one. And in `skip to` I need to specify a single classification definition name. The solution is to use the `subset` clause here in line 16 to make a definition name of a subset that covers both `up` and `same`:

```
...
11      one row per match
12      after match skip to last up_or_same
13      pattern (
14         strt (down | same)+ (up | same)+
15      )
16      subset up_or_same = (up, same)
```

```
17    define
18        down as price < prev(price)
19      , up   as price > prev(price)
20      , same as price = prev(price)
21  )
22  order by symbol, first_day;
```

Using the subset up_or_same in the after match skip to last clause in line 12 gives me the desired effect, which is that a search for a new match is begun on the *same* row as the last row of the previous match. This means that the last day of one match is also included in the next match as the first day, as seen here in the output and in Figure 17-4:

SYMBOL	MATCH	FIRST_DAY	LAST_DAY	DAYS
BEER	1	2019-04-01	2019-04-04	4
BEER	2	2019-04-04	2019-04-12	7
BEER	3	2019-04-12	2019-04-19	6

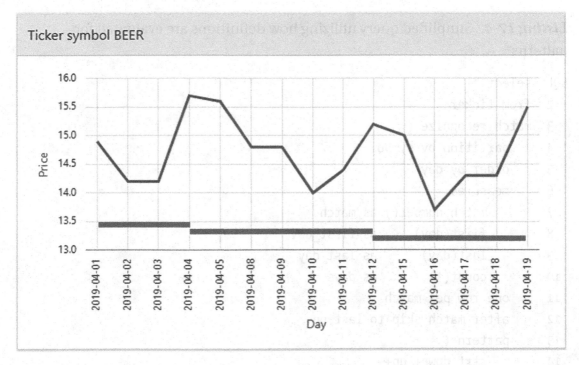

Figure 17-4. *The three V shapes entirely matched*

Revisiting if SAME is needed

This is nice that I could achieve my desired pattern matching using the three definitions down, up, and same and then a subset up_or_same. But could it be simplified?

Remember in the beginning of the chapter I tried using less-than-or-equal and greater-than-or-equal:

```
...
15        down as price <= prev(price)
16      , up   as price >= prev(price)
...
```

This was not working well when I simply was classifying single rows. But I promised to show that this is not always a problem – it depends on the pattern I use.

I can rewrite the query so it looks like Listing 17-4. Here I am not using any same definition, but only down and up in lines 17–18 – notice both are using -or-equal variants of less-than and greater-than. That also means I can simplify the pattern in line 14 and avoid the use of a subset, and then line 12 simply skips to last up.

Listing 17-4. Simplified query utilizing how definitions are evaluated for patterns

```
SQL> select *
  2  from ticker
  3  match_recognize (
  4     partition by symbol
  5     order by day
  6     measures
  7       match_number() as match
  8     , first(day)     as first_day
  9     , last(day)      as last_day
 10     , count(*)       as days
 11     one row per match
 12     after match skip to last up
 13     pattern (
 14       strt down+ up+
 15     )
 16     define
```

```
17        down as price <= prev(price)
18      , up   as price >= prev(price)
19  )
20  order by symbol, first_day;
```

The simplified Listing 17-4 gives me exactly the same desired result as I had before:

SYMBOL	MATCH	FIRST_DAY	LAST_DAY	DAYS
BEER	1	2019-04-01	2019-04-04	4
BEER	2	2019-04-04	2019-04-12	7
BEER	3	2019-04-12	2019-04-19	6

Now how did it do that? Why do I not seem to have the problem from the beginning of the chapter, where the row on 2019-04-18 incorrectly was classified as down? To find out, it helps to go back and see all rows per match (very often a good trick when debugging match_recognize) in line 10 of Listing 17-5.

Listing 17-5. Seeing all rows of the simplified query

```
SQL> select *
  2  from ticker
  3  match_recognize (
  4      partition by symbol
  5      order by day
  6      measures
  7        match_number() as match
  8      , classifier()   as class
  9      , prev(price)    as prev
 10      all rows per match
 11      after match skip to last up
 12      pattern (
 13        strt down+ up+
 14      )
 15      define
 16        down as price <= prev(price)
 17      , up   as price >= prev(price)
 18  )
 19  order by symbol, day;
```

Seeing all rows, I can also clearly see how 2019-04-04 and 2019-04-12 both are twice in the output – once as last row of one match and once as first row of the next match – so the total number of rows in the output is 17, even though the table contains 15 rows:

SYMBOL	DAY	MATCH	CLASS	PREV	PRICE
BEER	2019-04-01	1	STRT		14.9
BEER	2019-04-02	1	DOWN	14.9	14.2
BEER	2019-04-03	1	DOWN	14.2	14.2
BEER	2019-04-04	1	UP	14.2	15.7
BEER	2019-04-04	2	STRT	14.2	15.7
BEER	2019-04-05	2	DOWN	15.7	15.6
BEER	2019-04-08	2	DOWN	15.6	14.8
BEER	2019-04-09	2	DOWN	14.8	14.8
BEER	2019-04-10	2	DOWN	14.8	14
BEER	2019-04-11	2	UP	14	14.4
BEER	2019-04-12	2	UP	14.4	15.2
BEER	2019-04-12	3	STRT	14.4	15.2
BEER	2019-04-15	3	DOWN	15.2	15
BEER	2019-04-16	3	DOWN	15	13.7
BEER	2019-04-17	3	UP	13.7	14.3
BEER	2019-04-18	3	UP	14.3	14.3
BEER	2019-04-19	3	UP	14.3	15.5

But I'm really very interested in the row on 2019-04-18, which was originally classified as down, which led me to introduce same to get a proper classification. Why is it correctly classified as up here?

The reason is how things are evaluated when doing pattern matching. The database is not simply going through the definitions first to classify the rows and then checking if it fits the pattern. It tries to evaluate as little as possible. This means it will go along and evaluate something like this:

- When starting to look for a match, it will see if the first row matches strt – which any row will.

- Then it knows that if a match is to be found, the next row must be a down, so it checks if that is the case.

- The next row must be a down or an up, so it checks first if it is a down; if not, then it checks if it is an up. Repeat as long as it was a down that was found. So any row having less than *or the same* value as the previous row is classified down as long as we are in this part of the pattern, as down definition is evaluated first. The 2019-04-03 and 2019-04-09 rows are therefore both down rows.

- When the previous step found an up, it knows that the next row *must* be an up to make a valid match, so it checks if that is the case. Repeat checking for up as long as an up is found. That means that at this point, it will *not* evaluate a row *having same value* as the previous row to be down, because that definition is simply *not* evaluated at this point in the pattern.

- Therefore, since 2019-04-18 comes in the up+ part of the pattern, it will *not* be classified down, but up as we want it to.

This can be tricky when you have complex definitions and patterns. Life is simpler if the definitions are mutually exclusive like down, up, and same, but with knowledge of the evaluation method used by match_recognize, it is possible to utilize it to simplify a query like this, where rows that fall into more than one definition get the desired classification anyway, because the pattern dictates which definition is evaluated when.

V + V = W shapes

In stock ticker analysis, a W shape (also known as double-bottom) indicates a trend reversal, so it is an important pattern to search for in the data. Well, I already know how to find V shapes, so I simply expand the pattern clause in line 14 in Listing 17-6.

Listing 17-6. First attempt at finding W shapes

```
SQL> select *
  2  from ticker
  3  match_recognize (
  4     partition by symbol
  5     order by day
  6     measures
```

```
7       match_number() as match
8     , first(day)      as first_day
9     , last(day)       as last_day
10      , count(*)        as days
11    one row per match
12    after match skip to last up
13    pattern (
14       strt down+ up+ down+ up+
15    )
16    define
17       down as price <= prev(price)
18     , up   as price >= prev(price)
19  )
20  order by symbol, first_day;
```

Hang on; I was only expecting a single W match to be found, but my output shows two?

SYMBOL	MATCH	FIRST_DAY	LAST_DAY	DAYS
BEER	1	2019-04-01	2019-04-12	10
BEER	2	2019-04-12	2019-04-19	6

Looking at the graph in Figure 17-5, I can see that first I do match a W shape from 2019-04-01 to 2019-04-12; that is fine. But after that, the graph has only a V shape, but it is matched as a W shape? Why?

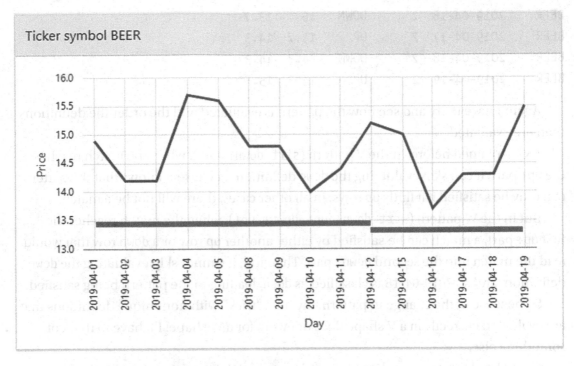

Figure 17-5. *Unexpected match of the last V as a W shape*

As usual I fall back to show the output of my W pattern using an `all rows per match` and that enables me to see that suddenly 2019-04-18 is again classified as a `down` row instead of the `up` that it should have been:

SYMBOL	DAY	MATCH	CLASS	PREV	PRICE
BEER	2019-04-01	1	STRT		14.9
BEER	2019-04-02	1	DOWN	14.9	14.2
BEER	2019-04-03	1	DOWN	14.2	14.2
BEER	2019-04-04	1	UP	14.2	15.7
BEER	2019-04-05	1	DOWN	15.7	15.6
BEER	2019-04-08	1	DOWN	15.6	14.8
BEER	2019-04-09	1	DOWN	14.8	14.8
BEER	2019-04-10	1	DOWN	14.8	14
BEER	2019-04-11	1	UP	14	14.4
BEER	2019-04-12	1	UP	14.4	15.2
BEER	2019-04-12	2	STRT	14.4	15.2
BEER	2019-04-15	2	DOWN	15.2	15

BEER	2019-04-16	2	DOWN	15	13.7
BEER	2019-04-17	2	UP	13.7	14.3
BEER	2019-04-18	2	DOWN	14.3	14.3
BEER	2019-04-19	2	UP	14.3	15.5

Again I have to try and see how the pattern is evaluated and the order the definitions then are evaluated.

As I explained before, in the V pattern (strt down+ up+), when the match reaches the up+ part, it can skip evaluating the down definition, because it knows that the pattern can only be satisfied if it finds up rows; in all other cases, there will not be a match.

But in the W pattern (strt down+ up+ down+ up+), when the match reaches the first up+ part, a match can be satisfied by either another up row or a down row that would lead the match into the second down+ part. Therefore it cannot skip evaluating the down definition, and so 2019-04-18 is classified as down, leading to the pattern being satisfied.

So because of the change in pattern, my little "trick" with nonunique definitions that are evaluated correctly in a V shape does not work for a W shape. I'll have to think of something else.

Could I go back to using down, up, and same and then use a pattern like in the following?

```
...
14          strt (down | same)+ (up | same)+ (down | same)+ (up | same)+
...
```

Well no, it would not help in this case. The last V shape on the graph would become classified like this:

```
...
```

BEER	2019-04-12	2	STRT	14.4	15.2
BEER	2019-04-15	2	DOWN	15.2	15
BEER	2019-04-16	2	DOWN	15	13.7
BEER	2019-04-17	2	UP	13.7	14.3
BEER	2019-04-18	2	SAME	14.3	14.3
BEER	2019-04-19	2	UP	14.3	15.5

And those six classifiers in that order will actually match that pattern, so it won't do.

Instead I'm going to put some more logic in the definitions in my define clause in Listing 17-7.

Listing 17-7. More intelligent definitions for W shape matching

```
SQL> select *
  2  from ticker
  3  match_recognize (
  4     partition by symbol
  5     order by day
  6     measures
  7        match_number() as match
  8      , classifier()   as class
  9      , prev(price)     as prev
 10     all rows per match
 11     after match skip to last up
 12     pattern (
 13        strt down+ up+ down+ up+
 14     )
 15     define
 16        down as price < prev(price)
 17              or (   price = prev(price)
 18                 and price = last(down.price, 1)
 19                 )
 20      , up   as price > prev(price)
 21              or (   price = prev(price)
 22                 and price = last(up.price  , 1)
 23                 )
 24  )
 25  order by symbol, day;
```

Looking at down, the idea is to replace the less-than-or-equal with a dual logic:

- If the price is less than the previous (line 16), it certainly is a down row.

- If the price is equal to the previous row (line 17), it is *only* a down row if the graph was sloping down right before it hit this place with equal prices. I can check that in line 18 by testing if the price in the row is equal to the price of the last row that was classified down. This can only happen if that last down row was just before the flat part of the graph.

345

And for up I use a similar dual logic in lines 20–23. With such a logic built into the definitions, Listing 17-7 produces only one match – the first W shape in the graph:

SYMBOL	DAY	MATCH	CLASS	PREV	PRICE
BEER	2019-04-01	1	STRT		14.9
BEER	2019-04-02	1	DOWN	14.9	14.2
BEER	2019-04-03	1	DOWN	14.2	14.2
BEER	2019-04-04	1	UP	14.2	15.7
BEER	2019-04-05	1	DOWN	15.7	15.6
BEER	2019-04-08	1	DOWN	15.6	14.8
BEER	2019-04-09	1	DOWN	14.8	14.8
BEER	2019-04-10	1	DOWN	14.8	14
BEER	2019-04-11	1	UP	14	14.4
BEER	2019-04-12	1	UP	14.4	15.2

Overlapping W shapes

The way I searched for the patterns in the last example meant that I looked on the graph as consisting of first a W shape and then a V shape. Looking at it that way means I only find a single W shape.

But I could look on the graph as having two overlapping W shapes, as marked out in Figure 17-6.

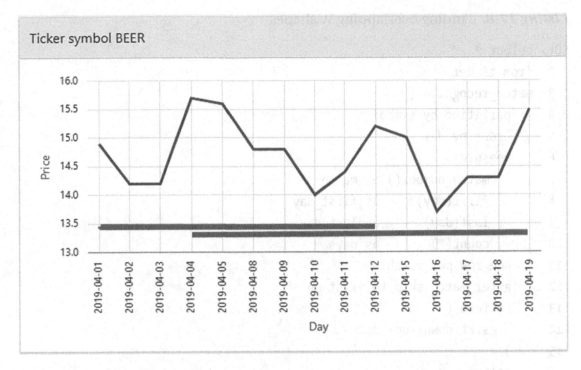

Figure 17-6. *The graph can be seen as having two overlapping W shapes*

Changing my code to enable searching for overlapping shapes is a matter of changing my `after match` clause, which in the previous examples was set like this:

```
...
11      after match skip to last up
...
```

That meant I never overlapped (except that strictly speaking a single row of each match would "overlap," like in Figure 17-4 with three V matches).

If I *do* want to overlap, I need to change where to skip to in order to make the search for the next match start at a suitable row. Ideally it should be the "last row of the first up+ part of the pattern," but that cannot be specified.

I could define two classifications, up1 and up2, with identical definitions, use up1+ for the first up-part and up2+ for the second up-part, and then `skip to last up1`. But there is an easier solution that will work here, as I do in line 12 of Listing 17-8.

Listing 17-8. Finding overlapping W shapes

```
SQL> select *
  2  from ticker
  3  match_recognize (
  4     partition by symbol
  5     order by day
  6     measures
  7       match_number() as match
  8     , first(day)      as first_day
  9     , last(day)       as last_day
 10     , count(*)        as days
 11     one row per match
 12     after match skip to first up
 13     pattern (
 14       strt down+ up+ down+ up+
 15     )
 16     define
 17       down as price < prev(price)
 18            or (    price = prev(price)
 19                and price = last(down.price, 1)
 20                )
 21     , up   as price > prev(price)
 22            or (    price = prev(price)
 23                and price = last(up.price  , 1)
 24                )
 25  )
 26  order by symbol, first_day;
```

When I do skip to first up in line 12, the matching will run like this:

- The first W match is found from 2019-04-01 to 2019-04-12.

- The first up is 2019-04-04, so it goes there and tries if a new match can be found from there.

- So 2019-04-04 is classified strt, 2019-04-05 is down, and it keeps classifying rows that match the pattern right until 2019-04-19.

- The second W match therefore is 2019-04-04 to 2019-04-19.

- The first up of the second W match is 2019-04-11

- 2019-04-11 is classified `strt`, 2019-04-12 is `up`, so the pattern is broken and no match.

- It moves on to 2019-04-12 and tries again for a new match, which will fail because it only matches a V shape, not a W.

- So it moves on to 2019-04-15 and tries again and fails.

- And so on until the end and no more matches are found.

And that is exactly the output I get when I run Listing 17-8, which matches the markings on Figure 17-6:

```
SYMBOL  MATCH  FIRST_DAY   LAST_DAY    DAYS
BEER    1      2019-04-01  2019-04-12  10
BEER    2      2019-04-04  2019-04-19  12
```

Lessons learned

In this chapter I've dived deeper into the stock ticker example than the Oracle documentation does, mostly showing the complexities introduced when "flat" parts of the graph needs to be considered part of either a down-sloping or an up-sloping part of the graph.

In the course of this walk-trough, I hope I've conveyed some knowledge about

- Using `all rows` vs. `one row per match` (often to debug the logic)

- How definitions in `define` are evaluated according to the fulfillment of `pattern`

- Different uses of `after match skip to`, with, or without `subset`

This knowledge should help you develop code for matching similar patterns yourself.

CHAPTER 18

Grouping Data Through Patterns

Grouping data with a group by clause requires you to find one or more values that are the same in those rows you want to belong to the same group. Often that is simply some columns or just as often a calculation on some columns.

Sometimes, though, the condition that tells you a row belongs to a group is *not* simply a condition you can calculate using *only* values from that row itself, but the condition is on how the row *relates* to other rows. A condition to group by could, for example, be that all rows with consecutive sequential values should be grouped – when a gap in the sequence is found, a new group is started. This requires a calculation *across* rows, which often can be handled by analytic functions – but sometimes not.

A solution here is to remember that in pattern matching when you use one row per match, that is in fact like an implicit group by, and you can use aggregates in the measures and get a result very much like if you had used a group by. And when you use match_recognize for grouping, the define and pattern clauses are just perfect for a grouping condition that depends on relations *between* rows in a certain order.

Two sets of data to group

To demonstrate grouping data with pattern matching, I use the tables in Figure 18-1.

351

© Kim Berg Hansen 2020

K. Berg Hansen, *Practical Oracle SQL*, https://doi.org/10.1007/978-1-4842-5617-6_18

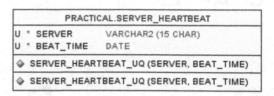

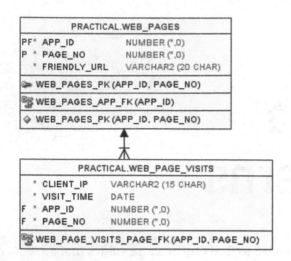

Figure 18-1. *Tables with server heartbeat and web page visits used for grouping data*

In the server_heartbeat table, a row is inserted every time a server sends a heartbeat (a call that basically just says "I'm alive"), which should happen every 5 minutes for every server.

The web_page_visits table stores every visit to every web page in the web applications of Good Beer Trading Co (i.e., every click a user makes). This table references the web_pages table, which I include in the figure just to give you the context, but the examples in this chapter use the web_page_visits table.

I'll show the data of both tables later, just before the relevant examples.

Three grouping conditions

I'm going to show you three different types of relational conditions you can use pattern matching to group:

- Data where all consecutive data belong in a group, where consecutive simply means that a value increases by an exact fixed amount for each row. It can be numbers that increase by 1 or 100 or dates that increase by 5 minutes or 1 day or similar definitions of consecutive.

- Data where rows belong to a group as long as a value is close to the value of the previous row, for example, as long as a date value is within 15 minutes of the previous date.

- Data where a group is rows within a fixed interval, for example, one hour. But not hours on the clock (like grouping by `trunc(date_col, 'HH')`), instead hours that begin by the first row in each group.

You can probably think of other types of conditions, but these three cover a lot of use cases.

Group consecutive data

First let me delve into grouping data that is consecutive. This part I'll cover more detailed to give you a ground base before going into the other two grouping methods.

For comparison I'll show you one method this could be done just with an analytic function and discuss why you might consider using `match_recognize` instead.

Analytic Tabibitosan vs. match_recognize

Before moving on to the example tables I've shown, I will walk you through the **Tabibitosan** method to find groups of consecutive integers using a single analytic function. This method was introduced by Aketi Jyuuzou on the Oracle Community Forums (back then OTN Forums).

I'll start with Listing 18-1, where I just use a `with` clause to generate some rows with numbers instead of creating a real table.

Listing 18-1. Difference between value and row_number

```
SQL> with ints(i) as (
  2      select 1 from dual union all
  3      select 2 from dual union all
  4      select 3 from dual union all
  5      select 6 from dual union all
  6      select 8 from dual union all
  7      select 9 from dual
  8  )
  9  select
 10      i
 11  , row_number() over (order by i)     as rn
```

```
12    , i - row_number() over (order by i) as diff
13   from ints
14   order by i;
```

Tabibitosan in Japanese means something like Mr. Pilgrim or Mr. Traveler. The idea is to imagine two walking pilgrims that both start at zero:

- The first pilgrim walks different distances each day, sometimes one mile and sometimes longer. His distance from the origin is represented by the integer value, in this case column i.

- The second pilgrim walks exactly one mile every day. His distance from the origin is represented by the results of row_number function that increases by exactly one for each row, in this case column rn.

The third column in the output is the difference between i and rn. In the analogy, this represents the *distance* between the two pilgrims:

I	RN	DIFF
1	1	0
2	2	0
3	3	0
6	4	2
8	5	3
9	6	3

Those days where the first pilgrim travels at a speed of one mile per day, the distance between them remains the same. If the first pilgrim walks more than a single mile in one day, the distance between them increases. The numbers are fairly clear as is, but it's even more clear when plotted on the graph in Figure 18-2.

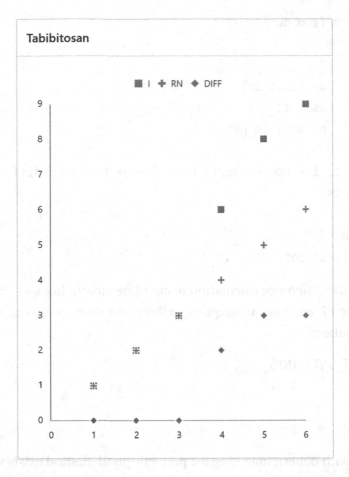

Figure 18-2. *Difference between the two pilgrims can be used for grouping*

In other words, the difference (the red diamonds in the graph) between the integer column and row_number will be *constant* for those rows where the integer column increases by exactly one per row (i.e., is consecutive), so I can easily group by this difference in Listing 18-2.

Listing 18-2. Tabibitosan grouping

```
SQL> with ints(i) as (
  2      select 1 from dual union all
  3      select 2 from dual union all
  4      select 3 from dual union all
  5      select 6 from dual union all
  6      select 8 from dual union all
```

```
 7      select 9 from dual
 8  )
 9  select
10     min(i)    as first_int
11   , max(i)    as last_int
12   , count(*) as ints_in_grp
13  from (
14      select i, i - row_number() over (order by i) as diff
15      from ints
16  )
17  group by diff
18  order by first_int;
```

Simply wrap the difference calculation in an inline view in lines 14–15 and group by the diff in line 17, and I get an output specifying the three groups of consecutive integers found in the data:

FIRST_INT	LAST_INT	INTS_IN_GRP
1	3	3
6	6	1
8	9	2

So why do it with pattern matching if a perfectly good method exists with analytic functions? Part of the answer is that it can become easier to adapt to changing requirements, as I'll show you. Part of it is about the efficiency of doing a one-pass operation while working through the data, instead of two passes – first the analytic row numbering and then the grouping.

In Listing 18-3, I show you how to get the exact same output as Listing 18-2, just using match_recognize instead of the Tabibitosan method.

Listing 18-3. Same grouping with match_recognize

```
SQL> with ints(i) as (
 2      select 1 from dual union all
 3      select 2 from dual union all
 4      select 3 from dual union all
 5      select 6 from dual union all
```

```
 6      select 8 from dual union all
 7      select 9 from dual
 8  )
 9  select first_int, last_int, ints_in_grp
10  from ints
11  match_recognize (
12      order by i
13      measures
14          first(i) as first_int
15        , last(i)  as last_int
16        , count(*) as ints_in_grp
17      one row per match
18      pattern (strt one_higher*)
19      define
20          one_higher as i = prev(i) + 1
21  )
22  order by first_int;
```

It is reasonably straightforward and reads like this:

- I define classification one_higher in line 20 to be a row where i is exactly 1 greater than the previous i – indicating it is consecutive to the previous row.

- The pattern in line 18 looks for any row (classified strt) followed by zero or more one_higher rows. So this matches a group of rows as long as they have consecutive i values – when it no longer is consecutive, the match stops.

- Instead of the group by in Tabibitosan, here I can simply specify in line 17 that I just want a single row output per match.

- Lines 14–16 get me the same values as Listing 18-2, just without grouping; here the pattern matching can work out the results as it walks along the data.

I've laid the ground rules with some simple integer data showing analytic function solution vs. pattern matching; now I'll move on to doing the same with a different datatype on more realistic data.

Consecutive dates instead of integers

In the server_heartbeat table, I should get a heartbeat stored from every server exactly every five minutes. In Listing 18-4, you see the data of the table.

Listing 18-4. Server heartbeat as example of something other than integers

```
SQL> select server, beat_time
  2  from server_heartbeat
  3  order by server, beat_time;
```

Observe there are two servers and there are places where one or more heartbeats have been skipped:

```
SERVER      BEAT_TIME
10.0.0.100  2019-04-10 13:00:00
10.0.0.100  2019-04-10 13:05:00
10.0.0.100  2019-04-10 13:10:00
10.0.0.100  2019-04-10 13:15:00
10.0.0.100  2019-04-10 13:20:00
10.0.0.100  2019-04-10 13:35:00
10.0.0.100  2019-04-10 13:40:00
10.0.0.100  2019-04-10 13:45:00
10.0.0.100  2019-04-10 13:55:00
10.0.0.142  2019-04-10 13:00:00
10.0.0.142  2019-04-10 13:20:00
10.0.0.142  2019-04-10 13:25:00
10.0.0.142  2019-04-10 13:50:00
10.0.0.142  2019-04-10 13:55:00
```

Can I use Tabibitosan to group rows that are consecutive with exactly 5-minute intervals? Yes, surely. I just need to adjust the "unit" used, so it becomes a 5-minute unit instead of a simple number 1. I do that in Listing 18-5.

Listing 18-5. Tabibitosan adjusted to 5-minute intervals

```
SQL> select
  2      server
  3    , min(beat_time) as first_beat
```

```
4    , max(beat_time) as last_beat
5    , count(*)        as beats
6    from (
7        select
8            server
9          , beat_time
10         , beat_time - interval '5' minute
11                    * row_number() over (
12                          partition by server
13                          order by beat_time
14                      ) as diff
15       from server_heartbeat
16   )
17   group by server, diff
18   order by server, first_beat;
```

What was i before in Listing 18-2 is now beat_time in line 9. In order to create something with a constant difference as long as the rows are consecutive, in lines 10–14, I multiply row_number with an interval of 5 minutes, which I then can subtract from the beat_time to get the diff value I can use for grouping.

Since (unlike Listing 18-2) I do this per server instead of on all rows at once, I use partition by in line 12. That way I get this output with three groups for each server:

SERVER	FIRST_BEAT	LAST_BEAT	BEATS
10.0.0.100	2019-04-10 13:00:00	2019-04-10 13:20:00	5
10.0.0.100	2019-04-10 13:35:00	2019-04-10 13:45:00	3
10.0.0.100	2019-04-10 13:55:00	2019-04-10 13:55:00	1
10.0.0.142	2019-04-10 13:00:00	2019-04-10 13:00:00	1
10.0.0.142	2019-04-10 13:20:00	2019-04-10 13:25:00	2
10.0.0.142	2019-04-10 13:50:00	2019-04-10 13:55:00	2

Multiplying row_number with an interval to make a "unit" adjustment is not hard, but it is not really very clear from reading the code in Listing 18-5 what this diff calculation is good for and what it does.

So let me try to similarly adapt Listing 18-4 to the 5-minute interval data and create Listing 18-6, which will give me the same output as Listing 18-5.

Listing 18-6. Same adjustment to match_recognize solution

```
SQL> select server, first_beat, last_beat, beats
  2  from server_heartbeat
  3  match_recognize (
  4     partition by server
  5     order by beat_time
  6     measures
  7        first(beat_time) as first_beat
  8      , last(beat_time)  as last_beat
  9      , count(*)         as beats
 10     one row per match
 11     pattern (strt five_mins_later*)
 12     define
 13        five_mins_later as
 14           beat_time = prev(beat_time) + interval '5' minute
 15  )
 16  order by server, first_beat;
```

I have given definitions and measures some other names than in Listing 18-4, so they represent the data better.

But the only *functional* change I made is in line 14 (compared to line 20 in Listing 18-4), where I replaced + 1 with + `interval '5' minute` – that is all it took to change the functionality, and it is very self-documenting.

You might have noticed that the data is very neatly exactly 5 minutes apart, which in reality is unlikely for such heartbeat data that probably arrives within some seconds either side of the exact time. I could create neatly aligned data by having a `before insert` trigger that rounded the inserted value to the nearest 5-minute value, but that would lose information (e.g., I might be interested in seeing that one server was always about 20 seconds late).

So rather than "massage" the data, I want to change my query to allow for a certain leeway rather than looking for exactly 5 minutes. With the Tabibitosan method, I'd have to round the values to the nearest 5 minutes at query time in order to achieve the "constant difference" for grouping. With pattern matching, it is much easier to simply adapt the definition and change line 14 of Listing 18-6 into a condition with a `between` clause to define that `five_mins_later` means somewhere between 4 and 6 minutes later:

```
...
12     define
13        five_mins_later as
14           beat_time between prev(beat_time) + interval '4' minute
15                       and prev(beat_time) + interval '6' minute
...
```

Again it is almost plain English and fairly readable and self-documenting.

But these queries found me groups of rows that are consecutive (for some unit of measurement). Often what I'm asked to find is the *gaps* between such groups; where are data *missing* that should have been there.

Gap detection

When I have the consecutive groups in the output from Listings 18-5 and 18-6, the gaps can be defined by the `last_beat` of one row (last beat before the gap) and the `first_beat` of the next row (next beat after the gap).

Getting a value from the next row naturally makes me think of using the `lead` analytic function. So I use `lead` in Listing 18-7.

Listing 18-7. Detecting gaps from consecutive grouping using lead function

```
SQL> select
  2     server, last_beat, next_beat
  3   , round((next_beat - last_beat) * (24*60)) as gap_minutes
  4   from (
  5     select
  6        server
  7      , last_beat
  8      , lead(first_beat) over (
  9           partition by server order by first_beat
 10        ) as next_beat
 11     from (
...
 27     )
 28   )
 29   where next_beat is not null
 30   order by server, last_beat;
```

361

The query of Listing 18-6 I put inside the inline view in lines 11–27, and then in lines 8–10, I use lead to find the value of first_beat of the next row.

But for the last row in the partition, lead will return null, and it doesn't make sense to talk of a gap after the last row. So I wrap in yet another inline view and filter away those last rows in line 29, giving me this output showing two gaps for each server (compare this with the output of Listing 18-5):

SERVER	LAST_BEAT	NEXT_BEAT	GAP_MINUTES
10.0.0.100	2019-04-10 13:20:00	2019-04-10 13:35:00	15
10.0.0.100	2019-04-10 13:45:00	2019-04-10 13:55:00	10
10.0.0.142	2019-04-10 13:00:00	2019-04-10 13:20:00	20
10.0.0.142	2019-04-10 13:25:00	2019-04-10 13:50:00	25

(If you noticed the round in line 3, this is simply because some of these gap_minutes values have teeny tiny rounding errors around the 20th decimal or so, because next_beat - last_beat is measured in days and in some of the cases has some values that create rounding errors when multiplied with 24*60 to get minutes.)

Now this works nicely, but it is actually possible to avoid having to use analytic functions on the output of match_recognize. In Listing 18-8, I show how to detect the gaps directly with pattern matching without any "post-processing."

Listing 18-8. Detecting gaps directly in match_recognize

```
SQL> select
  2     server, last_beat, next_beat
  3   , round((next_beat - last_beat) * (24*60)) as gap_minutes
  4   from server_heartbeat
  5   match_recognize (
  6     partition by server
  7     order by beat_time
  8     measures
  9       last(before_gap.beat_time) as last_beat
 10     , next_after_gap.beat_time   as next_beat
 11     one row per match
 12     after match skip to last next_after_gap
 13     pattern (strt five_mins_later* next_after_gap)
 14     subset before_gap = (strt, five_mins_later)
```

```
15   define
16       five_mins_later as
17           beat_time = prev(beat_time) + interval '5' minute
18     , next_after_gap as
19           beat_time > prev(beat_time) + interval '5' minute
20   )
21   order by server, last_beat;
```

This adds slightly more complexity to the pattern matching:

- I have *two* definitions in lines 16–19. One is the five_mins_later that I also used in Listing 18-6. The other is next_after_gap that classifies rows where beat_time is *more* than 5 minutes after the previous row.

- This enables me in line 13 to specify a pattern that begins like before: any strt row followed by zero or more five_mins_later rows. But then there should be exactly one next_after_gap row. So a match will consist of the group of consecutive rows *plus* the row after (that comes after the gap). This also means that for the *last* group, no next_after_gap row can be found, so it will not be matched – meaning I do not need to filter away the last group, as this pattern only finds the two groups (per server) that actually have a gap after them.

- From this match, I need the last beat *before* the gap and the first *after* the gap. The latter is easy; it is simply the beat_time of the single next_after_gap row (line 10). The first is a bit trickier, since it might be a value from a strt row (if the consecutive "group" consists of only a single row) or it might be a value from a five_mins_later row. Therefore I define a subset called before_gap in line 14, so that I in line 9 can specify that I want the beat_time of the last before_gap row.

- Finally, since I have included the next_after_gap row in the match, I need to specify that the next match should be searched for *from* this row (rather than normally from the row immediately following the match). This I do in line 12 in the after match clause, so that the next_after_gap row becomes the strt row of the next match (if any).

363

A little more complex, yes, but when you know the meaning of the different clauses in pattern matching, it still can be read and understood relatively plainly as English – especially if you have given the definitions meaningful names.

So far I've shown various queries grouping data that is consecutive, where consecutive means a column value increases by a specific fixed unit for every row. But there are cases where we want to group the data by other definitions.

Group until gap too large

One of these other definitions is that a row keeps belonging to the group as long as it is "close" to the previous row – by however you define "close." A group can become large and span a lot of rows, as the grouping doesn't stop until the gap between two rows is bigger than the defined "closeness."

A common example of this is doing the so-called **sessionization**. You log every page visit (click) to your web site without having a unique session id – but as long as the clicks from a given client (IP address) keep on coming without much pause between them, you consider those visits together to be a "session." Once the client has been away for a longer period (gaps in the page visit log), you consider his next visit to be the start of a new session.

Good Beer Trading Co has such a web page visit log table, whose content you can see in Listing 18-9.

Listing 18-9. Web page visit data

```
SQL> select app_id, visit_time, client_ip, page_no
  2  from web_page_visits
  3  order by app_id, visit_time, client_ip;
```

Two different IP addresses have visited different pages at different times on a given date:

APP_ID	VISIT_TIME	CLIENT_IP	PAGE_NO
542	2019-04-20 08:15:42	104.130.89.12	1
542	2019-04-20 08:16:31	104.130.89.12	3
542	2019-04-20 08:28:55	104.130.89.12	4
542	2019-04-20 08:41:12	104.130.89.12	3
542	2019-04-20 08:42:37	104.130.89.12	2

542	2019-04-20 08:55:02	104.130.89.12	4
542	2019-04-20 09:03:34	104.130.89.12	2
542	2019-04-20 09:17:50	104.130.89.12	2
542	2019-04-20 09:28:32	104.130.89.12	2
542	2019-04-20 09:34:29	104.130.89.12	2
542	2019-04-20 09:43:46	104.130.89.12	2
542	2019-04-20 09:47:08	104.130.89.12	2
542	2019-04-20 09:49:12	104.130.89.12	3
542	2019-04-20 11:57:26	85.237.86.200	1
542	2019-04-20 11:58:09	85.237.86.200	2
542	2019-04-20 11:58:39	85.237.86.200	2
542	2019-04-20 12:02:02	85.237.86.200	3
542	2019-04-20 14:45:10	104.130.89.12	1
542	2019-04-20 15:02:22	104.130.89.12	3
542	2019-04-20 15:02:44	104.130.89.12	2
542	2019-04-20 15:04:01	104.130.89.12	2
542	2019-04-20 15:05:11	104.130.89.12	2
542	2019-04-20 15:05:48	104.130.89.12	3

This is solved in Listing 18-10 pretty much like finding consecutive groups of rows, just adapting very slightly the criteria in the define clause.

Listing 18-10. Data belongs to same group (session) as long as max 15 minutes between page visits

```
SQL> select app_id, first_visit, last_visit, visits, client_ip
  2  from web_page_visits
  3  match_recognize (
  4    partition by app_id, client_ip
  5    order by visit_time
  6    measures
  7      first(visit_time) as first_visit
  8    , last(visit_time)  as last_visit
  9    , count(*)          as visits
 10    one row per match
 11    pattern (strt within_15_mins*)
 12    define
```

```
13          within_15_mins as
14              visit_time <= prev(visit_time) + interval '15' minute
15  )
16  order by app_id, first_visit, client_ip;
```

It's another table and other column names and a classification name that gives more meaning for this case, but apart from that, you should recognize this is rather much like Listing 18-6. The *functional* difference is simply line 14 that uses <= instead of =, showing how a match_recognize solution is easy to adapt with small changes, as the different parts of the logic have been separated out in mainly the define, pattern, and measure clauses. Adapting Tabibitosan to solve sessionization would have been a lot harder (if not impossible) as the logic is so dependent on creating a value that can be compared to a monotonically increasing value.

With this easy adaptation in Listing 18-10, I get four "session" groups created:

APP_ID	FIRST_VISIT	LAST_VISIT	VISITS	CLIENT_IP
542	2019-04-20 08:15:42	2019-04-20 09:49:12	13	104.130.89.12
542	2019-04-20 11:57:26	2019-04-20 12:02:02	4	85.237.86.200
542	2019-04-20 14:45:10	2019-04-20 14:45:10	1	104.130.89.12
542	2019-04-20 15:02:22	2019-04-20 15:05:48	5	104.130.89.12

Very often the logic used in pattern matching compares current rows to previous rows, but sometimes it can be a nice exercise to try and reverse the logic. Not that it changes much for this task, but knowing that you can do it with a "look ahead" logic can from time to time help in more tricky situations:

```
...
11      pattern (has_15_mins_to_next* last_time)
12      define
13         has_15_mins_to_next as
14             visit_time + interval '15' minute >= next(visit_time)
...
```

Most of the code is like Listing 18-10, but I changed the `pattern` and `define` clauses:

- Lines 13–14 define `has_15_mins_to_next` by comparing values to the next row – if the `visit_time` of the current row + 15 minutes is greater than the next row, I know it is within 15 minutes.

- And then the `pattern` in line 11 needs to be adapted to find zero or more `has_15_mins_to_next` rows followed by exactly one other row (which I call `last_time`) that is *not* classified `has_15_mins_to_next`.

This logic that looks ahead instead of back produces the same output as Listing 18-10.

I've shown that almost same logic can group rows that either has a fixed interval between rows (consecutively) or has at most a certain interval between rows. But what if the groups are defined by having to be within a certain interval of the *first* row?

Group until fixed limit

I could choose to define a session *not* by "as long as visits are happening at suitably small intervals," but rather define that the first page visit (click) starts a session, which then lasts for one hour. All the visits within an hour from the first visit are part of the session. The *next* visit after the hour has gone by (whether 2 minutes or 2 days thereafter) marks the beginning of a *new* one-hour session.

This can also be accomplished by a slight tweaking of the logic in the `pattern` and `define` of `match_recognize`, as I show in Listing 18-11.

Listing 18-11. Sessions max one hour long since first page visit

```
SQL> select app_id, first_visit, last_visit, visits, client_ip
  2  from web_page_visits
  3  match_recognize (
  4    partition by app_id, client_ip
  5    order by visit_time
  6    measures
  7      first(visit_time) as first_visit
  8    , last(visit_time)  as last_visit
  9    , count(*)          as visits
 10    one row per match
```

```
11      pattern (same_hour+)
12      define
13         same_hour as
14            visit_time <= first(visit_time) + interval '1' hour
15   )
16   order by app_id, first_visit, client_ip;
```

You'll quickly spot that it's not that much different from Listings 18-6 and 18-10. But there are a couple small, but important, changes:

- In the definition of classification same_hour in line 14, I am no longer comparing to prev(visit_time), but instead to first(visit_time). This does exactly what I wanted – whenever a row is within 1 hour of the first row in the match, the row will be included in the match.

- Notice in line 11 I no longer have a strt or similar undefined classification. This was needed when I used prev, which would yield *nothing* on the first row. But this time I am using first, and as a row is always *included* when evaluating the definition condition, the first row *itself* will be the result of the first call to first. This means that when testing the condition, it will always be true when it is tested on the first row (either the first overall or the first after a previous match has ended). Therefore I can skip having a strt and instead simply state that a match must be one or more same_hour rows.

With this altered logic, I get four different session groups than I did before:

APP_ID	FIRST_VISIT	LAST_VISIT	VISITS	CLIENT_IP
542	2019-04-20 08:15:42	2019-04-20 09:03:34	7	104.130.89.12
542	2019-04-20 09:17:50	2019-04-20 09:49:12	6	104.130.89.12
542	2019-04-20 11:57:26	2019-04-20 12:02:02	4	85.237.86.200
542	2019-04-20 14:45:10	2019-04-20 15:05:48	6	104.130.89.12

When you compare to the output of Listing 18-10, you see that where IP 104.130.89.12 before had a single 13-visit session that lasted over 1½ hour, that is now two sessions of 7 and 6 visits, because the visit 09:17:50 is more than an hour away from 08:15:42.

On the other hand, the same IP now has a single six-visit session starting at 14:45:10 and lasting about 20 minutes, whereas before that was split into two sessions because 15:02:22 is more than 15 minutes after 14:45:10.

For different use cases, both of these grouping methods are useful.

Lessons learned

In this chapter, I've been showing various uses of pattern matching to group data that doesn't have some key value to `group by,` but instead relates the rows by being consecutive or not too far apart. These examples should enable you to

- Consider `match_recognize` as an alternative to `group by` for cases where you cannot easily specify a grouping value from each row, but the grouping criteria are relations between rows.

- Express which rows are related and belong together with the `define` and `pattern` clauses.

- Use aggregate and navigational functions in the `measures` clause together with `one row per match` to achieve output like `group by.`

- Utilize the separation of logic in the different clauses of `match_recognize` with suitable aliasing and naming to make your code more readable and understandable.

Once you grasp the fundamentals of this approach, you'll find your own cases where you can substitute pattern matching for complex `group by` or analytic SQL.

CHAPTER 19

Merging Date Ranges

Lots of data have a date range for validity – when is or was the event or price or whatever active. Schedules, prices, discounts, versioning, audit trails, the list is endless.

It's common to want to merge rows (at least in report output) where the date ranges are right after one another or even overlapping. For example, you may have a production schedule for your assembly line having three rows with adjoining date ranges – producing the same product for three different sales orders. For production planning, you may want to output this as a single row with the total date range and the sum of the quantities you need to produce.

There can be many other examples of this – in this chapter I'll show you an example of merging job hire periods with the `match_recognize` clause.

Job hire periods

As an example of a table with date ranges, I'll be using the `emp_hire_periods` table shown in Figure 19-1, which has a foreign key relation to the `employees` table.

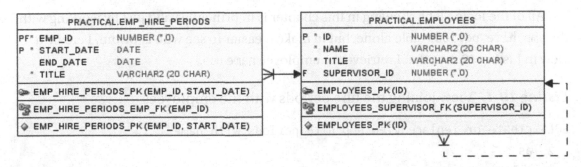

Figure 19-1. *The table of periods that employees have been hired for a given job*

© Kim Berg Hansen 2020

K. Berg Hansen, *Practical Oracle SQL*, https://doi.org/10.1007/978-1-4842-5617-6_19

A given employee can be hired in different periods for different job functions (indicated by the `title` column). The date ranges I have in the table follow these rules:

- A `null` value in `end_date` means the employee currently works at that function.

- When an employee stops working for Good Beer Trading Co, `end_date` is filled.

- If the employee is rehired, a new row is inserted.

- By promotion or change in job function, `end_date` is filled, and a new row is inserted with the new title.

- An employee can have more than one function at the same time, so the date ranges may overlap.

- The `start_date` is *included* in the date range and the `end_date` is *excluded* from the date range – often written as a [`start_date`, `end_date`[half-open interval.

You may find the last rule less than intuitive, but I'll get back shortly with an explanation of why this is a good idea.

Note   A *closed* interval [`start`, `end`] is `start <= x <= end`, while an *open* interval]`start`, `end`[is `start < x < end`. The *half-open* interval is then either]`start`, `end`] or (as in this case) [`start`, `end`[.

All of the logic I'll be showing in this chapter is in principle valid just by working with the `emp_hire_periods` table alone, but to make it easier to see who is whom, I create a view in Listing 19-1 so that I retrieve the employee name too.

Listing 19-1. View joining the hire periods with the employees

```
SQL> create or replace view emp_hire_periods_with_name
  2  as
  3  select
  4     ehp.emp_id
  5   , e.name
  6   , ehp.start_date
```

```
 7    , ehp.end_date
 8    , ehp.title
 9  from emp_hire_periods ehp
10  join employees e
11     on e.id = ehp.emp_id;
```

View EMP_HIRE_PERIODS_WITH_NAME created.

Querying the emp_hire_periods_with_name view in Listing 19-2, I can show you the data I have.

Listing 19-2. The hire periods data

```
SQL> select
 2     ehp.emp_id
 3    , ehp.name
 4    , ehp.start_date
 5    , ehp.end_date
 6    , ehp.title
 7  from emp_hire_periods_with_name ehp
 8  order by ehp.emp_id, ehp.start_date;
```

In the interest of saving a little space, I have not filled the table with data for all 14 employees, just a selection of 6:

EMP_ID	NAME	START_DATE	END_DATE	TITLE
142	Harold King	2010-07-01	2012-04-01	Product Director
142	Harold King	2012-04-01		Managing Director
143	Mogens Juel	2010-07-01	2014-01-01	IT Technician
143	Mogens Juel	2014-01-01	2016-06-01	Sys Admin
143	Mogens Juel	2014-04-01	2015-10-01	Code Tester
143	Mogens Juel	2016-06-01		IT Manager
144	Axel de Proef	2010-07-01	2013-07-01	Sales Manager
144	Axel de Proef	2012-04-01		Product Director
145	Zoe Thorston	2014-02-01		IT Developer
145	Zoe Thorston	2019-02-01		Scrum Master
146	Lim Tok Lo	2014-10-01	2016-02-01	Forklift Operator
146	Lim Tok Lo	2017-03-01		Warehouse Manager

147	Ursula Mwbesi	2014-10-01	2015-05-01	Delivery Manager
147	Ursula Mwbesi	2016-05-01	2017-03-01	Warehouse Manager
147	Ursula Mwbesi	2016-11-01		Operations Chief

When I visualize the same data in Figure 19-2, it's easy to see who has changed jobs along the way, who has been away from the company and returned in a different job, and who has had double jobs for periods of time.

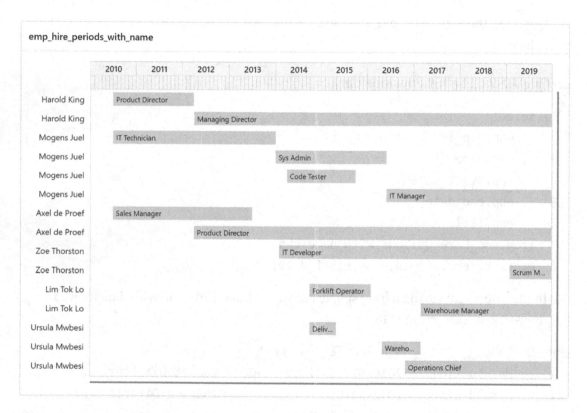

Figure 19-2. *Visualizing the data helps see the overlaps*

You'll notice that because I use the half-open interval I mentioned before, employees changing jobs have a start_date on the new job that is equal to the end_date of the old job. Why didn't I use closed intervals instead, so Harold King was product director from 2010-07-01 to 2012-03-31 – both dates *included*?

It might seem easier to use closed intervals, so you can simplify your code a little by using between instead of >= and < – but there's a problem. The date datatype can contain not only whole dates but also hours, minutes, and seconds. That means that with a closed interval end_date of 2012-03-31, Harold King would not be hired anymore at 1 second past midnight, and the entire day of March 31st, he would be out of a job until rehired April 1st at midnight.

"Easy," you say, "just put an end_date of 2012-03-31 23:59:59, and all is well." But is it? Possibly it'll be OK, but what if you need to switch to a timestamp datatype in the future and support fractional seconds? (Probably not the case for hire periods, but you can easily imagine other use cases for this.)

By using half-open intervals instead for your date ranges, you will never have the problem that Harold King in principle is not hired for a short time (a day, a second, a microsecond – no matter how small, with the closed interval, there will always be a piece of time that is not covered by the ranges).

When working with half-open intervals, it can help to think of both dates as from dates:

- The start_date is the exact moment *from* which the row starts being active.

- The end_date is the exact moment *from* which the row is no longer active (i.e., it *ends* being active *immediately* before that moment).

This thought process might have been helped by choosing column names like active_from and inactive_from, but the notion of *start* and *end* is just so commonly used that I'm doing the same.

Oracle itself has realized the usefulness of half-open intervals when they introduced **temporal validity** in version 12.1. So let me use this as a good opportunity for a brief detour and show you how temporal validity works. Afterward I'll get back to the date range merging.

Temporal validity

In Listing 19-3, you'll see the create table statement I used for creating the emp_hire_periods table.

Listing 19-3. Table defined with temporal validity

```
SQL> create table emp_hire_periods (
  2     emp_id           not null constraint emp_hire_periods_emp_fk
  3                         references employees
  4   , start_date      date not null
```

```
5   , end_date         date
6   , title            varchar2(20 char) not null
7   , constraint emp_hire_periods_pk primary key (emp_id, start_date)
8   , period for employed_in (start_date, end_date)
9   );
```

The interesting bit is line 8, which is the period for clause for defining temporal validity on the table.

In the parentheses, I've specified the two columns that contain the start and end point of the half-open interval. (These can be date or timestamp columns.) Both columns are allowed to be nullable; it is just for this use case I have set start_date to be not null as a job period will always have a specific starting point, whereas end_date allows nulls, because this means the job is still current.

Tip   If you do not specify the two columns, the database auto-creates two hidden columns to contain the interval. Normally I prefer to create the columns myself and specify them, but it might be handy if you have a use case where those who query are not interested in the actual interval, just whether the row is valid at a specific point in time or not.

Right after period for, you must name the period (give it an identifier), and I have carefully chosen employed_in. It is a good idea to give the name some thought, as a good name will be helpful in queries that use temporal validity, as I show it in Listing 19-4.

Listing 19-4. Querying hire periods table as of a specific date

```
SQL> select
  2      ehp.emp_id
  3    , e.name
  4    , ehp.start_date
  5    , ehp.end_date
  6    , ehp.title
  7  from emp_hire_periods
  8          as of period for employed_in date '2010-07-01'
  9        ehp
```

```
10   join employees e
11      on e.id = ehp.emp_id
12   order by ehp.emp_id, ehp.start_date;
```

In the from clause lines 7–9, I can use an as of syntax very similar to flashback queries, with the table in line 7, the as of specification in line 8, and the table alias in line 9.

When using flashback, I specify as of timestamp or as of scn, but with temporal validity, I specify as of period for and then the name of the period. This means that the name employed_in in line 8 helps self-document that I'm querying those that were *employed in* 2010-07-01, which was the start of the company, and there were only three people:

EMP_ID	NAME	START_DATE	END_DATE	TITLE
142	Harold King	2010-07-01	2012-04-01	Product Director
143	Mogens Juel	2010-07-01	2014-01-01	IT Technician
144	Axel de Proef	2010-07-01	2013-07-01	Sales Manager

If I want to find those that were employed 6 years later, I just change the date value in line 8:

```
...
8         as of period for employed_in date '2016-07-01'
...
```

And here I have five people (some of whom are the same, just with new titles):

EMP_ID	NAME	START_DATE	END_DATE	TITLE
142	Harold King	2012-04-01		Managing Director
143	Mogens Juel	2016-06-01		IT Manager
144	Axel de Proef	2012-04-01		Product Director
145	Zoe Thorston	2014-02-01		IT Developer
147	Ursula Mwbesi	2016-05-01	2017-03-01	Warehouse Manager

The query with as of is internally rewritten by the database into a regular where clause with suitable >= and < predicates; it is just easier to get it right with as of. Also the database treats it as a type of constraint – it will not let you insert data with an end_date that is before start_date.

This little aside showed you briefly how temporal validity can make things easier, and if you do use temporal validity, you'll also automatically get the benefits of the half-open intervals. Now I'll get back to the range merging, which you can do with or without temporal validity.

Merging overlapping ranges

What I want to do now is to take the data in Figure 19-2, find all places where hire periods of the same employee either adjoin or overlap, and merge those into single aggregate rows showing how many jobs (either successively or concurrently) the employee has had in that aggregated period. The result I want is shown in Figure 19-3.

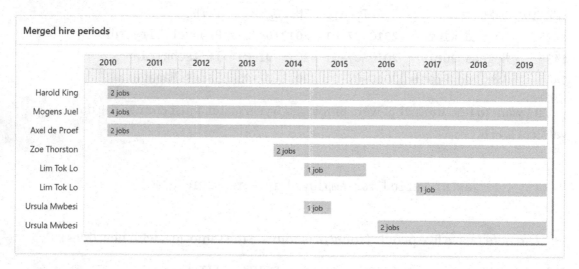

Figure 19-3. *Expected results after merging overlapping and adjoining date ranges*

I am now going to attempt solving this with `match_recognize`. To demonstrate trying out different approaches and changing the logic along the way, I will first show some attempts that do not quite work, leading up to a working solution in the end.

Attempts comparing to the previous row

In quite a few scenarios using `match_recognize`, it is typical to compare a value from the *current* row to a value from the *previous* row in order to make a row classification. So I'll try that first in Listing 19-5.

Listing 19-5. Comparing start_date to end_date of the previous row

```
SQL> select
  2      emp_id
  3    , name
  4    , start_date
  5    , end_date
  6    , jobs
  7  from emp_hire_periods_with_name
  8  match_recognize (
  9     partition by emp_id
 10     order by start_date, end_date
 11     measures
 12        max(name)         as name
 13      , first(start_date) as start_date
 14      , last(end_date)    as end_date
 15      , count(*)          as jobs
 16     pattern (
 17        strt adjoin_or_overlap*
 18     )
 19     define
 20        adjoin_or_overlap as
 21           start_date <= prev(end_date)
 22  )
 23  order by emp_id, start_date;
```

My simple definition in line 21 states that a row is overlapping or adjoining if the start_date is smaller than or equal to the end_date of the previous row. A match is then found by the pattern in line 17 of any row followed by zero or more adjoining or overlapping rows.

And sure enough, this rule does indeed merge *some* of the date ranges in this output:

EMP_ID	NAME	START_DATE	END_DATE	JOBS
142	Harold King	2010-07-01		2
143	Mogens Juel	2010-07-01	2015-10-01	3
143	Mogens Juel	2016-06-01		1
144	Axel de Proef	2010-07-01		2
145	Zoe Thorston	2014-02-01		1
145	Zoe Thorston	2019-02-01		1
146	Lim Tok Lo	2014-10-01	2016-02-01	1
146	Lim Tok Lo	2017-03-01		1
147	Ursula Mwbesi	2014-10-01	2015-05-01	1
147	Ursula Mwbesi	2016-05-01		2

But the output of, for example, Mogens Juel is not completely merged; there should have been a single row only for him with four jobs. The problem is that when I order his rows by start_date, the Code Tester and IT Manager rows are compared and *not* overlapping. A comparison like this to the previous row fails to discover that *both* rows are adjoining or overlapping to Sys Admin.

Thinking about it, I figured that maybe it would help simply to change the ordering in line 10 to order by end_date first:

```
...
10      order by end_date, start_date
...
```

The output has changed, but Mogens Juel still wrongly is shown twice:

EMP_ID	NAME	START_DATE	END_DATE	JOBS
142	Harold King	2010-07-01		2
143	Mogens Juel	2010-07-01	2014-01-01	1
143	Mogens Juel	2014-04-01		3
144	Axel de Proef	2010-07-01		2
145	Zoe Thorston	2014-02-01		1
145	Zoe Thorston	2019-02-01		1
146	Lim Tok Lo	2014-10-01	2016-02-01	1
146	Lim Tok Lo	2017-03-01		1

| 147 | Ursula Mwbesi | 2014-10-01 | 2015-05-01 | 1 |
| 147 | Ursula Mwbesi | 2016-05-01 | | 2 |

With the changed ordering, the first attempt at finding a match for Mogens Juel will try to compare the IT Technician row with the Code Tester row and fail to find an overlap.

No matter which ordering I choose, I cannot get *all* the overlaps in a single match by simply comparing a row to the previous row. I need a different way to handle this.

Better comparing to the maximum end date

Looking more closely on the rows of Mogens Juel in Figure 19-2, I decide that a better approach would be to compare the start_date of a row with the *highest* end_date that I have found so far in the match.

A first attempt at this approach *could* look like this, but *it would not work*:

```
...
 8   match_recognize (
 9      partition by emp_id
10      order by start_date, end_date
11      measures
12         max(name)        as name
13       , first(start_date) as start_date
14       , max(end_date)     as end_date
15       , count(*)          as jobs
16      pattern (
17         strt adjoin_or_overlap*
18      )
19      define
20         adjoin_or_overlap as
21            start_date <= max(end_date)
22   )
...
```

The reason it does not work is that when a definition condition like line 21 is evaluated, the row is *first* assumed to be classified `adjoin_or_overlap`, and *then* the condition is tested if it is true. Therefore the result of `max(end_date)` is calculated of all rows of the match so far *plus* the current row, which does not make sense.

In fact it makes so little sense that when I tested this first attempt, the query gave me either `ORA-03113: end-of-file on communication channel` or `java.lang.NullPointerException` depending on database version and which client I use. The database connection was then broken.

So do *not* use this first attempt. Instead you should try my *second* attempt, which is shown in Listing 19-6.

Listing 19-6. Comparing start_date of next row to highest end_date seen so far

```
...
 8  match_recognize (
 9     partition by emp_id
10     order by start_date, end_date
11     measures
12        max(name)         as name
13      , first(start_date) as start_date
14      , max(end_date)     as end_date
15      , count(*)          as jobs
16     pattern (
17        adjoin_or_overlap* last_row
18     )
19     define
20        adjoin_or_overlap as
21           next(start_date) <= max(end_date)
22  )
23  order by emp_id, start_date;
```

In Listing 19-6, I reverse the logic. Instead of comparing the current row with the *previous* row, I compare it with the *next* row:

- I go back to ordering by `start_date` in line 10.

- In line 21, I check if the `start_date` of the *next* row is less than or equal to the highest `end_date` seen so far in the match – *including the current row*, because the `max` call will assume the current row is part of the match when it is evaluated. That means that when a row is classified as `adjoin_or_overlap`, *that* row *should* be merged with the next row.

- The pattern in line 17 looks for zero or more `adjoin_or_overlap` rows followed by one single row classified `last_row`. As that classification is undefined, *any* row can match it – but since the row before `last_row` was classified `adjoin_or_overlap`, I *know* that the `last_row` should be merged too.

- If I find no `adjoin_or_overlap` rows, the row will become classified `last_row` because of the * in line 17 that says that zero `adjoin_or_overlap` rows are acceptable in the pattern. This means that when a row is not overlapping with any other rows, it will become a match of a single row classified as `last_row` and thus unmerged be part of the output.

- The measure `end_date` in line 14 is calculated as the largest `end_date` of the match. Since I am not qualifying the `end_date` in the `max` call with either `adjoin_or_overlap` or `last_row`, `max` is applied to all rows of the match no matter what classification the rows got.

This is a somewhat tricky `match_recognize` clause to understand. When I do conference presentations on this topic, I usually draw the date ranges on a whiteboard and step through the evaluation of the row classification row by row. As I cannot do an animated drawing in a book, I am going to simulate it using a series of figures from Figure 19-4 to Figure 19-8, going through the steps of finding a match for Mogens Juel.

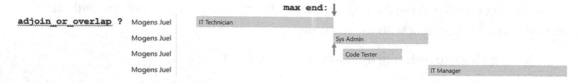

Figure 19-4. *Can first row be classified as adjoin_or_overlap?*

In Figure 19-4, I start by evaluating if the first row of Mogens Juel can be classified adjoin_or_overlap or not. Since I start by *assuming* it can, the max(end_date) in line 21 of Listing 19-6 evaluates to the end of the first row. The next(start_date) evaluates to the start_date of the second row. The two are equal, therefore adjoining, so the condition in line 21 is true, and the first row is classified adjoin_or_overlap.

Figure 19-5. *Can second row be classified as adjoin_or_overlap?*

Having classified the first row, Figure 19-5 evaluates if the second row can be classified adjoin_or_overlap or not. The max(end_date) evaluates to the end_date of the second row, while the next(start_date) is the start_date of the third row. The latter is less than the former, therefore overlapping, and the second row is classified adjoin_or_overlap.

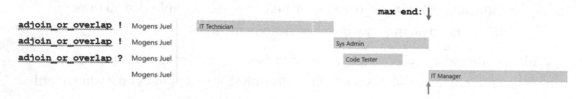

Figure 19-6. *Can third row be classified as adjoin_or_overlap?*

The pattern is still fulfilled, so in Figure 19-6, the classification evaluation is performed for the third row. In this case the max(end_date) does not move; it is still the end_date of the second row. The next(start_date) is the start_date of the fourth row. They are equal, so the fourth row is adjoining to the match found so far, and therefore the third row is adjoin_or_overlap.

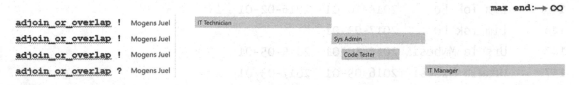

Figure 19-7. *Can fourth row be classified as adjoin_or_overlap?*

The match continues, and Figure 19-7 evaluates the fourth row. This time max(end_date) should be infinity as shown in the figure, because the fourth row has null in end_date. I am not *yet* handling this situation (more on this shortly), so in actual fact, max(end_date) would *wrongly* evaluate to the end_date of the second row. But since there are no more rows, next(start_date) evaluates to null, which makes the condition evaluate to Boolean *unknown*. Therefore the fourth row is *not* classified as adjoin_or_overlap.

Figure 19-8. *Fourth row classified as last_row and a match has been found*

When the fourth row is *not* adjoin_or_overlap, the pattern in line 17 of Listing 19-6 states that it should be a last_row in order to complete the match. So Figure 19-8 evaluates if the fourth row can be classified last_row or not. As last_row is an *undefined* classification, it *always* evaluates to true, and the fourth row *is* therefore classified as last_row, and the match has been completed.

This step-by-step evaluation of the row classification of Mogens Juel leads to the output of Listing 19-6, where the four hire periods of Mogens Juel have correctly been merged into a single row showing four jobs:

EMP_ID	NAME	START_DATE	END_DATE	JOBS
142	Harold King	2010-07-01	2012-04-01	2
143	Mogens Juel	2010-07-01	2016-06-01	4
144	Axel de Proef	2010-07-01	2013-07-01	2
145	Zoe Thorston	2014-02-01		1
145	Zoe Thorston	2019-02-01		1

146	Lim Tok Lo	2014-10-01	2016-02-01	1
146	Lim Tok Lo	2017-03-01		1
147	Ursula Mwbesi	2014-10-01	2015-05-01	1
147	Ursula Mwbesi	2016-05-01	2017-03-01	2

But I still have a couple of problems with this output.

Firstly several of the employees (including Mogens Juel) have a wrong value in the measure end_date. Those that are still employed should have null (blank) in the end_date column, and in this output that is *only* true for those with just a *single* hire period. For those that have had *more* than one job, the highest *non-null* end_date is wrongly displayed.

Secondly I notice that Zoe Thorston also has overlapping rows – the problem here is just that the end_date of both rows are null, meaning both rows are current and she has both job functions. With the null values, the simple comparison in line 21 of Listing 19-6 will *not* be true.

Both of these problems are because I am not handling the null values in end_date. This I will do now.

Handling the null dates

To handle these null values, I change a little bit more in Listing 19-7.

Listing 19-7. Handling null=infinity for both start and end

```
...
 8  match_recognize (
 9    partition by emp_id
10    order by start_date nulls first, end_date nulls last
11    measures
12      max(name)        as name
13    , first(start_date) as start_date
14    , nullif(
15        max(nvl(end_date, date '9999-12-31'))
16      , date '9999-12-31'
17      )              as end_date
18    , count(*)        as jobs
```

```
19    pattern (
20        adjoin_or_overlap* last_row
21    )
22    define
23        adjoin_or_overlap as
24            nvl(next(start_date), date '-4712-01-01')
25                <= max(nvl(end_date, date '9999-12-31'))
26    )
27  order by emp_id, start_date;
```

Even though this particular case only has null values in the end_date, for demonstration purposes, I have made the changes necessary to handle if there were null values in the start_date as well:

- In line 10, I make the order by a bit more explicit. If there had been null values in start_date, these would be considered earlier than any other start_date, so I use nulls first to make those rows come first. Similarly null values in end_date are considered later than any other end_date, so I use nulls last to make those rows come last.

- In comparisons I cannot simply use a nulls first to consider a null in start_date to be less than any other date, so in line 24, I turn a null into the smallest date possible in the Oracle date datatype.

- The aggregate function max ignores null values, so in line 25, I turn a null in end_date into the largest date possible in a date.

- To get a correct result in the end_date *measure*, I do the same nvl inside the max function in line 15. Then if the max results in the largest date, I use nullif in lines 14 and 16 to turn that back into null for output.

With these expanded rules, I get the final output where the rows of Zoe Thorston also are merged into one:

EMP_ID	NAME	START_DATE	END_DATE	JOBS
142	Harold King	2010-07-01		2
143	Mogens Juel	2010-07-01		4
144	Axel de Proef	2010-07-01		2

145	Zoe Thorston	2014-02-01		2
146	Lim Tok Lo	2014-10-01	2016-02-01	1
146	Lim Tok Lo	2017-03-01		1
147	Ursula Mwbesi	2014-10-01	2015-05-01	1
147	Ursula Mwbesi	2016-05-01		2

This output matches Figure 19-3, the result that I wanted.

Now I cannot merge any further – the rows of this output are all neither overlapping nor adjoining.

Lessons learned

This is just a single example of merging rows with date ranges in a report on employee job history, but it serves as inspiration and lesson to enable you to go ahead and do the same for other data.

In the course of the chapter, I've been explaining about

- The advantages of using half-open intervals for date ranges and how temporal validity can make it easier to query data with such intervals

- Using `match_recognize` to compare maximum values with next row to find overlapping or adjoining ranges and merge them into aggregate rows

- Expanding the rules to also handle situations where `null` indicates infinity

You'll likely find many places you can use these methods.

CHAPTER 20

Finding Abnormal Peaks

In many cases there's sequential data (often chronological) that's supposed to have a fairly steady value or increasing/decreasing at a fairly steady rate. If there are spots in the data where it is *not* fairly steady, you want to know about it. Or in other words, if you graphically represent the data, you want to find the abnormal peaks and spikes.

As a database professional, an obvious case of this situation is tablespace storage usage. Normally the number of GBs grows approximately the same rate each day/week/month – any excessive growth rate is indicative of an abnormal workload, which could be caused by a large scheduled onetime job or a bug causing a runaway process to falsely insert millions of rows.

Another use case is the one I'll use in this chapter – number of visits to individual web pages on the web site. Abnormal visit counts can mean denial-of-service attacks, high response to a marketing campaign, spam bots, and viral tweets – in all cases it'd be good to find such peaks in the data.

I think you can easily think of many other similar use cases, but how then to spot those peaks? Putting the data on a graph often makes such peaks easily visible to the human eye, but you can't make SQL code look at a graph – or can you? Well, in a sense, yes you can. I showed in Chapter 17 how to look for up-and-down patterns with `match_recognize` – it is a similar technique to find these peaks.

Web page counter history

As the example use case, I am going to use page counters for web pages – simply that each page on the Good Beer Trading Co web site has a counter that increments by 1 for every time someone visits that page.

Every midnight the current value of each page counter is stored in the `web_counter_hist` table shown in Figure 20-1, where you also see the `web_pages` and `web_apps` tables.

© Kim Berg Hansen 2020
K. Berg Hansen, *Practical Oracle SQL*, https://doi.org/10.1007/978-1-4842-5617-6_20

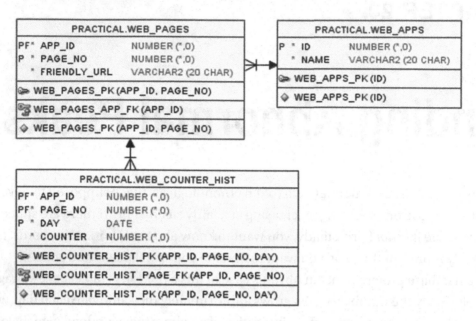

Figure 20-1. *The tables for storing web apps, pages, and counter history*

As the web_counter_hist.page_no column is not very human-friendly, in Listing 20-1, I create a view joining the three tables.

Listing 20-1. View joining web apps, pages, and counter history

```
SQL> create or replace view web_page_counter_hist
  2  as
  3  select
  4      ch.app_id
  5    , a.name as app_name
  6    , ch.page_no
  7    , p.friendly_url
  8    , ch.day
  9    , ch.counter
 10  from web_apps a
 11  join web_pages p
 12      on p.app_id = a.id
 13  join web_counter_hist ch
```

```
14       on ch.app_id = p.app_id
15       and ch.page_no = p.page_no;
```

View WEB_PAGE_COUNTER_HIST created.

Having set the stage, I am now ready to dive into the data.

The counter data

First, with Listing 20-2, I'll show you that my web site has only a single application with four pages in it.

Listing 20-2. The pages in my webshop app

```
SQL> select
  2       p.app_id
  3     , a.name as app_name
  4     , p.page_no
  5     , p.friendly_url
  6  from web_apps a
  7  join web_pages p
  8       on p.app_id = a.id
  9  order by p.app_id, p.page_no;
```

The application is the webshop, and the four pages each have a friendly_url, since it is nicer for us humans to use /About instead of /pls/apex/f?p=542:4::::::::

APP_ID	APP_NAME	PAGE_NO	FRIENDLY_URL
542	Webshop	1	/Shop
542	Webshop	2	/Categories
542	Webshop	3	/Breweries
542	Webshop	4	/About

And so I can use Listing 20-3 to see the counter history for each of the four pages of application 542.

Listing 20-3. Web page counter history data

```
SQL> select
  2      friendly_url, day, counter
  3  from web_page_counter_hist
  4  where app_id = 542
  5  order by page_no, day;
```

I get incrementing counter values for the 30 days of April 2019:

```
FRIENDLY_URL   DAY          COUNTER
/Shop          2019-04-01   5010
/Shop          2019-04-02   5088
...
/Shop          2019-04-29   7755
/Shop          2019-04-30   7833
/Categories    2019-04-01   3397
...
/Categories    2019-04-30   5033
/Breweries     2019-04-01   1866
...
/Breweries     2019-04-30   3115
/About         2019-04-01   455
...
/About         2019-04-30   586

120 rows selected.
```

These data I visualize on the graph in Figure 20-2. It's actually not that easy to spot abnormalities on these graphs. Mostly I can spot that the top line has a period of acceleration around the middle of the month, and the second line has a short burst near the end of the month. But to really find these spots, I'll be turning to SQL.

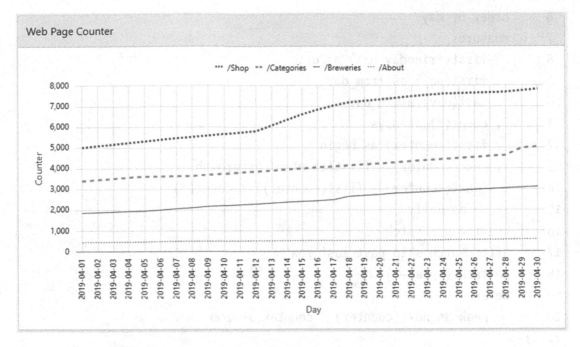

Figure 20-2. *Web page counter history data*

As I only have this one single application, I'm simplifying the rest of the SQL in this chapter and skip using `where app_id = 542` all over. The assumption for the rest of the code is a single application.

Patterns in the raw counter data

In this set of `match_recognize` examples, I'll be using these raw counter data as depicted in the preceding graph.

First I can try simply to find periods where a given page counter grew by at least a constant number every day. In Listing 20-4 I search for counter growth of at least 200.

Listing 20-4. Recognizing days where counter grew by at least 200

```
SQL> select
  2     url, from_day, to_day, days, begin, growth, daily
  3  from web_page_counter_hist
  4  match_recognize(
  5     partition by page_no
```

```
 6      order by day
 7      measures
 8         first(friendly_url) as url
 9       , first(day) as from_day
10       , last(day) as to_day
11       , count(*) as days
12       , first(counter) as begin
13       , next(counter) - first(counter) as growth
14       , (next(counter) - first(counter)) / count(*)
15            as daily
16      one row per match
17      after match skip past last row
18      pattern ( peak+ )
19      define
20         peak as next(counter) - counter >= 200
21   )
22   order by page_no, from_day;
```

In the definition in line 20, I state what a peak is: it is a day where the counter grew
by at least 200 on that day. Since the counter values are stored at midnight, the growth of
the counter during the day is the next value minus the current value. So any rows where
this is greater than or equal to 200 is classified as a peak row.

The pattern in line 18 can then be very simple – I'm looking for periods of one or
more consecutive days classified as peak rows. I output just a single row per period by
using one row per match in line 16. And the measures calculations in lines 8–15 give me
this output:

URL	FROM_DAY	TO_DAY	DAYS	BEGIN	GROWTH	DAILY
/Shop	2019-04-12	2019-04-15	4	5800	1039	259.75
/Categories	2019-04-28	2019-04-28	1	4625	360	360

That's exactly those two abnormalities that I mentioned in the preceding text I could
spot by eye on the graphs in Figure 20-2.

Note that since I did not specify any running or final in Listing 20-4, the output
specifically works because I am using one row per match – had I been using all rows
per match, most of the measures would have used running semantics and given me an
output I probably didn't want.

But I can also be explicit and specify that I actually want it to use `final` semantics, that is, evaluate the expressions as of the last row of the match. This would mean changing the `measures` expressions in lines 8–15 this way:

```
...
 8        first(friendly_url) as url
 9      , first(day) as from_day
10      , final last(day) as to_day
11      , final count(*) as days
12      , first(counter) as begin
13      , next(final last(counter)) - first(counter) as growth
14      , (next(final last(counter)) - first(counter))
15          / final count(*) as daily
...
```

It gives me the exact same output, but now I'd also get the same values calculated if I used `all rows per match`.

Note   As explained in the preceding text, using `next(counter)` in the `define` clause gets the value of the next midnight, so when I subtract the current value, I get the day's growth. To get the *total* growth of the period in line 13, the `final last` goes to the last day of the match – applying `next` then gives me the counter value from the following midnight *even though it is outside the match*.

I've now found growth peaks that exceeded a constant number, but the problem is that "at least 200" may be a good number for the most-visited pages, but is not appropriate for the least-visited pages.

So in Listing 20-5, I do not look for absolute numbers, but rather a relative growth in percent.

Listing 20-5. Recognizing days where counter grew by at least 4%

```
SQL> select
  2     url, from_day, to_day, days, begin, pct, daily
  3  from web_page_counter_hist
  4  match_recognize(
  5     partition by page_no
```

```
6      order by day
7      measures
8         first(friendly_url) as url
9       , first(day) as from_day
10      , final last(day) as to_day
11      , final count(*) as days
12      , first(counter) as begin
13      , round(
14          100 * (next(final last(counter)) / first(counter))
15               - 100
16        , 1
17        ) as pct
18      , round(
19          (100 * (next(final last(counter)) / first(counter))
20                    - 100) / final count(*)
21        , 1
22        ) as daily
23      one row per match
24      after match skip past last row
25      pattern ( peak+ )
26      define
27         peak as next(counter) / counter >= 1.04
28    )
29  order by page_no, from_day;
```

In line 27, I changed my definition of what is a peak row, so I do not look at the *difference* between the values of next and current midnight, but rather the *ratio*. If the next value is at least a *factor* 1.04 of the current value, the growth that day has been at least 4%, and the row is a peak row.

I keep most of my measures expressions, but in lines 13–22, I change from showing absolute growth to showing the total growth and average daily growth in percent:

URL	FROM_DAY	TO_DAY	DAYS	BEGIN	PCT	DAILY
/Shop	2019-04-12	2019-04-14	3	5800	14	4.7
/Categories	2019-04-28	2019-04-28	1	4625	7.8	7.8
/Breweries	2019-04-17	2019-04-17	1	2484	6.6	6.6
/About	2019-04-05	2019-04-05	1	468	4.9	4.9

In Listing 20-5, I look for periods where the growth in every day of the period has been at least 4%. But I can change the definition in line 27 to a slightly more complex calculation:

```
...
27          peak as ((next(counter) / first(counter)) - 1)
28                   / running count(*)  >= 0.04
...
```

With this formula, I look for periods where the average daily growth in the period has been at least 4%. The output shows me almost the same four matches, except that each of the first three periods is a little bit longer now, since some larger daily growths in the start of the periods mean that an extra day or two can be included in the end of the match. Even though those extra days individually have a growth less than 4%, the average in the period still stays at least 4%:

URL	FROM_DAY	TO_DAY	DAYS	BEGIN	PCT	DAILY
/Shop	2019-04-12	2019-04-16	5	5800	21.2	4.2
/Categories	2019-04-28	2019-04-29	2	4625	8.8	4.4
/Breweries	2019-04-17	2019-04-18	2	2484	8.4	4.2
/About	2019-04-05	2019-04-05	1	468	4.9	4.9

I've now shown looking for abnormal growth in terms of absolute or relative growth, but it might not be the best to do in this case. It might be better to look at daily visits.

Looking at daily visits

Some cases can usefully look for growth the ways I've shown in the preceding text, but when you think about it, maybe it isn't such a good idea for this case. Over time the counter value will just keep on increasing, so when the counter value over the years become orders of magnitude larger, a 4% growth rate needs a lot more daily visitors to satisfy.

So I'm going to try to look instead into how the daily visit counts behave. When you look at the data this way, it becomes clear that what I actually found in Listing 20-5 were periods where the daily visits were at least 4% of the counter value. That will unfortunately make the *same* daily visits give a high percentage in the start of the counter lifetime and a lower and lower percentage as time goes by and the counter increases.

To create a better solution, first, I'll use Listing 20-6 to just show the daily visits.

Listing 20-6. Focusing on daily visits

```
SQL> select
  2      friendly_url, day
  3    , lead(counter) over (
  4          partition by page_no order by day
  5      ) - counter as visits
  6   from web_page_counter_hist
  7   order by page_no, day;
```

The expression in lines 3–5 uses the lead analytic function to find the difference between the counter value next midnight and this midnight – same as I did before using next in the match_recognize syntax:

```
FRIENDLY_URL   DAY            VISITS
/Shop          2019-04-01   78
/Shop          2019-04-02   72
...
/Shop          2019-04-29   78
/Shop          2019-04-30
/Categories    2019-04-01   57
...
/Categories    2019-04-29   48
/Categories    2019-04-30
/Breweries     2019-04-01   21
...
/Breweries     2019-04-29   38
/Breweries     2019-04-30
/About         2019-04-01   4
...
/About         2019-04-29   5
/About         2019-04-30

120 rows selected.
```

And I visualize this output in Figure 20-3.

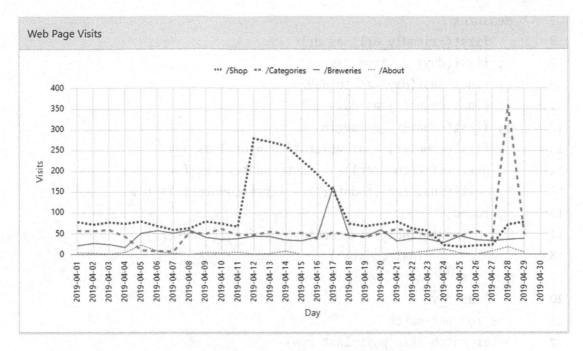

Figure 20-3. *Graphing visits instead of counter highlights peaks*

On this graph, it is much easier to spot the peaks compared to the graph in Figure 20-2. You can even see the small peaks on the lowest line – the /About page.

Then I'll proceed to finding patterns based on this graph.

Patterns in daily visits data

For starters, again I simply try to find patterns based on an absolute number. In Listing 20-7, I look for periods where the daily visits are at least 50 higher than the day just before the period.

Listing 20-7. *Daily visits at least 50 higher than previous day*

```
SQL> select
  2      url, from_day, to_day, days, begin, p_v, f_v, t_v, d_v
  3  from web_page_counter_hist
  4  match_recognize(
  5      partition by page_no
  6      order by day
```

```
 7     measures
 8        first(friendly_url) as url
 9      , first(day) as from_day
10      , final last(day) as to_day
11      , final count(*) as days
12      , first(counter) as begin
13      , first(counter) - prev(first(counter)) as p_v
14      , next(first(counter)) - first(counter) as f_v
15      , next(final last(counter)) - first(counter) as t_v
16      , round(
17           (next(final last(counter)) - first(counter))
18             / final count(*)
19          , 1
20          ) as d_v
21     one row per match
22     after match skip past last row
23     pattern ( peak+ )
24     define
25        peak as next(counter) - counter
26                   - (first(counter) - prev(first(counter))) >= 50
27   )
28  order by page_no, from_day;
```

Much looks similar to what I did before, but there are some differences:

- The definition of the peak classification in lines 25–26 works like this:

  - The next counter value minus current counter value in line 25 is the visits of the current day.

  - Taking the `first` minus `prev(first` in line 26 is identical to going back to the previous row and doing next minus current, or in other words this is the visits of the day just before the beginning of the match.

  - Subtracting the "day before" visits from the current day visits gives how much higher the current day is – if this is at least 50, the row is classified peak.

- In the measures I calculate these four values:

  - p_v is previous visits – the visits of the day before the first row of the match, as explained in the preceding text

  - f_v is first day's visits – the visits of the first day of the match

  - t_v is total period visits – the visits from the first to the last day of the match

  - d_v is daily visits – the average visits per day in the match period

All in all, the code produces this output:

URL	FROM_DAY	TO_DAY	DAYS	BEGIN	P_V	F_V	T_V	D_V
/Shop	2019-04-12	2019-04-17	6	5800	67	279	1386	231
/Categories	2019-04-28	2019-04-28	1	4625	37	360	360	360
/Breweries	2019-04-17	2019-04-17	1	2484	42	163	163	163

Which you'll recognize as the largest three spikes on the graph shown in Figure 20-3.

There was a lot of prev, next, first, and last used in Listing 20-7 to calculate visits based on the counter data. Alternatively I can pre-calculate the daily visits and that way simplify my match_recognize clause, like in Listing 20-8.

Listing 20-8. Pre-calculating visits for simplifying code

```
SQL> select
  2     url, from_day, to_day, days, begin, p_v, f_v, t_v, d_v
  3  from (
  4     select
  5        page_no, friendly_url, day, counter
  6      , lead(counter) over (
  7           partition by page_no order by day
  8        ) - counter as visits
  9     from web_page_counter_hist
 10  )
 11  match_recognize(
 12     partition by page_no
 13     order by day
 14     measures
```

```
15        first(friendly_url) as url
16      , first(day) as from_day
17      , final last(day) as to_day
18      , final count(*) as days
19      , first(counter) as begin
20      , prev(first(visits)) as p_v
21      , first(visits) as f_v
22      , final sum(visits) as t_v
23      , round(final avg(visits)) as d_v
24    one row per match
25    after match skip past last row
26    pattern ( peak+ )
27    define
28        peak as visits - prev(first(visits)) >= 50
29  )
30  order by page_no, from_day;
```

Lines 4–9 contain an inline view identical to Listing 20-6, where I calculate the daily visits with the analytic `lead` function. Then my `match_recognize` clauses become a lot simpler:

- Line 28 simply is the difference between current visits and visits from the day before the match start.

- The four measures described in the preceding text are much simpler in lines 20–23 by using navigational functions and aggregates.

The output of Listing 20-8 is identical to Listing 20-7.

It is worth noting that the database worked a little harder in Listing 20-8, since it had to first do the pre-calculation with analytic functions before it could do the pattern matching. On the other hand, the pattern matching processing became simpler, so depending on the data, it might offset this overhead – your mileage may vary, so test either approach on your own data.

It can also often be the case that your data already contains data in the form like "daily visits" instead of historical snapshot values of an increasing counter. If so, then it is easy to skip the inline view in Listing 20-8 and simply apply the pattern matching directly on your data.

Now, I do seem to get a better peak detection focusing on the visits than in the first couple of examples in this chapter, but it is still probably not good to look for an absolute like "at least 50 higher." So in Listing 20-9, I'm altering Listing 20-8 to search relatively for "at least 50% higher" instead.

Listing 20-9. Daily visits at least 50% higher than the previous day

```
SQL> select
  2      url, from_day, to_day, days, begin, p_v, f_v, t_v, d_pct
  3  from (
...
 10  )
 11  match_recognize(
...
 23      , round(
 24          (100*(final sum(visits) / prev(first(visits))) - 100)
 25              / final count(*)
 26          , 1
 27          ) as d_pct
...
 31      define
 32          peak as visits / nullif(prev(first(visits)), 0) >= 1.5
 33  )
 34  order by page_no, from_day;
```

In line 32 I switch from looking at differences to looking at ratios. If the prev row had zero visits, I cannot calculate a ratio, so I use nullif to make the entire expression null in those cases.

And then instead of a daily visits measure, I use lines 23–27 to calculate the daily average of the percentage of the day's visits compared to the "day before" visits.

I'm now finding quite a few more peaks in my data, or are they really peaks?

URL	FROM_DAY	TO_DAY	DAYS	BEGIN	P_V	F_V	T_V	D_PCT
/Shop	2019-04-12	2019-04-17	6	5800	67	279	1386	328.1
/Shop	2019-04-28	2019-04-29	2	7683	23	72	150	276.1
/Categories	2019-04-08	2019-04-29	22	3637	7	54	1396	901.9
/Breweries	2019-04-05	2019-04-29	25	1955	17	51	1160	268.9
/About	2019-04-04	2019-04-07	4	463	1	5	38	925
/About	2019-04-11	2019-04-11	1	508	3	5	5	66.7
/About	2019-04-13	2019-04-14	2	514	1	2	10	450
/About	2019-04-23	2019-04-24	2	531	4	8	21	212.5
/About	2019-04-28	2019-04-28	1	563	8	18	18	125

The problem with this approach is that when I have even just a single day with very low number of visits, practically all days afterward are 50% higher, even though there isn't really a peak. Like the output shows a 25-day "peak" for the /Breweries page.

So maybe instead I should go for searching periods where the daily visits are at least 50% higher than the *average* daily visit? I'll try that in Listing 20-10.

Listing 20-10. Daily visits at least 50% higher than average

```
SQL> select
  2      url, avg_v, from_day, to_day, days, t_v, d_v, d_pct
  3    from (
  4      select
  5        page_no, friendly_url, day, counter, visits
  6      , avg(visits) over (
  7          partition by page_no
  8        ) as avg_visits
  9      from (
 10        select
 11          page_no, friendly_url, day, counter
 12        , lead(counter) over (
 13            partition by page_no order by day
 14          ) - counter as visits
 15        from web_page_counter_hist
 16      )
```

```
17  )
18  match_recognize(
19      partition by page_no
20      order by day
21      measures
22          first(friendly_url) as url
23        , round(first(avg_visits), 1) as avg_v
24        , first(day) as from_day
25        , final last(day) as to_day
26        , final count(*) as days
27        , final sum(visits) as t_v
28        , round(final avg(visits), 1) as d_v
29        , round(
30            (100 * final avg(visits) / avg_visits) - 100
31          , 1
32          ) as d_pct
33      one row per match
34      after match skip past last row
35      pattern ( peak+ )
36      define
37          peak as visits / avg_visits >= 1.5
38  )
39  order by page_no, from_day;
```

My original inline view (lines 10–15) I wrap in another inline view, so that I can use analytic avg function in lines 6–8 to calculate the average daily visits for each page (by partitioning by page_no.)

Having pre-calculated the average visits, the expression in line 37 is pretty simple – if the ratio of visits to average visits is at least 1.5, the row is a peak row.

That gives me a much more realistic output that finds each of the three large spikes (that I also found with Listing 20-7) as well as the four small spikes on the /About page that I can see in Figure 20-3:

URL	AVG_V	FROM_DAY	TO_DAY	DAYS	T_V	D_V	D_PCT
/Shop	97.3	2019-04-12	2019-04-17	6	1386	231	137.3
/Categories	56.4	2019-04-28	2019-04-28	1	360	360	538.1
/Breweries	43.1	2019-04-17	2019-04-17	1	163	163	278.5
/About	4.5	2019-04-05	2019-04-06	2	31	15.5	243.1
/About	4.5	2019-04-14	2019-04-14	1	8	8	77.1
/About	4.5	2019-04-23	2019-04-24	2	21	10.5	132.4
/About	4.5	2019-04-27	2019-04-28	2	26	13	187.8

Using Listing 20-10 with the pre-calculated daily and average visits, it becomes easy to look for other things than simply spikes of 50% greater than average.

For example, I can change the definition in line 37 to find periods where the daily visits are at least 80% *less* than average:

```
...
37          peak as visits / avg_visits <= 0.2
...
```

That gives me periods where the pages might have had problems – particularly those periods where the /About page had absolutely no visitors at all:

URL	AVG_V	FROM_DAY	TO_DAY	DAYS	T_V	D_V	D_PCT
/Shop	97.3	2019-04-25	2019-04-25	1	18	18	-81.5
/Categories	56.4	2019-04-05	2019-04-07	3	25	8.3	-85.2
/About	4.5	2019-04-08	2019-04-08	1	0	0	-100
/About	4.5	2019-04-15	2019-04-20	6	0	0	-100
/About	4.5	2019-04-26	2019-04-26	1	0	0	-100

And I can make the pattern searching more complex as well in the next examples.

More complex patterns

With Listing 20-11, I can search simultaneously for high, medium, and low peaks.

Listing 20-11. Finding multiple peak classifications simultaneously

```
SQL> select
  2     url, avg_v, from_day, days, class, t_v, d_v, d_pct
  3  from (
```

```
...
17  )
18  match_recognize(
19      partition by page_no
20      order by day
21      measures
22          first(friendly_url) as url
23        , round(first(avg_visits), 1) as avg_v
24        , first(day) as from_day
25        , final count(*) as days
26        , classifier() as class
27        , final sum(visits) as t_v
28        , round(final avg(visits), 1) as d_v
29        , round(
30              (100 * final avg(visits) / avg_visits) - 100
31            , 1
32          ) as d_pct
33      one row per match
34      after match skip past last row
35      pattern ( high{1,} | medium{2,} | low{3,} )
36      define
37          high   as visits / avg_visits >= 4
38        , medium as visits / avg_visits >= 2
39        , low    as visits / avg_visits >= 1.1
40  )
41  order by page_no, from_day;
```

In lines 37–39 instead of just the single peak, I define three different classifications named high, medium, and low – each with a different minimum ratio between the day's visits and the average visits. The high is a ratio of at least 4, meaning the day's visits must be at least 400% of the average or 300% higher than the average, similar for the other definitions.

In the pattern in line 35, I state that a match must be either at least one high row or at least two medium rows or at least three low rows. A single low spike can be random, but three days in a row can be interesting to look at:

URL	AVG_V	FROM_DAY	DAYS	CLASS	T_V	D_V	D_PCT
/Shop	97.3	2019-04-12	4	MEDIUM	1039	259.8	166.8
/Categories	56.4	2019-04-28	1	HIGH	360	360	538.1
/Breweries	43.1	2019-04-05	4	LOW	217	54.3	26
/About	4.5	2019-04-04	3	LOW	36	12	165.6
/About	4.5	2019-04-27	3	LOW	31	10.3	128.8

I see in the output all the three different types of peaks has been found.

Note   The two last low peaks found both have an average daily visit count that is more than 100% larger than the total average, or in other words a ratio greater than 2 – so why are they not classified medium? In order to see why, switch for all rows per match, and remove all final keywords – I'll leave that as an exercise for you. You will find that the answer is that the first row of each of those periods has a ratio between 1.1 and 2, so it is classified low. Therefore, the next rows will not be tested as to whether they are medium or high, since that would be impossible according to the pattern. The only viable pattern that starts with a low row is to find at least three low rows, so the second and third rows in the bottom two matches are only evaluated as having a ratio of at least 1.1, which is true (even though they actually have a ratio of at least 2).

Instead of looking for multiple classifications simultaneously, I can mold a pattern to find a peak of a particular shape. For example, after sending out a newsletter with some links, I'd expect to find a sharp rise for one or a few days, which then tapers off to a medium rise and then low. Listing 20-12 finds such a shaped peak.

Listing 20-12. Finding peaks of a particular shape

```
SQL> select
  2      url, avg_v, from_day, days, hi, med, low, t_v, d_v, d_pct
  3  from (
...
```

```
17  )
18  match_recognize(
19      partition by page_no
20      order by day
21      measures
22          first(friendly_url) as url
23        , round(first(avg_visits), 1) as avg_v
24        , first(day) as from_day
25        , final count(*) as days
26        , final count(high.*) as hi
27        , final count(medium.*) as med
28        , final count(low.*) as low
29        , final sum(visits) as t_v
30        , round(final avg(visits), 1) as d_v
31        , round(
32              (100 * final avg(visits) / avg_visits) - 100
33            , 1
34            ) as d_pct
35      one row per match
36      after match skip past last row
37      pattern ( high+ medium+ low+ )
38      define
39          high   as visits / avg_visits >= 2.5
40        , medium as visits / avg_visits >= 1.5
41        , low    as visits / avg_visits >= 1.1
42  )
43  order by page_no, from_day;
```

Again in lines 39–41, I define three different classifications (slightly different ratio values as before but otherwise same principle.)

My pattern in line 37 then states I'm looking for a peak shaped with at least one high day, followed by at least one medium day and followed by at least one low day.

The measures `hi`, `med`, and `low` in lines 26–28 tell me how many days of each classification, so I can see how many days the visit count stayed `high` before it started to taper off:

URL	AVG_V	FROM_DAY	DAYS	HI	MED	LOW	T_V	D_V	D_PCT
/Shop	97.3	2019-04-12	6	3	2	1	1386	231	137.3

I found the single peak in the data that has the shape I was looking for.

Lessons learned

I've shown multiple examples here of looking for spikes in chronological data – techniques very similar to the up-and-down pattern search in Chapter 17 yet slightly different for slightly different use cases.

Having understood these examples, you should now know about

- Using the navigational functions `prev` and `next` (in conjunction with `final`) to access rows outside the match in the measures expressions

- Pre-calculating values to enable simpler pattern matching (test it to see if it hurts or helps performance)

- Having multiple classification definitions to use in patterns that find either any of the classifications or specific classification combinations in a certain order

There are many use cases of similar chronological (or just sequential) data where you can apply these types of pattern searches.

CHAPTER 21

Bin Fitting

Imagine packing your car to go on a holiday. Probably there's one person in your family that has the 3-D intuition needed to work out how to fit the suitcases just so, so that there's a nook free here to fit a pair of boots and a cranny free there to fit the odd-shaped gift you're bringing along to Aunt Mathilda. That one person always does the packing; the rest of you stay out of the way until the car is packed.

Such packing skills can be highly valued in certain industries, as it is not an easy task to make an algorithm that will do it perfectly. Variants are known as **bin fitting**, **bin packing**, **knapsack problem**, **cutting stock problem**, and more. Googling these terms you will find many algorithms for approximate answers, where typically the better the solution is, the longer time it takes to run.

The very best algorithms often require either several passes of the data or storing data in intermediate arrays for lookups. These are not easily translated to SQL and might even be examples of code where it is not optimal to do it in SQL. But with `match_recognize,` you *can* do some simple approximate bin fitting algorithms that are still quite useful.

Inventory to be packed in boxes

As an example of bin fitting, imagine that the Good Beer Trading Co is moving, so all of the inventory has to be packed into boxes (boxes being my specific example of the generic term *bin*) and moved to a new warehouse somewhere else.

I will be using the `inventory` and related tables I introduced to you in Chapter 13 on FIFO picking. In Chapter 13 I used more tables, but here I just use the ones shown in Figure 21-1.

© Kim Berg Hansen 2020
K. Berg Hansen, *Practical Oracle SQL*, https://doi.org/10.1007/978-1-4842-5617-6_21

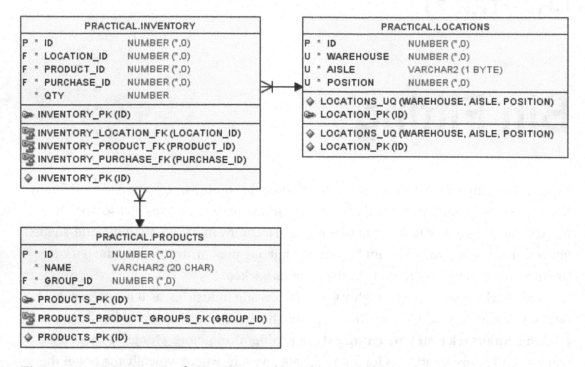

Figure 21-1. *Inventory, locations, and products tables used in this chapter*

In Chapter 13 I also introduced the view `inventory_with_dims` that joins the inventory with `locations` and `products`. This view I will be using throughout this chapter.

Observe the inventory data of one of the beers in Listing 21-1.

Listing 21-1. The inventory of the beer Der Helle Kumpel

```
SQL> select
  2      product_name
  3    , warehouse as wh
  4    , aisle
  5    , position  as pos
  6    , qty
  7  from inventory_with_dims
  8  where product_name = 'Der Helle Kumpel'
  9  order by wh, aisle, pos;
```

Most of the chapter examples show bin fitting for this beer:

PRODUCT_NAME	WH	AISLE	POS	QTY
Der Helle Kumpel	1	A	16	48
Der Helle Kumpel	1	A	29	14
Der Helle Kumpel	1	B	32	43
Der Helle Kumpel	1	C	5	70
Der Helle Kumpel	1	C	13	20
Der Helle Kumpel	1	D	19	48
Der Helle Kumpel	2	A	1	72
Der Helle Kumpel	2	B	5	14
Der Helle Kumpel	2	B	26	24
Der Helle Kumpel	2	C	31	21
Der Helle Kumpel	2	D	9	26

I'll try to pack these beers into boxes according to my bin fitting rules. First with limited capacity boxes.

Bin fitting with unlimited number of bins of limited capacity

This type of bin fitting is also a simple variant of the knapsack problem, which is a problem that is quite hard to solve exactly within reasonable time. In fact it belongs to a class of problems called NP-hard, which is out of the scope of this book to delve deeper into. Suffice it to say here that any solution I give will just be an approximation – more or less optimal.

I pack the beers into boxes according to these rules:

- A box can contain at maximum 72 bottles of beer.

- Quantities from different locations are allowed to be packed together in the same box.

- A quantity from a single location cannot be split into multiple boxes but must stay together in a single box.

   At first I am not worrying about trying to get close to optimal bin fitting. In Listing 21-2 I simply go through the warehouse in order of location and pack the beers into boxes. When I reach a location, if the quantity will fit into the current box, I will pack it into that box; otherwise, I will start packing in a new box.

Listing 21-2. Bin fitting in order of location

```
SQL> select wh, aisle, pos, qty, run_qty, box#, box_qty
  2  from (
  3     select
  4        product_name
  5      , warehouse as wh
  6      , aisle
  7      , position  as pos
  8      , qty
  9     from inventory_with_dims
 10     where product_name = 'Der Helle Kumpel'
 11  ) iwd
 12  match_recognize (
 13     order by wh, aisle, pos
 14     measures
 15        match_number()   as box#
 16      , running sum(qty) as run_qty
 17      , final   sum(qty) as box_qty
 18     all rows per match
 19     pattern (
 20        fits_in_box+
 21     )
 22     define
 23        fits_in_box as sum(qty) <= 72
 24  )
 25  order by wh, aisle, pos;
```

So what happens in this query? I'll explain:

- In the inline view lines 3–10, I simply limit the data to the beer I am packing at the moment.

- In `match_recognize,` I order the data by location in line 13.

- I define the classification `fits_in_box` in line 23 to be when the sum of `qty` is less than or equal to 72. When using an aggregate in a definition, it is evaluated using *running* semantics.

- The `pattern` in line 20 states I want one or more rows that are classified `fits_in_box`. This means that the `qty` of the first row is set as the running sum. If the running sum is not larger than 72, the row is added to the match. Then the `qty` of the second row is added to the running sum. If it still is not larger than 72, the row is added to the match and so on until a row causes the running sum to exceed 72, at which point the match ends.

- In the measures lines 15–17, I use the `match_number()` as the number of the box to be packed in, and I show both the `running` and the `final` sums.

When you look at the output, you can see this in action:

WH	AISLE	POS	QTY	RUN_QTY	BOX#	BOX_QTY
1	A	16	48	48	1	62
1	A	29	14	62	1	62
1	B	32	43	43	2	43
1	C	5	70	70	3	70
1	C	13	20	20	4	68
1	D	19	48	68	4	68
2	A	1	72	72	5	72
2	B	5	14	14	6	59
2	B	26	24	38	6	59
2	C	31	21	59	6	59
2	D	9	26	26	7	26

The first 48 beers are added to the running sum – it's not larger than 72, so it is assigned to box# 1. Then 14 beers are added making the running sum 62 – still assigned to box# 1.

Then it tries to add the 43 beers in the third row, which gives a running sum of 105 – it's larger than 72, so therefore the row is not classified fits_in_box, and the box# 1 thus stops with the first two rows. Instead the 43 beers in the third row become the first beers in the second match – box# 2.

And so it goes on until I end up having packed the beers from the 11 locations into 7 boxes. Fast and easy, but not very optimal. It's easy to spot that at the very least I could save one box by putting the contents of box# 2 and 7 together in a single box with 69 beers.

The problem is that packing simply in order of location does not take into account at all whether the quantities would fit together or not. Had the spread of quantities been different, I might even have gotten an even worse result using more than seven boxes.

One of the beauties of both analytic functions as well as pattern matching is that I can use different order by clauses for the logic and for the final output. So I can try to change the order by in the match_recognize in line 13 to order by the quantity in descending order (and then only use location as a tiebreaker).

To verify the output more easily, I also change the final order by in line 25 to the same (when making a packing list I can always change it back to location order):

```
...
 12   match_recognize (
 13       order by qty desc, wh, aisle, pos
...
 24   )
 25   order by qty desc, wh, aisle, pos;
```

I get an output that packs the beers quite differently than before:

WH	AISLE	POS	QTY	RUN_QTY	BOX#	BOX_QTY
2	A	1	72	72	1	72
1	C	5	70	70	2	70
1	A	16	48	48	3	48
1	D	19	48	48	4	48
1	B	32	43	43	5	69
2	D	9	26	69	5	69
2	B	26	24	24	6	65
2	C	31	21	45	6	65
1	C	13	20	65	6	65
1	A	29	14	14	7	28
2	B	5	14	28	7	28

But it isn't really any more optimal as I still use seven boxes. In fact this can even be called slightly worse, since here I cannot even take the two least-filled boxes and pack them together, as 28 + 48 would exceed 72.

There are various approximation algorithms that can get more or less close to the optimal solution. I have created a quite simplified version of a modified first fit decreasing (MFFD) algorithm. My simple algorithm works like this:

- First any quantity larger than 2/3 of a box capacity is simply assigned to individual boxes. (Any small quantities that might have "filled the holes" are likely to also fit into the rest of the boxes, so as approximation it won't be too far off.)

- The remaining quantities I sort in an interleaved manner:

  - First, the largest

  - Then the smallest

  - Then the second largest

  - Then the second smallest

  - And so on

- Then I pack as before, but using this sorted order, so that I get good chances that the interleaved large/small sorting creates pairs that fit together in a box.

This simple approximation algorithm I implement in Listing 21-3.

Listing 21-3. Using a simple best-fit approximation

```
SQL> select wh, aisle, pos, qty, run_qty, box#, box_qty
  2       , prio ,rn
  3  from (
  4    select
  5        product_name
  6      , warehouse as wh
  7      , aisle
  8      , position  as pos
  9      , qty
 10      , case when qty > 72*2/3 then 1 else 2 end prio
```

```
11        , least(
12            row_number() over (
13                partition by
14                    case when qty > 72*2/3 then 1 else 2 end
15                order by qty
16              )
17          , row_number() over (
18                partition by
19                    case when qty > 72*2/3 then 1 else 2 end
20                order by qty desc
21              )
22          ) rn
23      from inventory_with_dims
24      where product_name = 'Der Helle Kumpel'
25  ) iwd
26  match_recognize (
27      order by prio, rn, qty desc, wh, aisle, pos
28      measures
29        match_number()    as box#
30      , running sum(qty) as run_qty
31      , final   sum(qty) as box_qty
32      all rows per match
33      pattern (
34        fits_in_box+
35      )
36      define
37        fits_in_box as sum(qty) <= 72
38  )
39  order by prio, rn, qty desc, wh, aisle, pos;
```

With this modified algorithm, I get to use just six boxes. The first two have just a single large quantity, the next three all have a pair of quantities (one medium, one small), and in the last box fit three middlish/smallish quantities:

WH	AISLE	POS	QTY	RUN_QTY	BOX#	BOX_QTY	PRIO	RN
2	A	1	72	72	1	72	1	1
1	C	5	70	70	2	70	1	1
1	A	16	48	48	3	62	2	1
1	A	29	14	62	3	62	2	1
1	D	19	48	48	4	62	2	2
2	B	5	14	62	4	62	2	2
1	B	32	43	43	5	63	2	3
1	C	13	20	63	5	63	2	3
2	D	9	26	26	6	71	2	4
2	C	31	21	47	6	71	2	4
2	B	26	24	71	6	71	2	5

This algorithm is by no means the most optimal in all cases. I suggest you try out several methods for your specific use cases. But the most near-optimal algorithms can easily be harder to implement (perhaps almost impossible to implement in SQL, requiring procedural code) and use more CPU, so it will probably be a matter of a trade-off between a simple perhaps-good-enough algorithm like this and a very-good-but-too-slow algorithm.

Using the Der Helle Kumpel beer as example, I am now ready in Listing 21-4 to expand the algorithm to pack all beers in the warehouse.

Listing 21-4. Using partition by to bin fit all products

```
SQL> select product_id
  2         , wh, aisle, pos, qty, run_qty, box#, box_qty
  3  from (
  4     select
  5        product_id
  6      , product_name
  7      , warehouse as wh
  8      , aisle
  9      , position  as pos
 10      , qty
 11      , case when qty > 72*2/3 then 1 else 2 end prio
 12      , least(
 13            row_number() over (
```

```
14              partition by
15                  product_id
16                , case when qty > 72*2/3 then 1 else 2 end
17              order by qty
18          )
19      , row_number() over (
20              partition by
21                  product_id
22                , case when qty > 72*2/3 then 1 else 2 end
23              order by qty desc
24          )
25      ) rn
26    from inventory_with_dims
27 ) iwd
28 match_recognize (
29    partition by product_id
30    order by prio, rn, qty desc, wh, aisle, pos
31    measures
32      match_number()   as box#
33     , running sum(qty) as run_qty
34     , final   sum(qty) as box_qty
35    all rows per match
36    pattern (
37      fits_in_box+
38    )
39    define
40      fits_in_box as sum(qty) <= 72
41 )
42 order by product_id, prio, rn, qty desc, wh, aisle, pos;
```

Basically it's the same thing, but I include product_id in the inline view in line 5, so that I can use it to do partition by in line 29. That gives me an output that bin fits all the beers:

PRODUCT_ID	WH	AISLE	POS	QTY	RUN_QTY	BOX#	BOX_QTY
4040	1	A	13	48	48	1	51
4040	1	C	10	3	51	1	51
4040	2	C	28	48	48	2	53
4040	1	A	25	5	53	2	53
...							
7950	2	B	25	48	48	10	48
7950	1	C	24	42	42	11	42
7950	2	C	5	44	44	12	44

113 rows selected.

Note that since I use match_number() for the box# column, the box numbering restarts for each product; it is not a unique box number throughout the output. If I need that, then I need to add, for example, a dense_rank() over (order by product_id, box#) to the select list.

Listing 21-4 gave me details about which quantities to put in which box by using all rows per match. I can also get just the quantity of each box along with how many locations have been packed together by using one row per match in Listing 21-5.

Listing 21-5. Getting a single output row for each box

```
SQL> select product_id, product_name, box#, box_qty, locs
  2  from (
...
 26  ) iwd
 27  match_recognize (
 28     partition by product_id
 29     order by prio, rn, qty desc, wh, aisle, pos
 30     measures
 31        max(product_name) as product_name
 32      , match_number()    as box#
 33      , final sum(qty)    as box_qty
 34      , final count(*)    as locs
 35     one row per match
 36     pattern (
```

```
37          fits_in_box+
38      )
39    define
40          fits_in_box as sum(qty) <= 72
41  )
42  order by product_id, box#;
```

Besides changing line 35, I just change the measures, select list, and order by a bit to fit, so I get a simpler output:

PRODUCT_ID	PRODUCT_NAME	BOX#	BOX_QTY	LOCS
4040	Coalminers Sweat	1	51	2
4040	Coalminers Sweat	2	53	2
4040	Coalminers Sweat	3	54	2
...				
7950	Pale Rider Rides	10	48	1
7950	Pale Rider Rides	11	42	1
7950	Pale Rider Rides	12	44	1

```
86 rows selected.
```

So far I've been packing in boxes that had sufficient capacity to contain even the largest location quantity I have in the warehouse (72). What happens if I used boxes that were too small?

Showing where box capacity is too small

To demonstrate, I use the simple packing in location order from Listing 21-2 instead of the slightly more optimal modified first fit algorithm. The principle is the same no matter what algorithm, so I just keep it simple in Listing 21-6.

Listing 21-6. Problems when the boxes are too small

```
SQL> select wh, aisle, pos, qty, run_qty, box#, box_qty
  2  from (
  3    select
  4        product_name
  5      , warehouse as wh
```

```
 6        , aisle
 7        , position  as pos
 8         , qty
 9      from inventory_with_dims
10      where product_name = 'Der Helle Kumpel'
11  ) iwd
12  match_recognize (
13      order by wh, aisle, pos
14      measures
15         match_number()    as box#
16       , running sum(qty) as run_qty
17       , final    sum(qty) as box_qty
18      all rows per match
19      pattern (
20         fits_in_box+
21      )
22      define
23         fits_in_box as sum(qty) <= 64
24  )
25  order by wh, aisle, pos;
```

The difference from Listing 21-2 is simply that I use boxes with a capacity of 64 in line 23 instead of 72. What happens then in my output?

WH	AISLE	POS	QTY	RUN_QTY	BOX#	BOX_QTY
1	A	16	48	48	1	62
1	A	29	14	62	1	62
1	B	32	43	43	2	43
1	C	13	20	20	3	20
1	D	19	48	48	4	48
2	B	5	14	14	5	59
2	B	26	24	38	5	59
2	C	31	21	59	5	59
2	D	9	26	26	6	26

I only get nine lines instead of 11. The two quantities that are too large to fit in a box are not matched at all, so they do not appear in the output.

What if I want them to be shown in the output, just without a box#, so I can see that I have a problem with those? Well, I could try simply to change the pattern from fits_in_box+ to fits_in_box* in line 20:

```
...
20          fits_in_box*
...
```

Well, close, but not quite what I want:

WH	AISLE	POS	QTY	RUN_QTY	BOX#	BOX_QTY
1	A	16	48	48	1	62
1	A	29	14	62	1	62
1	B	32	43	43	2	43
1	C	5	70		3	
1	C	13	20	20	4	20
1	D	19	48	48	5	48
2	A	1	72		6	
2	B	5	14	14	7	59
2	B	26	24	38	7	59
2	C	31	21	59	7	59
2	D	9	26	26	8	26

The two rows with qty 70 and 72 appear as I want them to, but they are assigned a box# even though they do not match the rule in the define clause? This is because I use * that means *zero or more*, so match number 3 (box#) and match number 6 are actually *empty* matches.

The pattern matching syntax recognizes empty matches and has a syntax to exclude these from the output if you so desire:

```
...
18      all rows per match omit empty matches
19      pattern (
20          fits_in_box*
21      )
...
```

I simply add omit empty matches in line 18, and then the two empty matches no longer show in the output:

WH	AISLE	POS	QTY	RUN_QTY	BOX#	BOX_QTY
1	A	16	48	48	1	62
1	A	29	14	62	1	62
1	B	32	43	43	2	43
1	C	13	20	20	4	20
1	D	19	48	48	5	48
2	B	5	14	14	7	59
2	B	26	24	38	7	59
2	C	31	21	59	7	59
2	D	9	26	26	8	26

But notice in the box# column that match numbers 3 and 6 were actually assigned, just not shown. This could be appropriate in some circumstances, but it is not what I want.

Instead I go back to using + instead of * and use a different syntax:

```
...
18      all rows per match with unmatched rows
19      pattern (
20          fits_in_box+
21      )
...
```

The pattern uses + (*1 or more*) in line 20, but then I add with unmatched rows in line 18. This gives me the output that I want:

WH	AISLE	POS	QTY	RUN_QTY	BOX#	BOX_QTY
1	A	16	48	48	1	62
1	A	29	14	62	1	62
1	B	32	43	43	2	43
1	C	5	70			
1	C	13	20	20	3	20
1	D	19	48	48	4	48
2	A	1	72			
2	B	5	14	14	5	59
2	B	26	24	38	5	59
2	C	31	21	59	5	59
2	D	9	26	26	6	26

Here the quantities 70 and 72 are included in the output, but all of the measures of those rows are null, including box#, to show it is a row that was not matched at all – not even as an empty match. And you can see that the match number is not increased for the unmatched rows.

This is all well and good for the type of bin fitting that has unlimited number of bins of limited capacity. But there is a different type of bin fitting as well, so let me show that too.

Bin fitting with limited number of bins of unlimited capacity

Imagine we have boxes that are infinitely large – we can pack all the beer bottles into a box that we want. But we only have three such boxes, and we want to pack the beers as evenly distributed across the three boxes as possible. Still the rule goes that the quantity from a given location cannot be split across multiple boxes.

Let me recap the inventory of Der Helle Kumpel, but in Listing 21-7, I just show it in order of descending quantity instead of location order as I used in Listing 21-1.

Listing 21-7. The inventory of the beer Der Helle Kumpel in order of descending quantity

```
SQL> select
  2      product_name
  3    , warehouse as wh
  4    , aisle
  5    , position  as pos
  6    , qty
  7  from inventory_with_dims
  8  where product_name = 'Der Helle Kumpel'
  9  order by qty desc, wh, aisle, pos;
```

You see the by now familiar numbers, just in a different order:

PRODUCT_NAME	WH	AISLE	POS	QTY
Der Helle Kumpel	2	A	1	72
Der Helle Kumpel	1	C	5	70
Der Helle Kumpel	1	A	16	48
Der Helle Kumpel	1	D	19	48
Der Helle Kumpel	1	B	32	43
Der Helle Kumpel	2	D	9	26
Der Helle Kumpel	2	B	26	24
Der Helle Kumpel	2	C	31	21
Der Helle Kumpel	1	C	13	20
Der Helle Kumpel	1	A	29	14
Der Helle Kumpel	2	B	5	14

A fairly simple but good approximation algorithm for this type of bin fitting is to take the quantities in descending order one by one and put them in the box that has the least quantity already. Keep doing that, and at the end you'll have a pretty even distribution of the quantities.

So for three boxes, that means that at first, the three largest quantities are each put in a different box. Then the fourth largest is put in the box with the smallest total, and so on. I illustrate this in Figure 21-2, which starts at the fourth step and shows the following five steps of distributing the quantities. It goes on after that, but you should get the picture of how it works.

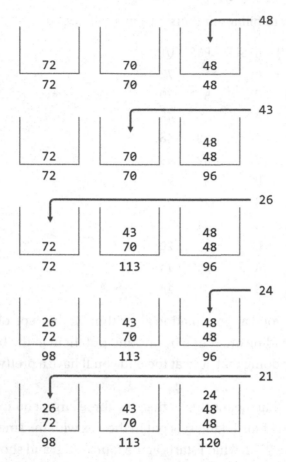

Figure 21-2. *Distributing in order of descending quantity*

To implement this with pattern matching, it is no longer sufficient to use simple define and pattern clauses to create one match at a time. In principle here I would need to work simultaneously on three matches, adding rows interchangeably to each of the matches. That's not how match_recognize works, however, so I need another way.

Instead in Listing 21-8, I can create a classification definition for each of the three boxes and utilize running sums on each classification variable.

Listing 21-8. All rows in a single match, distributing with logic in define clause

```
SQL> select wh, aisle, pos, qty, box, qty1, qty2, qty3
  2  from (
  3     select
  4        product_name
```

```
 5        , warehouse as wh
 6        , aisle
 7        , position  as pos
 8        , qty
 9      from inventory_with_dims
10      where product_name = 'Der Helle Kumpel'
11    ) iwd
12    match_recognize (
13      order by qty desc, wh, aisle, pos
14      measures
15          classifier()                as box
16        , running sum(box1.qty) as qty1
17        , running sum(box2.qty) as qty2
18        , running sum(box3.qty) as qty3
19      all rows per match
20      pattern (
21          (box1 | box2 | box3)*
22      )
23      define
24          box1 as count(box1.*) = 1
25                or sum(box1.qty) - box1.qty
26                      <= least(sum(box2.qty), sum(box3.qty))
27        , box2 as count(box2.*) = 1
28                or sum(box2.qty) - box2.qty
29                      <= sum(box3.qty)
30    )
31    order by qty desc, wh, aisle, pos;
```

This query requires some explanations:

- The pattern in line 21 is deceptively simple: I look for any number
  of consecutive rows that are classified either box1 or box2 or box3.
  But if you look in the define clause, only box1 and box2 are defined,
  not box3. This means that *any* row *not* classified box1 or box2 will
  automatically be classified box3, which in turn means that it is certain
  that all rows will be either box1 or box2 or box3, so that the pattern
  ends up *matching all rows*.

429

- In other words, I'm not really interested in creating multiple matches. What interests me is how the individual rows are classified as I walk along the rows in the one big single match in the order specified in line 13.

- The rows are classified in this way: The classification definitions that potentially can expand the match (in this case all three classifications) are tested one by one for truth in such a way that it checks if the condition is true *if the row is included in this classification*. At the first true definition, the row gets that classification. If neither box1 nor box2 is true, the row gets the undefined (and thus by default true) classification box3.

- So when checking if a row is to be classified box1, it makes the assumption that the row is box1 and then checks if the condition is true. Therefore, when in line 25 it evaluates the running sum(box1.qty), this *includes* the qty of the current row. But I want to check how much was in box1 *before* adding the current row, so I need to subtract the qty of the current row.

- Line 25 calculates how much is in box1 (excluding the current row). In line 26, I check if this is less than (or equal to) the smallest of how much is in box2 and box3. If this is true, then box1 is the box with the least in it (or at least one of them if more than one has the same smallest sum) and the current row should go into box1.

- If box1 was not the one with the least in it, I move on to test box2 by calculating in line 28 how much is in box2 (excluding the current row) and checking in line 29 if it is less than (or equal) to how much is in box3. If this is true, then box2 is the box with the least in it, and the current row should go into box2.

- If box2 was not the one, the row defaults to box3 – the only possibility left in the pattern.

- In lines 24 and 27, I check the count of box1 and box2, respectively. If the count is 1, then that 1 row is the current row (remember by evaluating the conditions it is assumed the current row will be classified box1 and box2, respectively) which means that the box was empty before the current row and therefore definitely the one with the least in it. Testing these counts eliminates worrying about null sums.

- As it is all one single match, line 19 outputs all of the rows. Line 15 then uses the classifier() function to show which box the row ended up in.

- Lines 16–18 show the running sums of the three boxes enabling me to inspect in the output if my algorithm worked. (Note that I haven't written running in the sums in the define clause – they are by definition running sums.)

Making the final order by identical to the match_recognize ordering makes the output explain what happens in the single match as the rows are handled in descending quantity order:

WH	AISLE	POS	QTY	BOX	QTY1	QTY2	QTY3
2	A	1	72	BOX1	72		
1	C	5	70	BOX2	72	70	
1	A	16	48	BOX3	72	70	48
1	D	19	48	BOX3	72	70	96
1	B	32	43	BOX2	72	113	96
2	D	9	26	BOX1	98	113	96
2	B	26	24	BOX3	98	113	120
2	C	31	21	BOX1	119	113	120
1	C	13	20	BOX2	119	133	120
1	A	29	14	BOX1	133	133	120
2	B	5	14	BOX3	133	133	134

You can see how for each quantity it is distributed into the boxes just like Figure 21-2, where columns qty1, qty2, and qty3 are the running sums that show how much so far has been put into, respectively, box1, box2, and box3.

The one slight drawback with this method is that the number of boxes needs a bit of work to change. If, for example, I have four boxes instead of three, I need to modify Listing 21-8 like this:

```
20      pattern (
21         (box1 | box2 | box3 | box4)*
22      )
23      define
24         box1 as count(box1.*) = 1
25              or sum(box1.qty) - box1.qty
26                    <= least(
27                            sum(box2.qty)
28                        , sum(box3.qty)
29                        , sum(box3.qty)
30                         )
31      , box2 as count(box2.*) = 1
32              or sum(box2.qty) - box2.qty
33                  <= least(sum(box3.qty), sum(box4.qty))
34      , box3 as count(box3.*) = 1
35              or sum(box3.qty) - box3.qty
36                    <= sum(box4.qty)
```

To complete it all, in Listing 21-9, I do this for every product, so that each product has three infinite-capacity boxes.

Listing 21-9. All products in three boxes each – output sorted by location

```
SQL> select product_name, wh, aisle, pos, qty, box
  2  from (
  3     select
  4        product_id
  5      , product_name
  6      , warehouse as wh
  7      , aisle
  8      , position  as pos
  9      , qty
 10     from inventory_with_dims
```

```
11  ) iwd
12  match_recognize (
13      partition by product_id
...
28  )
29  order by wh, aisle, pos;
```

This I accomplish with the `partition` by in line 13. If I skipped this line, all beers would be packed into the same three boxes.

And then I've ordered the output in location order, so this can be a packing list for packing everything from the warehouse:

```
PRODUCT_NAME        WH  AISLE  POS  QTY  BOX
Ghost of Hops       1   A      2    39   BOX1
Reindeer Fuel       1   A      3    48   BOX1
Hoppy Crude Oil     1   A      4    37   BOX2
...
Hazy Pink Cloud     2   D      23   17   BOX2
Reindeer Fuel       2   D      25   29   BOX2
Pale Rider Rides    2   D      28   40   BOX3

113 rows selected.
```

Maybe you think that it is not a very practical method for packing beers, as beer boxes of course in real life do not have an infinite capacity. But the principle is valid for other cases as well – a fairly common one is scheduling tasks on a given set of processors/resources. Instead of quantity, it is just time that is distributed as evenly as possible – putting a task on the processor with the least number of minutes in it is equivalent to putting it on the one that has the earliest available timeslot.

Lessons learned

Bin fitting in itself is a difficult problem to get as optimal a fit as possible; usually it is a matter of choosing either a complex solution with a nearly optimal fit or a simpler and faster solution with an approximate fit. What you choose is most often determined by how good an approximation you need for your business purpose.

In this chapter I haven't given you perfect fit solutions, but rather approximations – the bin fitting with limited number of boxes being reasonably good and the one with unlimited number of boxes being a relatively rough approximation. But with `match_recognize,` they're pretty fast, and they are good examples to teach you the following:

- Using running aggregates in the `define` clause to make the classification depend on summary values up to the current row.

- Creating calculated column values to support complex ordering to make the `match_recognize` clause walk through the data in very specific desired order.

- Having the `pattern` match *all* rows and utilize `define` to classify all rows can be an option to make `match_recognize` a tool to create a data manipulation algorithm rather than a data search tool.

- Using aggregates of other classification variables in the `define` clause to make the outcomes of different classification variables depend on each other.

- Utilizing the fact that an *undefined* classification variable is by default considered true, so it can be used as a kind of `else` option.

All in all, understanding these examples will help you gain the way of thinking that lets you really utilize all the power of `match_recognize`.

CHAPTER 22

Counting Children in Trees

Sometimes you'd like to do aggregation where a row is included in multiple rows of the output, for example, being counted multiple times or having the value added multiple times. An example of this is hierarchical data, where you want for every row to find the count of all the children in the tree – not just immediate children but also grandchildren and their children and so on, all the way down to the leaves of the tree.

It means that a given row is counted in the result for the parent, but also counted again in the result of the grandparent, and so on. It can look similar to subtotals created with group by and rollup, but with the hierarchy, you don't know how many levels down it goes, so you cannot simply use rollup.

One way I can solve this is using the after match skip to next row clause of match_recognize. Of course it could be used for other aggregates than count, but count is easy to understand, and once you know the technique, you can do the others easily.

Hierarchical tree of employees

The most classic table used to demonstrate hierarchical queries on Oracle is scott.emp table. Well, the Good Beer Trading Co also employs people, so my practical schema naturally has a table employees depicted in Figure 22-1.

© Kim Berg Hansen 2020

K. Berg Hansen, *Practical Oracle SQL*, https://doi.org/10.1007/978-1-4842-5617-6_22

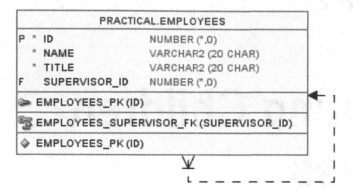

Figure 22-1. *The employees table with a self-referencing foreign key*

The column supervisor_id is a self-referencing foreign key that references the primary key id. Only one person has no supervisor – the boss of the company – for everyone else the supervisor_id contains the id of their immediate supervisor in the employee hierarchy. So I can show you the data of the table in a tree using Listing 22-1.

Listing 22-1. A classic hierarchical query of employees

```
SQL> select
  2      e.id
  3    , lpad(' ', 2*(level-1)) || e.name as name
  4    , e.title as title
  5    , e.supervisor_id as super
  6  from employees e
  7  start with e.supervisor_id is null
  8  connect by e.supervisor_id = prior e.id
  9  order siblings by e.name;
```

For a simple hierarchy like this, I tend to use the Oracle proprietary connect by query instead of the recursive subquery factoring I showed in Chapter 4. One of the things that are easier with connect by is, for example, the order siblings by I use here – that is more awkward to code with recursive subquery factoring.

So I start with the boss by specifying in line 7 to start with those with no supervisors. Then line 8 finds the immediate subordinates of the boss and then goes on recursively to find subordinates of those and so on:

ID	NAME	TITLE	SUPER
142	Harold King	Managing Director	
144	Axel de Proef	Product Director	142
151	Jim Kronzki	Sales Manager	144
150	Laura Jensen	Bulk Salesman	151
154	Simon Chang	Retail Salesman	151
148	Maria Juarez	Purchaser	144
147	Ursula Mwbesi	Operations Chief	142
146	Lim Tok Lo	Warehouse Manager	147
152	Evelyn Smith	Forklift Operator	146
149	Kurt Zollman	Forklift Operator	146
155	Susanne Hoff	Janitor	146
143	Mogens Juel	IT Manager	147
153	Dan Hoeffler	IT Supporter	143
145	Zoe Thorston	IT Developer	143

It's different persons, but you're likely to have seen a very similar output using scott.emp somewhere. And this query will form the basis for the rest of the SQL I'll show in this chapter.

Counting subordinates of all levels

The task is now for each row to do a count of subordinates all the way down the tree – not just the immediate subordinates one level down. If you look at the organization diagram in Figure 22-2, I need to find that Harold King has 13 subordinates (all employees except himself), Ursula Mwbesi has 7 subordinates total (2 immediately below her plus 5 that are a level further down the tree), Lim Tok Lo has 3 subordinates total (all just 1 level below and they have no further subordinates), and so on.

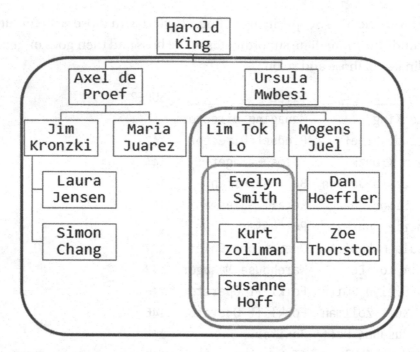

Figure 22-2. *Organization diagram with some of the subtrees marked*

A simple way to do this is using a scalar subquery as shown in Listing 22-2. The scalar subquery can find the relevant subtree in the hierarchy and count the nodes of the subtree.

Listing 22-2. Counting the number of subordinates

```
SQL> select
  2      e.id
  3    , lpad(' ', 2*(level-1)) || e.name as name
  4    , (
  5        select count(*)
  6        from employees sub
  7        start with sub.supervisor_id = e.id
  8        connect by sub.supervisor_id = prior sub.id
  9      ) as subs
 10  from employees e
 11  start with e.supervisor_id is null
 12  connect by e.supervisor_id = prior e.id
 13  order siblings by e.name;
```

The outer query is the same as Listing 22-1. The scalar subquery in lines 4–9 utilizes the same `connect by` query; only `start with` is not from the top of the tree, but instead `start with` in line 7 starts with those that are immediate subordinates of the current row in the outer query and searches the subtree from there and down:

ID	NAME	SUBS
142	Harold King	13
144	Axel de Proef	4
151	Jim Kronzki	2
150	Laura Jensen	0
154	Simon Chang	0
148	Maria Juarez	0
147	Ursula Mwbesi	7
146	Lim Tok Lo	3
152	Evelyn Smith	0
149	Kurt Zollman	0
155	Susanne Hoff	0
143	Mogens Juel	2
153	Dan Hoeffler	0
145	Zoe Thorston	0

The output is just what I'm after, but I've accessed the same rows of the tables multiple times – like Simon Chang that has been accessed four times: once in the scalar subquery for each of the three people above him in the tree and then once in the main query when it got to him in the tree. Also every time a leaf node in the tree was accessed, the database queried if there was anyone below him/her, so the four times Simon was accessed also incurred four lookups if he had subordinates.

All in all, it is a lot of repetitive work for the database. But luckily I have a way to reduce that amount of work.

Counting with row pattern matching

Using row pattern matching, I can create the query shown in Listing 22-3, which only needs to do the hierarchical query a single time and then do all the necessary counts on the retrieved tree without accessing the tables over and over again.

Listing 22-3. Counting subordinates with match_recognize

```sql
SQL> with hierarchy as (
  2      select
  3          lvl, id, name, rownum as rn
  4      from (
  5        select
  6            level as lvl, e.id, e.name
  7        from employees e
  8        start with e.supervisor_id is null
  9        connect by e.supervisor_id = prior e.id
 10        order siblings by e.name
 11      )
 12  )
 13  select
 14      id
 15    , lpad(' ', (lvl-1)*2) || name as name
 16    , subs
 17  from hierarchy
 18  match_recognize (
 19      order by rn
 20      measures
 21        strt.rn           as rn
 22      , strt.lvl          as lvl
 23      , strt.id           as id
 24      , strt.name         as name
 25      , count(higher.lvl) as subs
 26      one row per match
 27      after match skip to next row
 28      pattern (
 29        strt higher*
 30      )
 31      define
 32        higher as higher.lvl > strt.lvl
 33  )
 34  order by rn;
```

The output of Listing 22-3 is exactly the same as the output of Listing 22-2. I'll tell you how it works:

- I'm using a `with` clause for clarity as I taught you in Chapter 3.

- Inside the `with` clause lines 5–10 is an inline view containing the basic hierarchical query I've already shown you in the previous listings. Notice the `order by` in line 10 is inside the inline view.

- I place it in an inline view so that I can use `rownum` in line 3 (outside the inline view) and save it as column alias `rn`. I need to preserve the hierarchical ordering created by the inline view when I do my row pattern matching – this allows me to do so.

- Building my `match_recognize` clause, I start by defining in line 32 that a row that has a higher level than the starting row of the pattern is classified as `higher` – meaning that when it has a higher level, then it is a child/grandchild/greatgrandchild/... of the starting row (i.e., a subordinate).

- Of course, not everybody in the entire row set with a higher level is a subordinate – only those consecutive rows with a higher level that follow the row itself. Once I reach someone with the same level (or lower), then I am no longer within the subtree I want. I solve this in the pattern in line 29 by looking for a `strt` row (which is undefined and therefore can be any row) followed by zero or more `higher` rows – when a row is reached that is no longer classified `higher`, the match stops.

- In line 26, I've specified `one row per match`, and the employee I'm interested in outputting data from is the `strt` row, so I'm using `strt` columns in the measures in lines 21–24.

- In line 25, I'm doing a `count` on how many `higher` rows were in the match. If I just did a plain `count(*)`, I'd be including the `strt` row, but on that row anything I qualify with `higher` will be `null`, so counting `higher.lvl` gives me a count only of the higher rows, which is the count of subordinates that I want.

441

- With `after match skip to next row` in line 27, I'm specifying that once it has finished with a match of one `strt` row and zero or more higher rows, it should move to the next row that follows after the `strt` row. This is the part that makes rows be counted more than once – I'll explain in detail shortly.

That's all clear, right? Well, I'll dive a little more into the details to clarify why it works.

Note   A few words on why you'd consider using the long and somewhat convoluted Listing 22-3 instead of the short and clear Listing 22-2.

I tested this on an employee table where I had 14001 employees in it.

The scalar subquery method used about 11 seconds, nearly half a million consistent gets, and over 37000 sorts, due to a full table scan and many, many index range scans for the `connect` by processing.

The `match_recognize` method used less than half a second, 55 consistent gets, and four (four!) sorts, with just a single full table scan.

Your mileage will vary, of course, so test it yourself.

The details of each match

As I've mentioned before, very often a good way to see what happens is to inspect the detailed output using all rows per match. So this is what I do in Listing 22-4.

Listing 22-4. Inspecting the details with all rows per match

```
SQL> with hierarchy as (
...
 12  )
 13  select
 14       mn
 15     , rn
 16     , lvl
 17     , lpad(' ', (lvl-1)*2)
```

```
18       || substr(name, 1, instr(name, ' ') - 1) as name
19     , roll
20     , subs
21     , cls
22     , substr(stname, 1, instr(stname, ' ') - 1) as stname
23     , substr(hiname, 1, instr(hiname, ' ') - 1) as hiname
24   from hierarchy
25   match_recognize (
26     order by rn
27     measures
28        match_number()    as mn
29      , classifier()      as cls
30      , strt.name         as stname
31      , higher.name       as hiname
32      , count(higher.lvl) as roll
33      , final count(higher.lvl) as subs
34     all rows per match
35     after match skip to next row
36     pattern (
37        strt higher*
38     )
39     define
40        higher as higher.lvl > strt.lvl
41   )
42   order by mn, rn;
```

The with clause subquery is unchanged, as are the after match, pattern, and define clauses. I've changed the one row to all rows per match in line 34 and then created some different measures in lines 28–33:

- The match_number() function in line 28 is a consecutive numbering of the matches found. Without it, I couldn't tell which rows in the output belongs together as part of each match.

- The classifier() function shows what the row has been classified as according to the pattern and define clauses – in this case showing whether a row is strt or higher.

443

- When column names are not qualified, values of the current row in the match are used, no matter what classifier they have. When I qualify the column names with the classifier strt and higher in lines 30 and 31, I get the values from the last of the rows *with that classifier*.

- Aggregate functions like count in lines 32 and 33 can be running or final. In Listing 22-3, it did not matter, since I used one row per match, but here it does matter, so I output both to show the difference. Line 32 defaults to running (aka rolling count) which gives a result similar to an analytic function with a window of rows between unbounded preceding and current row, while line 33 with final keyword works similar to rows between unbounded preceding and unbounded following.

The output of Listing 22-4 has far more rows than are in the table, but I have 14 matches (one for each row in the table) identified by 1–14 in the mn column. So if I step through the output, here's the rows for the first match:

MN	RN	LVL	NAME	ROLL	SUBS	CLS	STNAME	HINAME
1	1	1	Harold	0	13	STRT	Harold	
1	2	2	Axel	1	13	HIGHER	Harold	Axel
1	3	3	Jim	2	13	HIGHER	Harold	Jim
1	4	4	Laura	3	13	HIGHER	Harold	Laura
1	5	4	Simon	4	13	HIGHER	Harold	Simon
1	6	3	Maria	5	13	HIGHER	Harold	Maria
1	7	2	Ursula	6	13	HIGHER	Harold	Ursula
1	8	3	Lim	7	13	HIGHER	Harold	Lim
1	9	4	Evelyn	8	13	HIGHER	Harold	Evelyn
1	10	4	Kurt	9	13	HIGHER	Harold	Kurt
1	11	4	Susanne	10	13	HIGHER	Harold	Susanne
1	12	3	Mogens	11	13	HIGHER	Harold	Mogens
1	13	4	Dan	12	13	HIGHER	Harold	Dan
1	14	4	Zoe	13	13	HIGHER	Harold	Zoe

As my pattern matching is ordered by rn, it starts at rn = 1 (Harold) and classifies him strt (since any row can match strt) and then repeatedly checks if the next row has a lvl greater than the lvl of the strt row, which is true for all of the remaining 13 rows, as everybody else has a lvl greater than 1. That means that the first match does not stop until it reaches the end of the rows.

Match number 1 has now been found, containing 1 strt row and 13 higher rows as shown in the cls column. In the strt row, no higher rows have been found *yet*, so when I qualify a column with higher (and I am not using the final keyword), the result is null, as you can see in column hiname. This also means that when I do the total (final) count of higher in column subs, the strt row is not counted, and the result is the desired 13 subordinates.

You can also see in the output how the running total goes in column roll and that strt.name in column stname keeps the value of the last (in this case only) strt row.

So when the first match is finished, I specified after match skip to next row, which in this case is rn = 2 (Axel). He'll be the strt row of match mn = 2 in the continued output:

```
2   2   2      Axel        0   4    STRT    Axel
2   3   3       Jim        1   4    HIGHER  Axel    Jim
2   4   4        Laura     2   4    HIGHER  Axel    Laura
2   5   4        Simon     3   4    HIGHER  Axel    Simon
2   6   3      Maria       4   4    HIGHER  Axel    Maria
```

After Axel as strt, this match finds four higher rows, because row rn = 7 (Ursula) has lvl = 2, which is *not* higher than Axel (it is the same), and therefore the match stops with Maria. The counting of subordinates works just like before – even though there are five rows in the match, there are only four that are classified higher and are counted. These rows were also included in the count of Harold King's subordinates in match number 1, but because of skipping back up to rn = 2 to find the next match, these rows are included once more.

The next row after Axel is Jim, who'll be the strt row of match mn = 3 that is the next in the output:

```
3   3   3      Jim         0   2    STRT    Jim
3   4   4       Laura      1   2    HIGHER  Jim     Laura
3   5   4        Simon     2   2    HIGHER  Jim     Simon
```

Match number 3 ends up with one strt row and just 2 higher rows, since Maria (who follows Simon in the rn order) does *not* have a lvl higher than Jim. So Laura and Simon are counted as Jim's subordinates – just as they also were counted under Axel and under Harold.

445

The output moves on to match number 4, which starts with Laura classifying her as a `strt` row. After her comes Simon, but he has the same `lvl` as Laura. Therefore, he cannot be a `higher` row, and the match becomes a match containing only a single `strt` row and no `higher` rows, leading to a subordinate count of 0 in the output:

```
4   4   4           Laura   0   0   STRT   Laura
```

And so it goes on and on, until at the end, the match number `mn` = 14 is found, containing just Zoe:

```
...
14  14  4           Zoe     0   0   STRT   Zoe
```

The details of this long output are good to learn how the different pieces of `match_recognize` work for this solution. But I can also take just some of the columns of the `all rows per match` output and use `pivot` in Listing 22-5 to visualize the rows that are part of each match.

Listing 22-5. Pivoting to show which rows are in which match

```sql
SQL> with hierarchy as (
...
12  )
13  select
14      name
15  , "1", "2", "3", "4", "5", "6", "7"
16  , "8", "9", "10", "11", "12", "13", "14"
17  from (
18      select
19          mn
20      , rn
21      , lpad(' ', (lvl-1)*2)
22          || substr(name, 1, instr(name, ' ') - 1) as name
23      from hierarchy
24      match_recognize (
25          order by rn
26          measures
27              match_number()      as mn
```

```
28        all rows per match
29        after match skip to next row
30        pattern (
31           strt higher*
32        )
33        define
34           higher as higher.lvl > strt.lvl
35      )
36  ) pivot (
37      max('X')
38      for mn in (
39          1,2,3,4,5,6,7,8,9,10,11,12,13,14
40        )
41  )
42  order by rn;
```

The only measure I am using is match_number() in line 27, and then in lines 19–22, I select just mn, rn, and the name. This allows me to do a pivot for mn in line 38 specifying the 14 match numbers in line 39, thereby getting rn, name, and 14 columns named 1–14 (these column names must be enclosed in double quotes, as they do not start with a letter).

The value of the 14 match number columns is the literal X if the rn of the row is included in the match, otherwise null. So I can select the mn column and the Xs and just use rn for ordering the output:

NAME	1	2	3	4	5	6	7	8	9	10	11	12	13	14
Harold	X													
Axel	X	X												
Jim	X	X	X											
Laura	X	X	X	X										
Simon	X	X	X		X									
Maria	X	X				X								
Ursula	X						X							
Lim	X						X	X						
Evelyn	X						X	X	X					
Kurt	X						X	X		X				
Susanne	X						X	X				X		

447

```
Mogens      X                   X                   X
   Dan      X                   X                   X   X
   Zoe      X                   X                   X           X
```

In this pivoted output, it is easy to use the Xs to check that all rows are included in match number 1, the rows from Axel to Maria are included in match number 2, and so on.

Fiddling with the output

Having examined the detailed output, I'll return to the one row per match version to fiddle a bit more and show you a couple of things.

First, I'd like to make it clear that although Listing 22-3 with one row per match only has a single aggregate measure, and so far I've only shown multiple aggregate measures in Listing 22-4 using all rows per match, it is perfectly legitimate to use multiple aggregates or uses of functions like first and last together with one row. Take a look at Listing 22-6.

Listing 22-6. Adding multiple measures when doing one row per match

```
SQL> with hierarchy as (
...
 12  )
 13  select
 14     lpad(' ', (lvl-1)*2) || name as name
 15   , subs
 16   , hifrom
 17   , hito
 18   , himax
 19  from hierarchy
 20  match_recognize (
 21     order by rn
 22     measures
 23       strt.rn            as rn
 24     , strt.lvl           as lvl
 25     , strt.name          as name
 26     , count(higher.lvl)  as subs
 27     , first(higher.name) as hifrom
```

```
28      , last(higher.name)  as hito
29      , max(higher.lvl)    as himax
30    one row per match
31    after match skip to next row
32    pattern (
33        strt higher*
34    )
35    define
36        higher as higher.lvl > strt.lvl
37  )
38  order by rn;
```

In lines 26–29, I am using both navigational functions and aggregates. Remember that when I use one row per match, it makes no difference if I use running or final for the aggregates, so even if I didn't specify final, I get the same result:

NAME	SUBS	HIFROM	HITO	HIMAX
Harold King	13	Axel de Proef	Zoe Thorston	4
Axel de Proef	4	Jim Kronzki	Maria Juarez	4
Jim Kronzki	2	Laura Jensen	Simon Chang	4
Laura Jensen	0			
Simon Chang	0			
Maria Juarez	0			
Ursula Mwbesi	7	Lim Tok Lo	Zoe Thorston	4
Lim Tok Lo	3	Evelyn Smith	Susanne Hoff	4
Evelyn Smith	0			
Kurt Zollman	0			
Susanne Hoff	0			
Mogens Juel	2	Dan Hoeffler	Zoe Thorston	4
Dan Hoeffler	0			
Zoe Thorston	0			

So my first point was the use of multiple measures for whatever output I want in the various columns. Can I fiddle with the rows in the output as well? Say, for example, I want to output only those employees that actually have subordinates (or in other words are not leaf nodes in the tree).

449

Sure, I could put the entire query in an inline view and then use a `where` clause to filter on `subs > 0` and that way not get any leaf nodes in the output. It would work fine, but my second point to show you is a better alternative that filters away the non-leaf nodes earlier in the processing.

In Listing 22-3 line 29, I'm using a pattern of `strt higher*` which is a pattern that by design will be matched by *any* row that will be classified `strt` – it is just a question of how many `higher` rows will follow after that `strt` row. So Listing 22-3 will by the nature of the pattern output all rows of the table.

Let me in Listing 22-7 change just one character – otherwise, it is identical to Listing 22-3.

Listing 22-7. Filtering matches with the pattern definition

```
...
29          strt higher+
...
```

I have changed * to + which means that any given `strt` row will *only* cause a match if it is followed by at least one `higher` row. So the leaf nodes, which are *not* followed by any `higher` row, will not cause a match – instead the database simply moves one row along and checks if it can find a match using the next row as `strt` row. This leads to only supervisors being output:

ID	NAME	SUBS
142	Harold King	13
144	Axel de Proef	4
151	Jim Kronzki	2
147	Ursula Mwbesi	7
146	Lim Tok Lo	3
143	Mogens Juel	2

Doing it this way allows the database to discard the unwanted rows immediately as it works its way through the pattern matching process – rather than the inline view that lets the database build a result set of all rows and then afterward removes the unwanted ones again.

Lessons learned

In this chapter I've demonstrated that with a suitable ordering, the `after match skip to next row` clause can very efficiently allow `match_recognize` to process the same rows multiple times in different groupings without accessing them in the table multiple times. In the demos I covered

- Preparing the source query by creating an ordering column that allows `match_recognize` to work in the hierarchical order

- Setting a `pattern` that for each row finds the group of rows that are in the subtree below

- Using `after match skip to next row` to use the pattern search on every row, even if it was included in previous matches

- Changing the `pattern` to ignore those rows not having a subtree below

These methods you can use on any hierarchical data. They can also be useful on other data with an ordering that is nontrivial, where you can set up a more complex query to prepare the data and preserve the ordering, before you process the data with `match_recognize`.

Index

A

Accumulated sum, *See* Rolling sum
Analytic functions
  avg
    sliding windows for centered
      moving average, 292
  dense_rank, 223–225
    restart ranking using partition
      by, 251
  lag, 267
  last_value
    case expression to create null on
      rows of group except the first, 279
    ignore nulls, 278
  lead, 361–362, 398, 402
    case expression to create null on
      undesired rows, 277
    emulating connect_by_isleaf in
      with clause recursion, 71
    ignore nulls, 276–280, 283
    look more than one row ahead
      using second parameter, 272, 277
    null at end of partition, 270, 272,
      274, 276, 277, 279, 283
  ntile, 41, 42
  order by clause
    analytic order by different than
      query order by, 199, 246
  over, 209
  query partition clause, 196, 197

  rank, 222–225
  regr_intercept, 298, 299, 305
  regr_slope, 298, 299, 305
  row_number, 220–222, 353–356, 359,
    418–420
    emulating minus all, 35–37
    emulating multi-column scalar
      subquery, 8
  sum (*see also* Rolling sum)
  windowing clause
    default window clause
      dangers, 208–212
    number of rows preceding or
      following, 211, 292, 293
    range between, 206, 210
    range on current row may include
      following rows, 206–208
    rows between, 200, 312, 313
    shortcut with implicit
      between, 201
    unbounded following, 204, 211
    unbounded preceding, 210, 211,
      312, 313
    values preceding or following, 211

B

Bin fitting
  approximation algorithm, 411
  evenly distributing in bins, 423
  limited number of bins, 426–433

© Kim Berg Hansen 2020
K. Berg Hansen, *Practical Oracle SQL*, https://doi.org/10.1007/978-1-4842-5617-6

Bin fitting (*cont.*)
  modified first fit decreasing
      (MFFD), 417
  unlimited number of bins, 413–422

C

Collection, *See* Nested table type
Collection operators, *See* Multiset
      operators
Common table expressions, *See* with
      clause
connect by queries, *See* Queries,
      hierarchical
Conway's Game of Life
  oscillator, 104
Creating delimited text
  large delimited text
      distinct in listagg, 182
      ORA-01489 when using listagg, 185
      on overflow subclause in
        listagg, 186
  using collect
      specifying nested table type using
        cast, 175
      using apex_string.join, 176
      using apex_string.join_clob, 189
  using json_arrayagg
      returning clob using
        json_value, 188
  using listagg, 172–173
  using stragg ODCI aggregate function
      supporting distinct using map
        member, 177, 178
  using xmlagg
      getclobval, 188
      using xmlelement, 182
      using xmlparse, 183, 184

D

Date intervals
  half-open intervals
      advantages compared to closed
        intervals, 372, 374–376
Dynamic SQL
  expression evaluation with execute
      immediate, 70

E

execute immediate, *See* Dynamic SQL
Expression lists
  in pivot measures, 143

F

Forecasting future values
  centered moving average, 292–293
  deseasonalizing, 295–298
  linear regression
      interception point, 299
      slope, 299
  reseasonalizing, 301–305
  seasonality factor
      partition by month of
        year, 290
  time series, 287–292
  trend line, 298–300
Forecasting reaching minimum
  adding values when minimum
      reached
      using model clause
        iteration, 319–321
      using with clause recursion,
        316, 319, 322
  summing expected values from
      budget, 308

Functions
    add_months, 289, 315, 317, 320
    analytic functions (*see* Analytic
        functions)
    extract, 289, 295
    greatest, 312, 313, 317, 320
    least, 245, 418, 419
    listagg
        visualizing two dimensions, 91
    mod, 250, 263
    nullif, 294–297, 403
    numtodsinterval, 315, 317, 320
    regexp_count, 154, 164
    regexp_substr, 154–156, 163–164
    replace, 147, 158, 159, 165
    trunc, 309, 314, 317, 320

G

Gap detection
    using lead, 361–362
    using match_recognize
        first row of next group using skip
            to last, 362
        using value of subset in
            measures, 362, 363
Grouping rows
    on cross-row conditions using
        match_recognize
        consecutive data, 358–361
        within fixed interval from first
            row, 367–369
        until gap in data, 364–367
    Tabibitosan method
        on consecutive dates, 358–361
        on consecutive integers, 356
    using last_value, case and ignore
        nulls, 280

H

Hierarchical queries, *See* Queries,
    hierarchical

I

Inline views
    as alternative to scalar subquery, 9
    correlating
        cross apply, 11–12
        lateral, 3, 9–12
        outer apply, 13–14

J

JSON
    json_arrayagg
        returning clob, 188
    json_table
        individual elements of JSON array
            in path, 156
        treating delimited string as JSON
            array, 155–156
    json_value, 188

K

Knapsack problem, *See* Bin fitting

L

loop
    exit when, 148

M

match_recognize
    after match
        compare to last row of specific
            classification using last, 336

match_recognize (*cont.*)

    compare to previous row using prev, 328

    complex row-classifying condition, 341

    default, 336

    evaluation depending on pattern, 327

    mutually exclusive definitions, 329

    skip past last row, 336

    skip to last, 284, 336–339, 342, 362

    skip to next row, 440, 442, 443, 445, 447, 449

    undefined classification always true, 331

  define

    compare next row to max of rows so far, 381–386

    compare to following row using next, 361, 367, 382–383, 398, 408, 435

    compare to previous row using prev, 366, 368, 379–381

    compare to specific row using classification name, 434

    compare to starting row using first, 367–368

    complex row-classifying condition, 407, 415

    evaluation depending on pattern, 407

    simple row-classifying condition, 283

    skip to first, 348

    truth assumption when evaluating condition, 430

    undefined classification always true, 368, 383, 385, 430, 434, 441

    using running sum, 430

  gap detection (*see* Gap detection)

  measures

    classifier, 443

    final semantics, 395, 396, 444, 445, 449

    match_number, 328, 333, 334, 338, 339, 342, 414, 418, 420, 421, 423, 443, 446, 447

    running semantics, 394, 415, 444, 445, 449

    using first, 284, 334, 335, 360, 379, 381, 382, 394–397, 400, 448

    using last, 284, 334, 335, 360, 379, 381, 382, 394–396, 400, 448, 449

    using last on subset, 362, 363

    using max, 379, 381, 382

    using next, 394–396, 400, 449

    using next on last, 284, 400, 418

    using prev, 327

    using prev on first, 395, 396, 400

  omit empty matches, 424

  order by, 327, 328

  output

    all rows per match, 327, 328, 333, 334, 336, 338, 342, 414, 418, 420, 421, 423–425, 429, 442–443

    one row per match, 328, 334, 336, 338, 342, 348, 349, 394, 396, 400, 402, 405, 407, 421, 448–449

  partition by, 327, 328, 334, 338, 339, 345

  pattern

    | alternator (or), 327, 328, 330–333, 407

matching all rows in
one match, 429

* quantifier, 283

* quantifier, 364, 379, 440, 441, 443,
446, 450

+ quantifier, 332–336, 338, 341, 394,
396, 400, 402, 405, 409, 425, 450

subset

after match skip to last of a
subset, 336–339, 342, 362

with unmatched rows, 425, 426

model clause

any, 92

cv() cell addressing, 97, 320

dimension by, 91, 92

consecutive number using
row_number, 320

ignore nav, 92

iteration_number, 97, 320

measures, 92, 320

partition by, 319

rules

iterate, 97, 98, 320

sequential order, 320

upsert all, 97

Modularization of SQL, *See* with clause

Multiset operators

default differences compared to set
operators, 38

disappearing values by multiset
except distinct, 32

multiset except
compared to minus, 34–37

multiset intersect, 30–31

multiset union, 28–30

using all, 28, 32

using distinct, 28

N, O

Nested table type

aggregated output of collect, 184

iterating elements with first and
last, 174

output of pipelined table function, 147

P

Pipelined table function

apex_string.split, 152–153

custom built, 152

pipe row, 147

PL/SQL functions

in with clause (*see* with clause,
PL/SQL functions)

PRAGMA UDF, 77–80

reducing context switching
overhead, 78, 79

Q

Queries

cross join

generate dynamic unpivot
dimension mapping, 123–128

generate grid, 89

generate rows for manual
unpivoting, 121–122

generate variable number of rows
using lateral, 151

lateral, 10

Expression lists

in unpivot measures and
dimensions, 114–116, 119, 122

fetch first (*see* Top-N calculations,
using fetch first)

Queries (*cont.*)
  fetch first rows
    in correlated inline views, 10
  hierarchical
    connect by, 59, 436
    connect_by_isleaf, 60
    connect_by_root, 60
    level, 58, 436
    order siblings by, 60, 436
    start with, 58, 436
    sys_connect_by_path, 60
  outer join
    partitioned, 290
    using lateral and on clause
      together, 12
  pivot (*see below* pivoting)
  pivoting
    column naming by aliasing,
      140, 141, 143
    expression lists in measures, 143
    implicit group by aggregation,
      136, 137, 280–281, 435
    keeping only needed columns for
      implicit group by, 137
    multiple measures and
      dimensions, 139–144
    single measure and dimension,
      134–137, 139–144
    using group by and case
      expressions, 138
    using pivot, 138, 282, 446–447
  refcursor variable
    opening with dynamic SQL, 124
  table keyword
    adding (+) as outer join
      equivalent, 150
    column_value for scalar
      output, 149

  cross apply, 151
  outer apply, 159–160
  temporal validity
    null for infinity, 386–387
    as of period for in select, 376
    period for in table creation, 376
  unpivot (*see below* unpivoting)
  unpivoting
    group by and aggregates on
      unpivot output, 118
    multiple measure and
      dimension, 113–119
    single measure and dimension, 110
    using dimension tables
      dynamically, 123–128
    using dimension tables
      manually, 121
    using generated dimension
      rows, 112–113
    using generated numbered
      rows, 111–112
    using unpivot, 118

R

Recursive subquery factoring, *See* with
    clause, recursion
Rolling sum, 237–265, 307–322
  of all previous rows, 243–245, 255, 256,
    258, 328
  including current row, 241, 243, 255,
    256, 312, 313
  null when window has no rows, 245
  partitioned, 241, 312, 313, 319, 320
  sum interval from previous to current
    row, 317, 320
    join overlapping
      intervals, 258–260

Row pattern matching, *See* `match_recognize`

Running total, *See* Rolling sum

S

Scalar subqueries
  concatenated values, 6–7
  hierarchical, 438, 439, 442
  multiple, 5–9
Sessionization, *See* Grouping rows, on cross-row conditions using `match_recognize`, until gap in data
Set operators
  concatenating sets (*see below* Set operators, union all)
  default differences compared to multiset operators, 20
  implicit distinct, 25, 37
  `intersect`, 25, 26
  `minus`
    compared to `multiset except`, 334
    emulating `minus all` using `multiset except all`, 35
    emulating `minus all` using `row_number`, 36–37
  order by column aliases, 24
  `union`, 25, 26
  `union all`, 25
Splitting delimited text
  Oracle Data Cartridge Interface (*see* Creating delimited text, using `stragg` ODCI aggregate function; *see below* Splitting delimited text, using ODCI function)
  using `apex_string.split` to split to rows
    using `substr` to split to columns, 147

using generated rows
  using `regexp_substr` to split to columns, 154, 155
using `json_table`
  JSON array of scalar values, 156
  transformation to nested JSON arrays of rows and columns, 165–168
using ODCI function
  real column names instead of generic `column_value`, 161
using PL/SQL in pipelined table function, 147
String aggregation, *See* Creating delimited text
Subquery factoring, *See* `with` clause

T, U, V

Top-N calculations
  handling ties
    avoiding indeterminate output, 228
    using `dense_rank`, 230–231
    using `rank`, 229
    using `with ties` subclause of `fetch first`, 229–230
  Olympic rule, 217
  partitioned
    avoiding indeterminate output, 228
    using `dense_rank`, 233
    using `fetch first` and `lateral` inline view, 233–235
    using `rank`, 232
    using `row_number`, 231–232
  top-rows rule, 217
  top-values rule, 217
  using `dense_rank`, 222–225, 227, 230–232

Top-N calculations (*cont.*)
  using `fetch first`
    not able to do Olympic
      rule, 226
    `rows only`, 225
    `rows with ties`, 226
  using `rank`, 222–225
  using `rownum`, 222
  using `row_number`, 222, 223
Turning columns into rows, *See* Queries,
    unpivoting
Turning rows into columns, *See* Queries,
    pivoting

W, X, Y, Z

Warehouse picking
  batch picking
    assigning picks to
      orders, 252–262
  different picking
    principles, 246–248
  FIFO, 240–246
  First-In-First-Out (*see above*
    Warehouse picking, FIFO)
  picking route
    aisle numbering, 249, 251
    odd-even switching `order by`
      direction, 250
`with` clause
  column names list, 52–53
  modularization, 44–47

successive named subqueries
  emulating Excel column
    calculations, 287
optimizer handling
  creation of single-use temporary
    tables, 50
  forcing materialization using
    `rownum`, 50–51
  `materialize` hint, 50, 51
  substitution like views, 49
PL/SQL functions
  compiled like `PRAGMA UDF`, 81, 82
  dynamic evaluation, 69–70
  encapsulation in view, 83–85
  multiple functions in `with`
    clause, 81–82
  use for tools or read-only
    database, 83
preserving hierarchy before
  `match_recognize`, 440–442
recursion, 319
  emulating `connect_by_isleaf`, 71
  emulating `connect_by_root`, 60, 64,
    66, 69, 71
  emulating `level`, 71
  emulating `order siblings by`, 60, 63
  hierarchical, 61
refactoring nested inline views, 46–47
test data creation
  overloading a table, 53–55
using named subquery multiple
    times, 48

Printed in the United States
By Bookmasters